NAKED IN THE
PROMISED LAND

NAKED *in the*
PROMISED
LAND

LILLIAN FADERMAN

THE UNIVERSITY OF WISCONSIN PRESS

The University of Wisconsin Press
1930 Monroe Street
Madison, Wisconsin 53711

www.wisc.edu/wisconsinpress/

3 Henrietta Street
London WC2E 8LU, England

5   4   3   2

Printed in the United States of America

Library of Congress Cataloging-in-Publication Data
Faderman, Lillian.
Naked in the promised land / Lillian Faderman.
   p. cm.
   Originally published: Boston : Houghton Mifflin, 2003.
   ISBN 0-299-20014-0 (pbk. : alk. paper)
   1. Faderman, Lillian. 2. Scholars—United States—Biography.
3. Lesbians—United States—Biography. 4. Jews—United States—Biography.
I. Title.
CT3990.F33 A3   2004
2003070541

To ensure the privacy of certain persons who appear in this book,
some names and identifying characteristics have been changed.

FOR AVROM

ACKNOWLEDGMENTS

My deep gratitude goes to the many friends who read this book in its numerous versions, made helpful suggestions, and gave me encouragement: Rosie Pegueros, Ruth Schwartz, Linda Garber, Barbara Blinik, Ruth Blinik, Joyce Aiken, Rosalind Ravasio, Charlie Bolduc, Joyce Brotsky, Virginia Hales, Sharon Young, and Olivia Sawyers. Special thanks to Frankie Hucklenbroich, Steve Yarbrough, and Beatrice Valenzuela.

It would have been impossible for me to finish the manuscript without the gift of time from my colleagues and the administration at California State University, Fresno. I'm especially grateful to Luis Costa and Michael Ortiz.

My editor, Elaine Pfefferblit, believed in this project from the start and has made me feel her support. Thank you. Sandy Dijkstra continues to be a great friend and a terrific agent.

I'm blessed in my family—Avrom Irwin Faderman and Phyllis Irwin. Thank you for your sweet nurturance.

CONTENTS

LILLY

1   HOW I BECAME AN OVERACHIEVER

How could I not have spent years of my life lusting after the golden apple—the heft of it, the round, smooth feel of it, the curve of it in my small hand? When I was three months old and a war was raging across the ocean, my mother rocked me in her arms in a darkened theater. On the silver screen, here in America, in the Bronx, was Charles Boyer, a duke with a mansion in Paris, another in the Loire, another in Corsica. His sumptuous abodes were concocted by a lunatic confectioner: furniture, curtains, ceilings, walls—all of billowy whipped cream. If the movie had been in Technicolor, everything would surely have been ivory, heaven blue, sun gold. My mother—a shopgirl, an immigrant, no husband—stared with open mouth, rapt, all but drooling at Boyer and paradise. When she remembered, she dandled me a bit in her arms, praying I would be silent long enough to let her see—one more glimpse of the duke, of his mansion, of the story. This she told me.

I did not cooperate. From fitful sleep I awoke to bawl, to shriek with new lungs, with all my strength.

To the lobby and back with me. One more glimpse for her, and to the lobby again.

"See," she softly crooned. "Look, see." Standing in the back of the theater, she held me up to better see the screen. It was the handsome duke she wanted us to see, and the many mansions. For a moment my mouth was open too in rapt attention.

We went home together, I in her arms, in the late October cold sunset to our little rooms in the Bronx. She wrapped the blanket tighter around me and held me to her breast so that no cold could reach me. But her head was full of Duke Boyer with his bedroom eyes and kissy mouth and mansions.

For my first three months we'd been living on "relief," as welfare was called in New York in 1940, and my mother didn't have to work. We could go to movies together to our hearts' content. But it couldn't last.

"You have to sue the baby's father," the relief worker told my mother in the loud voice she used for people who didn't speak English well. "The Bronx can't be supporting you and her forever." She printed the address of the public lawyer in big, careful letters and told my mother what subway to take.

"That's not my baby," my father swore on the stand, and the judge believed him. He didn't have to pay my mother a cent.

The Bronx didn't have to pay any more cents either, the relief worker said. That was when my aunt—*the funny monkey*, my mother called her—came to live with us and take care of me, and my mother went back to the garment factory where she'd been a draper before I was born. No more movies and outings in the cold for me.

My aunt kept me well bundled in the cramped and overheated apartment and crooned Yiddish lullabies to me all day long. *Unter Lililehs viegeleh . . . Under little Lilly's cradle stands a pure white goat. The little goat went to market, to buy you raisins and almonds.* A foghorn voice came out of her short body. I stared up at her with huge love eyes. She held me to her heart and I crawled in forever, she said. *A kush on dyneh shayneh bekelech, a kush on dyneh shayneh pupikel*, a kiss on your pretty little cheeks, on your pretty little belly button. *Smack, smack* would go her lips in big goopy kisses on my briefly exposed skin, and I was beside myself with glee.

My mother called her Rae, and I'd never heard the word *aunt*, so when I began talking I called her My Rae. I became roly-poly because My Rae was always sticking into my mouth big spoonfuls of whatever she was cooking in our small kitchen—prune compote, potato and carrot *tzimmes*, boiled chicken with noodles, My-T-Fine Chocolate Pudding. "Open the *moileleh*, the little mouth," she said and grinned ecstat-

*My Rae and Mommy:
immigrant girls in
American finery, 1920s*

ically when I did. In went the compote, in went the *tzimmes*. "A *michayeh*, a pleasure," she said. I learned to walk months later than most kids because when My Rae wasn't cooking or making her sewing machine go *whirr, whirr* with the piecework she did for money, she never let me out of her arms.

They were the only two of their family who, in 1923, had made it to the safe shores of America, long before Hitler marched through Prael, their shtetl in Latvia, and wiped out everyone else—a crippled brother, two sisters, the sisters' husbands, the sisters' five children. It was not supposed to work out that way. "This is what you must do," the grandmother I never saw told her eldest daughters, my mother (a sylph, an eighteen-year-old beauty) and my aunt (a bulldog, the chaperone). The poorest of the poor were going off to America and sending back dollars and pictures of themselves dressed like the nobility. Why should her two daughters be any less lucky? They were to marry rich men in America and bring the rest of the family over.

They'd been in America for almost twenty years, their parents had died, and neither my mother nor my aunt had married, not even by the time I was born to my mother and her lover in 1940. She'd been with him for eight years. He'd told her from the beginning that he wasn't the marrying kind, but she loved him, so she couldn't help herself.

Then, not long after my mother lost the paternity suit against my father, Hitler invaded Latvia. When the silence from Prael continued, month after month and year after year, 1941, 1942, 1943, 1944, my mother blamed My Rae for all of it.

"You! It's all because of you. I could have brought them, but you said no. 'First we get married,' you said with your big mouth. Lousy bitch, I'll tear you to pieces like a herring. A fig on you," and she thrust her thumb between her index and middle fingers, waving it in front of My Rae's nose in a shtetl version of giving someone the finger. I sat on the bare floor and bawled. "And Moishe would have married me, but you had to butt your lousy two cents in."

"The cholera should take me. I should die in their place." My aunt wept for her multiple sins.

The Hebrew Immigrant Aid Society was getting dribbles of information during the war about the fate of those overseas. My aunt went to them and kept going back. Nothing. Then at the end, in 1945, came the tardy news that in the summer of 1941 the Jews of Prael had been made to dig their own graves and were murdered on the spot. No one survived.

My mother shrieked, tore her hair, fell to her knees. I fell on top of her, shook her to remind her, "You have me, Mommy. Mommy, don't cry." I didn't know to weep for the relatives I'd never seen, but something terrible was happening to her. I wailed. Now we shrieked together, high keening sounds, and my scalding tears were fluid fire down my cheeks.

My aunt, wailing herself, still remembered me. She lifted me up and held me to her heaving breast.

ABOVE: *Lilly, about one and a half years old*
RIGHT: *Lilly, about five years old*

My mother sat upright on the floor and stared. "Everything you took from me. Now you want to take my baby," she screamed. "*A mameh ohn a boich vaytik*, a mother without a bellyache you want to be. You lousy bitch, you can't!" She threw a shoe at my aunt's head.

Maybe my aunt reasoned that since so many in the family had been killed, she had a moral responsibility to remain alive. She left us still keening and came back to the apartment a couple of hours later with a train ticket to California in her hand.

"I can't no more. I'll die," she yelled at her sister as she threw things into a cardboard valise. She wet my face with kisses and more tears and left me alone with my mother. I was five.

I cried even louder and harder than my mother for a long time. And

How I Became an Overachiever   7

then My Rae's image faded from my mind. As hard as I tried, I could only remember her foghorn voice and her long blue eyes.

My mother cursed the walls, naming both her sister and her lover, my faithless father, whom she hadn't stopped loving. Then, despite the paternity suit, she and my father began again. Maybe they'd never stopped and I didn't know about it because my aunt had kept me distracted with lullabies and *tzimmes*. Now we moved into a furnished room on Fox Street, "by a Missus," my mother called it, who would take care of me while my mother worked and on Saturday nights and all day Sunday, when she was with her lover. Mrs. Kalt, the woman's name was. She talked to me in Yinglish and patted my back with gruff, absent-minded strokes when I cried because my mother was gone, and sometimes she gave me three pennies so I could run to the dark, sweet-smelling candy store on the corner and buy myself a charlotte russe with a little mound of whipped cream that I could wrap my tongue around.

My mother and I slept in the same bed, and some nights I was startled awake by soft whimpers, like a forlorn child's, but they were my mother's. Was she crying for Moishe? For the lost relatives? I didn't know, but I cried too, the same wretched little sobs. We held on to each other and whimpered together.

But we weren't always miserable. Some Saturday mornings, to my ecstasy, she took me to Crotona Park. I struggled to reach her arm as we walked along the paths. "Mother and daughter," she said. Our skirts blew in the gentle breeze, and I held on to her tightly.

Sometimes we'd stop to rest on a bench and she'd sing—her voice sliding up and down—songs from "Your Hit Parade" that she must have heard from the other women in the shop. *It had to be you, wonderful you. It had to be you, wonderful you,* she knew the lyrics imperfectly. "On this bench me and Moishe sat the first time I went out with him," she confessed to me or the wind one morning.

Of course our movie-going resumed: *All This and Heaven Too, Together Again, Back Street*—that was her favorite; I saw it at least four times. "What's a backstreet, Mommy?" I asked. If she knew, she never told me.

Though I didn't understand most of what I saw, I learned to speak

English without a Yiddish accent through the movies. And it was there that I came to understand female gorgeousness: women with glossy waved coifs, spider-leg eyelashes, and bold lipstick, elaborate drapes and flounces over statuesque, well-corseted figures, shapely legs (but never as shapely as my mother's) in seamed nylons and high heels; women who were sophisticated, glamorous. My mother tried to copy them on the Saturday nights she went out with my father.

I watch as she looks at her face in the speckled mirror. She burns a wooden match and the cooled tip becomes a brush that she draws across her lids once, twice, a third time. I hold my breath just as she does in her concentration. The smudges are uneven, and she rubs her fingers over them, smoothing them out. Now her eyelids look heavy over her eyes, which are luminous and large.

Next she takes her tube of lipstick and pokes her pinkie finger over the top of the worn-down stick, then dabs the color on each cheek. She rubs, rubs, rubs, rubs with her finger, and her cheeks become rosy. I know those cheeks well because I have kissed them with loud, smacking kisses and with soft, butterfly kisses. I don't know if I like the new color, but I know from movie posters that glamorous women must have rosy cheeks.

Her lips are next. She applies the blood red stick directly. I see she has not followed their lovely outline. The blood red laps over and makes her lips larger, like Joan Crawford's. For a moment I want their delicate pink back, the graceful shape I sometimes studied while she slept. But now they look like a movie star's lips, and she nods at them with satisfaction.

"Hubba, hubba," I say in my best Bud Abbott voice. She smiles, but I'm not sure whether she is smiling at me or something she sees in the mirror.

Next she combs her dark curls, then puts Pond's cold cream on her already creamy shoulders and neck.

My eyes do not leave her for a second; but after she kisses my cheek and slips out, they well up with tears.

Him I never see.

I watched her so many times as she made up her face to look right with her makeshift cosmetics. Did she see in the old mirror the beautiful face that I saw? Did he tell her how beautiful she was?

Her lovely figure should have clothes like the movie stars', I thought. But I knew, because she told me, that we were too poor for her to buy herself nice clothes. "Someday, I'll wear the beautiful dresses," I promised myself, trying to picture my grownup self in them and not remember the sound of the door closing behind her.

It was through the movies that I learned to think big: I would become a movie actress, since my mother admired them so much. Though she hardly read or wrote English, and she never lost her Yiddish accent, she knew the names and lives of all the actresses as though they were her sisters: Bette Davis, Marlene Dietrich, Greer Garson, Greta Garbo, Joan Crawford, Barbara Stanwyck—those were her favorites. She remained in love with Charles Boyer. "He looks like Moishe," her lover she meant, my father. I hated Boyer and his big lips.

Her eyes and mouth almost always looked sad when she didn't make them up, but on Saturdays during the day and in the evenings during the week I had her to myself, and I was happy just being close to her. What else could I need? We had "kitchen privileges" with our furnished room, but she didn't like to cook, and we both loved to dine out, as she called it. Sometimes we went to the Automat, where you could put nickels in a slot and, like magic, the little window popped open so you could take out the wonderful *goyishe* dishes on display. Lemon meringue pie. Peanut butter and jelly sandwiches on squishy white bread. Mashed potatoes and gravy with ham steak—forbidden and for that reason delicious.

Or we went to a little restaurant on Southern Boulevard, with a menu in Yiddish and white tablecloths. Calves liver and fried onions. *Gedempfte flaysh* with apricots. Stuffed cabbage in a sweet and sour sauce. "What will madam have?" the waiter, who wore a little black bow tie, asked my mother, and me also. He wrote our order on a pad with the stub of a yellow pencil he pulled from behind his ear.

Or we took the subway all the way across the city, with me clinging to her skirt so I wouldn't lose her, and we went to the Katz Deli on Delancey Street, with sawdust on the floor and great bowls of sour pickles on the table. Huge corned beef sandwiches, so big that she and I could split one. Lox and cream cheese on Russian rye bread. Scrumptiously greasy potato latkes.

I was almost always the only child in those restaurants, and I forgot I was a child. I took my ordering very seriously. I saw how the men at the other tables did it for themselves and their wives, and I did the same: "I believe I will have . . ." I said, in a voice I tried to deepen so I would not be mistaken for a child.

How many dresses she must have had to drape for such outings. I think whatever money she had after paying for the furnished room and the sitting services of the Missus she spent on our entertainment. Though we could afford nothing better than a furnished room, we lived lavishly on movies and dining out.

"Mother and daughter," I said as we walked back home through the Bronx streets in 1946. Now I was six years old, and it wasn't so hard to reach her arm.

I don't know why we moved to an even smaller furnished room on Longwood Avenue, but it was then that my mother enrolled me in P.S. 62. I went to school until three o'clock and then to a day care center a block away—a *nursery school*, it was called—until my mother came to collect me after five.

That first winter in day care I was taken with the other children to a holiday pageant, where a play was performed about an infant and a stable and wise men. "Jesus is God," the little actors shouted at the finale.

I'd been bored, but now I was troubled. My mother or aunt told me about words such as "Jesus" and "Christ" and "gentile," and I knew they meant some ancient horror, Cossacks galloping on fiery horses, running swords through women and children and setting fire to the shtetl at Eastertime after the village priest enraged them against the Jews. Whenever we passed two nuns on the street, my aunt said it meant bad luck and you were supposed to say "Tsu, tsu, tsu," like spitting something out. One nun could mean good luck, but it was safest not to pass any.

I was so shaken to hear the dangerous words in an auditorium that I must have been oblivious when my schoolmates were ordered to form a line and walk to the yellow bus on which we'd come. Soon I found myself surrounded by strange children in maroon uniforms.

I stood there, stunned, at the end of the row where I'd been sitting with my schoolmates. A harried woman wearing glasses that slid down her nose appeared out of nowhere and barked at me, "Underprivileged or Catholic?" I'd never heard either of those words, and I stared at her with an open mouth. "Underprivileged or Catholic?" she repeated.

One of the teachers who was herding a group of children out overheard her and peered at me. "She looks like a little Eye-talian or Porto Rican."

My inquisitor took my hand and rushed me toward a bus packed with more children in maroon uniforms. "Up you go," she said.

I obeyed her and squeezed into a seat near the front, next to a red-faced fat boy who stuck his tongue out at me and yelled, "Oooh, cooties."

I looked around, thinking I'd move to more hospitable ground, and there, in the middle of the bus, shooing children into seats, were two nuns in black, their gigantic crucifixes gleaming on their breasts. I burst into exasperated, horrified tears, which caught the attention of one of them.

"She's not Catholic Elementary," she said, and gruffly taking me by the hand led me out of her bus and finally settled me in the right one, with my underprivileged schoolmates.

I'd learned two new words.

Though I'd looked forward to going to school, I wasn't happy there. One day I cut my finger on the jagged edge of something in the playground, and the other children gathered around me to see the ooze of blood.

"Ooh, look how bright it is," one little girl observed. "Her blood looks so clean, and she's so dirty."

I must have been dirty. In the hot months, my mother came back from the shop sticky and dripping. She ran a cool bath for herself in the little bathroom we were allowed to use, pulled her clothes off, threw them in a pile on the floor. Then she sank into the tub while I sat on the edge.

Sometimes I cooled myself by placing my lips on the delicious wetness of her back. "Onekiss, twokiss, threekiss, fourkiss." I could count up to a hundred and aimed to give at least a hundred kisses, though always she said, "Enough, Lilly, enough," before I could get out of the twenties.

But I don't remember ever being in the bathtub myself. Baths were to get cool in. Probably her mother had never cleaned her in a bath when she was a child either. They probably had had no baths in the shtetl.

The children at school must also have noticed my hair. It was a long time before I realized that a comb was supposed to go through one's hair with ease, that knots were not inevitable if you combed your hair every day, that most people in America washed their hair. My black head was a tangled mass of unruly curls. The hair seemed to grow out in a great bush rather than down. In the morning, when she got me ready for school, my mother sometimes passed a comb over my head, but if she combed deep enough to hit the knots, the pain was awful. "Stop, stop," I screamed at her, and she did, leaving my head to announce to the world the story of her hopeless parenting.

One day my first-grade class went to the Bronx Zoo on a field trip, and Victor, an immaculate blond boy who wore a clean, starched white shirt every day and a little gold ring on his pinkie finger, ended up next to me on the bus. "I'm not going to sit there," he proclaimed after one look at me and popped up, then cried when the driver yelled back at him to sit down and shut up.

I squeezed myself toward the window, trying to give him as wide a berth as possible so there would be no further protests, and I clamped my lips together so I wouldn't cry too.

It didn't matter, I tried to tell myself. Because what did matter to me, passionately, was Miss Huntington, my teacher—a blond *goya*, my mother would have called her. She was a woman in her forties, not beautiful the way the movie actresses were beautiful, I knew, but to me totally captivating. Her eyes were blue, as I remembered My Rae's had been, and she was tall like my mother. But in no other way was she like them. She was an American. Her voice was low and cool. She had no accent when she spoke, and she could read English. She smiled a lot and laughed at things. Someone like that didn't carry heavy burdens on her heart, dark sorrows that made her whimper in the night. Though I felt a little guilty toward my mother and maybe even toward the memory of My Rae, I was madly in love with Miss Huntington.

Would I have been so attentive to learning otherwise? I hung on her every word. I watched her lips form the letters she had written on the board and I copied her accent; I modulated my voice to imitate her tones. Ay, Bee, Cee—it was easy for me. Many of the letters looked like they sounded, *S* like a snake, *K* like a crash, *L* like a leap, *O* like an oooh. I memorized them right away, hearing her voice in my ears.

"Who can say the whole alphabet?" she asked, and my arm shot up.

"Me, Miss Huntington. I can." I ripped the letters off at great speed while some of the children tittered at my intensity.

One day she explained silent letters to us, and cases when letters made unusual sounds: "'*G-h*' sometimes has a *fff* sound," she told us. Then she wrote letters on the board. "Who knows what this word is?" The class was silent.

"E-n . . ." I struggled with the code. I knew it! *"Enough!"* I shouted, floating through the air on diaphanous wings. The secret of reading was mine. The class murmured, awed by my miracle. "Wonderful, Lillian," she said, beaming at me, pronouncing my name in American, making it sound as wonderful as she was.

One morning we lined up in the schoolyard, waiting for Miss Huntington to come and take us in to class as she always did. Instead the vice principal, Miss O'Reilly, came, a no-nonsense woman of great girth and steely gray hair. "Miss Huntington is sick," she announced, "and I will be with you today."

But Miss O'Reilly had important administrative papers to tend to, so she had no time to stand in front of the class and deliver lessons. "You must be very good boys and girls, very quiet," she told us, passing out the picture books that were reserved for reward days.

She sat at Miss Huntington's desk, absorbed in writing and figuring, ignoring the din until it couldn't be ignored any longer, then rapped on the desk with a ruler. "Silence. Do I have to give out demerits?" The roar died down briefly, then rose on a wave again.

"All right," she announced. "We're going to have a contest. Whoever can be the quietest for the longest will get a very valuable present, a toy that you'll love." The class tittered, but she had struck a chord. There was silence for a while, then only occasional whispering. From time to time she looked up. "It's something everyone would love to have," she reminded us.

The boy in the row next to me was sitting with his hands folded, eyes straight ahead, lips sealed. "Look at Shlomo," she said. "Are you going to let Shlomo be the one to get the valuable present?" Some imitated his posture for a few minutes, then tired of the game.

Shlomo's shoes had low tops and were made of the smooth, rich, dark brown leather such as I had lusted after, not like my cheap-looking, scuffed high-tops. He carried his lunch and his homework to school in a leather satchel with a picture of Pinocchio on it. I had seen him one day walking with his father and a happy-looking mother and sisters. He had everything. It was I who needed the valuable present.

I folded my hands and extended them in front of me, much farther than Shlomo's. I peered into the distance with glazed eyes. I pressed my lips together tightly, as though I never cared to open them again. I became as rigid as a soldier, a corpse. A fly buzzed around me and I did not acknowledge it. Only once in a while did I dare to glance over at Shlomo to see if he were still in the running. I mustn't let him beat me—he couldn't beat me.

It felt like hours later when Miss O'Reilly announced that it was time for our nutrition break. "I have finished my work," she said. "And now I will keep my promise." She left as the monitor passed out milk and graham crackers, and she returned with a large paper bag. "Class, which student do you think should get the present?"

My heart sank. She was leaving it up to them. They would never choose me. I had no friend who would speak out for me.

"Barbara Ann," one girl said, naming the prettiest girl in class.

"Barbara Ann is a chatterbox," Miss O'Reilly said abruptly. "Lillian, come up here."

She had noticed. There was justice in America! My blood beat a joyful tattoo.

"Shlomo, you come up here, too." For him she pulled a big box out of the bag. "Shlomo, do you know who Albert Einstein is? This is a chemistry set. You work hard with this chemistry set and someday you,

Shlomo Schwartz, will be another Albert Einstein." There was a bored pattering of applause as Shlomo returned to his seat.

To me she said, "Now, Lillian, you have a choice. Would you like a toy or a useful present?"

She looked at me expectantly. I knew the answer I was supposed to give. But maybe she had a doll with blond hair and blue eyes that opened and closed in that bag. I had never had a doll before. Maybe it was a pair of skates, or a bow and arrow, or something else more wonderful than I could even imagine. My classmates held their collective breath along with me. They would have chosen the toy, I knew. And the toy, the lovely, frivolous luxury of it, was what I wanted.

"Come on, Lillian," she prompted. My name had never sounded so heavy, so adult before. I hated the way she pronounced it, impoverishing me even more by cutting a whole syllable out of it: *Lil-yun*. I could not open my mouth to say what I knew she wanted me to say, what a little girl who was so serious that she would sit for hours as still as a corpse in order to win a valuable present should say.

"I would like the toy, please," I blurted out.

"What?" she asked in disbelief, or perhaps to bully me into reconsideration.

"I would like the toy," I said again.

"Shame on you," she came back. "I know how hard your mother has to work to support you, a girl without a father. Don't you want to help her out? Don't you want something serious that will help her out?"

I expected my classmates to giggle at the news of my fatherless state, but they were silent, as solemn in the battle now as I was.

"I would like the toy, please," I repeated.

A half dozen of them clapped their hands; one cheered, "*Yeaa.*"

"Quiet," Miss O'Reilly admonished them. "All right, Lillian. I'm surprised at you. That was not a good choice, but you may have it." She took out of the sack a book with a worn gray cover. "*The Last of the Mohicans*," she informed me. I sucked in my breath in disappointment, and it seemed to me that I heard the class echo my sound.

"And because your mother needs all the help she can get, I'm going to give you the serious present too." Now she handed me a little bag. I opened it just enough to see that it contained beige cotton stockings.

"But in the future, I want you to remember to make a wiser choice," she said, dismissing me back to my seat.

They applauded for me again, and this time all of them joined in. I couldn't decide if it was in commiseration over the way I'd been tricked or preached to or if I'd really won their admiration by standing firm for my desire.

When we went out to the playground at noon, I was alone again, as though their tribute had never happened. But I felt somehow that I'd tasted a victory over forces that weren't sympathetic to me. I'd learned that I could win, I could earn applause, but, even better, I could be strong enough to demand my desire. I might not get it, but I would get the satisfaction of knowing I couldn't be daunted.

Those Saturday evenings when my mother dressed up and left me I knew where she was going, though she never told me. I knew she would never be finished with him, that man she thought looked like Charles Boyer. The more I became aware of how overwhelmingly I loved her, the more I despised him.

"You have me, Mommy," I said one Saturday evening when she didn't make up her face to go out and I found her crying in our room.

"It's not the same thing." She made a sad little smile. And I knew for sure that she was crying now not about the lost relatives but about Moishe and how much she missed him when she wasn't with him. "To who can I let out my bitter heart?" she sighed to the air.

Moishe, that hated name. I wanted her not to need anyone else. I wanted to be everything to her.

But her life was so hard, so full of losses, her work so exhausting. She had to stand on her feet the whole day, she told me, because it was her job to drape the dresses on the tall, stuffed mannequins. "No sitting," the forelady barked at any draper who might be weakened for a minute by her period or her troubles and tried to pull up a stool from the finishers' station. In the steaming New York summers it was especially bad: My mother's mannequin was next to the pressers, and she'd be bathed and scalded by vapors from their hot machines. And there was no escape: She had to support us. "My whole body is breaking from tiredness," she'd sigh as we walked the block and a half together from my nursery school, and I could feel the tremor of her tiredness in the fingers I clutched. Once in our room, she threw off her clothes and stretched naked and immobile on our bed, where I, sitting on a corner of it, watched over her as she stared up at the ceiling until she could drag herself to cool off in the bathtub. *"Rateveh mich,* save me. Save me from the shop, Lilly," she said once, gazing at the ceiling with a little smile on her lips that confused me. My mother didn't joke. Was she joking now? "Save me from the shop," she said again and sighed.

"How, Mommy? What should I do?" I asked, primed to do anything in her service.

"You can't," she admitted. "How could you?" Then, "Become a movie star."

Did she mean it? Could I become a movie star? I would do it, I promised myself. That's what I would become! She needed my help, and I would not fail her!

One evening, when my mother and I returned home after our long day, a squat little person was waiting in our room, wearing a small brown hat and veil, balancing an enormous black patent leather purse on her lap, sitting stiffly on the edge of the room's only chair.

"She's back. My *Malech Hamovas* is back," my mother said to the air. "Angel of Death, now you come back, after you left us for so long alone!" she turned to the veil and yelled.

My Rae lifted her veil, gathered me into her arms, wet my cheeks with her tears. *"Shepseleh meine,* my little lamb."

"My Rae!" I threw myself at her, then pulled away. My mother wouldn't like it.

"The *mameh ohn a boich vaytik* is back, the mama without a belly-ache," my mother translated bitterly for my benefit, though I didn't need the translation.

"Why you didn't answer my letters?" My aunt wept to my mother in English. "Why you disappear and my letters come back to me? Thank God the old super heard where you moved and took pity on me. You want to kill me? You almost killed me," she shrilled.

"You're the murderer, you!" My mother outdid her, resuming the litany I hadn't heard in a while. "You cockroach, you. You bigmouth, you."

But after my mother emptied herself and my aunt shed all her renewed tears, after both women yelled themselves to hoarseness, My Rae suddenly declared, as though they hadn't been screaming about death and destruction for the last hour, "The baby needs eats."

We went to the Automat. Neither woman spoke to the other, but both piled my plate high. They had no family except each other, no children in the next generation except me, and they were signaling a kind of truce, one we would live with for a while.

"Look how pale and skinny she is." My aunt felt my ribs.

"I need you to tell me how to take care of my *kind?* Where were you when I needed you? Now we don't need you. Go back to California." My mother tossed her hand and grumbled, yet, it seemed to my ear, less vehemently than before.

My aunt did go back to California, but not alone.

I'll never know what got into my mother a few weeks later. I'd been watching her in the mirror, just as I had on so many Saturdays, while she put on her makeup. This time, though, I wasn't sad because My Rae had said she would take me to the Automat. She stayed with us now, sleeping on the Missus's couch in the living room. It hadn't taken me any time at all to remember how much I'd loved her.

"When you were a little tiny *puttzeh-ruttzehleh*," she reminded me to my giggly glee, "I took you into my arms and I held you next to my heart. And you know what you did, little *gonif*, little thief? You crawled right in, and you never crawled out again."

Though I'd lost the image of her over the last couple of years, she had crawled deep into my heart too, I realized. I'd never stopped loving her. How I loved her now! But different from the way I loved my mother. My mother I would have to take care of. My aunt would take care of me. I needed them both, desperately.

"Can I have lemon meringue pie? And then can we go see the Rockettes at Radio City Music Hall?" I'd asked for the biggest treats I could think of, and I knew as sure as I knew the sun would rise the next day that she would give them to me.

My mother looked distracted now as she put on a blue low-necked dress, but suddenly, as though she'd resolved something that was troubling her, her face in the mirror was suffused with a brightness, and she turned to me and cried, "Lilly, I'm taking you."

"Where am I going?" I asked. *What about the lemon meringue pie and the Rockettes?*

She didn't answer. Instead she pulled me to her and passed a comb through my knotted hair. "Let's make you look nice." From somewhere she produced a big wrinkled bow that I remembered seeing only in a picture of me that My Rae had had a photographer take long before she'd left us. My mother pinned the bow to my head with a bobby pin that scraped my scalp.

"Ouch!" I yelled, but she didn't seem to hear me.

"Where are you taking the baby?" My Rae cried.

"I have to try just one more time."

"Mary, you crazy, leave the baby here with me," My Rae yelled, her hands scrabbling for me.

But my mother clutched my wrist and pulled me down the stoop. "We're late!" She seemed like a different person—excited, worried, but happy too, all at the same time.

A big yellow car passed. "Taxi," my mother cried and waved at it until it pulled up to the curb.

I'd never been in a taxi before. "They're for rich people," she'd told me once, though now we were rattling along in one. I pressed close to her, but she seemed to have forgotten I was there. The taxi driver stopped in front of a restaurant that I'd never been to in all my excursions with her, and she clutched again at my wrist to pull me out. The strangeness of it all. My mother looked up and down the street and I looked with her, but none of the passing people was the one she wanted to see.

Who were we waiting for? It was him, I was sure, the one she dressed for every Saturday and left me for. I stood with her in front of the restaurant, squeezing her hand hard, leaning my weight on her arm, balancing on one foot, then on the other.

The El train roared above us. Now she freed her hand from mine and paced up and down.

I hopped to the lamppost near the curb and twirled round and round it, making myself dizzy. I didn't want to think. A starched pink and white little girl about my age walked by, snug between her father and mother. She stared open-mouthed, as though I looked funny, and I put my thumb to my nose and wiggled my four fingers at her, making a rude sound with my tongue and lips.

She did the same to me. "Stop that, Marsha." Her father slapped her hand down, and they walked on.

When I next looked at my mother, she was talking to a man who was wearing a gray suit and a pearl gray Homburg. Charles Boyer. I held tight to the lamppost, watching them.

I saw him glance over at me, and his lip curled before he turned back to my mother. "Why did you bring her?" I heard him say in Yiddish, his mouth twisting around the words.

The El train again roared overhead and I couldn't hear my mother answer, but her back was bent, her hands open, imploring.

He shook his head, then glanced at me again. Was this stranger my father?

My mother came to me and I clutched hard at the lamppost.

"Come, Lilly, come," she said and pulled at my hand. "Say hello to your father." She nudged my back.

Father. I knew what the word meant, but what did it mean to me? I stared at the gray cloth of the man's coat in front of my eyes. "Hello, Father," I said, raising my eyes, suddenly shy.

"I'm not your father. This is crazy," he snapped to my mother.

"No, Moishe, please," she cried.

"What are you trying to do?" His voice dripped distaste. Then he turned, and I watched his legs scissor away from us. He must have been wearing taps on his heels. *Tap, tap, tap, tap,* his shiny black shoes went, and my mother stood there weeping.

I was glad to see his form grow tinier and tinier. He hated us. I nuzzled hard into her chest, wrapped my arms tight round her waist, and she only sobbed louder.

That night My Rae tucked me into bed, but I wasn't asleep when she stood in the hallway with my mother and told her, "You leave and you'll see. He'll come after you. What do you have here? There we'll be together." My mother answered with groans. "You stay here," my aunt kept on, "and he won't stop thinking you're his *kurveh*, his whore."

Then, a few weeks later, I was taken to Gimbel's department store, and My Rae bought me two dresses, dark plaid, "so they shouldn't show the dirt," and a dark green coat, "to travel," she told the saleswoman. And then my mother and I were sitting together with My Rae on a train, chugging across the continent.

"To California," my mother answered when I asked where we were going. "Where the movie stars are."

So she really had been serious! She did think I could do it. She did want me to become a movie star and rescue her from the shop!

My mother had taken me to see Al Jolson in the movies. He was a big star, she said, and he was Jewish. I knew enough about anti-Semitism by then to understand that being Jewish could be a handicap. But he had made it. With my Semitic hair and eyes and my nose that was slightly convex where it should have been slightly concave, I knew already that I would never be beautiful like the *shiksas*, Marlene Dietrich, Joan Craw-ford, Barbara Stanwyck. But I could be like him. I had heard him sing "Mammy" and "California, Here I Come." I could do that just as he did, falling on one knee with my arms open wide. My mother told me that sometimes movie directors found their stars in the most unexpected places. Lana Turner was discovered at a drugstore soda fountain, she said.

I did a soft-shoe up and down the aisle of our train as we sped west for four days: "California, here I come, right back where I started from." I waved my arms and belted out my chant. "Where bow wows of flowers bloom in the sun, where birdies sing and everything." No one had ever told me that songs had tunes that your voice was supposed to follow. When my mother had sung, on her good days as we walked together in Crotona Park, it was her words I heard, not the tune—she had no tune. She just let her voice slide up and down: "Oh, my man I love him so, he'll never know," she half sang and half said. "When he takes me in his arms the world seems swell." I put great expression in my voice, like Jol-son did. Some of my trainmates smiled at the intense, scruffy seven-year-old. Others looked irritated or buried their noses deeper into their magazines or embroidery. I continued regardless. How could you tell what a movie director looked like?

I knew I'd failed when my aunt said we were arriving in Los Angeles early the next morning. No movie director had discovered me; my mother would have to find another job in a shop.

But how could anyone feel like a failure in the Southern California sunshine? It had been cold when we left New York, but when we stepped off the train in Union Station it was springtime. He, her lover, was thousands of miles away. He would not come for her, I knew. And hadn't she forgiven her sister? She'd agreed that we would go to California together. The future seemed as cheery as what I remembered of the end of *All This and Heaven Too*.

Outside the station the lawns were green, like the ones in Crotona Park. In Los Angeles, I saw, the streets were like parks. Even better. There were tall, skinny trees with huge zigzaggy leaves that sprouted only on the trees' very tops, like messy wigs on long giants. They were as enchanting as the pictures in the Dr. Seuss book that Miss Huntington read to the class for a special treat. I had been transported to another world, where the sun shone even when winter was not over, where everything looked magical and amusing. I would live happily ever after with my mother and My Rae. It was more wonderful than if I'd been given the doll with blond hair and blue eyes. What joy! What joy!

And I would be discovered. I would learn to sing and dance and act, and maybe to ride horseback or play the violin, and I would become a child star. I would work hard. I would never be lazy. I would get up early in the morning and start practicing, and I would practice until late at night.

Every nerve of me was set for the race. Not just for that moment, there at Union Station, but forever. It might take a bit of time, but a movie director would discover me.

And then I would rescue my mother from the shop.

2   Going Crazy in East L.A.

THE NAME OF OUR NEW Missus was Fanny Diamond. That first evening, without teeth in her mouth, her nose and chin almost meeting, she looked to me like a scarier twin sister of the wicked witch in *The Wizard of Oz*. (Her teeth, as I later discovered, always sat in a glass of water near her bed when it wasn't mealtime.) While she showed the dining room with a cot where My Rae would sleep and the bedroom where my mother and I would sleep, I lagged behind because I wanted to examine a row of glass jars I'd spied on a living room shelf. They held floating objects that looked from a distance like marbles: Now I could see that they were blue or brown or green at their centers, and they had big borders that were wrinkled and yellowish or milky blue and smooth. The smooth ones looked as though they'd just been plucked from a person's head. Yes. There was no mistaking what they were. Eyeballs! My stomach contracted. I ran at a gallop to find my mother, who was following Fanny to the kitchen now.

"It's all right. My Marty is a eye doctor," Fanny cackled.

"Can we go now?" I begged, grabbing at my mother's arm, but she didn't hear me because she was listening to Fanny tell her how to turn on the old gas stove.

I tugged at the sleeve of My Rae's blouse to make her bend down. "I don't like it here," I whispered in her ear.

She stage-whispered back, "When we get some money for furniture, we'll take an apartment. For now we have to live with a Missus."

There were twin beds in our room, but that first night I lay in my mother's bed, clutching her arm until she said, "I have to turn over now, Lilly." I glued my body to her back and wouldn't let go of her because I couldn't get the floating eyeballs out of my mind.

When I awoke in the early morning, it was to an awful odor that I remembered from long before, in New York, when I'd burned my pinkie finger on an iron that my aunt kept hot so that she could press her piecework. Fanny's house was on a corner, next door to a kosher chicken market, and when the wind was wrong, the smell of singed feathers and skin was powerful. That first Friday on Dundas Street, I went to the market with my mother and My Rae to select a chicken. I breathed through my mouth, trying vainly to block the smell. Live chickens, hundreds of them, were packed tightly into cages, to be freed only when a housewife pointed and said to the chicken man, "Gimme this one." Then he extricated the chosen one by its legs while the other chickens squawked an uproar, and he handed it over to a *shochet*, a kosher slaughterer, who tied its legs to a noose that hung from the ceiling.

I watched it all, unable to look away after My Rae had selected our chicken. Its mournful little head and beak pointed downward, and with one deft stroke of his razor, the *shochet* sliced its throat. The blood dripped and puddled onto the sawdust floor until the chicken was cut down and ran in little circles, its almost-severed head flopping grotesquely, ribboning blood, its still-undead wings beating frantically. When it finally collapsed on the sawdust floor, another man, wearing a big leather apron, singed its feathers off, wrapped the naked bird in a newspaper tied with string, and gave it to me.

I carried home the warm bundle, a dead baby placed eerily in my arms by the big jolly executioner. Then my aunt unwrapped it, spread it on the drainboard, sawed it into pieces with a big knife, and sprinkled the dissected parts with the coarse salt that she poured into her hand from a yellow box bearing the word KOSHER in English and Yiddish. I ran out of the kitchen. But when I had to go back for a drink of water, I couldn't help looking again at the nude, hacked-up thing that had been a white-feathered, squawking creature only a short while before. A couple of hours later, the pale yellow pieces were bobbing and dodging bits of carrots and onions in a big pot of water that sat over a flame on the gas stove.

At supper I gagged with my first bite. I could still smell the singed feathers and skin, and I ran from the table out to the rickety front porch, my aunt running after me with a drumstick in her hand. I clamped my lips tight and shook my head violently until she retreated.

"No appetite," I heard her mutter as the screen door creaked shut behind her. "Wrists skinny like a chicken bone."

"Ooh, look, the witch's daughter," two passing boys about my age hooted at me as I stood on the porch. "Witch, witch, come out on your broomstick," they shouted at the house through cupped hands.

But the three of us were together again. On Saturdays my mother and My Rae and I took a bus to Hollenbeck Park and walked in the sunshine amid the lush California greenery, or we pressed close, I in the middle, on a silvered wooden swing the size of a loveseat that overlooked a dark pond alive with quacking ducks. "Lift your legs and I'll swing you," I ordered them, standing on my tiptoes to push us off. My mother had a dreamy look in her eyes and a faint smile on her lips.

"Look at who's Samson," My Rae said.

"Me!" I chortled, making our collective three hundred pounds swing back and forth.

They left the house together every morning and took three buses to get to their shops in the downtown neighborhood of tall buildings where the garment manufacturers were. In the late afternoon they came back together, and when I heard their voices on the porch I rushed to throw myself at them, first my mother and then My Rae. I shadowed my mother through the house, happy that the long day at a strange school (where the funny way I said *waata* and *singk* had already been noted) was over and we were together again.

But even before she put her purse down, she went to find Fanny. "Did I get any letters?" she asked.

"Not a single thing." Fanny's answer was always the same.

In the beginning my mother nodded and smiled. As the weeks and months went by she stopped smiling. "Nothing?" she'd ask again.

"Listen, the only thing the letter carrier ever brings is big bills for me."

"Watch me do Eddie Cantor," I'd beg my mother, pulling at her skirt, arresting her there in Fanny's dark and dusty hallway. I made my big eyes bigger and rolled them round and round. "Oh, you beautiful doll, you great big beautiful doll," I sang, and I gestured grandly, first to my heart and then to her person, with open-fingered hands.

"I'm so proud of my little girl," my mother said. But I knew her thoughts were elsewhere.

"Watch me do Jack Benny now," I demanded, following her in a soft-shoe dance, playing my air violin and humming a screechy tune that I ad-libbed. "Mommy, wait, look." She flopped on her bed and stared up at the ceiling.

"Can I read to you?" I asked, positioning myself at the side of the bed with one of the books I'd gotten from the Malabar Public Library. She moved over to make room for me, but she didn't take her eyes from the ceiling. "Are you listening?" How could I pull her back from where she was in her head? I put all the expression I could muster into the words. "The outlook wasn't brilliant for the Mudville nine that day," I orated. "The score stood four to two with one inning left to play . . ."

But she didn't look interested in what Casey could do at the bat. I switched books. "Tell me not, in mournful numbers, Life is but an empty dream!" I didn't understand all the words, and I knew that she understood even less than I did, but I put plenty of voice music into it, making solemn low sounds and then, for contrast, high happy sounds. I held the book with one hand and waved the other in the air. I declaimed to the end of the poem and then read her another and yet another. "Did you like it?" I asked anxiously.

"I'm so proud of my little girl," she said again, and she held me in her arms when I lay down next to her, but her face was like pale stone, and I knew I hadn't taken away her sadness.

More and more, as the months wore on, when My Rae came to say supper was ready, my mother told her, "I can't eat" or "Who wants food now?"

"Well, the baby needs to eat," My Rae said the first time my mother shooed her away. She took me by the hand and pulled me toward the torn oilcloth-covered kitchen table.

"I'm not a baby anymore. Haven't you noticed?" I sassed her and bucked free and scurried back to my mother, to put my arms around her, pat her soft dark curls, make her feel better. When would she stop missing him?

My mother stopped putting lipstick on her beautiful lips. I never saw her burning a match anymore to make herself eye shadow. The blouse she wore to work had half-moons of yellowish stain under the arms, and the hem drooped and dangled threads from the bottom of her skirt, but she wore them that way week after week.

"Fix yourself," my aunt said gruffly, "for the sake of the baby. Forget about *vus iz gevehn*, what was. It's over. Moishe, Europe, over and done with."

My mother bared her teeth at My Rae like a mad dog, like she used to do in New York. "I don't need you to tell me nothing," she growled.

Something bad was happening to her, but how could I stop it? What if she drove My Rae away again? We'd be alone, in a strange house and a strange room in a strange city. I wanted the old times back, when the three of us pressed together on the wooden swing and my aunt called me Samson. But I couldn't be with both of them at the same time, and it was my mother who needed me most, so it was in our bedroom, reading on her bed while she stared up at the ceiling, that I spent the evenings. Sometimes, though, when my mother was asleep or in her trance, I slipped out to find My Rae in the dining room. I'd throw my arms around her furtively and bury my head in her big, sheltering bosom, as I knew I mustn't do in my mother's presence. "I know, Lilly, I know," My Rae said, and pressed her lips to my forehead before I broke away and ran back to my mother.

At the end of the summer, my aunt bought some forest green worsted and paid a dollar to the cutter at Bartleman's, her shop, to snip out the pattern for two dresses. For weeks she stayed late at work. "Who needs her to ride home with me on the bus," my mother grumbled.

On the first morning of the High Holidays, before it was time to go to the synagogue, My Rae called me into the dining room. She was wearing a beautiful new dress, with gold disks running all the way down the front, and she held up its miniature, an exact copy, and buttoned me into it with nimble fingers. "For Rosh Hashanah." She turned me round and round to examine her handiwork. "*Oy vee shayn*, how beautiful!" she exclaimed. "Who's the love of Rae's life?" she sang as she puffed my sleeves and fiddled with my collar.

I looked down at myself. I adored the Robin Hood color, the big gold buttons that were just a little smaller than hers, the way we matched. "Who's the love of Lilly's life?" I sang back, making sure to keep my voice low so my mother wouldn't hear.

The next week, I sat again with my mother and aunt in the cramped upstairs hall of the Breed Street Synagogue while the men downstairs droned their Yom Kippur pleas to Yahweh, and the women above who could read Hebrew bent over their prayer books and chorused along with them. When it was time to say *yizkor*, the memorial prayer for the dead, we kids were superstitiously ushered out. "Hurry, go," the mothers said, shooing us, because only those whose loved ones had died said *yizkor* or even remained in a room where it was being said. I hurried off, as superstitious as the grownups. I sat on the concrete steps, watching some girls play a quarreling game of hopscotch in front of the synagogue, until, twenty minutes or so later, a big kid came out and called to his little brothers down the street, "Hey, get back here, I think they're finished."

"Why did you say *yizkor* for them?" I could hear my mother even as I was walking back through the upstairs doors. Her eyes blinked out of control. "You louse," she hissed at my aunt's face. "Hirschel's not dead! You want to kill him by making believe he's dead?"

There was spit on my aunt's cheek. She swiped at her face with the sleeve of her dress. "Mary, control yourself in the *shul*," she whispered hoarsely.

The people in the rows around us who'd been fanning themselves against the heat with prayer books or pledge envelopes stopped and stared. The loud *davening* of the men downstairs could not drown out the whispers of my mother and My Rae.

"They're not dead! None of them! How do you know they're dead?" My mother forgot now to try to whisper.

"Shaddup for the baby at least," My Rae moaned.

"You lousy bitch!"

My Rae jumped up and sidled out, knocking against the legs of the women in our row.

"What's going on here?" a large angry woman in a black cloche demanded.

"*Mishugenehs*, crazy people," a lady in a polka-dot blouse yelled. Her eyes were red from *yizkor* weeping.

Now my mother jumped up, following My Rae, shoving aside the same legs.

"*Tsk! Tsk! Tsk! Tsk!*" I heard all around, and a buck-toothed girl sitting down the row bent over to stare at me as though I were a bug.

"Excuse me," I begged, passing the legs. "Excuse me. Excuse us," and I fled down the synagogue stairs after my mother and my aunt.

The week before Thanksgiving, the teacher passed out big new boxes of Crayolas and white stenciled sheets, and I lost myself in the lavish variety of the wax sticks. Tongue between my teeth, I gripped the Crayolas and colored Indian faces Carmine Red (because we'd been told they were red men) and pilgrim dress Midnight Black and Earth Brown. I solved the problem of their "white" English skin by leaving their faces and hands uncolored. Chartreuse and magenta and teal were the colors of the heaps of food they shared with the red men. I yearned for a peace in our house like the peace between the pilgrims and the Indians. Those idyllic afternoons at Hollenbeck Park were already a far memory. They fought all the time now.

"Forget the past!" My Rae always yelled at my mother. "Forget Moishe, he should grow a cancer in his heart! Forget Europe."

But my mother couldn't. "Moishe would have married me, but you had to take us away."

"He wanted you to go again for another abortion," my aunt once hollered in her own defense. "He told you to give her up for adoption," she shouted another time.

Both times my mother pulled me to her, protecting me again from annihilation (and letting my aunt know to whom I belonged). "I would die first," she vowed ferociously each time, as though the threats against me were imminent still.

That Thanksgiving morning I jumped out of bed and raced. I'd heard my mother's voice screaming from the dining room, "You *choler-yeh*, you cholera-infected one! You brought me and the baby to this dump, and now you're going to leave us alone?" She stood in her thin nylon nightgown, its straps fallen to her arms, looming over my shriveled aunt. My Rae looked as paper-pale as the pilgrims in my crayoned pictures. She was dressed, a brown coat buttoned up to her chin, a little navy hat perched on her head. She gripped a bulging cardboard valise.

"What are we supposed to do now? Answer me!" My mother's breasts flopped as she moved, and my breath caught at the glint in her eyes that was like those of the crazy women I'd seen in a movie, *The Snake Pit*. And we were alone, the three of us, because Fanny had left the night before to spend Thanksgiving at the eye doctor's house.

"Lilly!" my aunt cried when she saw me. "If I go I can help you." She straightened and ran to draw me to her, but I squirmed to get away. She knew she mustn't do that in my mother's presence! She pulled me back, and my nose shoved against her bosom, choking me. "*Shepseleh, meineh.*" She kept her fingers on my head. "I can't do anything for you if I stay here."

I broke free and ran to my mother's side. What was happening here? What did my mother mean, "leave us alone"?

"With Mr. Bergman I can make a home and help you."

What was she talking about?

"Do you know what that bloodsucker is doing?" my mother bellowed.

My aunt moved toward the door, my mother at her heels. I held on to the table, my head thrumming, the floor tilting. Then I forced my knees to unbuckle, and I bolted after them.

"Do you know what she's doing?" my mother shrieked again.

Now, through the glass panes on the door I saw a little man in a brown hat walk up the porch steps. He opened the screen door and rang the bell formally, though he must have spied the three of us peering at him from the other side. We froze for an instant, all four of us, like characters in a funny papers cartoon. Then my aunt unfroze, opened the door, and shut it behind her.

"My Rae! No!" I cried.

"Don't go after that louse!" My mother's arm held me back.

I broke away and threw myself at the door, but my hand remained stuck to the doorknob, as though under a spell. They stood on the porch. I could see my aunt's shoulders heaving. Mr. Bergman, who'd taken his hat off in her presence, held it in one hand and patted her back with the other. He moved his lips, saying words I couldn't hear. She turned to look back at us, and I opened my mouth to cry "Come back," but nothing came out. He was old, much older than my aunt, with a bald head and a kind, round face, and he wore an immaculate beige suit and polished brown shoes. He put his arm around her, led her to a black car that was parked in front of the house, settled her in, and drove off with her.

"Do you know what that *choleryeh* is doing?" my mother yelled. "She's getting married!"

My mother and I live in the front bedroom of Fanny Diamond's house. Though my mother often says we're going back to where we came from, the black metal trunk that we brought with us from New York stands unpacked. It makes up part of the furniture in our room. Through the years, my dresses and blouses and skirts that can't fit on the hook behind the door I pile on top of the trunk, my only closet. In my mother's small closet are stuffed all the dresses she used to wear when she went to see her lover.

If the window shades were up, there might be sunshine in our room, but they're always down, hiding us because we're separated from the pavement outside by only a two-foot swath of grass. But the shades have serious rips on their sides, and if a peeping tom or kids egging each other on want to, they can peek in and see my mother running naked up and down our narrow room, bumping into the twin beds, the dresser, our metal trunk, tearing her hair until it stands straight up. "Hirschel," she cries to her crippled brother. "I didn't kill you! Don't you know how I love you?" I close the door so that Fanny won't hear her, but I can't do anything about the people who walk by on Dundas Street and can see and hear it all.

I run back and forth in the room, following my mother, keeping up with her pace, two chickens cut down from the noose. "He's okay, Mommy. He's not dead."

"Zay hargenen yidden, they're killing Jews!" Her eyes are shut tight,

and she screams as though under her lids she can see it. "Gevalt! Help! I did a terrible thing!" she shrieks with her mouth open wide. When she drops onto her bed, I cradle her head; I smooth her wet forehead; I place the tenderest kisses on her ash-colored face. I know I am all she has in the world.

When I'm home alone, I watch myself in the mottled dresser mirror as I practice my routines. I recite "To Think That I Saw It on Mulberry Street" in my six-year-old-boy voice, but with dramatic flourishes and great urgency. How will I get a job as an actress? What can I do to get discovered? If my mother didn't have to go to the shop every day, she could rest and get well. "When my baby smiles at me," I belt out my sing-say. I throw my head back, hand on hip, shoulder forward. I lift my skirt to my thigh and pose my leg. Would I look more like Betty Grable if I could dye my hair blond?

One Saturday I was startled from sleep by my mother, hair spiked, a wild woman, banging on her head with her fists. "I killed him! Oh, my God, help me!"

I jumped up and took my place behind her in the chicken dance. "It's okay, Mommy. He's okay. Everything's okay." Where was My Rae? Who else could help me with my poor sick mother? *Come back, I need you, I can't do this alone!* But I didn't even know where to phone her.

It was afternoon before my mother stopped, like a wound-down clock. She flopped onto her bed, stared at the ceiling like someone hypnotized, then sank finally into sleep. I sat on the edge of the bed, watching over her, a mother with a sick child. The world was silent except for her soft snores. What would become of us? Through the ripped window shade, I looked out at a slice of empty street.

When a black car stopped in front of the house, I leaped to my feet and pulled up the shade. She was here. But for how long? Had she changed her mind? I watched as they both got out. My aunt was wearing a shiny dress that came down to her ankles, and a gardenia corsage was pinned at her heart. Mr. Bergman was decked out too, in a powder blue suit, smiling amiably. My aunt's eyes were red and puffy, and she carried a big cooking pot in her hands.

My head buzzed and bumbled. She was here. Finally. But not to stay. I raced to the front door, but Fanny had already opened it, and I lagged behind her, suddenly shy before that stranger with a pot.

"Look what I brought for your supper," my aunt cried when she saw me.

I hadn't eaten all day, and I could smell the *gedempfte flaysch* even through the screen door. At the rich odor my stomach rose, but I ignored it. It had been weeks since I'd laid eyes on My Rae. I loved her more than anything in the world, except for my mother. How could she have abandoned me? "Go away!" I shouted from behind Fanny and saw Mr. Bergman's expression change from amiability to shock and then sternness. I wanted to scream at her, *You said that when I was a baby you held me to your heart and I crawled right in forever, and now you've left us alone to get married!* But all I yelled before I ran back to my sleeping mother was, "I don't want your *gedempfte flaysch.*"

Fanny Diamond was not a witch, she was a *schnorrer*. That's what my mother and My Rae called a stingy person who acts like a beggar. She owned the kosher chicken market on the corner, and she also owned the dark little grocery store next door to the chickens, where you could buy sour pickles from briny barrels. But every afternoon Fanny donned her dead husband's woolen overcoat and wing-tipped shoes in order to preserve the raggedy dresses and down-at-the-heels shoes that were her daily costume, and, almost disappearing in the clothes of someone who'd been a head taller and a hundred pounds heavier, she watered the tiny patch of manicured lawn in front of our house's tattered screens and chipped stucco. "You live there?" my schoolmates said, fascinated and repelled when they found out that I shared the dilapidated, spooky house on Dundas Street with the witch lady.

Fanny must have heard my mother's wailing, but if she knew what went on behind our closed door, she never let on. Maybe she figured that since my mother went to work every morning, as though she were perfectly well, and paid the forty dollars' rent on the first of every month without fail, nothing very bad could be happening behind the door.

Or maybe she figured that she would help where she could and not interfere where she couldn't. From her daughter Ruthie's home in Beverly Hills she brought me barely worn, maid-starched, and maid-ironed dresses — a peach organdy with puffed sleeves and an orange-ribboned belt, a yellow dotted swiss with a Peter Pan collar, a dress-up buttons-and-bows green velvet. Sally and Becky, her granddaughters, had outgrown them, and Fanny's daughter wanted to give them away to somebody who needed them. Of course the dresses didn't stay in mint condition for long, but at least now I had a lot of different clothes to wear. "Little *momzer*," Fanny called me affectionately when we were alone together. I didn't learn until I was an adult and she was long dead that *momzer* means "bastard."

Not only did Fanny give me her granddaughters' dresses, she gave me her wisdom too. "So, what do you want to be?" she asked one afternoon as I sat at the kitchen table reading a comic book and she stood at the sink eating sardines out of a can.

"I dunno," I answered, a little embarrassed. "Maybe an actress." I'd wanted success always for the sake of my mother, but that ambition had become a part of who I was, and now I wanted it for myself too. Yet I was almost ten years old, and I'd made no progress toward realizing my glorious dream. I still didn't know how to begin.

"Don't be a silly girl," Fanny said, confirming my fears. "Everybody wants to be an actress, but how many actresses do you see in the world?"

In fact, I'd just recently been thinking of a backup plan. Unlike child stardom, which would allow me to rescue my mother right away, with this new plan she'd have to wait for years, but still, it was better than nothing. I remembered seeing Myrna Loy play a judge in *The Bachelor and the Bobby-Soxer*, and I had just seen Katharine Hepburn play an attorney in *Adam's Rib*. They wore gorgeous dresses and had beautiful hairdos and lived in big fancy houses. "Maybe I'll be a lawyer, then," I told Fanny with a shrug.

She cackled. "*Narreleh*, little fool, poor girls don't become lawyers. You better pay good attention in school and you can be a secretary. Like that you can help out your poor mother."

I felt a hot sting in my eyes. She couldn't be right. Mrs. Patrick, my teacher, had told us about Abraham Lincoln, who was poor, and he became the president. "In America anyone can become anything," she'd said. Why shouldn't I believe it? Mrs. Patrick knew more than Fanny.

. . .

Every night as I'm trying to fall asleep I comfort myself with happy fantasies. Lights! Camera! Action! and I, dressed in star-spangled leotards and a star-spangled top hat, break into my whirling, twirling, high-kicking, splits-in-the-air tap dancing routine. Fred Astaire and Danny Kaye dance beside me, beaming broadly at their little co-star's brilliance.

But those child star images give way after a while to images from my comic books. Sometimes I'm clad in red tights, like Mary Marvel, sometimes in blue tights, like Supergirl. Lilly the Kid, that's who I am. Always I fly through the air with a muscled mighty man on one side of me and a muscled mighty boy on the other. I name our missions, and they follow. We grab up into the air the evil men with big lips and Homburg hats, and we deposit them behind jail bars before they can do more harm to women and children. We rescue emaciated and terrified victims, like those I've seen in the movie newsreels, who are only seconds away from their death in concentration camp ovens.

My mother doesn't know for a long time that I am Lilly the Kid, the real brain behind these great deeds that fill the movie newsreels and the Yiddish papers. And then I tell her. Mighty Man and Mighty Boy stand at my side and confirm what I say.

"I'm so proud of my big girl," she tells me every night in my fantasy before I drop off to sleep.

A half-dozen kids from my fourth-grade class stood in a knot on the playground, entranced by the story that Melvin Kaplan and his little sister were telling: "She was walking down the street all naked. Her titties and everything was showing." A couple of them tittered, the rest opened wide eyes. "Our dad saw her. It was like six o'clock in the morning." Melvin and his sister raced each other to tell it. "And then somebody calls an ambulance and says, 'There's a naked lady walking on the street,' and they came to take her away. My dad says they put her in a place for crazy people."

Now they all giggled, and I could hear my heart pounding as though some animal were trying to break out of it.

"And you know what else?" the sister shrieked. "She was sucking on her own titties when the ambulance came. On her own titties!" she yelled, outdoing her brother, relishing the detail.

The girls from my class let out sounds of disgust; a boy whooped.

It was Arthur Grossman's mother they were talking about. Arthur, a boy with curly black hair and large black eyes who looked so much like me that he could have been my brother. He wasn't in school the rest of that week, and when he returned the following Monday, he had a sheepish look, as though he'd done something wrong. On the playground he wandered around by himself, pretending to examine ant trails or little pebbles. I watched him. I wanted to say something to him, but I didn't know what words to use.

The other kids didn't leave him alone for long. "Hey, Arthur, how's your mom?" Sandra Schulman asked with a high-watt smile when we filed out for lunch. He ducked his head and moved off.

In class I couldn't stop watching him. I knew that if he'd been there with his mother that morning, he would have thrown a coat over her and led her by the hand back to their house and closed the door and hidden her from the eyes of the neighbors who told their kids about her shame. But he must have been sleeping the morning it happened. Probably he didn't even know she'd left the house. Probably the ambulance sirens woke him up.

A few weeks later he was absent again, and he never came back to school. Melvin Kaplan and his little sister said that Arthur's father couldn't take care of him, so he had to go live at the Vista Del Mar Home, which was for kids who didn't have any parents. Would I be sent to the Vista Del Mar Home someday?

But sometimes my mother seemed all right. She'd be with me and talk to me as though nothing terrible had ever been wrong, and I'd almost forget how sick she'd been. Sometimes she'd even talk about her family in Europe. We'd be in a restaurant maybe; I'd fiddle with my milkshake straw or try to act casual in some other way, but I'd hold my breath to listen. I yearned to know something—anything—about where I came from, though I never dared ask lest my questions trigger another bad episode.

"When I was ten years old," she reminisced on my own tenth birthday in 1950, when she took me to the Famous Restaurant on Brooklyn

Avenue, "I already worked in seven different jobs." She enumerated them on her fingers. First, she helped out in her *mameh's* tiny grocery store; then she sold onions and cabbages in the shtetl market; then she was a maid for a rich family in Prael; then she took care of children for a family in Dvinsk, the city fifty miles away; then she untangled balls of wool in a Dvinsk shop where they wove cloth; then she was a milliner's apprentice; then she was a tailor's apprentice.

"All those different jobs I had by the time I was ten years old. Then when I knew what I needed to know, I went to work by a tailor as a regular seamstress." She held her teacup with delicacy, her pinkie finger raised like some fine lady's in the movies, and sipped. "So that's what I did in my life until I was eighteen and came to America," she sighed.

"But why did your parents let you go away to work when you weren't even ten?" I knew she'd never *ever* let me go away from her.

"We had no food. If I lived somewhere else, the people there had to feed me. If I lived at home, my *tateh* and *mameh* had to feed me, and they had plenty other mouths to feed without me," my mother said without rancor. "At home, most of the time we got only black bread and potatoes to eat, and maybe a few carrots or cauliflower. Maybe, if we were lucky, on Friday night everybody got a little piece of fish or some meat in a tablespoon."

It had never occurred to me that anyone could be that poor. Though we lived in an ugly furnished room, I always had food, and here we were in the Famous Restaurant and I'd just filled my belly almost to bursting with lamb chops and potato latkes and chocolate cake.

One evening in a Brooklyn Avenue delicatessen she'd ordered a plate of chopped herring for herself. That was when she talked about Hirschel, whose name I'd heard before only through her shrieks. "I was maybe nine years old," my mother said now, "so that means Hirschel was a year old, and my *mameh* gave me a few kopeks and told me go to the market and buy a herring." Enchanted now, I saw my mother as a little girl, a nine-year-old with big dark eyes and curly black hair. "I always carried Hirschel around with me in my hands when I was at home because he was the baby, and my *mameh* was busy with everything else she had to do and couldn't watch him all the time. He was so darling, with his round little head and his little hands with dimples on them." We laughed together at this sweet vision, as though he, a baby still, were happily cooing before our eyes, and I adored them both, my mother, who was a child, and my uncle, the baby, whom I would never see at any age. "We loved each other like I was the one who was the *mameh*," my mother said.

"So I go to the market and I'm carrying Hirschel, and I buy a herring just like my *mameh* told me, and the lady wraps it in a little piece of paper. I carry Hirschel, but I'm so hungry that I can't stand it no more. With my teeth I unwrap the piece of paper, and I just lick at the herring. It's so good, just to have at least a little bit of the salty taste. I lick and lick — and Hirschel falls out of my hands. Right away I got worried, because he was crying till his little face was red like fire. When I get home with him and the herring, he's still crying, and I'm crying too. We're both crying our heads off, and it's black in front of my eyes. I have to tell my *mameh* what happened, but she didn't say much because it didn't look like he was hurt bad, only a few scratches. Except that when he started walking, he had a big limp. And my *mameh* said it was because of me, that I dropped him because I was busy licking the herring and I was the one who made him a cripple." I leaned my head against her bare arm and stroked her fingers that rested on the table. So that was why it was always his name that she cried. If I'd been her *mameh*, I'd never have said those things to hurt her.

When my mother wasn't sick, it was sometimes hard to believe that there would be crazy times again. She bought a little radio, a brown plastic box, and on Friday nights we cuddled on her bed, my leg draped over hers, and we listened together to Dorothy Collins or Snooky Lanson or Gisele MacKenzie sing the romantic songs she loved on "The Lucky Strike Hit Parade." Later I rose on my knees in the bed and sang them again for her, or sometimes I hopped down and did a tapless tap dance or a wildly acrobatic ballet to accompany my singing. "Again" was her favorite. I was pretty sure she was thinking of my father when she heard it, but it didn't really matter because she was looking at me and listening to me and he was thousands of miles away. I pirouetted around as I sang, and my mother moved her lips along with me, bobbing her head in agreement at the important phrases. "Again, this couldn't happen again," we sang. "This is that once in a lifetime. This is that thrill dee-vine."

"I'm not a good mother to you," I heard her say one night after she turned the lights out and I lay in my own bed, waiting for sleep, the words of songs still going through my head.

"Don't say that!" I scolded in the dark. "You're the best mommy in the world."

"I don't know why I get so crazy sometimes," she sighed. "I can't help it."

For a while, Rae and Mr. Bergman would come to take us for a Sunday drive to Ocean Park Beach, but he didn't like it when my mother said my aunt was a *choleryeh*, and finally he wagged his finger at her and told her that in the future she'd have to ride the streetcar if she wanted to go to the beach. But he was really a kind man, and when it came right down to it, he'd do anything my aunt wanted. He'd drive her across town to East L.A. so she could bring us some dish she'd made, and no matter how mad he was at my mother, he'd always slip her five dollars and instruct her, "Buy something nice for *Lilileh*," little Lilly, as he called me. "She's a good girl. Good as gold," he said.

"Good as gold." My aunt bobbed her head, defending me now and against all future incidents and slipping a dollar bill into my own pocket before she left. "What else do I still work for?" she said when I once tried to give it back because I was afraid my mother wouldn't like it.

But most weeks Rae was a ghostly memory. She lived far away, on the other side of town, and I was alone with a sick mother. I could tell by looking at my mother's face when a bad time was coming: there would be a deep flush on her cheeks and neck and chest, and her mouth would change. She'd keep swallowing her lips, or she'd spit out an imaginary speck that would not be gone from her tongue. Her eyes would change too. Someone else looked out from them, a person who barely saw me, not even when I stood in her line of sight to distract her attention from the terrors in her head.

"I did a bad thing!" she howled, and I knew—I had figured it out now—that it wasn't just because she'd dropped her baby brother. It was also because she'd been busy with Moishe when she should have been finding a way to rescue her family. "God punishes me," she wept. She beat her head, her chest.

"Mommy, stop it, stop it, you'll hurt yourself!" I groped for her banging hands. "You have to be all right—what will I do if they take you away?" I cried, hunting for the words that would make her stop.

Something always triggered the spells; often it was a May Company bag. The women at Schneiderman's, her shop, brought their work dresses with them and changed from their street clothes. One woman, a Hungarian whose three brothers had been killed by the Nazis, carried her work dress in an old May Company bag, and that created an excruciating dilemma for my mother. If she carried her own work dress in a May Company bag it would mean that, like the Hungarian woman, she didn't have a brother anymore. But maybe her own brother hadn't been killed. Nobody knew for sure that he had. No one knew anything except that the Jews who were in Prael the summer of 1941 were all murdered. But maybe Hirschel wasn't in Prael that summer, or maybe he escaped and hid somewhere. Maybe he was a displaced person now and would show up in America soon.

But if she carried her work dress in the May Company bag, she was "making" him be dead. It didn't mean that! It did mean that! She forced herself to shop at the May Company, fighting her superstitions. The bags sat in a folded pastel green heap on the dresser and she eyed them, tormented. She put her work dress in a May Company bag with trembling hands, she took it out, she put it in again, she took it out again.

Through the whole ordeal, no matter how long the spell lasted or how bad it was, she got up at six-thirty and was out the door by seven. She almost never missed a day of work. How she controlled herself, how she steadied her hands enough to drape dresses on a mannequin so that she could support us, I can't imagine.

From the Malabar Public Library I borrowed "adult section" books. "They're for my mother," I swore to the blue-haired librarian who wanted to foist *The Secret Garden* and the Nancy Drew books on me when I brought up to her desk for a check-out stamp *Personality Maladjustment and Mental Hygiene, You and Psychiatry, Keeping a Sound Mind.*

I didn't understand most of what I read, but, sitting on my bed or on the milk crate that Fanny kept as a chair on the front porch, I kept reading as though it were a matter of life and death. On the next page might be the simple answer, and I'd learn what to say or do to help my mother. Someone had to do something. Who else was there but me?

I grew up in the shadow of my mother's tragedy.

And, for a while, I caught her sickness. It didn't take the same form; it wasn't full-blown, but the germs were there.

"Good night, Mommy," I said every night from my bed to hers.

"Good night, Lilly."

"Sleep tight, Mommy," I said.

"You too. Sleep tight."

"See you in the morning, Mommy."

"Okay. See you in the morning."

"Good night, Mommy." I waited for her response to the trinity again. "Sleep tight, Mommy." "See you in the morning, Mommy." And then a third time, "Good night, Mommy. . ." She had to chorus back each statement. If she didn't, she would be dead before the night was over. I was certain of it. She must have understood the unspoken rules because she always answered me.

I had another ritual for the mornings, before she left for work. "Watch the way you cross the street, Mommy," I said. "Look both ways, Mommy." "Don't come home late, Mommy." She had to acknowledge each warning, and I had to repeat this trinity three times as well. If we didn't do it right, I knew that something terrible would happen to her that day and I'd never see her again.

Even if we did do it right, most days I was afraid I'd never see her again. At four-thirty every weekday afternoon, I waited at the bus stop across from the Evergreen Cemetery until she came. I never let my toes point directly toward the cemetery because that would mean her death. The second the bus slowed, I peered through the windows, trying to decipher her form in the rush-hour crowd, feeling my face flush hot and hotter. I placed myself squarely in front of the door the instant the bus stopped, and the people who descended before she did had to walk around me or trip over me. When I saw her I was swept by a torrent of cooling relief, and I threw myself at her as though she'd been gone for a month.

If she wasn't on the four-thirty bus, I forced myself to pretend calm and wait for the four forty-five bus. If she wasn't on that one, waiting for the five o'clock bus was like being under a sentence of death and watching without hope for a reprieve. I paced up and down the sidewalk, running to the corner every couple of minutes to look at the big street clock whose hands dragged in diabolically slow motion. I was almost certain she wouldn't be on the five o'clock bus, and that could mean only one thing.

I learned the meaning of the expression "to be beside oneself" at that bus stop: when she wasn't on the five o'clock bus, my mind took leave of my body, which ran up and down the street, frenzied, possessed, the decapitated chicken cut loose from the noose, crying scalding tears that I was aware of only because I couldn't breathe through my nose, and my face smarted as though coals had pelted it. She'd been killed, I was certain of it. I would be sent to the Vista Del Mar Home now. I had nobody in the world anymore because Rae had left me to get married and my mother was dead.

3 CRUSHED

WHEN SHE CAME to see me these days, Rae didn't say I was skinny like a stick anymore. Alone in bed at night, nightgown hiked up, I ran my hands over my body, and it felt as though it belonged to someone else. Where it had been flat and bony on the top part of me, now there was a startling, unfamiliar, soft roundness. Where it had been smooth on the bottom part of me, now I could feel tiny, wiry hairs.

One morning, after my mother left for work, I stripped my nightgown off and gazed at my naked self in the dresser mirror. The reflection confirmed what I'd felt even more than looking down at myself could. My waist was the same, but my hips had definitely grown out of their little-boy shape. And farther, down there, little tendrils spread from the center like delicate new twigs on a tree. But it was the flesh on my chest that awed me the most — not like my mother's full breasts, but beautiful in its own way, soft and so tender, almost like something seen through mist.

No doubt about it, I was on my way to becoming a woman. Standing there opposite the mirror, I envisioned myself in the ravishing trappings of womanhood that I'd adored on actresses — flounced and draped gowns and opulent furs, seamed nylons and high heels, glossy lips and come-hither eyes. But the pleasure in my new self was bittersweet, really. I was leaving childhood. I would never be a child star. I'd failed in my life's first mission.

. . .

In a decayed old building on the corner of Wabash and Evergreen avenues, there was a radio and phonograph repair shop, and in its window stood an ornate record player and a cunning statue of a dog whose head wagged perpetually at his master's voice coming from a giant horn. Most days on my way home from school I stopped to stare at the dog and the record player and, farther back in the window, the dusty assortment of wooden radios and tape recorders with big reels. Suddenly they were all gone. Through the window I could see that the shop was empty of everything but dust. For weeks it stood empty.

Then, a few months before my twelfth birthday, two plaster masks —comedy and tragedy—appeared in that same window (spotlessly clean now), surrounded by pink satin toe shoes and black patent leather tap dancing shoes, and above, in a grand flourish with gilt paint, a sign announced, THEATRE ARTS STUDIO! OPENING SOON! REGISTER NOW! Next to it hung a picture of a woman—with blond hair that fell to her shoulders in shiny waves, full lips that turned up in a fetching smile, a scooped blouse that revealed creamy skin. IRENE SANDMAN, EXECUTIVE DIRECTOR, it said under the picture (the title alone dazzled me, though I had no notion what an executive director was). I could hear myself breathing through my mouth. Could it be true? Could there suddenly be a place like this in East Los Angeles, with a woman who looked like a movie star, an EXECUTIVE DIRECTOR who might show me the way to Hollywood?

I came back every afternoon to try to find out what REGISTER NOW! meant and to gaze, slack-jawed, at the beautiful picture, but the door was always closed.

One day, finally, though the inside was still dark, the door to the Theatre Arts Studio was open, and there stood the woman of the photograph, hanging a watercolor of little tutued ballerinas on the wall. My heart shook. I'd never seen anyone so splendid-looking in the flesh, so statuesque on her high heels and long legs, her deep slim waist clenched by a broad golden belt. I stood at the door and her heavy perfume reached me. My head whirled.

Her arms stretched gracefully to straighten the framed picture, then she turned. I'd startled her, and she blinked. Violet blue eyes with long dark lashes. I hadn't known such eyes existed off the movie screen.

"May I help you?" Her voice was movie-actress rich. Later, when it played itself in my head over and over, I called it *liquid gold*, though I'd never seen such a thing. I imagined liquid gold would be as bright as a brand-new penny, yet mellow somehow, and smooth.

My cheeks felt stiff. My tongue—a dry, useless wad—must have mumbled something.

"We'll be starting classes on April first," she answered. "What aspect of theater arts are you interested in?"

I must have said acting. Later I remembered that she'd said I could take private lessons for $1.50 an hour. I must have left the magical dimness where Irene Sandman stood and gone back outside to the daylit street. I must have gotten home. But I know I didn't see anything that was in front of my eyes, and my ears were deaf to everything but her golden voice.

My mother gave me the money. I knew she would, because wasn't this the beginning of what we'd dreamed about for so long? My teacher was Sid Sandman—the Acting Director of Theatre Arts Studio, Irene called him. He was waiting for me the afternoon I went for my first lesson. He took me into the large room, which was separated only by a thin whitewashed partition from the little front office where I'd first seen Irene Sandman's gorgeousness. I recited "To Think That I Saw It on Mulberry Street" for him, and he watched with judicious eyes, legs crossed, chin resting on the palm of his hand. With his black lacquered hair and pencil-thin mustache and his brown belted jacket with a scarf around his neck, which he tucked under his shirt like an ascot, he did look as I'd dimly imagined a director might. He nodded approvingly at my attempts to sound like Milo, in wonderment at the marvels of Mulberry Street. "I'll write a dramatic monologue for you," he declared.

At our next meeting, I pronounced the lines of the script he handed me with all the histrionics I'd been practicing for years: "My . . . my name is Rachel Hoffman. My mother? I don't know where she is. *They* took her away. I haven't seen her in a long time." When I was eight years old, I'd overheard some woman in a store say about me, "Doesn't that child look like a little refugee?" Sid must have thought so too. Halfway through the monologue, I was to push up my sleeve and display to my invisible, kind interlocutors the concentration camp number branded on my arm. "What? She's in the other room? Waiting for me?" I was to exclaim at the end of my four-minute performance before I ran off, joyfully shouting, "Mommy! Mommy! Mommy!" I had no trouble imagining devastating separation from my mother. I had no trouble imagining emotional wounds inflicted on me by the Nazis.

For weeks we went over the piece, only he and I in the entire place, the office room dark. "Very fine!" Sid Sandman said solemnly, or "Take it from 'the number on my arm?'"

Always I listened for a noise in the outer room or hoped that the door would open. But I saw the luminous Irene only in my dreams.

One day, though, the light was on in the office when I arrived, and there at last, sitting at the desk and holding a receipt book, was Irene Sandman. I felt myself turn paler than dead grass.

"I'll just pay you now for the whole month," a woman said.

"One month for Sissy Simpson . . . and that's for the Wee Ones Dance Movement Class," the lovely voice said.

I watched her elegant white hand with its well-shaped red fingernails writing out the receipt. The woman took it and left, brushing by me.

"Lillian, hello," Irene Sandman said.

She remembered my name!

"Sid says you're making terrific progress."

I barely squeaked out an "Oh, thanks," though I could have wept for joy.

"I'll sit in on your session today," she said, smiling brilliantly at me. Neon spots swirled before my eyes. How would I be able to speak if those radiant violet eyes were upon me?

But I did. I was Rachel Hoffman in every inch of me, with only the tiniest fraction of my mind aware that Irene was poised elegantly on the bench next to her husband. When I ran out of the room shouting, "Mommy! Mommy! Mommy!" in my eyes there were real tears that sprang miraculously from nowhere.

"Wow!" Irene let out as I came back to stand before them.

Could I believe what I was seeing? There were tears in her eyes too. I'd moved Irene Sandman to tears! In Mary Marvel's cape I floated just under the ceiling.

"Lillian." The mellow tones arrested me a half-hour later as I floated still, now out the door. "I'd like you to bring your mother with you next week."

I landed with a thump. Dear God, my mother! Whatever for? My mother never wore lipstick anymore. The shadows under her eyes had become even darker, and there was so much gray in her hair now. And her accent! I loved her more than my own life, but how could I bring her to stand in the presence of this glorious personage?

"I've had our lawyers draw up a personal management contract, which Theatre Arts Studio will sign with our most gifted students." Irene's exquisitely lipsticked lips smiled. "And you're one of them."

I have no idea how I maneuvered the streets that day again, but I know I must have galloped because I was panting as I bolted up the porch steps on Dundas Street. I had just enough breath left to shout toward the bedroom, where my mother was lying down, "I've been discovered! I made it!"

"We're from Chicago," Irene said to my mother, but my mother was staring at the tutued ballerinas on the wall and her mouth was ajar. I was mortified. Why didn't she know how to behave in such a momentous situation? What would Irene think? Fanny's furnished room showed on us, I was sure. I'd selected my mother's dress from out of her now-unused New York collection. I'd made her wear lipstick and go to the beauty parlor to get her hair done, but still she looked shabby and dim next to Irene Sandman. Who wouldn't?

"Both of us were very involved in Chicago's theater arts, but we decided to come to Los Angeles because that's where the theater world has moved."

My mother looked at her now and made little "Dat's nice" sounds. *We must seem like dolts to Irene Sandman.* Though she didn't address me, I nodded my head vigorously at whatever she said to make up for my mother's virtual silence. I arranged my face into what I hoped was an intelligent expression, and I kept it plastered there.

"The theater used to be very alive in Chicago. Mel Tormé was my best friend in high school," Irene said, laughing. So charmingly. My toes curled. My mother was looking at the picture on the wall again. Was she even listening to Irene? "Steve Allen was our buddy too. He was always very funny, but he didn't know how to play the piano. I'm the one who taught him. Though he was very quick to catch on," Irene added demurely. "He didn't need much teaching."

My mother recognized the name Steve Allen. "Iz dat soll," she said, and I shrank as I heard her mispronounce the American idiom. It was better when she said nothing. We were lost here, in the presence of this heavenly being who had a direct pipeline to Hollywood.

"Do you have any questions?" Irene asked. My mother shook her head.

"What if one of us has to end the contract?" I said in a wavery voice. I couldn't imagine such an eventuality on my part, but I hoped that if I asked an adult-sounding question Irene would think I was thoughtful and worldly and wouldn't notice my mother's incompetence.

Irene looked at me without expression. I wanted to evaporate. "You don't get married thinking about divorce," she finally said. "We'll need a stage name for her," she said in my mother's direction. "Lillian Faderman doesn't sound much like an actress."

"How about Lilly the Kid?" It had been my fantasy name for so long, the words just blurted out of me.

To my mortal shame, those beautiful lips now spread and seemed to begin a guffaw, but she arrested it. "I was thinking of something more along the lines of Lillian Foster."

My contract stated that our arrangement would last for seven years, renewable in perpetuity. I knew what *perpetuity* meant, and I prayed for it in association with Irene Sandman. It also said that Irene would be my sole representative and would receive ten percent of my earnings. That sounded wonderful—there would be earnings!

To celebrate, my mother and I went downtown on Saturday and—at $3.50 for her, $1.50 for me—we took a Tanner Grey Line Bus Tour of movie star homes, Robert Mitchum, Greer Garson, Spencer Tracy, Anne Baxter, each more fantastic than the last. So there really were palaces right here in Beverly Hills, California, just as in the movies, with great expanses of blue-green lawn and tall iron gates and uncountable gables and turrets. My mother and I devoured it all.

"When you become an actress," she said to me dreamily as our bus lumbered up and down the glittering streets of Beverly Hills and spewed exhaust fumes into the rarefied air, "which house do you want us to buy? We have to find a tutor for you, you know, because if you're making movies you can't go to school regular. Then we'll both have a maid, and we'll have a chauffeur," she said, recalling movies she'd seen about the rich, who always had a whole staff of servants, "and a man butler to answer the door and the telephone—and what else?"

"And I'll buy you the most beautiful winter coat in the world," I promised, remembering the shabby, thin jacket she'd worn every winter since we'd come to California.

"Why just one? I'll need a long white ermine, and a brown mink stole, and maybe a Persian lamb jacket," she enumerated with a sweet smile.

Did Irene have an ermine coat? I wondered. How splendid ermine would look beneath her spun-gold hair.

"I'd like you to sing for me before your acting lesson," Irene announced when I arrived for my next session with Sid. I chose "Again," and I wasn't nervous because I'd been singing all my life. She played a little introduction on the piano and then nodded for me to begin. For a few seconds she scrambled around the keyboard, trying to find my key. Then she realized there wasn't any. She shook her head, and I cut off my caterwaul, puzzled. "Lillian, you need to listen to how the music sounds and match your voice to it."

It was a revelation to me. I felt my skin prickle and beads of sweat form above my lip.

"We'd better start you on singing lessons." Singing lessons? My dreams were crumbling like a dried mudpie! My mother gave me the $1.50 a week gladly for my acting lessons, but she couldn't afford singing lessons.

"How about working in the office on Saturday mornings?" Irene said, as though she'd read my despair, "and you can pay for all your lessons that way."

I would have worked in the morning and the evening and on Sunday —and the rest of the week too—just to be around her. "Oh, yes, that would be wonderful," I managed to gulp in a torrent of gratitude. "Oh, yes."

I loved Saturdays. I arrived before 8:00 A.M. to open the studio for the little kids' ballet class (taught by a Bulgarian woman with stringy hair and b.o.). By nine, Irene came to take my place behind the desk. "Will you go to the cleaner's and pick up some things for me?" she'd ask, and I'd run to fetch Sid's pants or a dress or blouse of hers (which I'd furtively kiss through the clear wrapping). "Will you go over to the Elite and bring me back a cup of coffee?" she'd ask next. Whatever she needed I carried as though it were a sacred chalice through grimy streets, and my lips moved in fervent prayer. "Irene, oh Irene, Irene," were the only words.

She began teaching at ten o'clock, after the Bulgarian finished her Modern Dance for 12–15-Year-Olds. I sat again in the gray metal chair, now warm from Irene's perfect bottom, and opened my nostrils wide to inhale Emir, her heady perfume that lingered in the purple Orlon cardigan she often left draped over the chair. Alone in the office, I ran my hands up and down the soft material. "Irene, oh Irene." I spoke it in my head.

I listened intently, entranced by every syllable, as she instructed a pimply, bespectacled girl at the piano, then a dark and very handsome young man who was a singer, then a class of six adolescent tap dancers. With the handsome singer—Tony Martinez, his name was—she laughed a lot, though it never seemed to me that his remarks were very witty. ("Can I take that one again?" Tony would say. *Ha, ha, tee hee hee,* they'd carry on.) What did he do to make her so happy?

Never did I permit dreamy passion to interfere with efficiency. "Hello, this is Theatre Arts Studio. May I help you?" I answered the phone in a low voice that sounded professional, as I'd heard Irene do. I collected money with aplomb. I wrote receipts with a secretarial flourish that Fanny would have approved of. I greeted all comers with grace and verve.

For three years, there was nowhere in creation I would rather have been than behind the desk at Theatre Arts Studio, inhaling Emir and feeling soft Orlon between my fingers while I worked to pay for my lessons.

Eddy St. John (I later found out his real name was Edward Fromberg) walked through the door one Saturday morning. "I have a singing lesson with Mrs. Sandman at twelve o'clock," he said, his voice fluttering up and down. He took the chair closest to me and flipped through the stack of sheet music he'd brought with him. I could see that the one that crowned the pile had a picture of a sequin-gowned Marlene Dietrich on the cover sheet. "See What the Boys in the Back Room Will Have," it was called. I watched him as he studied the music. He had the longest eyelashes I'd ever seen on anyone, and his hair was a coppery color I'd never seen before. He moved his head in time to the music in his mind, and he waved a long, slim hand, totally without self-consciousness. His lithe shoulders swayed.

He looked up to see me watching. "I just love Dietrich songs, don't you?" He flashed me a disarming smile.

"Let's try something else for a change. How about 'On Top of Old Smokey'?" Irene threw out to Eddy from time to time over the next months.

"Not my style," he'd rebut. "Let's do 'The Man That Got Away.'"

"How about 'The Tennessee Waltz'?" she'd suggest.

"How about 'Stormy Weather'?" he'd insist. He was only three years older than I, but what self-possession! Maybe he didn't know that Irene Sandman was a goddess.

Eventually she gathered several of us together into a troupe that performed at homes for the aged, Hadassah luncheons, mental hospitals, and other such places. Eddy was the star, dressed all in black, with a fedora tipped just above his eyes, singing dramatic, breathy torch songs. He had an expressive high tenor that he could make husky and intimate à la Dietrich or heartbreakingly plaintive like Judy Garland. There were also the Starlets, two twelve-year-old girls with matching fat brown Shirley Temple curls, who sang in harmony while they shook silver-dusted maracas. And there was a fourteen-year-old with her seven-year-old sister, both dressed in powder blue leotards, with dark blue stuffed-cloth tails attached to their pant seats. They did a monkey act, balancing acrobatically all over each other.

And there was me, Lillian Foster, Mistress of Ceremonies, introducing each act with the energetic, smiling spiel that I'd rehearsed with Irene. "And now Theatre Arts Studio is *dee*-lighted to present the *fab*-u-lous (or mag-*nif*-icent or a-*stound*-ing) . . ." Irene said that a Mistress of Ceremonies needed a gown, so my mother gave me ten dollars and I went to Brooklyn Avenue to buy one—pink satin, strapless and back-less, with pink netting over the skirt. When it was time for my mono-logues, I quickly slipped into the Hadassah kitchens or rest home bath-rooms and changed to adolescent-girl clothes. I acted Rachel Hoffman as well as another piece that Sid wrote for me about a French orphan who is adopted by a kindly couple ("zz-zz-zz," he instructed me when-ever I forgot and sounded a *th*), and I did a monologue that he pieced together from Lillian Hellman's play *The Children's Hour*. I was a twelve-year-old named Mary who fabricates an accusation against two women, her teachers. "Unnatural!" I was supposed to yell in a disgusted voice.

"We have a show to do next Sunday!" I would come home with the gift of the news, and it seemed like a wonder tonic for my mother. Eight of us squeezed into the Sandmans' green Ford, and Irene drove us to our shows. Even if it was a spell-time, my mother's anguish was suspended for a while. Whenever I came out onstage, I could see her in the front row, her head cocked birdlike at me in rapt attention. I worried a lot that Irene might mind that my mother came with us, but she never said a word. I made sure my mother always wore lipstick and a New York dress.

Irene follows me everywhere. Into Fanny's house. To my classes at Hollenbeck Junior High School. In the street I look for her car, and I imagine I see it con-stantly. She is with me when I walk arm-in-arm with my mother down Wabash Avenue. At school I tell the girls with whom I'm friendly that I'll be en-

tertaining at an opening of a Thrifty Drugstore in Bellflower. "Irene Sandman is our director," I say. I just want to hear myself pronouncing her name.

Mr. Bergman and Rae come again to take us to Ocean Park Beach. I leave my mother sitting with them on a boardwalk bench, and I walk down near the green water, where I can write her name in the sand — IRENE SANDMAN IRENE SANDMAN IRENE SANDMAN. The ocean comes up to wash it away, and I write it again and leave it there. Maybe she'll happen by before the ocean comes again. She'll find it and wonder who is so in love with her.

How can I make her say "Wow!" again, the way she did when she first heard me do Rachel Hoffman? "Wow!" I hear her voice in the dark in my bed at night, and I kiss my pillow as though it were her skin.

Has anyone ever felt this way? What is this? Everything but Irene has gone out of my head. How bizarre I feel, as though something is wrong. I go to the Malabar Public Library for more psychology books because I've never heard anyone talk about such a thing. "Crush," it's called. I have an "adolescent crush" on a woman. "Very common," the books say.

But one book with a brand-new cover, Attaining Womanhood: A Doctor Talks to Girls About Sex, *by Dr. George W. Corner, says something else. I don't understand all the words, but I understand enough to be petrified. "There are a few women who develop a deep-seated and even permanent need to be sexually attracted only by members of their own sex. This condition may apparently be an inborn trait; in other circumstances it is believed to be set up as a result of unfortunate circumstances in youth."* What circumstances could be more unfortunate than mine? *And then his sentences get even more alarming. "The thought of it is disagreeable to people who do not have such impulses, but the person so affected must be regarded not as sinful but as the victim of a disturbed temperament."* I am the victim of a disturbed temperament.

"A girl should avoid a woman who exhibits lavish fondness toward her," Dr. Corner concludes, "or who insists on constant companionship, or indulges in intimate fondling." What bliss I would feel if Irene were such a woman, *I think; the irony is not lost on me, though I am in tears.*

To whom could I talk about this? Who would help me understand? Not my mother. I took the buses to Rae's apartment.

"What happened?" She paled at the sight of me.

I threw myself face down on her bed. "I'm in love with Irene Sandman," I wept.

"Oy! You scared me so much. I thought you were sick," my aunt cried. Then, "What do you mean you're 'in love'? She's a lady. How can you be in love?"

"That's just the problem," I moaned.

"Don't talk foolish," Rae said. "There's no such thing. A girl can't be in love with a lady. Wait, you'll meet a nice boy soon, and you'll see what 'in love' means."

One afternoon I arrived early for my acting lesson. Theatre Arts Studio was dark, but the front door was open just a crack, as though someone had forgotten to close it.

"Do you take me for a goddamn idiot? Do you think I don't know what's going on?" It was Sid's voice, loud and angry, coming from the big room.

"Oh, for God's sake, he's only twenty years old," Irene shouted back. "I'm not interested in babies." I smelled her perfume even at the door.

"I don't give a damn what you say. Your lipstick was smeared all over your face, your blouse was open—what am I supposed to think?" Sid yelled. "You be careful, damn you, or we'll lose this place!"

"What about Silvia, you bastard?" she screamed at him. "Do you think I've forgotten Chicago?"

I backed out on tiptoe. Who were they fighting about? That handsome Mexican boy she gave singing lessons to! I walked around the block, dazed, images of Irene and the boy floating before my eyes. What had she done with him? Her blouse open, her lipstick smeared all over her face. Tyrone Power kissing Maureen O'Hara in *The Black Swan*. Had he forced her? What had they done together?

When I returned to the studio, the light was on and Irene was no longer there. Sid was sitting on the bench in the big room, staring at nothing. He jumped up when he saw me and put on a business face. "Let's hear that Linda Loman monologue first," he said.

I watched for Tony Martinez the next Saturday; I was sure he was the one. What did a person need to look like for Irene to let them smear her lipstick and open her blouse? I wrote receipts and answered the phone, but on my lips I felt her creamy skin where I'd pulled her blouse open—though my lips, confusingly, were Tony Martinez's.

But he didn't show up for his lesson. I paged through the appointment book. No, he hadn't been shifted to another time. When I checked the ledger the following Saturday, a red line had been drawn through *Tony Martinez*.

Eddy invited me to come over to his house and listen to records after we'd worked together in the troupe for a few months. I really liked him, but not in the way my aunt meant. I was sure he didn't like me that way either.

He led me to his bedroom at the back of his family's sprawling house. "Have you ever heard of 'lip sync'?" he asked, plopping me into an overstuffed chair. "Watch!" On a phonograph that sat in a scratched wooden cabinet Eddy put a 33⅓ record of the Andrews Sisters singing "Bei Mir Bist Du Schön" and sped it up to 45. He performed a hectic charleston all around my chair, moving his hips and lips at racing speed —the Andrews Sisters as spastic chipmunks.

"Now close your eyes," he demanded.

Billie Holiday intoned "Gloomy Sunday."

"Open!" Eddy cried, and I did. He stood decked out in a white feather boa and a black picture hat, with a woman's long cigarette holder between his fingers. For a minute it felt weird to see him like that, but then I liked it. He looked like a truly glamorous actress—like the ones I loved best. Billie Holiday's yearning, lazy tones came out of his mouth.

Evelyn, his older sister, threw the door open. "Eddy, I don't think Ma-*ma* wants you to entertain girls behind closed doors. No offense," she said to me with a smile and winked.

Evelyn was big and smiley. She sewed spangles and sequins on cheap sheath dresses for Eddy's secret costumes. She was good-natured too. In the Fromberg house there were always innumerable cats, with or without stripes, with or without tails, with or without whole ears, slinking around her feet and tripping her. They'd be attracted to the Frombergs' front porch by the saucers of milk she put out for them, and then she couldn't resist letting them inside. It was through Evelyn that I met Chuck.

I carried slim volumes of plays with me everywhere in those days. I was Laura, shyly telling her gentleman caller about her glass animals; I was the girl in white, nostrils flaring, lips distorted in disgust, in the presence of the Hairy Ape. I was ready for the day Sid and Irene would say it was time for my Hollywood audition.

"Wadda ya know, a young girl that reads! You don't see that much nowadays," Chuck said in lieu of a wolf whistle. Eddy had invited me over to show off his new suede pumps and elbow-length black gloves. I could feel Chuck's gaze follow me down the hall. No male had ever done that to me before. It felt funny. Did I like it?

In the late afternoons, Chuck was almost always drinking coffee with Evelyn at the Frombergs' kitchen table. He wore a gray uniform with a Mason's Market logo over one shirt pocket and his name, Charles Augelli, monogrammed over the other. "So wadda ya reading today?" he'd ask me every time. "I'm a poet myself," he said. "Ya like poetry? Ever hear of Robert Service? William Rose Benét? Those guys are great."

I shook my head, memorizing the names. I'd look them up at the library.

"How about William Ernest Henley? That's my favorite. Out of the night that covers me black as the pit from pole to pole," he expostulated, waving his sloshing coffee cup in time to an irregular beat. "I am the master of my fate, I am the captain of my soul."

Chuck was short for a man, only a few inches taller than I. His face was long, and his black caterpillar eyebrows and marble-round eyes gave it an almost comical effect. But he was muscled, wiry, and had a certain feline grace to his movements. His uniform was starched and crisp, even though it was always the end of the day when I saw him, and I'd never met anyone else before who could recite poems by heart. I surprised myself at how I felt robbed of something when I went to visit Eddy and Chuck wasn't sitting in the kitchen.

"Lillian, I have to speak to you after your lesson today," Irene said. She looked disgruntled. Had I done something wrong in the office?

"You're not concentrating," Sid snapped after I'd repeated the same gesture he'd criticized for a third time. "Let's just cut it short for today," he said, dismissing me to my fate.

"Lillian," she began, as I stood before her in the little office. I watched her full red lips, my throat dry. "I'm sorry to have to ask you this, but I'm afraid it's necessary." I will implode under her gaze, I thought. Where to put my eyes? How to hold my mouth? "The car is really crowded with eight people, and this Sunday we're going to Norwalk. Your mother really doesn't belong at these shows. You'll have to ask her to stay at home, all right?"

I stared at Irene, mute. I couldn't even pronounce the usual inane words I'd manage to muster in her presence. What would I tell my mother? I'd wanted to do all this in the first place just for her. I couldn't hurt her this way. I dragged myself out the door, down Wabash Avenue to Dundas Street, seeing nothing but the empty years ahead because I'd have to quit Theatre Arts Studio.

"I just won't go. I'll quit," I offered, looking at my hands instead of my mother's face. What if she said, *Yes. Quit?*

Those words would kill me.

"I enjoyed myself so much," my mother said. "I always looked forward." She wasn't trying to disguise her disappointment. I tensed, waiting for the hammer blow.

"But I want you to keep going." Her rough palm stroked my cheek. "Don't worry for me," she said.

I drew air to my lungs to protest, then shut my mouth and threw my arms around her instead, ready to bawl with relief. But relief was followed by guilt: I'd betrayed my mother, there was no other way to see it. Now I admitted to myself as I held her that even if she'd said, "Without me you can't go," I would have kept going secretly if I had to. How could I give up Irene Sandman?

"It's probably just for a little while," I said, keeping my eyes to the ground, feeling black despair that Irene, the woman I would gladly have died for, had no compassion, that I had no honor. "Norwalk is so far away, and the car's not that big. But there'll be other shows," I chirped, hating myself for a lying magpie.

Boys were all that the girls in the eighth grade talked about. "Juan gave me this heart he made in shop," "Joe called last night," "Steve asked me out again for Saturday." They said the word *love* a lot. Who did I have to love that would love me back?

"Can I take you for a soda?" Chuck jumped up from the kitchen table as I was leaving Eddy's house. He said the words so quickly that I almost didn't understand him.

"Chuck!" Good-natured Evelyn was miffed. "She's fourteen," she huffed, as I stood awkwardly by the door.

"So? Don't fourteen-year-olds drink sodas?" he said.

After that first time, he waited for me in his Mason's Market truck a block away from Hollenbeck Junior High every afternoon, and we went to a malt shop nearby. He recited long poems that he knew by heart. Edgar Guest, Eugene Field, Rudyard Kipling.

"I'm deeply in love with you. You know that?" he said after we'd been meeting for about three weeks. We sat in his truck, parked under a dripping jacaranda tree up the street from Fanny's house. From his shirt pocket he pulled a little cardboard box that held a gold-colored heart on a long chain. "How about a kiss now?" he asked as he slipped it over my head.

There was a shock when I felt his scratchy stubble above my lips, and then I liked it. It was strange but also pleasant to have his wiry arms around me. Is that what Irene felt when Tony kissed her? I remembered Tony's big hands and the crisp black hairs that showed on his chest through his open shirt.

"I've never met a girl like you before," Chuck said.

"Do you know what Miss Lillian Dumdum is doing?" Eddy tattled to Irene. He disapproved, just like his sister, and I hated him. Why did he have to tell Irene?

"He's *how* old?" she asked, looking at me, her violet eyes darkening. I pulled at my nails under the desk.

"Well, we're just good friends," I defended myself, worried, but a little pleased too that she was interested in me enough to be upset.

"Doesn't your mother tell you not to go out with someone that old?" Irene sounded genuinely shocked, and I fought back the smile that wanted to pop out on my lips.

"This is for you." Chuck grinned the next Monday when I got into his truck. He placed a piece of lined paper that had been folded into small squares in my lap. On top of the sheet was written: "Its Crazy But Its Grand!!!" and verses were penciled on both sides in his schoolboy handwriting. "I'm 24 yrs old and I've been down lifes strand," his poem began.

> Tho your only 14 darling let me take your hand.
> I know everyone says its crazy.
> It may be crazy but its grand!!!

"It's really nice," I said, secretly pitying him. This wasn't the first time I'd realized that Chuck wasn't very smart.

"Let's not go for a soda today," he said. "Let's just talk," and he headed his truck up City Terrace. He parked in an empty lot with tall yellow weeds and gently pulled me to him. When he kissed me this time, he slipped his tongue into my mouth, and I jumped as from a bee sting and pushed at his arms, averting my head.

"It's okay, it's okay," he whispered, his fingers light on my chin, his brown eyes loving. I didn't fight him when he lowered his mouth to mine again, and this time I liked it. I could get lost in the sweet, new comfort of it. His mouth tasted like Sen-Sen. I'd heard girls talk about kisses like this—*french kissing*, they called it.

Chuck's hand slinked down from my shoulder and neatly cupped my breast. "No!" I jumped, and my hand clamped his, moving it off me, though not without a twinge of regret. That was called *second base*. He brought his fingers back and I let them rest there, only for an instant. He'd made a warm sensation flow all through me, but I couldn't let him lull me, because "second base leads to third base," the girls had said, "and third base leads to diapers and baby bottles." I shifted away from him.

"I'm sorry, sweet darling," Chuck crooned, "I won't do that. You can trust me." He turned me to him, and I let his tongue find mine again.

"You know what we're doing when you're sixteen?" he asked on the drive back to Fanny's house. "You and me are gonna get married."

My breath caught. Could he be serious? I didn't want to contradict him because he was nice to me and seemed so sincere, but how could I be an actress, married to him?

. . .

As I lay in the dark at night, ignoring my mother's soft snores, I thought about what it would be like to kiss Irene the way Chuck kissed me. I became Tony Martinez again. I saw myself, with Tony Martinez's hands, touch Irene where Chuck wanted to touch me. I saw the perfect shape of her upturned breasts in the lavender pullover she often wore. What would it mean to get to *third base* with her? My mother turned over in her bed, and I cast Irene out of my head until the little *puff-puff* sounds resumed. Then my thighs clamped together. I tingled where I never had before.

But those night visions didn't stop me from liking Chuck's kisses and wanting the next afternoon to come quickly so I could get more of them.

The lines between Irene's eyebrows knitted a lot when she looked at me now. I was thrilled. If she worried, it must mean she thought I mattered, at least to Theatre Arts Studio. Or maybe she was being a concerned grownup because she thought that my mother was crazy and there was no one else to be concerned. It didn't matter. All that mattered was that she noticed me. I wanted her to worry, though I was certain that there wasn't anything worrisome about what I did with Chuck in his truck on City Terrace.

"Are you still going around with that man?" she asked before my singing lesson. She was ruffling through sheet music, but I could tell by her frown that she'd been thinking about it a lot.

"Yeah," I said innocently. "I see him after school every day. He just dropped me off."

"I'm worried, Lillian. We need to talk. I'll take you to a drive-in for a burger and a milkshake," she said the next Saturday after the last student left.

Delirium! To be in Irene's car with nobody else to share the small, closed space with us . . . It had never happened before. I was near enough to hear the swish of her nylons as she shifted her legs to press the clutch, the brake. Her Emir permeated the air. I was near enough to reach out and touch the smooth rayon of her dress. What if I were brave enough to do it? My fingers stroked her thigh in my mind.

I sipped the milkshake, but the smell of food was nauseating. The burger she ordered for me tasted like raw oats, and I chewed and chewed before I could swallow. She didn't touch her own salad. I stared at her manicured deep red fingernails as they thrummed on the wheel.

"You're very young, Lillian, and I know you don't have the happiest life with your mother." I looked up. She'd turned her magnificent eyes on me, and now I swam in them. But I wished she would leave my mother out of it; I still smarted from the thought of my treachery. Yet if Irene thought that my mother was a normal person, I'd never be sitting here with her. *Let her think what she wants about my mother*, I decided; I'd luxuriate in every second I could be near Irene.

"Unhappy young people sometimes do unfortunate things," she said, and my face muscles shaped themselves into a mask of tragedy. How could I prolong these moments? I felt like a klutz in the gazelle-like grace of her presence. Could she see the nervous tic that had started just under my eye? "I don't want you to make a mistake, like I did," she went on. "I married very young."

Oh, the wonder of the moment! Irene Sandman was confiding, in me, about her life. Once, when we did a talent show at the Wabash Playground and Sid, decked out in a white suit and black bow tie, was the Master of Ceremonies, he introduced her to the audience as "my gorgeous wife" (*gorgeous*, I thought; *you can say that again!*). She glided onto the stage wearing a diaphanous summer dress, a flowing flowered scarf around her neck, and she and her husband seemed to lock eyes in mutual admiration. Could it have been an act? When he sometimes came into the studio on Saturday mornings, Irene looked at him as though she were annoyed. Except for the fight about Tony, I'd never even heard them say more than five words to each other. Oh, what would she tell me now about their life together?

"I met Sid when I was eighteen and he was thirty. I know how it is to get carried away, and I wanted us to talk because Eddy got me worried about you. You mustn't run off with this man."

"Run off with him?" I was stupefied.

"Elope."

"I don't even like him that much," I blurted out.

Irene looked puzzled.

"Well . . ." I'd said the wrong thing. "I mean . . ." What could I tell her now that would impress her? Interest her? "I don't ever want to get married. I'm going to devote my life to the theater."

"To what?"

"You know . . . acting."

A smile played around her lips, and I wanted to sink beneath my seat.

"Lillian, you have a lot of growing up to do," she said. She shook her majestic head, and despair shook me in its cruel claws: I was nothing but a silly child to her. "Well, anyway, Eddy misled me." She waved her hand dismissively. She was interested in me only if I was in trouble; maybe she just wanted to make sure I wouldn't leave the studio. I wanted to slam the dashboard with my fist, to make her jump. *Look at me, listen to me*, I wanted to shout. *Why can't you feel about me the way you felt about Tony Martinez?*

"If you're not going to run off with him, there's no problem. So why are we here?" Irene laughed. "Better finish your hamburger; we should get going," she said absently, flashing her lights for the waitress to bring the check.

I sank, I crumbled, I was crushed. I'd ruined my golden opportunity. What had I hoped for? I didn't know. I just needed to hold her attention. I didn't expect from her what she gave Tony Martinez. There was nothing in me that could make her want me. But I just needed to be near her.

I would throw myself at her now, heedlessly. I'd have no other chance like this. "I love you," I would implore her. My heart raced at the vision. She would let me . . . what? I sat frozen to the seat. I peered at her as she drove. She was a distant star, glittering always. She was a zillion miles away. She didn't even know I was in the car anymore.

I looked out the window, unable to make sense of anything before my eyes. It was over. "*You dumb dimwit . . . dope . . . nincompoop!*" I shouted at myself inside. "*I hate you! Drop dead with a cancer on your heart! Die!*"

4 MEN I

I'M AS TALL AS my mother's waist, walking in open spaces between her and My Rae—Hollenbeck Park, the Moroccan desert (but no Gary Cooper is in sight). Where we are doesn't matter because we're together.

"Balance me!" I demand. They know the game and comply. Mommy on the right, My Rae on the left, every few steps their warm, upturned hands bear my forty pounds, and I swing my legs in the air. This is more delicious than a bottle of warm milk.

A pea green puddle pops into our path out of nowhere, and we pause to contemplate its mystery. We can't go straight ahead so we'll go around. "But we have to put you down," Mommy and My Rae say in one voice.

My feet hit the ground, and a snake pops out of the water. It is beautifully mottled, smiling as in a cartoon. I don't know whether to laugh or be scared. I blink, and my eyes open just in time to see My Rae dragged under the opaque water.

Again the snake pops up, ringed with power. I ready my mouth to scream, but before breath reaches my vocal cords, the snake arches, slashes like a whip, and my mother is gone.

In the daylight I knew it was only a dream, but for weeks the images came back so clearly that my stomach would contract to my spine. I felt bereft of something I had no power to keep for myself, though it was vital to me.

I did nothing about Chuck, but sometimes I wished he would be the one to say it was over. Yet if he did, wouldn't it be awful to be rejected? Every

time I thought I'd tell him that I couldn't see him anymore, another reason not to say it would pop into my head: What if I broke up with him
and then I never found another person to love me, just like my mother
never found anyone after Moishe? What if I really did love him now—
like Rae once said I'd love a boy—but I didn't know it because all I'd
ever seen of that sort of love was the crazy lose-your-head-and-ruin-
your-life way my mother did it? I just couldn't figure out what was true
or what to do. So I drifted.

A few weeks before the end of the year, Chuck told me over sodas
that he'd made reservations for New Year's Eve at the Sinaloa Club. I
knew exactly where it was—just a few doors away from the delicatessen
on Brooklyn Avenue where my mother and I went to eat. Sometimes I'd
see men with black jackets and ladies with beautiful long gowns step
from sleek cars in front of the Sinaloa Club. When the men held the
padded pink door open for their dates, the street would be filled with a
woman's sultry voice belting songs that always rhymed *amor* with *dolor.*
Though I never got a look inside, I was sure that the Sinaloa Club was
the closest thing in East L.A. to what I'd seen in movie magazines of
Hollywood nightspots like Ciro's or the Mocambo, where the stars met
to sip martinis and be sophisticated. "I'm rentin' a tux and steppin' out
wid ma baby," Chuck sang now in the empty soda shop and got up to do
a goofy jig and a Charlie Chaplin bow in front of me. I could wear my
pink satin Mistress of Ceremonies gown and the silver stiletto heels that
Eddy had given me.

But what would my mother do on New Year's Eve if I went out with
Chuck? Always, since we'd come to Los Angeles, we'd spent the last
hours of the year drinking hot chocolate and listening to the radio—
"Your Hit Parade" and then the midnight countdown at Times Square.

I never really decided what to do, but when the sun went down on
the last day of 1954, I found myself taking a bath and then standing at
the mirror putting on rouge and eye shadow from little plastic boxes, remembering how I'd watched my mother in the mirror those Saturday
nights in New York as she applied her makeshift cosmetics. How beautiful she'd been.

I took my pink gown down from the hook behind our bedroom
door.

"You didn't tell me you had a show tonight," my mother said. She stood behind me while I examined a little tear in the gown's netting.

"I've got a date." I turned to face her. I hadn't said anything about it earlier because I didn't know myself what I was going to do. I'd never even said I had a boyfriend. *Stupid!* I should have told her I'd been invited to the Frombergs' party. I should have arranged to meet Chuck down the block. Now it was too late to say anything but the truth. It all came out—where I met him, that he was Italian, his age, his truck—and with every word I said she looked more upset.

"You're fourteen years old!" my mother yelled.

She'd never yelled at me in anger before.

"So what?" So what if I was fourteen? She'd never treated me like a child. I'd always been an adult.

She stomped from the room, and seconds later I heard her screaming into the telephone, "You know what she's doing?"

It didn't take twenty minutes. From the rip in the window shade I could see the black car pulling up in front of our house and Rae, in a little maroon hat, rushing out, then bending back in to wave a worried Mr. Bergman off, as if she didn't want him to witness this.

I returned to what I was doing, but now I was mad. I dusted talcum powder on my armpits in huge puffs, I pulled old socks and new movie magazines from under my bed and tossed them over my shoulder as I rummaged for Eddy's high heels.

My mother stormed in with my aunt behind her, both of them on the same side at last. "Are you *mishuga?* You're going out with a *Talyener goy* who's ten years older than you? On New Year's Eve yet?" My aunt bellowed each question louder than the last. "New Year's Eve, when the *goyim* get *schicker*, drunk? In a truck?"

"I'm not a baby!" I yelled. "I'm going." I grabbed the silver high heels I'd just found and the strapless gown from my bed, then locked myself into the bathroom, to dress and comb my hair in peace. What was this? All of a sudden they were going to tell me what to do? Since when?

"What's going on here? What's the commotion?" It was Fanny now, come to join the fracas because she'd heard Rae and my mother pounding on the bathroom door. "Are you crazy?" she said when they told her. "You'll let her go in a truck with a man?" I kept dressing.

My mother and aunt sobbed more words on the other side of the door; "*Goy*" was the one that came through clearest. I squirted some Emir on my hair.

Then the doorbell rang, and rang again, and then Chuck knocked on the screen door and called "Hello? Hello?" I threw open the bathroom door and ran past my mother and my aunt and Fanny, kicking a fusillade on the floor with my silver stilts, gripping the bottom of my gown so I wouldn't trip. "Let's go!" I shouted, banging the screen door behind me, pulling on Chuck's tuxedo sleeve. I ran, Chuck ran; my mother, Rae, and Fanny ran too.

"What's happening?" Chuck shouted, wheezing beside me. I glanced as we ran and saw his caterpillar eyebrows, a clear plastic box with a purple bow that he clutched in his hands, his tuxedo that shone a rust color by the light of the street lamp and looked high at his ankles. I didn't know if I felt like laughing or crying. Then I did both, at the same time, as we flew up Dundas Street. "What's wrong?" he shouted again, and I just shook my head and kept running and sobbing and giggling. The white carnation in his buttonhole dropped, and my silver heel trampled it.

His truck was all the way up the block. Over my shoulder I saw that my mother and Fanny had given up, but Rae was right behind us, then right behind me when I opened the door on the passenger side. She pushed me aside, hoisted herself like a gymnast up into the seat, then settled her squat frame there, arms folded and face stony. "You're not going!" she yelled at me.

"Lady, please get out of my truck!" Chuck cried.

She didn't budge.

How dare she carry on like this when she'd left me alone all those years with my mother in Fanny's furnished room? How dare she butt in now, when my childhood was over? "Rae, get out! Dammit! The whole neighborhood is looking," I hollered, though the streets were empty.

"Not till you go back into the house." She glared at me, unfolded her arms, then emphatically folded them the other way.

"I'll . . . I . . . I'm calling the cops to get her out of my truck," Chuck sputtered. His face and ears were red. I could see the plastic box with an orchid corsage inside sitting on the sidewalk.

"You should be ashamed of yourself. A grown man with a fourteen-year-old girl!" My aunt yelled at him now, and her heavy jaw jutted forward like a bulldog's. "You think I don't know what you want?"

"I don't care what you say. I'm going out tonight!" I screamed at her.

"Do you know what men like that do?" she screamed back.

"Lady, get out!" Chuck banged on the hood with a mallet fist, and with each bang I could see Rae's maroon hat jump a little on her head.

An hour later my aunt descended from the truck, her eyes puffy with weeping. I stepped up to take her place, as though triumphant. But I was acting. By now I was really tired and miserable, and what I truly wanted was to go home, with her, to forget the whole awful scene and Chuck and New Year's Eve—all of it. I watched her walk down the empty street.

Chuck jumped behind the wheel, breathing as though he'd just done hard physical labor, and I could see his temple throbbing. As we drove off, I spied the orchid, still on the sidewalk in its clear plastic box with the big purple bow.

"Chuck . . . I'm sorry." I was embarrassed for all of us that she'd accused him as she did. I touched his white-knuckled hand that gripped the wheel, but he pulled away as though he were disgusted with me. I sat, baffled about what to say or do next.

He drove to our spot on City Terrace. "I don't feel like going to a nightclub now," he muttered. "I didn't do anything to deserve that." His voice rose like a little boy's and he pounded his fist on the dashboard so hard that the truck shook.

It scared me a little, though I couldn't blame him for being so upset. "Chuck . . ." I opened my mouth to sympathize, to say how angry I was at my aunt, but he turned to me and grabbed me, his fingers digging into my bare arms, then his tongue thrusting down my throat, his stubble scratching my skin and hurting. I fought to break loose but he pinned me. With one hand he snatched at the long skirt of my gown, tugging it up. The more I struggled, the harder he gripped me. His fingers wrestled with my garter belt, with the band of my panties; his knees pushed at my thighs. "Chuck, stop!" I screamed.

And he did. He loosened his hold on me, then moved back to the driver's seat, his breath coming in whistles through his mouth. He gripped the wheel and banged his head on it, again, then again. "I'm an idiot," he moaned. "She just got me so angry." He slumped over the wheel and stayed that way for so long that I thought he'd fainted. My teeth chattered as if I were sitting in a refrigerator. What should I do?

When he snapped his head up, I jumped. "We're going to Evelyn's party," he announced, backing the truck out of the weeds so quickly that the tires spun. I pressed up against the passenger door, moving as far away from him as I could, and he didn't say another word. I wasn't scared of him now as much as I was angry. Where had that monster sprung from that tore at my clothes and hurt me with his hands and mouth? What had that been about?

I followed Chuck up the Frombergs' steps, and Evelyn swung open the door. Over Chuck's shoulder I could see that people were kicking in a conga line. Evelyn blew loudly at an orange noisemaker that snaked from her lips and then shouted, "Hap-py New Year!" She wore a tiny gold cardboard tiara on her head and a red and purple gown sausaged her big body. He entered first. Then she took one look at me and her jaw dropped. "You bastard, get out," she spat at Chuck. "You son of a bitch!"

How had she known?

"Okay, okay." He threw up his hands as if he were fending off a blow. "You're right. I'm a bastard son of a bitch." Then he slunk off like a kicked alley cat—even more pathetic because of the funny tuxedo. I could hear Evelyn breathing through her teeth. I kept my eyes on him till he turned the corner, and then she drew me to her big bosom in a motherly hug. "Sweetie, go change and then come back to the party," she said gently. I left, fighting back the rush of tears that her kindness had loosed. It wasn't really his fault. Rae had made him angry. But why did he have to terrify me? I was mad at him, but I was also sorry that he might lose Evelyn's friendship and, because of me, never sit in her kitchen and sip coffee again.

My mother was in bed with the light off, and the house was mausoleum-quiet. As a kid, I used to panic when I couldn't see her breathing or hear her snoring: What if she were dead? Standing now at the threshold, wide-eyed in the spook-filled dark, I listened as I used to. I shouldn't have left her alone. I heard a squeak of springs as she turned over.

Then I tiptoed into the bathroom, closed the door behind me, and turned on the light. For an instant I didn't recognize the girl in the mirror. Now I saw what Evelyn had seen. My cheeks and chin were blotchy red from the friction of Chuck's stubble, my lips blurry with lipstick smear, my hair wild. I looked like I'd been raped.

It had been three years since Irene signed me to an exclusive management contract, and though Lillian Foster had done scores of shows in the pink gown, Irene had called them all "charity performances." "It's good experience and exposure," she told the troupe in her mellow amber voice. Despite my crush, I wondered what good the experience and exposure could do when she didn't send me out on a single Hollywood audition. How would I ever earn money to help my mother? Years had passed, and I'd accomplished nothing toward her rescue. The hot seasons were still the worst, when she came home dripping and exhausted from Schneiderman's unventilated top floor and the steam of the pressing machines. "Save me from the shop!" she cried, flopping on her bed in a dress wet with sweat, as in New York; but now it was to the ceiling that she cried, as though she'd lost faith in our dream. I'd lost faith too.

One Saturday, tacked on the wall above the briny pickle barrels in the grocery store, I saw a penciled message in Yiddish and English, "*Shadchen*, Matchmaker," it said. "I will find you Your *Besherteh*, Your Destined Mate. Reasonable Rates!" It was signed "Mr. Yehuda Cohen."

My mother had sent me to get a quart of milk, but I almost forgot. I stared at the wrinkled piece of paper with the shaky handwriting for a long time. My mother needed rescuing, and as hard as I'd tried, I hadn't been able to do it. What if I gave her into someone else's loving hands now—like a poor woman who couldn't take care of her baby might give it to a rich woman who'd be so happy to have it? A few days later, I went back to the grocery store after school and wrote Mr. Cohen's telephone number on the inside cover of my geography notebook. For a week or more I kept looking at it as I sat in my classes. By now, though I could scarcely admit it to myself, I knew there was another reason too that made me want to call Mr. Cohen: I'd begun to understand that if I were all she had in the world, I'd never be able to live my own life. Someday I'd want to do things, to travel places . . . like Chicago, maybe . . . or France. With my mother in tow, how far could I travel? I wouldn't even be able to go to college if I always had to take care of her. I hated my selfish thoughts, but I couldn't help them: I needed to give her to some-one else—a husband.

My mother sat on the milk crate looking out at nothing, her face blank, as if she were a million miles away. She wore a torn plaid wrapper—her weekend uniform these days.

"Mommy? I've been thinking a long time about something." I knelt at her feet, pausing dramatically, to impress on her the seriousness of what I was about to say. "You can't keep working in the shop. We need to find you a husband."

"A husband?" She jumped as though I'd waved something noxious in front of her nose. "What do I need a husband for?"

"Mommy, listen to me," I kept on: "I don't think I'll ever get my break in Hollywood; I can't help you." I came back to it every hour; I dogged her. "We don't want to live in a furnished room at Fanny's for-ever." "Your spells are worse when you get so tired out by your work. It's killing you!" It was all true.

"Who'd even want me now?" she said that afternoon in front of the dresser mirror, turning her head at different angles to scrutinize the ex-tent of the wrinkles on her face, the extent of the sag under her chin. I could tell she'd started thinking seriously about it, though she was still far from convinced.

That evening she poured borscht from a Manischewitz bottle into two bowls for our supper. "Moishe . . ." she began.

I didn't want to hear it. "Mommy, he'll never want us. And I hate that bastard! I hate him!" I screamed. *Slam* went my hand on the table, and my mother cringed, and the red liquid jumped from the bowls and puddled on the oilcloth. I didn't care. I had to convince her!

I searched the kitchen counter for a rag to sop up the spilt borscht. Finding none, I wadded old newspapers from the stack Fanny kept to put on the floor after she mopped on Friday afternoons. How could I make my mother understand? I blotted and rubbed at the spill, but my efforts left red streaks on the table. I threw the newspaper wad down, defeated, and sank onto a chair, covering my head with my hands. "I want a father in my life!" It popped out of my mouth as if I were Charlie McCarthy, and I stopped, shocked. Did I really, after fourteen and a half years without a father, feel that I needed one now? I'd always been happy there'd been no man to come between us. Then why had I said it?

"You want a father?" she cried.

I looked my mother in the eye. I couldn't back out now. "Yes. I need a father."

She sipped at her soup, taking quick, nervous slurps. I stared at the red liquid in my bowl. After that day, I always hated borscht.

Mr. Yehuda Cohen had a long white beard like the ones I'd seen in pictures of biblical patriarchs, and he wore the same long black overcoat in all seasons. He came to Dundas Street to examine us and set the terms — three dollars per introduction. He smelled of fried fish, but he sent a procession of potential *beshertehs*.

In consideration of the novelty of a gentleman caller, Fanny let us take the dusty, yellowed sheets off the furniture in the living room, where we'd never been allowed to sit before. ("The couch is old. I don't have money to buy a new one when it falls apart," she had always said.) I piled stacks of library books in front of the jars of floating eyeballs to hide them.

On the morning of my mother's first date, I walked with her to the beauty parlor on Wabash Avenue so she could get a henna tint in her hair. That afternoon, as she let me dab my own rouge on her cheeks and brush her lashes with my Maybelline, I studied the face I'd loved so much. What would a suitor think? The years in East Los Angeles had really aged her. There were fine little wrinkles all around her eyes and deep lines between her eyebrows that gave her a permanently pained expression. Her cheeks, which had been firm and opalescent, looked saggy and sallow. I was stung by my love for her, which was even greater now that she no longer looked young and beautiful. "Please let him be nice to her. Please let him be a loving man," I prayed to I-didn't-know-who.

Jake Mann's hair was marcelled into shiny, tight blond waves, and he wore electric blue or burnt sienna suits. "What a little doll!" he said in a gravelly voice as I went to the kitchen to fix him a glass of tea on his first visit. His fingers clasped my hand instead of the glass when I handed it to him, making the dark liquid slosh over the rim. "Oh, she burned her pretty fingers," he said to no one in particular, relieving me of the glass and then lifting my hand to his mouth for a wet kiss—"to make it feel good."

He invited my mother out for "cocktails." "You're invited too." He winked at me.

"He's a real sport," my mother said, glowing, when she came back after midnight. I'd waited up, sleepless, missing her cruelly. "He took me to a nice place for a Tom Collins. Then he took me to Chinatown for a big dinner." In her fingers she twirled a yellow toothpick-and-paper umbrella, which she proffered to me as though I were six years old. "It was in the Tom Collins," she said, beaming.

I took it from her, holding it awkwardly in my palm. What was I supposed to do with it?

Mr. Mann came to take my mother out again the next week. "So where's that little princess?" I could hear him from the bedroom.

"Why don't you go say hello?" my mother asked me when she came in for her purse.

If she married Mr. Mann, we'd all have to live together until I finished high school. More than three years. So I had to be friendly. I followed her out. "Say, give us a hug," Jake Mann said avuncularly. He pulled me to him, pressing himself against me for what seemed like a long time. I broke away, befuddled. My mother stood at the front door, purse in hand, smiling like a stranger, waiting for him. I'd never had a fatherly hug. Was I imagining things?

"He really knows how to treat a lady," my mother said at the end of the evening, and her face looked bright and a little excited. I marveled how quickly she'd gotten into the spirit of this thing. She sat on her bed, and I watched as she rolled her seamed nylons down her still-lovely legs. "He's a nice dresser, too. Not like Moishe," she sighed, "but still nice. And he took me to an Italian restaurant, and then we went on a wonderful drive near the beach and saw the stars." She enumerated Mr. Mann's virtues and her pleasure. "On Sunday he wants to take us both to Ocean Park Beach," she said, pulling her pale pink nightgown over her head.

I remembered Mr. Mann's tight hug. "No, you go alone with him," I said lightly, rummaging through my mind for an excuse that would keep me home.

"He wants to take us both. You come too," my mother insisted, pulling the covers over herself. I got up to turn the light off, then lay in the dark in a muddle of feelings while my mother breathed softly in sleep.

"Whoop! Where's the bathing suit?" Jake Mann exclaimed on Sunday morning when he saw me in a white skirt and blouse. "We're all going swimming on such a beautiful day."

My mother wore her green one-piece bathing suit under a floral print dress. "Put your suit on underneath," she encouraged me. "It's a beautiful day to go in the water."

Jake Mann opened the rear door of his long automobile for me, and as I slid in, I felt his hand brush lightly against my buttocks. I turned to look at him, astonished. But what could I say there in his car, my mother in the front seat? Perhaps I'd imagined it, or maybe it was an accident.

In the beach parking lot he stripped down to his bathing suit, and my mother did the same. "We'll lock our clothes in the trunk," he said. "That way we don't have to worry about them when we go into the water." I disrobed, self-conscious, not knowing what else to do. He handed my mother a blanket to carry, and he took a little portable radio from the trunk.

I felt his eyes inspecting my black two-piece suit, my thighs, my breasts, as he walked between me and my mother down to the beach. I was aware of the oppressively huge expanse of his naked flesh next to me, the blond-gray hairs that covered his chest and legs and arms.

My mother spread the blanket, plopped down, snapped on the

radio. *"Hey there, you with the stars in your eyes,"* she hummed along with Frank Sinatra.

"Let's go for a swim!" Mr. Mann seized my hand and held me up just as I was about to sink down near her, onto the gay red and green stripes.

"I don't know how to swim," I told him, forcing myself not to sound sullen and pulling my fingers away. "Why don't you two go?" I turned to my mother.

"You never taught her to swim?" he scolded. "What's the idea of that? I'll teach her."

"Go, Lilly, let him teach you how to swim." My mother smiled contentedly at the sun.

He pulled at my arm. "Up-sy!" He grinned and lifted me to my feet, ignoring my protestations that the water was too cold for me. "Don't be a scaredy-cat," he said.

I walked down to the water with him. How was I supposed to act? Didn't my mother see that there was something funny in the way Mr. Mann behaved with me? And there was something else troubling me. I'd seen men in bathing suits before, of course, but the sight of Jake Mann down below was disquieting. His member looked huge under the flimsy red material of his trunks. Didn't everyone see the funny way it protruded? Wasn't he embarrassed by it? By the time we reached the water, the red strip looked like a little tent under his belly. Alarm fought with nausea inside me. Where could I put my eyes?

The water felt frigid on my feet. "Come on, don't act like a teeny, tiny baby," he mocked, dragging me by the hand. Would he drop my mother if I insulted him? How could I keep him for her but keep him away from me? I half went and half was pulled deeper into the water. I couldn't protect my thighs, my belly, my chest, from its iciness. My teeth chattered.

"I'm going to teach you to swim," he said, his voice still jovial and booming above the waves. "You're old enough to know how, for God's sake. Now lay down against my hand and I'll show you to kick." He pushed the back of my head down and my legs went up, then he held me afloat with his hand on my belly. At least the lower part of him was covered by the water and I didn't have to see it. "Okay, keep your legs straight and kick. I've got you. Nothing to worry about," he said now in a businesslike manner.

I couldn't stop shivering. It was hard to breathe. I kicked as he commanded me to, and he moved us some steps farther from the shore. What if I couldn't touch the ocean floor with my feet? What if the water was above my head? I would be at his mercy. The ocean was huge around us, and I didn't know how deep it was below me now. I swiveled my head quickly to look at him, and water filled my nose. I coughed and sputtered and clutched at his arm.

"Don't get scared. You're doing good," he told me. I relaxed my clutch and kept kicking. "Atta girl!" he said.

Then he righted me and dropped his hand from my belly. I could feel the bottom with my feet and sighed in relief. I stood on tiptoe to keep my head well above the water.

"Now, how about a little thank-you kiss for your first lesson." He grinned hideously, a huge shark in the middle of the ocean. He pulled my chin up with one hand and clamped his mouth down on mine. With the other hand he pulled my buttocks toward his member.

I struggled, and the undulating water pushed me off balance. His mouth was hard on mine, his hand firm on my buttocks, keeping me upright. I felt him rub against me.

"Stop it," I freed my mouth and shouted. There were other people in the water but no one close by. If I broke away from him, would I drown?

"Come on, be a good girl," he said, knocking his hips against me, not relinquishing his hold on my buttocks. "Don't you like it?"

"Goddammit, leave me alone!" I snarled in the most menacing voice I could muster. He tightened his grip, and my nails raked down his wet back with all the strength in my fingers. He dropped his hand, looked surprised and startled. I broke free and landed on tiptoe, my chin barely above the water. I swerved toward the shore, not looking back, my arms and hands flailing to push the ocean aside until I got to the shallow water.

"Little bitch," I heard him sneer a good distance behind me. But he wasn't following me. I hobbled frantically through the water and then over the sand, breathless, back to the blanket and my mother.

She sat there, still placid, innocent of thought. *"That's what a woman is for,"* Peggy Lee was singing on the radio. "Where's Jake?" my mother asked, smiling. "Did he show you how to swim?"

How could I answer her? I scrutinized the water, but he was nowhere in sight. Maybe he'd drowned.

This was the same strip of beach where I'd written IRENE SAND-MAN over and over in the wet sand. I held the thought of her violet eyes now, like a holy relic.

Later Mr. Mann came lumbering, scowling and silent, across the sand. "How'd you get so many scratches? Your back's bleeding," my mother cried, touching his skin solicitously.

"I fell on those lousy rocks out there," he said, tossing his hand in the direction of our combat.

Whenever the phone rang during the next weeks I heard my heart thud in my ears, but it was always for Fanny. "I don't understand," my mother said. "I thought we got along so good." And then, maybe a month later, I saw her standing in front of the dresser mirror, her fingers lifting her cheeks. "I hear Marlene Dietrich had four facelifts," she said.

"You don't need a facelift. You're beautiful," I told her, meaning it, but she didn't seem to hear me.

"'Mary, you have such shining eyes, such *lichtege eigen*,' Moishe used to say to me," my mother sighed. "All gone now. Nothing left of it."

I kept my secret about why Jake Mann had disappeared because I thought it was better for her to be a little hurt and baffled than to learn the truth. But anxiety squeezed at my chest whenever I thought of him. "Let's forget the husband," I wanted to tell my mother. Yet how could we? Nothing had changed. Not a single problem had gone away.

"So one don't work out, what's to worry?" Mr. Cohen said with good cheer. He had many more names on his list, and for three more dollars there was always another.

Shmuel Glatt, a redheaded German Jew, was next. Shmuel had numbers tattooed on his forearm from the concentration camp where he'd lost his whole family. He was stocky and short, barely taller than my mother. His small brown eyes had heavy undershadows that gave him a permanent lugubrious look, but he smiled a lot and told jokes in long strings, like Eddie Cantor or Jack Benny. His Yiddish accent was heavy, and it made his jokes, which were almost always about anti-Semites (*antizsemeeten,* he called them), funnier — or more disturbing. *So Rasputin says to Czar Nikolai, "Your Majesty, the Jews are complaining that you're anti-Semitic. For that, you should kill them all." "They're damn liars," the Czar says. "I'm not anti-Semitic, and I'll prove it. I'm only going to kill half of them." So a Jew is walking in the street, and he bumps into a Nazi. "Swine," says the Nazi. "Pleased to meet you. I'm Garfinkel," the Jew says. So Mr. Horowitz goes into this nice restaurant and sits down. And the goy waiter comes over to him and says, "We don't serve Jews here." "That's okay," Horowitz says. "Jews I don't eat. Give me a vegetable soup."*

My mother didn't know how to react to Shmuel Glatt in the beginning, but later she laughed at his jokes, and I did too. She dressed in the New York clothes whenever he came, and she put on the Emir I'd bought her for Chanukah. In the months she went out with him, she had hardly any spells. I was a little sad that it wasn't I who had the power to make them go away, *but the important thing is, he's good for her,* I told myself.

"He's a gentleman," she said after their third or fourth date. I'd heard them on the porch. He asked her for "a kiss goodnight," and there was a brief silence. "I had a very nice time, Shmuel," she said less than a minute later, and then I heard her key in the door.

He'll do, I thought. He even brought me Baby Ruth candy bars and Hershey with almonds, as though I were a kid, extracting them from a pocket on the inside of his jacket and presenting them to me with a magician's flourish. If my mother had to marry someone — and she did — Mr. Glatt wouldn't be a bad choice. He was all right.

It was his *lantsman* Falix Lieber, with whom he'd been liberated, barely alive, from the Bergen Belsen extermination camp, who became the bogeyman that lodged in my psyche and shook me for a long time.

"I got three free tickets for the Workmen's Circle bazaar," Shmuel Glatt announced one Saturday evening. "We'll have *pickelehs* there, we'll have *gribbines mit schmaltz* there, we'll have bellyaches there," he sang. It was there that my mother and I met Falix. "He helped me so much in the camp," Shmuel said, serious now, clapping Falix's back when he introduced him. Falix was in his thirties, with dusky skin and a soft black beard and hooded dark eyes set deep in his head. He wore a white shirt with half-rolled sleeves, his tattoo of numbers visible, like Shmuel's. Falix kept an arm around his seven-year-old daughter, Shayna, to whom he spoke in Yiddish. *"Maydeleh,* little girl," he called her. Later in the evening I watched as he fed her right out of his hand from the potato knish that he'd bought, lifting it to her pretty lips and then taking the tiniest nibble of the heavy dough himself, making her giggle immoderately.

"And you, *maydeleh?*" He turned to me after they'd finished the knish. "You want me to feed you too?"

I shook my head no, feeling foolish.

"And why not?" He winked at me. He followed us around the bazaar, never letting go of Shayna except to buy a dish of ice cream, which then he fed her and himself alternately, from the same spoon.

"So what do you do for a living?" he asked me.

Was he joking? Didn't he know I was a kid? "I'm in junior high school," I answered, discomfited by my own bashfulness. "In the ninth grade."

"Without Falix there wouldn't be a Shmuel Glatt here today," I heard Shmuel tell my mother again, tears in his small eyes. We all sat together and waited for the balalaika concert to begin. "I was ready to die. What did I need to keep living for? 'No,' Falix says. 'You have to show those bastards.' He made me eat when I didn't want to eat anything. He made me keep up my strength."

The next Sunday, when Shmuel banged on our screen door, Falix was right behind him. "On such a nice day I've come to drive everybody to the park," Falix announced. He wore a hat well back on his head, and the sleeves of his white shirt were rolled up again, exposing the terrible tattoo. "Madam." He extended his arm for me to take in imitation of Shmuel, who walked down the porch steps with my mother on his arm.

"Come on, Lilly. You come too," my mother said happily, still holding on to Shmuel's arm as she stood near Falix's old DeSoto.

"Madam?" Falix repeated more emphatically, his arm still extended at an exaggerated angle, and I took it, not knowing what else to do, and let him lead me into the front seat of his car. My mother and Shmuel climbed into the back.

"We better walk faster," I told Falix in the park. He'd insisted we stroll arm-in-arm, like my mother and Shmuel, and I felt self-conscious and embarrassed. "They're way ahead of us."

"Yes, but who's got the car keys?" he answered with a wink. "When they need to go home, they'll come back and find us. Sit here." He led me to a bench under a tree.

"They'll be worried," I said, struggling awkwardly to free my arm from his grip as we sat on the bench. Maybe he saved Shmuel's life, but he was acting a little like Jake Mann, I thought. I was irritated with my mother for making me come with them and then abandoning me.

"Relax," he said, placing his arm around my shoulder. "Who's going to hurt you? Am I hurting you?" He lifted my chin and looked into my eyes. I tried to rise, but he pulled me back, planting his lips on mine, ignoring my push at his chest.

I wasn't strong enough to get him away from me. Where was my mother? When would someone come by? Finally he took his mouth from mine. "Don't you know how to kiss?" he whispered. "A big girl like you? What would it hurt if I showed you?" I struggled against him again, pushing at his shoulders, trying to clamp my mouth. It was useless. There was no more fight in me. I relaxed my hands, my lips. I let myself sink, like a drowned girl. My mother had disappeared. "Isn't this nice?" he raised his head to say, and returned to my lips.

But then his hand cupped my breast, and a shiver waved through me when his fingers moved over my nipple. "Don't," I said with clenched teeth, and my hand flew up to stop him.

"*Maydeleh*, what's the excitement?" he laughed and crooned. "What's so bad here?" He bent to my lips again, his breath warm on me, his hand on my breast again. My own hand covered his, but I didn't try to remove it.

He heard their voices at the same time I did, and he jumped up and settled two feet away from me on the bench. My mother and Shmuel were walking down the path toward us. I wanted to run to her, but what about Shmuel? I sat glued to the bench. Didn't she see what Falix had been doing? Why didn't she yell at him like My Rae had yelled at Chuck?

"You had a nice tree to sit under," Shmuel said cordially.

"Yes," my mother said. "It's nice and shady here."

If there was a Mrs. Lieber I never saw her, and I never saw little Shayna after that first time at the bazaar. When Shmuel came to court my mother now, Falix was almost always with him. Didn't my mother understand what he was up to?

Falix talked to me as though I were an adult. He spared me nothing. "I have a good friend"—he was gleeful one Sunday—"who just married a beautiful lady with a beautiful daughter, fifteen." He stretched the vowels out as though he were tasting delectable little bites of knish—"bee-ooo-tii-ful," he said with feeling, and his eyes shone. "In the night he has the mother and in the day he has the daughter." His hand cupped my knee, moved to my thigh.

"When my Shayna is twelve years old," he said dreamily, a hint of melancholy in his voice, "I'll find her a *geliebte*, a lover. A girl shouldn't go longer than twelve without a man to love her."

He crooned at me always, whether I was fighting him off or tired of fighting him off. He sought me in the kitchen, on Fanny's crumbling back porch, in the bedroom as I sat on the floor doing my homework. Sometimes I let him touch me where he wanted, pretending more struggle than I felt. Then I hated myself for it.

But when I lay in bed, my mother asleep in the bed next to mine, and I remembered where and how he touched me, I was also overwhelmed by physical sensations in deep places where I'd never had them before. They weren't like the sweet throbbings I'd had at night when I thought of Irene. They came in great scary waves and were out of my control. When I thought about Falix Lieber in the daylight my face flamed. Could people tell about that dark thing by looking at me?

It went on for a couple of months, and then Falix disappeared, along with Shmuel, just as Jake Mann had. I was relieved never to have to see Falix again and Shmuel, who brought him and must surely have guessed what was going on. But even years later, Falix Lieber sometimes sneaked up on me to scare me, to lull me, in fantasies that popped out of nowhere, crooning, "*Maydeleh*, what's so bad here?"

I think my mother was really upset to be dropped by Shmuel. I know she'd felt a special link to him—they'd both suffered because of the Nazis, they'd both had terrible losses, and now they might help each other forget a little bit and snatch some happiness from life. But not even that had worked out. "I can't no more," my mother cried. "They don't like me. I'm old. Who would want me now anyway?" She flopped on her bed and threw her eyes heavenward once again, and I stood at the door feeling more helpless than ever. I had no idea what we could do next.

But Yehuda Cohen had another one: Albert Gordin, "a nice, honest man," the matchmaker said, collecting our three dollars and folding them into his moth-eaten wallet. "Has a steady job. A bachelor." Mr. Cohen enumerated the new man's virtues.

Albert arrived on a Sunday afternoon with a little bouquet of pink carnations wrapped in newspaper. He was seven or eight years younger than my mother. (She'd lied about her age to Mr. Cohen, and never—in twenty-five years—did Albert learn the truth.) He wore a new-looking plaid jacket that was too big across the shoulders and too long in the sleeves and a yellow-and-blue-striped tie that also looked new. He removed his hat from time to time—only to wipe his brow in the L.A. heat. When he lifted it, I could see two deep indentations on the top of his head, which was bald as a baby's.

He didn't offer to take my mother out anywhere. He got to the point, sitting on Fanny's couch. "I'm looking to get married. Mr. Cohen says you're looking for the same thing."

"Yes, I wouldn't mind getting married," my mother said. Her voice sounded to me as shaky as a little old lady's.

"Mr. Cohen told me you're a good, honest person," he said.

"Yes," my mother said guilelessly.

"I make a good living. Not too much, but enough for a wife."

"I wouldn't have to work?" my mother asked, getting to the point herself. She'd had too many painful months to be coy now.

"Not you and not your daughter."

"So I could stop my job right away if we got married?"

I held my breath.

"I'll tell you," he said. "My mother says to me a couple months ago, 'Albert, I'm going, and now you have to settle down with a nice lady.' And then she passes away. She was almost eighty-four years." He swiped at a tear in the corner of his eye, but I don't think my mother saw it because she was studying the floor as though the faded flowers of Fanny's carpet were tea leaves that could foretell her future. "So if we like each other, we'll get married right away and you don't have to work no more, okay?" Albert asked.

The next day he came in the evening, right after my mother got home from work. He wasn't going to waste any time. On this visit he was more relaxed and a lot more voluble. Whenever he was about to launch into a monologue he abruptly stood up. "Those doctors I work with at Cedars of Lebanon Hospital, they're so smart," he proclaimed, "they know everything—*everything*. You can ask them a question, any question you want, and they can tell you the answer. That's how they got where they are." He plopped down again on Fanny's couch.

My mother nodded her head after each sentence, but her eyes looked glazed.

"Dr. Friedman, my big boss," Albert said, standing up again, "he's sooo rich that he's not a millionaire—he's a mul-ti-mill-ion-aire." He punctuated every syllable with a pointed finger.

"Would you like some coffee?" I squeezed in between his monologues.

Albert shook his head no. "He writes a book and ev-er-y med-i-cal stu-dent in the whooole country has to buy it. It costs them one hundred dollars for a book by Dr. Friedman."

After he left, I followed my mother to our room, and for a minute I thought we were going to do the chicken dance again, but she stopped her pacing after one turn and plopped down on her bed. I plopped with her. I could smell the sickly sweet dead-flower-and-sweat odor that her skin always had when she was really upset. We both stared up at the ceiling now, with eyes open like two corpses.

"Lilly, what should I do?" This after a long time.

"I don't know!" I tried to think it out, but I couldn't. Here was the person who might finally rescue her from the shop. But he was weird. Yet if he was a nice, honest man with a steady job, like Mr. Cohen said . . . But how could she live with him?

The next time we heard Albert's steps on the porch and his banging at the front door, my mother pulled frantically at my arm, even though I was doing my math homework. "You come too and sit with us," she implored.

"Why? You're fine," I whispered, and extricated myself from her clutch. He didn't require much conversation from her—she didn't need my help in that area. But I could see in her eyes that she wasn't fine. I wasn't either. She went, head down, as if to her death. I sat on my bed, chewing my nails. I couldn't even add five plus five now. I jumped up to join her.

"Without me," Albert, on his feet, was saying, "the doctors can't do nothing. I'm the one who knows where everything is," and down he plopped again.

"I'm the one who keeps the knives sharpened for them," he rambled the next time he came. "'Albert,' they tell me, 'without a sharp knife I'm lost.' I'm in the pathology labatory almost all the time."

I didn't know what a pathology laboratory was. He cleaned, he straightened things up, I figured out. He kept doctors' instruments in order. It took me a while to understand that it was autopsies he was cleaning up after, and that one of his main jobs was to be sure that the scalpels and saws were sharp. My guts twisted at the insight, but I never told my mother. Why upset her needlessly?

A few weeks later, Albert arrived holding more carnations wrapped in newspaper, a bouquet identical to the first one. In his other hand he carried a small box. As soon as I opened the door I knew something was different.

"Lee-lee," he pronounced my name. "Hullo." His nervousness was palpable. "I have news for your mother. Where is she?"

My mother came out, as scared as he. I retreated to the bedroom.

"Look what I bought for you," I heard through the walls less than a minute later.

"Oh, my God!" my mother exclaimed.

"So, you want to get married now?" Albert asked seconds after that.

I covered my eyes with my hands. I covered my ears, my mouth. *Oh, God! Oh, my God!* I did the chicken dance by myself up and down our room. Then I forced myself to stop. *He doesn't try to put dirty paws on me.* I sat on my bed, repeating his good points like a mantra: *he has a job, he'll let my mother quit the shop.*

As soon as the screen door closed behind him, my mother rushed to our room. On her face was animal panic. On her left hand was a gold ring with a tiny diamond. "Lilly, what should I do? Tell me!"

I flew to her, held her tight, as in a death grip. "I don't know," I cried. Then, into her shoulder, "Marry him, Mommy." My voice sounded in my ear as if it came from underwater.

I felt her nod her head, again and again, as though she was agreeing, convincing herself.

The next evening Albert showed up with two immaculately tailored men in their fifties, both bald, one tall and big-bellied, his forehead showing blue veins, and the other inches shorter, with a round, fat face. A new pastel blue Cadillac convertible, which I'd seen before only in billboard ads, was parked in front of the house. "This . . . this is my older brother Jerry, and this is my . . . other older brother Marvin." Albert's expression was sheepish, like a kid's whose parents have come to school on account of his bad behavior. They sat down on Fanny's couch, Albert hemmed in between his brothers.

"Albert says he wants to marry you," Jerry, the shorter one, said to my mother.

"Did he tell you he was in a mental institution for three years?" Marvin asked, a businessman with no words to waste.

Their family had emigrated from Russia to Mexico at the start of the 1930s because they couldn't get into the United States. Jerry told the story while Albert looked down at his shoes. Marvin and Jerry became jewelers—big successes, I gathered. Albert, still in his teens, wandered off to work with a traveling peddler, and in the heat of Vera Cruz, "a hundred and fifteen degrees," Jerry emphasized, he had to be hospitalized. "He had a nervous breakdown."

"Do you understand?" Marvin asked my mother, staring at her with cruel, ironic eyes. "He went crazy. They even had to do an operation and open his head."

"To save his life," Jerry added quickly.

Marvin ignored him. "You still want to marry Albert?" His mean mouth smirked.

Now Albert looked up and rose to his feet. "I'm not crazy no more," he uttered with a quiet dignity that I hadn't seen in him before.

"Yes, he's all right now. He's not stupid, you understand," Jerry said, as though Albert, who stood near my mother now, weren't in the room. "He holds down a job and he can speak five languages—Russian, Polish, Yiddish, Spanish, English," he enumerated. "And he reads Hebrew better than a lot of rabbis." Jerry sounded almost proud of his poor younger brother.

"He's all right now," Marvin agreed, "but we thought you needed to know about it. Now we wash our hands, and what you do is your business." He got up to leave at once, holding the screen door open peremptorily for both his brothers. Albert gave my mother a shame-faced, pleading, backward glance.

From the window I watched them usher Albert down the steps and into the back seat of the Cadillac. I felt sorry for him, how he'd sat hemmed in between the fat-cat brothers, disgraced like a culprit. Yet how could my mother marry him? I ran to her. "Mommy, what should we do?" I cried.

My mother was bent over the couch, patting smooth the yellowed sheet where the brothers had sat. Then she straightened, shrugged her shoulders high, and let them fall. "They told me he's not stupid, he keeps a job." She sighed. "I'll marry him. What else can I do?"

5 SHEDDING

I LOST HER. I made myself an orphan by giving my mother up to a crazy man with holes in his head. They got married, and he moved in and slept in my bed; I suppose he slept in her bed too, where we used to snuggle and listen to "Your Hit Parade." I was cast out of my shabby paradise and had to go sleep on the old army cot in the dining room, where Rae used to sleep before she left to marry Mr. Bergman. The first nights I stuck my knuckles in my mouth so my mother wouldn't hear me sobbing, slobbering, because it was Albert and not I who'd rescued her from the shop.

Yet it had all gone just the way I'd planned. She'd quit her job the very day they went downtown to City Hall and became man and wife, and now she was safe and I'd be free. So why did I feel that she'd betrayed me, that I had to break away from her, just as she'd broken away from me?

I stare into the full-length mirror in the dressing room of the girls' gym. A tough girl with a furious face stares back at me. I've shaved off the thin end of each eyebrow and replaced it with a penciled black line that aims straight up, two rapiers poised above my scowling eyes. My blood-red lipstick is drawn high on my upper lip to make it look socked-in-the-mouth full. My head is crowned by a huge pompadour. I might be hiding a knife in there, so you better watch out. My blouse is see-through nylon, and my skirt is pachuca-tight and pachuca-short.

"Is that the way you dress?" my aunt says with a voice that slides all the way up from her deep foghorn the first time she sees my transformation.

"Yeah, that's the way I dress," I tell her. What does she know about surviving at Hollenbeck Junior High? She's never even been to school. She doesn't know anything except how to take care of Mr. Bergman.

"Oy vey iz mir, oh, woe is me," she says, slapping her cheek.

I've bought a silver metal belt at the 5&10, and I clasp it breath-quenchingly tight around my waist. Why should I hide what I've got? I've measured myself with an old cloth tape measure that Rae left behind. I'm 36-22-36. The world can like it or lump it.

Most of the Jewish kids have moved west, to a nicer part of town, the Beverly-Fairfax area, away from the Mexican kids and the Negro kids and the Japanese kids who spent their first years of life in relocation camps. Only a handful of Jewish kids are left behind to graduate from Hollenbeck Junior High School. Who cares? What good did the Jewish kids ever do me anyway? I was always an outcast, an odd girl, with my crazy mother, no father, Fanny's furnished room. With them or without them, I'm alone.

The Jewish kids that remain titter at the way I dress, and I don't give a damn. I always liked the Mexican kids better anyway because they're poor too, so why would they look down on me? Though I have no gang, I dress like the pachuca gang girls who look so tough, just the way I want to be.

Carlos used the current expression of admiration to introduce himself. "You built like a brick shithouse, baby." His dimples and strong white teeth looked beautiful against his dark skin, and I liked the rolling shuffle of his walk, a tough guy bop. "Hey, *ese*, how you doin' man?" I'd hear him say to other pachucos. I loved its lilt. I'd practice saying it too when I was alone. "Hey, *ese* . . ." How cool it sounded.

"I gotta rumble with them *pinche cabrones* alla time 'cause they call me a black Mexican," he said with a sneer about the light-skinned Mexican boys who watched us with narrowed eyes as we walked past them holding hands. "*Tu madre*," he muttered in their direction, but under his breath, and he raised a middle finger at them, though they were already behind us, so only I could see it. He seemed to be a loner, just like me, and that made me like him even more. I loved that he risked being seen with me though I wasn't a real pachuca, not even a Mexican. I loved his clothes, the sharp-creased pachuco khaki pants, the dark, long-sleeve shirt with the collar raised in back. I loved his shiny black hair, a duck's ass, slicked on the sides with Vaseline, and sex curls—that's what the girls called them—dangling on his forehead.

"Hey, baby, I made this for you in shop." He didn't look at me as we walked, but he handed me a red and green plastic heart, like those I'd envied on other girls. When you wore a heart like that, everyone knew you had a boyfriend. "I don't have no chain, but you get yourself one and wear this round your neck," Carlos said in his pachuco rhythm. He grasped my waist as we bopped down the street together. "You don't got to go home right now. Let's go talk in the park," he said.

"We can sit on my porch and talk," I offered. It didn't matter if I took him to Fanny's ugly house because he probably lived in a bad place too; and I really didn't want to go back to Hollenbeck Park. I had such a long history there already, swinging with my mother and My Rae, fighting Falix off. *Did my mother see what Falix was doing? Did she?*

"No, it's better in the park," Carlos said, and led me with his firm grip on my waist. I let myself be led because I wanted to keep being his girlfriend. Near the familiar pond we lay side by side under a low willow tree, a droopy umbrella hiding us from the world. I willed myself to cast my mother and aunt from my memory and feel only how warm his breath was on me and how soft his lips were. His mouth lowered to my neck, and his teeth made gentle little bites and sucks on my exposed skin. Then his tongue found its way in and out of my ear, and he shifted to lie on top of me. A bird sang its heart out on the branches above us, and I was paralyzed by languor under his fifteen-year-old's expertise. When I closed my eyes, I still saw the bright dizzy green, and the leaves were tangled with birdsong. "Hey, baby, let's go in that boathouse. Don't nobody come in there during the week." Carlos looked down on me, a young boy's look that surprised me with its sly hopefulness. Through all the layers of our clothes I felt him harden.

"No, let's just stay here." I knew I mustn't go in there with him because outside I could control things a little, but in the boathouse there'd be nothing to stop us, and I wouldn't be able to say no. I wanted it too, but what if I got pregnant? My mother's fate.

"We can't do nothing more here, and if the cops or them *pinche cabrones* come . . . Shit . . . Let's go in there," he said, the tough guy again, pressing down harder on my pelvis.

"No, let's stay here," I begged. "Please." I planted a placating kiss on his shoulder. I was more scared than I cared to show.

He made an annoyed sound through clenched teeth, and I felt him moving on me, first slow, then fast and faster, his breath coming quicker and louder. I lay there stiffly, not knowing what to do, and in no more than a few minutes, before I could figure anything out, he uttered one soft cry and it was over. He lay perfectly still on top of me, a deadweight. My fingers pressed the rough grass, and under my nails I felt the dirt. A confused owl hooted from an invisible branch.

"Come on, I'll walk you home." He scrambled off me and onto his feet seconds later, then pulled me up abruptly. "Oh, shit, I can't go now!" he exclaimed, looking down at a stain around the zipper of his pants. "Look, here's a bus coupon, baby. You go. I'm gonna see you tomorrow." He pecked my forehead, and I watched his retreating form until he vanished through the trees, his footsteps crunching the fallen leaves. I still tingled from him, but I felt relieved too, as though I'd gotten off easy.

Hot and cold skipped around in me the rest of that afternoon while I bent over my English essay at the kitchen table. "I don't want anything," I told my mother when she came in to fix supper, and I left. I hid out on the weed-strewn patch of backyard, filled with dreamy longing, though I was unable to escape the dull sounds of pots and plates and forks coming through the kitchen window as my mother and Albert ate. All I could think of while I finished my homework on my cot later was how Carlos had kissed me; and when I went to sleep I could feel his body on top of me.

In homeroom the next day, I stood at the door waiting for Carlos until after the bell rang; then Miss Miller scowled at me and told me to take my seat. Carlos sailed in much later. I waved to him, smiling hugely, and he nodded, but his handsome face was expressionless, and when I looked back at him in the last row he seemed very intent on carving something on his desk with a big nail. As soon as the bell rang, he disappeared in the spin of milling bodies before I'd even gathered up my books. Something bad must have happened. I had to find him and ask what was the matter.

"Hey, how you doin'?" It was Ramon behind me, one of the boys Carlos told me he was always rumbling with. "Wanna go out with me after school?" He leered at me, an insinuating grin that said he knew all about me.

"No, I'm busy," I said, squeezing as quickly as I could through the crowd.

"*Puta*," I heard Ramon snigger.

I saw Carlos one other time that day, talking to Joe, another kid he'd said he always rumbled with. When he spotted me in the distance, he shifted his body with his back to me, as though to hide.

That was almost the end of it, except that two days later, when the kids in sixth-period art class lined up in front of the teacher's desk to claim the work that she'd graded for the last unit, I felt someone pushing at my back and pressing against my buttocks. I jumped away, bumping into the girl in front of me, then spun around into the crude grin of Martin, another one of the rumble guys. "Don't you like it?" he mouthed, then emitted a soft, mean laugh. "I heard you did."

So now I knew. Guys talked. If you let one of them paralyze you in sweet languor, they'd all swarm like scavengers to carrion. It was a nasty game.

Suddenly guys everywhere were acting like that, as though Carlos had telegraphed the whole male world about me or as though I gave off some scent only they could smell. In school, in the streets, on the bus, in the stores, it was impossible to escape their salvos: "Hey, girlie, want a lift? I'll drive you to heaven!" "You shake it like you gonna break it!" "Hey, sexy, you givin' me a heart attack!" *Smack, smack, whistle, whistle.* Was it the way I dressed? But I liked the way I looked — the grownup, been-around mask of my face, the drop-dead hourglass costume of my body. Why should I change because of those *pinche cabrones? Kiss my ass,* I thought *(but I'll be crafty enough to keep you from getting that close).*

Still dark, maybe 5 A.M., only weeks into my mother's marriage. The smell of cigarette smoke that drifted in from the porch through the dining room window pulled me from sleep. "Ohboyohboyohboy," I heard, and the heavy shuffle of Albert's shoes back and forth across the loose porch planks. Then once more: "Ohboyohboyohboy."

I dozed off but was awakened again a few hours later. Fanny was banging loudly on the door of their bedroom. "Open up!" she yelled.

I dashed out to the hallway.

My mother, still in her light nightgown, bleary-eyed, opened the door. "Yes?" Over Fanny's shoulder I could see Albert's empty, unmade bed.

"Your crazy husband woke me up again," Fanny said, her long nose twitching, toothless jaws working, incensed. "Five o'clock in the morning, and I hear his 'ohboyohboyohboy.' Tell him I'm sick and tired of it."

My mother chewed her lip. "I'll tell him," she said in a little voice, "just as soon as he comes back from work."

That evening she sat on the milk crate on the porch, waiting for Albert. I perched on my cot doing homework, and through the dining room window I could see how worried she looked. What could I do about it? Did she understand now she'd married a crazy man? I'd resolved to be polite to him, but I wouldn't go near him unless it was absolutely necessary.

I saw her stand up as his car came down the street, and she paced on the porch till he parked. "Fanny says you woke her up," she stage-whispered to him frantically as he walked up the creaky stairs.

Fanny appeared from nowhere and threw open the screen door, letting it slam behind her. "Mister, you woke me up at five o'clock in the morning with your crazy 'ohboyohboyohboy.' This is the third time. What kind of man talks to himself at five o'clock in the morning?"

There was quiet for maybe three heartbeats as Albert stood glued at the top of the stairs. Then, "You go to hell," he roared, lunging with open claws, tripping on the air. "You're the crazy one. You!"

Fanny scampered back into the house as though running from a mad cat, and the screen door slammed. She held it to with one hand, shaking the other one at him in a fist. "*Mishugeneh!* I'll make you to move," she yelled.

"*Choleryeh,*" he hollered, "witch!" and his spittle hung on the screen door.

"A devil boils in you," Fanny yelled, "you *paskudnyak* you, you no-goodnik!"

"Your flesh should be torn from you in pieces," Albert one-upped her from the porch.

I heard Fanny's footsteps retreating at a run to her room.

"Mary, we're moving out," Albert hollered to my mother, who sat huddled on the milk crate.

Moving? Oh, yes! But where could we go if we left East L.A.?

That same night, at about midnight, Albert's cigarette smoke and pacings and mutterings woke me up again, and the following morning too, and many other nights and mornings, but Fanny said nothing more; she just avoided him. Whenever he referred to her now, he called her "*choleryeh* witch," but he didn't seem interested in fighting with her again, and he and my mother never even began to look for a new place to live.

Every atom of me wanted to go. There was no reason to stay at Fanny's now. There was the whole world outside, and I wanted to know it. The only question was, how was I going to get out when I wasn't even fifteen years old and still had another month of junior high school?

"Do you think I can start going out on auditions?" I kept asking Irene, though I still felt like a mouse in her lofty presence.

"You have to be ready first," she kept answering me with an absent-minded shrug. "Any phone calls I need to return before I start teaching this morning?"

But I *was* ready. What was she waiting for?

Suddenly one Saturday, as she shrugged at me yet again while she read the neat list of phone messages that I'd printed for her, I saw right through my idol as clearly as if her flawless skin were cellophane. She didn't know any better than I how things were done in Hollywood. Why else would she be living in East L.A. and booking a bunch of kids at Thrifty Drug Store openings and Hadassah luncheons? I admitted to myself what I'd probably guessed for a long time: she and Sid had no more connections in Hollywood than my mother. If I wanted to move up, I'd have to find the way by myself—the Sandmans had nothing to offer but dreams. Yet I couldn't bear to go, never to see her again.

It was Sid who shoved me. "You have to convey a more wistful feeling: 'Ah've always relied on the kindness of strangehs.'" He modeled the intonation one afternoon at my lesson. "Arms out and palms up." He pulled at my wrists.

"'Ah've always relied on the kindness of strangehs,'" I repeated, twisting my lips into a wistful Blanche DuBois smile, with Blanche's fey tilt to my head. I sensed her easily. I had no trouble imagining what it would feel like to be so vulnerable, to allow yourself to yield to everyone. I could play her, though I would *never* be her.

My arms were extended and my palms were pointed up as he'd directed, but Sid still hadn't let go of my wrists. I glanced at him, breaking out of Blanche. His expression as he stared at me in the big room was not teacherly. "You know," he said in a voice I'd never heard before—low and sort of choked—"when you came here three years ago, I thought, 'My God, I've never seen such a pathetic-looking little girl.'" His face was close enough for me to see beads of sweat glistening on his thin mustache. "And now . . ."

He didn't finish his sentence, this husband of the gorgeous wife, but I knew very well from Jake Mann and Falix Lieber what he wanted. Should I laugh? Should I break away and run into the street? Could innocence or pathos save me? My mind bubbled and then cooled. I assumed a little-girl voice. "You've been like a wonderful father to me all these years," I squeaked. He was breathing as if he'd just run a marathon, and his hands moved to my shoulders. Words were my weapon, and I shot them. "You and Irene have been the mom and dad I never had." My voice rose higher, a child's grating whine. "I was going to tell her next time, when I see her in the office, how good you've been to me."

I could read the expressions on his face—surprise first, then fear, then cunning. His look shifted to a studied nonchalance. "Let's take that 'strangehs' line again," he said.

The whole incident hadn't lasted more than two minutes, and that was the end of it. But how could I keep on at Theatre Arts Studio now?

About a week later, close to my fifteenth birthday, I looked through the Yellow Pages of the Los Angeles telephone directory under "Theaters." "Geller Theatre and School of Dramatic Arts," the biggest ad said. "Professional Productions Staged by Our Students. The Stars of Tomorrow. Conveniently Located Steps from Hollywood."

"So it's good riddance to the bottle blonde you were so maaad about, you fickle little thang." Eddy-as-Scarlett taunted me on the steps of his porch.

I ignored his calling my beloved a bottle blonde because I'd never been to the Westside except on the Tanner Grey Line Motor Tour of the movie stars' homes, and if Eddy went with me it wouldn't be so scary. "Come on," I begged. "This can be the break we've been waiting for."

"She's ready for her close-up, Mr. DeMille!" The spidery fingers spread in perfect and annoying imitation of a demented Gloria Swanson. "Batty, batty. She really believes that someone is going to put two little Jewish girls from East L.A. into the movies. But this little Jewish girl"—he pointed to himself—"is not as dumb as this one"—he rubbed an elegant forefinger into my collar bone.

"To hell with you," I said, slapping his hand away and stomping down the steps. Why couldn't he take serious things seriously? Why wouldn't he go on this brave adventure with me? "Stay here if you want," I tossed at him over my shoulder. "I'm going where there's a chance for something good to happen."

But how do you get to Wilshire Boulevard and Fairfax Avenue from East L.A.? One bus from Wabash Avenue to Brooklyn Avenue, I discovered; another from Brooklyn Avenue to Olvera Street; a third down Wilshire Boulevard to another universe, on the border of Hollywood. I sat in the front seat of each bus, looking out the big window, traveling west. On the Wilshire bus I could see a gloriously gaudy crimson and platinum sunset that promised everything.

The lobby at Geller's was full of glamour. I'd never seen so many blondes at once. Almost everyone, men and women, had golden hair, even those with eyebrows and eyes darker than mine, even those with conspicuous black roots. Most of the men wore tight James Dean jeans and white T-shirts. A lot of the women wore shin-length capri pants and high, high heels. A lone dark-haired beauty—Babette, everyone called her—was decked out in a lacy white dress that billowed over piles of crinoline petticoats, and she carried a Little Bo-Peep parasol to complete the little-girl-cum-southern-belle look. ("Her father is a big movie director," I heard one newcomer whisper.) Another woman batted Joan Crawford eyes at everyone and called them "dahling." She was much older than the others and was wearing a slinky black sheath; Hollywood dripped from her pores. My silver stilettos would not have been out of place, but I was in my silly pachuca garb, looking like an East L.A. barrio girl. What was I doing here? Eddy was right.

No! I wouldn't get scared off. They didn't have to know who I was or where I came from. I was an actress. I'd just act as though I were someone else. I sneaked into the ladies' room, where two women who looked like starlets were combing their shiny hair in front of the mirror, and I slipped into a stall.

"So this guy promised that he'd introduce me to somebody who works at the William Morris Agency," one said. I'd wait until they left.

When the doors swung closed behind them, I scrubbed the pachuca lipstick off my lips and started over, following the outline. I erased the black rapiers over my eyes and with my Maybelline eyebrow pencil drew new lines in to look more natural. I combed the wild pompadour down. I could do nothing about my pachuca clothes, but at least my face and hair looked less like those of a Hollenbeck Junior High gang girl.

The lobby was dense with blue haze. Everyone smoked. Some puffed away through ivory or ebony cigarette holders. The most muscled boy held his Chesterfield between a thumb and an index finger, eyes narrowed as he puffed. A rival dangled his own cigarette from his lips and puffed on it, a squint in his eyes that was at least as cool as the thumb-and-index-finger chap's. I smoked my first cigarette in the lobby of Geller's, offered to me from the pack of the lip-dangler. Before that summer was over I was smoking two and a half packs a day. Smoking made me look older.

That first evening I auditioned for the acting school with a dozen other people. When Mr. Lord, the director of Geller's, called my name, I walked onto the stage and did a monologue from *The Member of the Wedding*. Though I still wore my pachuca clothes, I knew how to hold my body in Frankie's girl-boy stance, I knew how to make my voice sound boyish and confused and full of longing, a lost adolescent.

"I'm E. J. Smith," whispered a big, pink-skinned man who leaned over my chair as I took my seat in the audience again. "You were terrific." He offered me his great paw to shake. He was dressed in a striped three-piece suit and a tomato-red bow tie, and his hair and eyebrows and lashes were white-blond. I'd never seen anyone up close who looked like that. "A real *goy*," my mother would have said of him. "I'm working in a talent agency," he told me. My head spun. *Was it happening already?*

"Can we see that *Member of the Wedding* again?" he asked with authority when the other auditions were finished.

"Sure, we have some time," Mr. Lord said amiably, and he called me up again. I saw the audience lean forward to watch, and I became Frankie once more. When I finished they all applauded, though they hadn't applauded for any of the others.

"Work-Study scholarship," Mr. Lord said, when I told him later that I could not afford the forty-dollar-a-month tuition. "You can address theater advertisement envelopes for us, ten hours a week."

I was on my way.

"You were *goood!*" a young woman said as I drifted ecstatically toward the bus stop. She had platinum blond hair and a high Judy Holliday voice with a New York Jewish accent. "Simone Deardon," she introduced herself. (Months later I caught a glimpse of her driver's license. Sonya Dubinsky, it read.)

"Lil Foster," I replied. I wouldn't be "Lilly"—that was the illegitimate girl who grew up in a scroungy furnished room and looked like a refugee child. And I couldn't be Lillian—that was such a somber name. I could be absolutely anyone I wanted to be here, I realized—acting was what it was all about. "Eighteen," I said when Simone asked how old I was. She was twenty.

"Lee-lee." Albert opened the door before I got up the steps. I saw my mother's pale face over his shoulder. "Your mother was driving me crazy. What's the matter with you, to stay out all night?"

"Don't yell at her," my mother yelled at Albert. "Do you want to make me sick?" she yelled at me. "Where were you?"

It was 1 A.M. The buses had stopped running by the time I got to Olvera Street, but I'd waited a long time at the bus stop before I figured that out. When an elderly Mexican lady and her husband stopped at the traffic light, I asked them for a ride. She made her husband pick me up. They'd just closed their bar on Olvera Street, she said. Then she shook a motherly finger at me. "Terrible things can happen to a young girl alone on the street."

Now I had to shed Irene too. I was supposed to take a singing lesson with her the next day. "I have to talk to you about an important matter," I'd say, looking straight at her. "There's something very important . . . *extremely* important . . . I need to say to you." I rehearsed the lines out loud, pacing in the dining room between my unmade army cot and the lopsided lion's claw table. But I couldn't think of what I'd say next because the recollection of her statuesque form emptied my head.

I got there thirty-five minutes early, just to sit alone in the cool office for a while and listen through the partition to the lesson she was giving and think about how I used to pet her Orlon sweater. I stared at the old print of the tutued ballerinas that had been part of the furniture of my life for more than three years. *"Every time we say good-bye, I die a little."* It was Jamie, one of her voice students, singing in a jazzy, syncopated rhythm as Irene pounded the piano. *I'd* come to say good-bye. It smote me like a cudgel on the heart.

"Okay, that's it," Irene announced, and they were coming out. I'd forgotten that Jamie had only half-hour lessons. I heard Irene's high heels click against the wooden floor of the big room, then Jamie's tapped heels and toes behind her, and I wanted to scurry under my chair like the scared mouse that I was.

"Hi!" Jamie waved at me and left.

"Your lesson's not until four. What's up?" Irene asked.

I didn't answer because my tongue had stopped working again. I managed a deep breath.

"Don't tell me it's still that man? I thought it was over."

Chuck, she meant. That seemed like a century ago. I shook my head.

She sat down behind her desk on our gray metal chair. "So what is it?" She'd sounded impatient about Chuck, but I must have looked tragic, because now she regarded me with softened eyes.

I couldn't face those eyes. I studied my balled fists. When I looked up—after an eternity—her hand was extended across the desk, palm up. I dared, I grasped. At last, her silk skin, her warm clasp, I was touching Irene Sandman! I would never let go.

"You can tell me," she said softly.

"I have a terrible crush on you" tumbled out of my mouth when I opened it—the ventriloquist's dummy again—and I couldn't stop: "I'm afraid this is how homosexuals begin." I felt her fingers twitch in surprise but I held firm, a drowning clutch. "I think I'd better leave" bubbled out now (where had that come from?) "because I don't want to be one of them." I hadn't rehearsed any of those lines that escaped from me. "And I know that's what will happen if I stay here because I can't help myself." *No, why was I saying that? There was Carlos. If he'd been different I'd still be his girlfriend.* I forced up the memory of his lips on my neck; then I inhaled her perfume and the scent filled my brain and washed everything else out. I just looked down at our clasped hands, my dark olive fingers against her pink-white palm, the miracle of it, and I clutched harder. I could hear the clock *tick-ticking* on the wall, right above my head. *Tick-tick, tick-tick, tick-tick.*

When I finally looked up, I saw tears in her beautiful eyes. I hadn't seen anything like that since she'd said "*wow*" the first time she saw me do Rachel Hoffman. She sniffed. Or did she have a cold? No—the wonder of it—I'd moved her once again! It didn't matter about being an actress anymore. There were tears in her eyes for me! I would stay, just to be near her.

"I know this is hard for you," she murmured, and her fingers moved under my grip. "These things can be terrible. Sid and I had a good friend in the theater in Chicago who . . ." I fixed on her violet eyes, afraid of what she would tell me yet needing to hear. But she stopped.

"Who what?"

"You're so young, Lillian," she sighed. She'd changed her mind about telling me, I could see; she was retracting the tantalizing, scary tidbit. Now she wriggled her hand free of mine and dabbed at her nose with a Kleenex. "You're probably right," she said. "It would be better for you to go."

What was she talking about? *No, it's a mistake,* I wanted to cry out. I would fall to my knees and kiss the hem of her dress! I would grab her hand back. I would be her little dog! *Please let me stay,* I would beg.

But I couldn't stay. I needed to become somebody else. And maybe it was true—that what I'd felt for her was the way homosexuals begin, and I didn't want to be one.

I didn't know what was true anymore.

She rose and extended her hand again, only for a handshake this time.

I rose too, weak with confusion. "Thanks for everything," I said, struggling for the well-modulated tones I'd learned from her, and I touched her hand for the last time.

"Sid and I will miss you," she answered. Then, head bowed, I limped out the door on rubber legs.

"I've lost the love of my life," the mask of tragedy inside me bleated.

"Free, free," the mask of comedy exulted.

"So you won't have to take all those buses," my mother said. We were moving to the Westside, where the famous corner of Hollywood and Vine was, where the movie studios were.

"So you can go to the high school with *Yiddisheh kinder* again," Rae said. She and Mr. Bergman were moving to the Westside too.

For the first time in her life, my mother bought furniture. And now she and I and Albert would live in an apartment of our own, without a Missus. We were leaving Dundas Street!

I walked around Fanny's house as in a spell. Would I really be free of this place? Good-bye to the floating eyeballs! Good-bye to the dusty yellowed bedsheets that covered the broken living room furniture! Good-bye to the room where I grew up, the beds in which I'd slept and dreamed before they became Albert's beds! One last peek in the mottled mirror that had seen me as Betty Grable and Eddie Cantor and Mary Marvel. That mirror had also witnessed my mother's flailing and screaming for her dead brother, and me, running behind her, year after year, two decapitated chickens. I'd been miserable in that room, yet it had been home to me and I'd been happy too. But all that was the past. Who would I be next year at this time, looking into a mirror somewhere else?

"Watch yourself with that crazy bastard," Fanny told my mother when we stood together in the ugly living room for the last time. Albert paced the strip of sidewalk in front of the house, his hat pulled over his ears.

"I'll miss you," I said to Fanny. It was true. She'd been one of the few adults in my daily life. She'd lavished her granddaughters' dresses on me as well as, for better or worse, her opinions and advice. I wanted to hug her now, but I was shy, despite our years together.

"No, you won't miss me." Fanny tossed her hand dismissively. She was dressed in her dead husband's shoes and coat, ready to water the green patch of front lawn as soon as we left. "You'll forget all about me and Boyle Heights in a week. That's the way life is, little *momzer.* Don't worry about it."

"I'll never forget Dundas Street," I swore. "I grew up here. It formed me."

"Formed, shmormed," Fanny mocked. But then we did hug each other, for the first time in all those years.

I never saw her again. I left all of East L.A. behind me for a very long time.

LIL

6 HOLLYWOOD

PARAMOUNT STUDIO, RKO, *the corner of Hollywood and Vine, all are only a few miles away from Geller Theatre and School of Dramatic Arts. You could almost reach out and touch those shimmery shrines.*

"Someone has to make it," Simone says logically. "They need talent, and we've got it."

"Right," we chorus. "Why shouldn't it be us?" After class we crowd the booths at Tiny Naylor's and talk Hollywood talk until 2 A.M. This is "the gang," as Simone calls us, the dearest comradeship I've ever had (though my harrowing fear is that they'll find out I'm only fifteen years old and think I'm a baby).

"John Wayne in a romantic comedy! For crying out loud, his agent is nuts if he lets him take that picture," one of us says. The movie stars are our glittering second cousins. We're so close — by profession, by geography. Of course we worry about them, though they don't yet recognize us as family. We keep up with their doings through the Hollywood Reporter *or* Variety — *the family chronicles we read religiously.*

"You guys," Nick announces, still stunned by his luck, "my cousin's agent just promised to get me on as an extra for The Ten Commandments. *Twenty-five smackers a day for at least two weeks. Thirty-five if you get to say something or grunt."*

"Terrific!" Simone cries, patting him on the back, and we all cheer.

I don't have a lot to add yet, but I'm new to the game. Most of them have been in Hollywood for years.

"Can I give you a lift home?" Simone asked the first time we all went to Tiny Naylor's. She drove a new pink convertible with a white top. *But what if she saw my mother? "This girl comes from a family of slobs,"* *she might tell them at Geller's. Or Albert? "From a family of crazies," she* *might say. She wouldn't even be able to understand their Yiddish accents.*

"You can just drop me off here," I said at Stanley and Oakwood, my hand poised to open the car door the second she stopped, and I'd flee, like Cinderella at the ball, so she wouldn't see which building I went into.

"Sweetie, I gotta tell you somethin', for your own good," Simone began as she stopped the car at the corner. *What did she know about me?* *My age! I'd been so careful — how could she know?* "That striped blouse with that tweed skirt have gotta go," she said, her Betty Boop eyes fluttering sympathetically. "You got talent, but you don't know how to dress."

Their house was a white-pillared mansion, with an upstairs and a downstairs and real oil paintings on the walls — sunsets and oceans and puppies, in big gilt frames. I followed Simone across the white brocaded carpet, fearful that my shoes might leave a smudge. "This is the greatest actress in the school," she gushed to her elegantly coiffed mother.

"Well, isn't that nice." Her mother stretched tight lips over perfect teeth while she surveyed me, head to foot.

Her father, who wore a gray suit and steely businessman spectacles, came home later. Through the picture window in the living room, I could see the shiny, big car he parked in the driveway. "I'll be upstairs till dinner," he told his wife, sifting through his mail without looking up. He threw a "g'day" toward me when Simone told him who I was.

Simone's room had a pink satin canopy bed; a thousand dolls left over from childhood were ranged against the wall on built-in shelves. Her walk-in closet, bigger than my whole bedroom in the new apartment, was stuffed with movie-star clothes. "These don't fit me anymore. You try them on." Simone pulled out one glamorous piece after another, tossing them munificently onto her bed. Form-hugging ankle-length capri pants; a red dress ("marvelous décolletage," Simone said) made of soft, cloudlike material; a glittery black blouse, scooped low at the bosom, pinched tight with elastic at the waist. "I'm through with these, too. Betcha they'll fit," she said, her cheeks flush now with Pygmalion's pleasure as she reached into a tower of shoes and fetched toeless three-inch heels, backless four-inch heels, clear plastic platform sandals that were almost invisible on the foot.

"Now you don't look tacky at all," she said, gratified by her efforts as I modeled the red dress and the four-inchers for her.

"So now we do somethin' about that hair," she told me when I next showed up at her house, wearing her purple capris and the toeless three-inchers. She wanted me platinum, like herself, but we compromised on raven's wing black with a thin swath of copper running through the left side. She sat me on the pink padded stool in her marble bathroom and expertly draped my shoulders with a plastic sheet, then painted my head with the smelly black dye, dipping her brush into the bottle with the flourish of an artist dipping from a palette. She stepped back to examine her handiwork and noticed she'd accidentally gotten a splash of dye on the tip of my nose. She rubbed at it with a washcloth, her face straining in worry, but it remained. "What should we do?" she cried.

I examined the black splash in the mirror. It was the size of a dime and made my nose look fat. Now I rubbed until the skin all around it colored like a rose, but the spot got no dimmer. "That's okay." I shrugged to hide how upset I really was. "Walt Disney will hire me to do Minnie Mouse."

Simone looked ready to cry, but the sob that escaped from her sounded like a laugh. That was all I needed. A guffaw broke through my lips, and then we chortled and snorted together until we hiccuped, and still we couldn't stop. "Let's try cold cream," Simone sputtered through her hysteria. She ran to bring it from her medicine cabinet. Biting her lip in concentration, she smeared it hard on my poor bespattered and berubbed nose. It did the trick. But for the rest of the afternoon we laughed like two schoolchildren over nothing, for the sheer fun of laughing. She was the girlfriend I'd never had as a kid.

"You look just like Elizabeth Taylor," generous Simone said as I was leaving.

I couldn't believe my good fortune. It was she who usually organized our treks to Tiny Naylor's, and now I sat next to her in the pink convertible, with the rest of the gang crowded into the back seat, as we sped down Wilshire Boulevard after classes or rehearsals. Almost everyone liked Simone, and she'd found something in me to like. *Oh, don't let anything ruin it.*

"Simone has the emotional depth of a post when she tries to act," catty Babette whispered to me on a break when Jesse, the James Dean look-alike, held Simone's eyes with his as he lit her cigarette. "She's just here to find a great-looking guy, don't you think?"

"Simone's wonderful," I answered, defending my friend.

"Well, she still can't act her way out of a paper bag," Babette said with a smirk.

Simone swiped at Jesse's face, a playful slap.

I had secrets I had to keep, even from Simone, but she also had secrets she kept from me. For a while after the slap, she went around with a faint smile on her lips and a distant look in her eyes. It was about Jesse, I was sure, though she never mentioned him. Then the smile faded, the look became dark, and for the first time since I'd met her she wasn't chatty. I found out why, standing outside what I'd thought was an empty classroom, waiting for seven o'clock. Gloria, the older woman who called everybody "dahling," was already inside. "I've never seen Nick so pissed," I heard her say. "Jesse asked to borrow his apartment when Nick went to Vegas, and then, dahling, Nick came back to find bloody sheets. Blood all over his bed! Can you believe that Jesse? He didn't even bother to clean it up."

"Yuk! Well, she got more than she can handle, the silly bitch." It was Babette's voice. "He'll drop her now, 'cause all he wants is cherry."

It had to be Simone they were talking about. Poor Simone. How awful that Nick talked, and now Babette and Gloria were talking, and pretty soon everyone would know. This wasn't the first time I understood that girls can't get away with very much.

My mother cried a lot about me in those days. "What do you mean, you're not going any more to school? You used to be so good in school. Albert, hear what she wants to do!"

I'd had a summer of acting classes and performances and late nights at Tiny Naylor's and weekends at the beach with the gang. Albert and I had already had tiffs because I came home in the early morning hours, and my mother wouldn't let him sleep until she heard my key in the door. "Every night I have to hear it. 'Something terrible happened to her!' 'She got killed by a car!' 'She got kidnapped!'" He mimicked my mother's frenzied pitch. "Enough already!"

"Well, she's stupid to worry," I tossed off. I knew how to live my life better than she did. In the beginning, I'd tried to reassure her. "We rehearse late, and then Simone always drives me home. I'm just learning to be an actress," I'd told her reasonably. "What are you worried about?" But I gave up.

"She says she's quitting school," my mother cried to Albert again.

"She can say all she wants, but she gotta go till sixteen. They throw you in jail if you don't go."

"I just got a job—I'm a receptionist—for this lawyer—downtown—a criminal lawyer," I embellished when Simone invited me to go window-shopping. I'd already spent four furtive days in the tenth grade, and I hated it. I'd heard that the prissy Lane's dresses the girls wore cost forty-five dollars apiece, and their fathers were dentists or CPAs or owned shops like the ones in which my mother used to work. They cracked their gum on their back teeth and had cowlike expressions on their faces, and all day long they brushed and primped at their beauty-parlored hair as though it were their life's work. Jewish-American princesses. They never even saw me, but it didn't matter because I had my own gang.

I had to become a double agent. Actually, when I wasn't scared that I'd be found out, it was almost fun. To Fairfax High School I wore dirty brown and white oxfords, with gray-white socks that bunched around my ankles, refusing to stay up on my calves. I camouflaged my body in long, drab skirts and wrinkled blouses that wouldn't remain tucked in at the waist. This was my costume, my disguise. In anticipation of my wonderful evenings, I set my hair in bobby pins and wore an old-lady babushka over my head.

"Ooh, where you going tonight?" a nosy girl might ask from a neighboring desk, surprised at my hairpinned head—as if such a sloppy creature could have anywhere to go.

"No place," I'd answer, barely lifting my eyes from my book of plays. Let them stew.

Each afternoon I went home from school and donned the other costume. This took a couple of hours: Max Factor base — dusky and mysterious; eye shadow and lipstick and rouge, the way Simone had taught me to apply them. I brushed the pincurls out into a sophisticated do, back behind my ear on one side, falling exotically over a mascaraed eye on the other — a raven-haired Veronica Lake, I hoped. "Diamond Lil," Simone had called me when I tried on the last pair of capris she gave me, stretch material in a harlequin effect, one leg all black, the other all white.

"Diamond Lil," I chuckled to myself in algebra class, snug in my slob disguise. I *loved* that name.

When I was with my Geller's gang, Fairfax High School was my shameful secret, because I could never let them know I was a kid. Sometimes I woke from a nightmare as if I'd been dropped into a pit: *They've discovered the truth. "She's only fifteen years old!" Babette points a shaming finger at me, and the others hoot, even Simone: "Baby, baby, kindergarten baby!"*

Okay, the less I talked the better: I'd be a silent, smoldering beauty. I was an actress, and I could act any role I wanted.

"How's your new job," Stan asked.

"Fabulous," I drawled, a mysterious smile playing around my lips. End of discussion. A snake vanishing between two rocks.

The truant officer came to our apartment two or three times. "Well, your daughter had twelve absences last month." I heard the precise nasal voice addressing my mother the first time. I peeked out from my room and saw the woman's lace ruff collar and tight blue-gray hairdo that sat like a helmet on her head, and I dashed back to my bed on noiseless tippy-toes. I buried my head under the pillow, simulating the high snores of deep sleep, but she didn't barge in. *Should I be scared? Could they really throw me in jail? Or reform school? They probably thought I was an immigrant girl, poor family. They wouldn't bother with me much because they'd figure I'd be sixteen soon enough and quit to get married.*

"She hasn't been feeling good," my mother said, excusing me another time.

"Then you need to take her to a doctor, and she has to bring a letter from him to school. In America, children have to go to school," the truant officer lectured, enunciating carefully. "She can go to work or get married or whatever you want her to do when she's sixteen."

"Okay," my mother said, tremulous before American authority. "I'm gonna tell her to get better." My mother screamed at my door when the truant officer left: "Lilly, what's the matter with you? You want to make me sick?"

"Leave me alone," I screamed back. "I know what I'm doing."

I hated it when the truant officer came to see my mother, who'd then get hysterical, but I couldn't bear to drag myself to school in the morning after I'd stayed out until 2 or 3 A.M. And I wasn't learning anything from the teachers anyway. I'd sit in the back of the class and read plays. No one stopped me, or even noticed, and I could finish almost three a day. I knew more about Tennessee Williams, Arthur Miller, Maxwell Anderson, and William Inge than anyone at Geller's.

Algebra—D, my report card said, *English—C, Geography—D, History —D, Latin—F* (why in the world had I taken Latin?). But what did it matter? I only had a few more months to go, and then I could quit school and devote myself to my acting career.

Though I now gave my mother new things to worry about, the truth was that as soon as she'd married Albert, her old madness vanished— maybe because she didn't have to work anymore in an unventilated sweatshop, on her feet with her arms extended all day long; maybe because she didn't have to see the Hungarian woman and hear the tragic stories of lost brothers that made her think of her own; or maybe it was just that now she had new responsibilities—shopping for food, cooking supper every night—and they took up a lot of space in her mind. Whatever it was, though my mother never looked happy, she wasn't running around the room naked either, pulling her hair and screaming "Hirschel!" How could I not be grateful to Albert for that?

In other ways, though, her life was still horrible. I knew from the movies and the songs she'd loved and the way she'd pined over my father for all those years after he betrayed her that she'd been a very romantic, very sexual person. But I couldn't imagine her making love with my stepfather. Did they ever have sex? On the nights I was home I listened from my bed, curious and ready to be repelled, but no sounds came through the thin plasterboard that separated the two bedrooms except for Albert's wall-rattling snores and my mother's tossing and turning, her pillow or head hitting the wall.

On weekend mornings I was often awakened by Albert's voice from the kitchen: "*Nu*, are you gonna deal today or tomorrow?" Then a long silence. "So, your turn! Am I playing this game by myself or with some-body else?" Then with passion: "Hah, I got you!" and I could hear him slam his victorious cards on the table. Did they play gin rummy instead of having sex? *Why, oh why, had she made me push her into this? Why, why, with all her voluptuous beauty, wasn't she able to get Moishe to marry her?*

During the week, the minute Albert came home from work he sat at the kitchen table, dealt out a solitaire hand from his grubby deck, and waited for my mother to deposit his food in front of him. When she stood beside him with his plate, he pushed the cards aside to clear a space and lifted his knife and fork without a word, without a nod of ac-knowledgment. *What if he goes crazy again and does something violent to her?* But he never did. He wasn't a normal person, but he worked and brought home the money, and she cooked his suppers. It was a busi-nesslike arrangement. They never talked.

I never talked either when I was home for supper. The table was silent except for Albert's *chomp* and *slurp* and my mother's *crunch* and *crack*. It was her sounds, even more than his, that grated in my ear, set my teeth on edge, like steel screeching on steel. Sometimes, sitting there at the table, I hated her with a visceral fury that made me clench my fists. *Why hadn't she managed to make her life any better? I would never lead a life like hers!* But my hatred was followed almost always by a gush of pity. I'd loved her so passionately once, when we were the center of each other's world. And now she was stuck.

We never walked arm-in-arm anymore, the way we used to on the streets of the Bronx or East L.A. We never went anywhere together any-more. "Mother and daughter," we'd said in New York. I tried not to let myself think about it. Whenever I remembered I felt a claw in my gut, but I could escape in my mind by thinking about Geller's and my friends and my hoped-for career. I had to make my own life.

. . .

"I hear that William Morris himself came to see *Anna Christie* here last month, and he actually signed one guy on," somebody whispered on audition night, the first time I went to Geller's.

"Elia Kazan was in the audience a couple of years ago. That's when he discovered Eva Marie Saint here," somebody else whispered.

Did we all wait with secret hope after each performance for the fabulous knock on the dressing room door? "William Wyler's out front and says he has to talk to Lil Foster!"

But though we were practically next door to them, the big shots weren't coming around to the school productions. So where did they find their talent? How did you get discovered? I still hadn't a clue, and there was no one at Geller's to advise us. We took classes and were on our own. Jack Lord auditioned the students, but then, like a god in a mechanistic universe, he virtually disappeared. We joked about the appropriateness of his name.

I'd thought, the night of my audition, that I'd already been discovered by E. J. Smith because he worked in a talent agency and told me I was terrific, but he never said anything more after that night. What could it hurt to talk to him now? "Oh, that's when I was at the Mel Kaufman Agency. I quit there," he told me when I asked how I could get an appointment. "I'm trying to get started someplace else. But you can just go into the Mel Kaufman Agency on your own. Take some photos," he said easily.

"Did you go?" he asked weeks later when we ran into each other in front of Geller's. I'd given up right away because I had no money for professional photographs. I'd seen the kind you were supposed to take around with you. Gloria had had some done. "Publicity pictures," she said they were called: black-and-white glamour shots, moody large eyes staring intently into space, glossy wet lips. The photos were backlit, with shadows that spoke of high drama and mystery. She told me what they cost. A fortune.

"If you need pictures, I've got some ideas," E. J. said. His close gaze made me feel prickly, and I was still intimidated by his large, white-blond goyishness, but I stayed to listen. "I know this guy who's a photographer, likes to do pinups on the side." I must have looked startled because E. J. spread his fingers upright in a gesture that indicated *noth-*

ing to worry about. "Very professional stuff," he said with a businesslike air. "I know he'd trade publicity stills for a couple of hours of a pinup shoot. He'll give you what you need."

I said nothing as E. J. tore the title page off the typescript he was carrying, Tennessee Williams's *Baby Doll*, and scribbled a name and phone number on it, then stuck it in front of me. For a second I hesitated, but I'd seen pinup photos of Betty Grable. A backless bathing suit, long legs ending in high heels, a bright smile over her shoulder, flirting with the camera. It would be just one more role.

I wore Simone's harlequin capris and plastic see-through platform heels to the shoot in Wes Martin's studio. Framed portraits adorned the windows—a glowing bride in miles of swirled white satin, a pouting little redheaded boy holding a puppy, a debutante looking fresh and virginal. "Miss Foster?" Wes Martin asked, coming out from another room when I opened the door that made a buzzer ring. He was wearing gray work pants and a workshirt with rolled-up sleeves, a thin, balding man with an efficient air.

I can do this, I assured myself. "Gigi," I ad-libbed. "My professional name is Gigi Frost." Lillian Foster or even Lil sounded far too serious for a pinup model.

"Let's try a few shots in the outfit you're wearing. Looks great." His smile was impersonal.

The poses I took weren't much different from the ones I'd practiced in the mirror at Fanny's from the time I was eight years old: hands on hips and chin tilted down, a "come hither" expression in my eyes; arms in the air, an ecstatic expression on my lips; a cross-legged pose, back arched and chest forward, a naughty-girl moue on my face. Then in his tiny bathroom I hung my capris and cotton pullover on a hook, folded my panties and bra and placed them on the floor, and changed into my two-piece bathing suit.

"Okay. Okay. Okay," he said to each new pose I struck with his umbrellas and scarves and ukuleles. It was fun, I thought, surprising myself at the flirty way I could be with a black box. It wasn't me—it was some glamour girl, or rather it was me playing the role of a glamour girl.

"Now can we take just a few figure shots?" Wes Martin said.

"Like the first ones?" I asked, meaning the harlequin pants and high heels, standing full-figure instead of seated or kneeling.

"No," he said. He glanced sharply at me, and his pale cheeks became pink. "'Figure' means 'nude,' 'no clothes.'" He seemed as embarrassed as I.

Nude. He wanted me to take my clothes off in front of him? I hadn't been completely naked in front of anyone since I was a baby. What if my mother or Rae saw nude pictures of me? "This is what a Jewish girl does?" Rae would yell. My mother would bawl.

But how would they ever see them? Why shouldn't I let him take some "figure" photographs, as he called them. I needed those publicity pictures if I was really going to make the next step in my career, and I could see there was nothing to fear from Wes Martin. Hadn't Marilyn Monroe gotten her start that way?

"There's a big towel in the bathroom you can use for a wrap. I'll set up a plain white background, okay?"

The air felt cold when I removed the white towel from my torso and stood on the huge sheet of heavy background paper. As the big lights warmed my nipples and my belly, my teeth stopped their little castanet clacks, but I couldn't shift my eyes to look at him. Nor could I flirt with the camera now. Naked, I posed sedately, as I imagined an artist's model would. "Good job, good job," he said, still entirely businesslike, to every new pose I struck. Then, "That's three rolls. Great!" And I went back to the bathroom to dress as he set up the lights for the glamour head shots I needed to take to the Mel Kaufman Agency.

A week later, I returned for the contact sheet he'd made of twelve head shots and fifteen eight-by-tens of the one he thought was the best. I held the photo up gingerly, by the edges, delighted. I looked like a film noir actress.

"Would you like to see some of the pinups?" he asked matter-of-factly.

"No, that's all right," I cried. The memory of my nude posing had really agitated me, bothered me all week, as though I'd let myself be robbed of something. I hurried out of the studio as quickly as I could; but with the publicity photos in the cardboard envelope that Wes had given me, I soon pushed the nagging scruple aside. I'd needed professional pictures to hand to an agent, and now I had them. Good ones.

I stared at the eight-by-ten again as I sat alone on the back seat of the bus. No, I didn't look like Elizabeth Taylor, I thought, critical now, a little disappointed. But still . . .

I studied the picture for days. Something was very wrong. My nose. Where it should have been button or turned up, like Debbie Reynolds's or Doris Day's, like all the noses of the most popular actresses of the 1950s, it had a bump and it was too big. It was my mother's nose. I'd always thought she was so beautiful, but now I saw that I wasn't at all beautiful. Not with that nose.

I'd known girls at Fairfax High who started the school year with convex noses, and before the first semester was over their noses were concave. A "nose job," it was called, plastic surgery. "A lot of girls are doing it," I heard someone whisper when Annette Kessler came back to school after a week's absence, looking like a movie star.

"I've got to ask you something important," I told E. J. when he wanted to see the publicity stills Wes Martin had taken. Who else could I ask about what it takes to make it in Hollywood? "Do I need plastic surgery on my nose?"

He gave a low whistle and studied me judiciously, cupping my chin to turn my head left and then right in profile. "You're talking about a lot of money there," he said, "but I'll tell you, there's something you can do that's much cheaper." He slipped an arm around my shoulder as though we were good friends. "For your teeth."

"My teeth?" I'd never thought about them.

"They're called Hollywood veneers. A dentist fits them on you, and it gives you a perfect smile. You just slip them off when you eat or sleep. They cost something like a hundred bucks."

I laughed an exasperated laugh. I didn't have even one buck.

"Look, if you didn't mind the session with Wes," E. J. said, "I can put you in touch with this agent, Andy, who books only pinup and figure. You can make a hundred bucks in a few hours' work. Do yourself a favor." He smiled, showing his own big pearly teeth.

I slipped into the women's dressing room the instant he walked off and studied myself in the mirror, forcing my lips into a jack-o'-lantern grin. I said the alphabet slowly, exaggerating each letter, to see how I looked to people when I talked. He was right. How hadn't I noticed my teeth before? They were hideous hobgoblin teeth pointing every which way, yellow, uneven, crowded like grave markers in an ancient cemetery that I'd seen in a photograph.

Pictures of young women in various stages of undress plastered the walls of Andy's Santa Monica Boulevard office, and scattered on his desk were glossy black-and-white photos of women—in tiny bikinis, in baby doll nightgowns slipping off a shoulder, in sheer peignoirs that were molded to breasts and stomachs and thighs, in nothing at all, the pubes covered only by a beach ball or a coyly raised knee. He was a smiley man, about sixty, with a beer-belly and a fluffy Santa Claus beard. "Let's see what you look like, little darlin'," he said. "You can get undressed over there." He waved toward another room.

I looked at him blankly, suddenly scared.

"There's a robe in there. Just wrap it around you and come on out," he said a little impatiently. "Nobody bites around here."

I could give it up, I thought as I walked to the dressing room. What had I wanted this for in the first place—a Hollywood career? My mother and I had dreamed it together, but those dreams were finished.

Yet what was there for me if I didn't become an actress? It was the only goal I'd ever seriously thought about, and I was good at it. Everyone said so. I couldn't give it up now.

I undressed in front of the full-length mirror that leaned against the wall in the dressing room. How dirty my bra looked. I couldn't remember when I'd last washed it. It was the only bra that I owned, and one strap was held up with a safety pin. I wadded it and shoved it into my large purse, then wrapped the flimsy nylon robe around myself and stepped out quickly.

"Okay, little darlin'." Andy motioned me mechanically to a raised platform. "If you'll just drop the towel, please." He switched on two large, blazing photography lights and adjusted their beams to aim at me. "Now, turn sideways."

I posed, smiling with closed lips.

"Outstanding," he now cried, accenting the first syllable, "Absolutely *out*standing!"

Most women don't know how to please a man, declares lovely Gigi Frost, and no one is more qualified to illustrate this than Gigi, who is a student of romantic languages at USC. "Sometimes a girl must realize she has to vary her mood to keep a man interested, and there is no better way than to apply some of the tactics foreign women use in winning and keeping a man."

I'm In The Mood To Please

"Girlie mags. My mother and Rae would never go to the newsstands that sold those magazines."

Back in the dressing room I pulled my blue sheath over my naked skin, shivering as though all my synapses were exploding like cherry bombs. "I can put you to work right away," Andy called at me. "Mario Parma does spreads for mags—*King, Adam*, first-rate stuff—and he's always looking for new faces. Fifty bucks a day, and he's the one pays my commission, not you. Should I give him a call?"

Magazines. Girlie mags, they were called. I'd seen them on Hollywood Boulevard newsstands, and the pimply boys and round-shouldered old men who leafed through them. But my mother and Rae read only the *Forward*, the Yiddish newspaper that they bought in little Jewish grocery stores. They'd never go to the newsstands that sold those magazines. Fifty dollars a day. That was almost as much as Albert earned in a whole week.

"Sure," I answered as I stepped out of the dressing room.

Andy wasted no time. "I've got something new and fantastic for you," he said into the receiver of his black telephone. "Gigi Frost's her name. Incredible! About 38-21-36. Right?" He confirmed it with me.

I nodded. *My God, what was I doing?*

"Doesn't own a bra," Andy said, looking at the bodice of my blue sheath approvingly. "Doesn't need one."

Mario Parma let me schedule the shoot for the Monday before Easter, though I never told him that I wanted to do it then because I'd be out of school. One day of work turned into a second, then a third and a fourth. Two hundred dollars for four days of work! I signed the release form: "I, Gigi Frost, cede to Mr. Mario Parma the sole, exclusive, and non-conditional right to use photographs taken of me on March 26–29, 1956, for purposes of publication or in any venue he deems fit." Two hundred dollars was a small fortune. I could use the money to get Hollywood veneers and clothes that weren't Simone's hand-me-downs—and who knew what else?

I cashed his check at the Bank of America on Fairfax. Oh, the heft in my hand of twenty new and crisp and green and lovely ten-dollar bills. So I really could have saved my mother from the shop if only we'd been patient for a little longer.

. . .

"You'll do real good for about three months," Crissy told me. I saw her in Andy's office when photographers came to pick her up for location shoots or when she did a session on the premises. She was a pert redhead who just missed being really pretty by her rabbity front teeth. "They're always interested in a new bod, but once your pictures come out in a lot of magazines, that's the end of it."

"Yeah, it's shits," Olga said in an Eastern European accent. She was Crissy's sidekick, and I never saw one without the other. Olga wore her hair in a single, sleek blue-black pigtail that dangled past her buttocks, but her most startling feature was her eyes: she accented both the upper and lower lids with heavy black liner, which gave her a staring-raccoon appearance. "The only jobs you get are amateurs," she said, "and they don't hardly never pay you more than twenty-five, thirty dollars." She'd been with Andy's agency for about six months.

"You gotta watch out for them too," Crissy said cryptically, looking not at me but at my reflection in the mirror.

"This girl was killed a couple months ago." Olga shook her head ominously, and the pigtail swayed in mournful agreement. "She went with amateur man to shoot in Topanga Canyon, and next thing anybody hear was they find her body, all cut up and scattered round."

"They never got the guy who did it," Crissy said. She and Olga looked at each other and tittered nervously.

"I'll be careful." I shrugged, hiding my horror, half-wondering too if they were just trying to scare off the competition.

"Never let those creeps take beaver shots," Crissy warned me, wrinkling her small nose. "They're not supposed to, but they like to try, and then they sell them illegally."

I arrived at Tom Eakins's studio early, another fifty dollars for a few hours of work. "I hear good things about you," he said, smiling affably. "Gimme a couple minutes to set up the lights. My office doubles as a dressing room, so you can change in there."

As I folded my capri pants over a swivel chair, I couldn't help seeing a note that he'd scribbled in pencil on a desk pad that stuck out from under the telephone: Gigi Frost great figure bad face. Someone must have said this to him over the phone. Bad face? I was wearing the Hollywood veneers when I went out on jobs now. It couldn't be my teeth anymore. It was my damn nose. Did it really look that bad? I could see my profile in Tom Eakins's three-sided mirror. Yep. It looked awful. My nose took up my whole face. I'd been ridiculous to think I could break into Hollywood with a nose like that. I had to have that nose job; I had to model long enough to be able to pay for plastic surgery.

"How come we never get together on weekends anymore?" Simone complained when she drove me home from Tiny Naylor's. "You got a boyfriend?"

I'd take the plunge, I decided, with just this one thing. We sat in the car on the corner of Stanley and Oakwood, and I offered her one of my cigarettes. "I'm working a lot on the weekends. I have modeling jobs." I lit us both up.

"That's terrific," she said, clearly impressed. "In a store or what?"

"No, for photographers. I do pinup and figure."

Simone turned to look at me, her huge lashes fluttering. "Pinup?" She was puzzled. "What's 'figure'?"

It was too late to hold back now. "You know," I said, "nude modeling." I coughed in the smoky, closed car.

"You model nude?" She stared.

"Yes."

"In front of men?" Her voice rose to an outraged squeak. "I think that's terrible. Naked in front of strange men? How could you?" She tapped the cigarette out angrily in the pink-lacquer ashtray. "What about morals?"

Morals? I knew about her and Jesse. How was what I did any worse? He'd just used her, didn't even bother to clean up her hymen's blood from Nick's sheets. At least nobody touched me when I worked. And what did she know about it anyway, about anything, with her canopied bed and a million dolls left over from when she was a kid and a closet stuffed with nice clothes. I had to bite my lip to keep from lashing out; she'd been good to me. But now it was I who was angry, damn her. When she was my age she'd had braces; her father could afford them. She didn't know a thing about the hunger I'd felt my whole life.

"I need the money" was all I said, opening her car door. It clapped shut behind me, that substantial sound the lock of an expensive automobile makes. Neither of us said good-bye.

Simone avoided me after that. She even stopped organizing treks to Tiny Naylor's. Once in a while I went there with other people, but it wasn't the same thing anymore. Sometimes in the lobby my eyes and Simone's would meet by chance, and she'd look away. She'd been the only close girlfriend I'd ever had, and I missed her, but soon I looked away too.

Mario Parma gave me a dozen of the pictures, and I kept some for myself and let Andy have the rest. He put them in the big black leather folio that photographers came by to check, and he said he could send me out on a shoot every day if I wanted to go. "I get a lot of requests for you. How come you can only work weekends now?" he complained.

"Oh, you know," I said airily. "Things. Boyfriends. Stuff." I couldn't tell him that I had two more months of the tenth grade to complete before I was through with school forever.

What could I do with all the money I was making? I'd save most of it for a nose job, of course, but why shouldn't I give my mother a little happiness? Albert never took her anywhere. "I don't have an acting job yet," I told her one evening as I led her by the hand into my room. I closed the door behind us. This would be our secret. "But I've been making money as a pinup model, like Betty Grable." She knew who wholesome, happy Betty Grable was. I pulled a leopardskin bathing suit picture out of the envelope Mario Parma had given me. "A famous photographer took it," I said. "He's going to put it in a magazine."

My mother studied the black-and-white picture for a long time. Was she going to be upset, like Simone? "How beautiful you look," she finally said, and ran her finger over the gloss of the bathing suit and the thighs. She turned wet eyes to me. "I used to have legs like that," she reminisced, "and such a flat, nice belly."

Simone once told me her parents had taken her on her birthday to the best restaurant in Los Angeles, a place called the Café de Paris. Though I was only fifteen, I could afford it. I'd just made a hundred dollars from a Japanese photographer who did a two-day shoot with me at Paradise Cove. I'd skipped school because he said the Cove was jammed with people on the weekend and he could only hire me if I would work during the week. "I'm making a lot of money as a model," I bragged to Rae next (omitting the figure part of it, of course), "and I want to take you and my mother out." It would be the three of us alone again.

"Party of three, Lil Foster's the name," I said over the phone when I made the reservation, remembering with nostalgia my suave, childish ordering voice when my mother and I went to restaurants in New York.

"Rae, you're not supposed to pick it up, for God's sake!" I whispered frantically. Here we were in this elegant setting, she'd ordered the T-bone steak, and she was holding it in two hands, gnawing with her front teeth like a bear. I looked sidelong to see who was watching.

"Don't bother me. I eat the way I eat," my aunt grumbled, pursing her lips. She picked the T-bone up again and took a big bite, chewing defiantly.

"Rae, please," I begged, "they'll make us leave." Was the maître d' watching? He was. His nostrils were distended in disgust. I shriveled. This wasn't the world Rae belonged in: Why had I brought her here? But it was the world I wanted—this delicious extravagance, this luxury. Yet I needed Rae, too, and I loved her. I just had to learn to keep my worlds separate.

"So much fat." My aunt grimaced, dropping the cleaned-slick bone on her plate with disdain. "And they charge so much money."

My mother was holding her knife and fork with delicate fingers. I adored her for it. When she sipped from a teacup at the end of the meal, her pinkie was extended in a patrician arc. Her eyes were shiny as she looked at the plush red chairs, the velvety red wallpaper, the waiters in tuxedos. "So nice," she breathed. "Everything so beautiful." It didn't re-ally matter if Rae couldn't appreciate it. This was something my mother and I shared, and I'd brought her pleasure, and myself too. This is what a little money could do. "Take it all in, Lilly," my mother whispered to me, as though we were two kids who'd sneaked into a palace.

I bought her a tiny gold Bulova wristwatch with my earnings from the next two jobs and a dozen red roses in a box covered with gold foil.

"Where do you get so much money to waste on flowers?" Albert said, but when I invited him to come along with me and my mother to the Cocoanut Grove he did, because it was Dr. Nathan Friedman's favorite nightclub.

By the time summer began, I discovered that Crissy was right: I'd been modeling for three months, and once the professional photographers took all the pictures of you they thought they could sell, they looked for a fresh face. The calls at fifty dollars a day came seldom now. Of course there were still the amateurs, who walked into Andy's agency wanting girls to shoot. The pay wasn't so good and it might be dangerous, but still, it was work.

"They just want to jump into the bed with you," Olga complained again as four of us prepared in Andy's dressing room for a group shoot.

"It would pay a hell of a lot better than this," Corinne said bitterly to the mirror. "I tell you, sometimes I'm tempted."

"I bet none of those guys even have film in cameras." Olga snickered.

I got my clothes off and slipped into a fuchsia lambskin modeling bikini that barely covered nipples and pubes. Was Corinne serious? Those amateur photographers were usually old men in their forties or fifties, maybe older. How could you let men like that put their hands all over you. Repulsive. I shivered, remembering Jake Mann and Falix Lieber. It was one o'clock now, and at five I'd leave with twenty dollars in my purse. Twenty dollars for four hours was still about five times what you could make behind a counter somewhere. That's all I needed to think about right now.

A dozen men with cameras packed the studio room, waiting to descend on us. Hungry coyotes, I thought. But Olga was wrong about none of them having film in their cameras. They looked through their lenses and snapped, and light bulbs popped incessantly as the four of us twisted and turned in various postures. One man, though, with too-black hair, a too-black pencil-thin mustache, and a sly leer that he didn't bother to conceal, perched his Rolleiflex on a tripod and spent most of the four hours looking through the lens, his hands jiggling coins in his pockets. I worked as far away from him as I could manage because he reminded me of Sid.

My arms and legs were shaky with fatigue as I got back into my street clothes at the end of the session; we'd had only two ten-minute breaks the whole time. When I emerged from the dressing room, I saw that the mustachioed man hadn't yet left. He was standing in the dim hallway with Corinne, who now wore a tight, off-white knit dress, and she was telling him something that he was writing down on a match-book cover. I passed them and then, at the door, dropped my purse to the floor and straightened a nylon, a snoop.

"Room two-sixteen, seven o'clock." I looked up as he addressed her barely covered bosom; then she turned from him, scurrying away on her red high heels, but not before he grabbed a pinch of buttock between his thumb and index finger. "A little appetizer." He grinned.

"See you soon." She waved over her shoulder, a smile plastered on her face like greasepaint. She didn't make eye contact or speak to me, though she passed within three inches.

Don't do it! I wanted to shout. But what if she said, "Why not?" or "I really need the money"? or "Maybe I like it"?

"Bye," I called after her, embarrassed at what I'd seen and heard.

"Bye," she returned weakly, still not looking up, closing the door behind her.

Is that what happens when the big modeling jobs run out? Would that happen to Crissy and Olga? *Not me. Not me.*

"How'd you like to do a location shoot with . . . ?" Andy mentioned the name of a famous silent film star.

I'd seen one of his movies with my mother at the Classic Silent Film Theater on Fairfax Avenue just a couple of weeks earlier. Now I'd be working with him. My mother would be so excited to hear that I'd met him in person. I'd edit the story of course. She'd reminisced, "I remember him from when I first came to this country, such a fine actor." He'd been a boy comedian with a world-famous zany smile in an innocent face.

"He likes to shoot at this big old house in the Hollywood Hills," Andy mentioned. "Fifty bucks for a couple hours, and you don't even have to sign a release because he doesn't sell the pictures."

"That's Harry Houdini's old mansion," Crissy said. "It's so much fun. I've been there lots of times with amateurs."

The Silent Film Star was no longer the thin, bespectacled goof of the silver screen. His weight had increased by probably half, most of it around his abdomen, which was bisected by a tight belt with a big silver buckle that displayed a cougar rearing up on its hind legs, its teeth chomping the air. He'd lost two fingers on his left hand; and on the thumb and index finger of the other he wore large silver and turquoise rings.

"Pleased to meet you, Gigi Frost." His zany smile hadn't changed, and he was still illustrious enough to make me mute with shyness.

"My mother really admires you" was on the tip of my flustered tongue to say, but that would make me sound like a kid. "Happy to meet you," I said instead, with knocking heart.

We drove north into the hills, to an area of mansions as lavish as those I'd seen in Beverly Hills so long ago. But now I was in the presence of real Hollywood royalty; I'd come a huge distance.

The old Harry Houdini mansion—if that's what it was—looked like a gray stone castle, with turrets and moats and an expanse of green that went on forever. The Silent Film Star took three cameras from the trunk of his long Cadillac and slung them over a shoulder. "All set." I followed him up white marble stairs, gulping for air. I'd never been inside such a place. It made Simone's mansion look like Fanny's furnished room.

A maid, her black uniform covered by a crisp white apron, answered the mellifluous chimes, greeting the Silent Film Star by name. "Would you like the west room again, sir?" she asked discreetly, never looking at me. I could see the high sheen of the black oak floors that bordered the dark, intricate oriental carpets. Such gorgeousness! A huge ivory statue of a unicorn stood on the floor next to the bright brass double-door entry.

"No, no, we're here for a shoot today," he said brusquely.

"Oh, of course," she whispered, glancing at his cameras now. "So sorry."

A man in a white suit and a girl in a tight black dress came out of nowhere and walked down a winding, highly polished staircase. "You can go round the house, if you like," the maid said, ushering us out awkwardly, and now I knew for certain this was the kind of house I'd heard Olga and the others snicker about.

But the Silent Film Star had brought cameras. Surely it was all right. "I know the way," he said, clearly displeased with the maid. "I just wanted to let you know we're here." He led me by the arm through the iron gate. "Dumb cluck," he grumbled. "Didn't she see my gear?"

In the grand, manicured garden, I slipped out of my sheath and my underwear while he readied the cameras. Then I posed, kissing mossy iron satyrs that leered hungrily and reached with muscled arms. I embraced nymphs, naked like me, that simpered with concrete mouths. I sprawled beneath a fountain that spouted from the big marble lips of four turbaned giants. I could smell gardenias everywhere, and the sun shone, strong and seductive, on my bare skin. How I loved the grandeur of the place! I worked hard for him, anxious to please, and he shot alternately with each of his three cameras. But images of what I'd seen in the house kept playing in my mind. What had the maid thought? Of course I knew—that we were there for what Corinne had talked about. What had the man in the white suit and the girl done together? As I kissed and embraced and sprawled, I kept seeing their twisting naked limbs and his hands all over her. I couldn't turn the vision off. Did she like it?

At one point in the session the Silent Film Star lifted my arm for a pose, and his hand brushed against my breast—an accident maybe, but I remembered Sid and shifted quickly. "I can do it," I cried, taking the pose he wanted. He frowned. But overall he seemed pleased with my work. "Very artistic," he said, smiling from time to time at a pose I'd strike and snapping away. He'd taken his suit jacket off, and I could see the wet rings of perspiration on the underarms of his shirt. "That's fifteen rolls," he said, wrapping up after three hours.

"This is an incredible setting," I ventured, once dressed. I hadn't dared to utter much before other than "Is this pose all right?"

"Yeah, this house has quite a history," he said. "Would you like to see some more of it? I can give you the Cook's tour."

Was it once really Harry Houdini's mansion? I could imagine the star-studded parties—the Pola Negris and Clara Bows and Mabel Normands in lavish, flowing gowns who'd once paraded in its romantic opulence.

He led me through the glass door that opened onto the marble patio, and he walked in front of me up the winding staircase. The maid who'd offended him wasn't in sight. "Would you look at this tapestry." He pointed to a carpet that covered most of the wall at the head of the stairs. Through its muted colors I could make out horses and bare-chested riders with shields who were lifting up or treading down naked, terrified women. "Seventeenth-century French," he pronounced, like an art connoisseur.

"This is my favorite room." He put his hand on the small of my back familiarly, and I let myself be steered through a door of ornately carved black wood into a chamber of mirrored walls, shiny mahogany bedposts, a dark fur bedspread.

"It's beautiful," I said inanely. Then he pulled me to him. I averted my face and could see his left hand with the missing fingers digging into my shoulder.

"Wouldn't you like me to triple your shoot fee? A hundred and fifty dollars," he rasped.

The green vision of bills snaked round in my head. A hundred and fifty dollars was almost four weeks' wages for a lot of women, and I could make it in a few hours. His spicy cologne mixed with the sour smell of his sweat. I stared at the mangled hand that sat on me. *My mother. Her abortions.* "No! My parents are expecting me." The words flew from my lips on their own. "I've got to get home."

"What are you, a little girl?" he scoffed, and his mouth came down on mine.

A panicked voice inside me cried, "Bite his tongue!" but the image of his innocuous face on the silent screen rose before me. *He's got Holly-wood connections. I could rescue my mother from Albert.* "*No!*" the panicked voice yelled inside me, and I pushed hard at him. "No!" I shouted aloud.

"Okay, little girl," he said, freeing me. "Here's your fifty dollars." His smirk looked like disdain, and he peeled two twenties and a ten from a wad. "I'll drive you back to Andy's," he grunted over his shoulder as I followed him, lost, down thickly carpeted stairs I hadn't seen before.

I am in danger, I thought on the ride down from the Hollywood Hills. *I am on the verge of going out of control.* The Silent Film Star looked straight ahead, maneuvered the wheel with both hands, and said noth-ing, emphatically. He'd dismissed me, left me alone with my thoughts.

How puny I felt in the deep black leather seat. *A girl alone in the world is a rabbit chased by a pack of hungry coyotes.* I cringed at the vision. It was only a matter of time before the rabbit would be caught and torn apart.

My mother's hair spiked straight up as though tugged, and she looked as she used to when she screamed "Hirschel." "Oh, my God, Lilly, my God!" she shrieked at me when I pulled open the screen door. "You're killing me. Why do you want to punish me like that?"

"What? What's wrong? What happened?"

"I said to Mrs. Frank next door, 'My daughter is a model for bathing suits.'" My mother sobbed the words. "'Look,' I said, 'I'll show you her beautiful pictures.' I didn't know the terrible things you had in that envelope. Naked!" she howled. "I was so ashamed. I can never show my face again to the neighbors."

The figure photos. I hadn't hidden them because I never thought she'd look in my drawers. I slammed the wall with my fist, masking chagrin in outrage. "Does Albert know?"

"Albert! I have so much shame I want to die. How should I tell Albert?"

"Don't tell Rae either!" I shook my mother by the shoulders, a bully's shake. "Promise," I snarled at her. I couldn't bear the thought of my aunt's screeching and carrying on also.

"It's my fault. I didn't give you a good childhood," my mother said, weeping noisily. "How can you do it?" she yelled again. "Is that the way a nice Jewish girl behaves?"

Nice Jewish girl? How am I Jewish? What do I have to be nice about? "Dammit, shut up," I screamed, and covered my ears to drown her out. "Please please please shut up! I'll never do it again. Quit crying!" The worse I felt, the louder I screamed. "Dammit, shut up!"

I wanted to stop. I saw Corinne with the mustachioed guy, the girl in the tight dress with the man in the white suit. Bile bubbled into my mouth. I had to stop before it happened to me. I knew it for sure. The coyotes would get me.

7 MY MOVIE-ACTRESS NOSE

ONCE MY MOTHER discovered the pictures, she had a whole new set of fears—her daughter, naked for the world to see, careless and vulnerable, was going astray and was fated to turn out just like her. What a danger, what a woe women were to themselves, if they didn't keep a rein on their sex and weren't clever in their dealings with men. Her own life had taught her that lesson at a terrible price: Instead of finding a way to get her family out of the Nazis' path, she'd let a man and sex distract her from a sacred mission.

The fact is, there was probably no way she could have succeeded in her mission. She and Rae had been ignorant teenage girls shipped off from the shtetl to America with only each other as guide in a stupefying new world. My mother tried her best. The right man never came along, and what could a woman do about it? She failed in the marriage department, but year after year the alarm clock rang at six-thirty and she was out the door and off to the shop by seven o'clock, no matter how lousy she felt, no matter how rotten Moishe was being. And for as long as mail continued to be delivered in their shtetl, she and Rae sent money orders to Prael from their meager paychecks every month. It was enough money to buy a little more food, an occasional new coat, a pair of shoes maybe, though it wasn't enough to rescue the family—neither she nor Rae ever made enough. But I think that somehow my mother's failure to save them must have gotten mixed up in her head with her affair with my father. Those years she was going crazy in our furnished room, she must have believed that the death of her brother and sisters was directly connected to her sexual mistakes. What else could her punishing guilt have been about? And now I, her only child, the last remnant of her slaughtered family, had also shown the signs of sexual foolishness.

"Terrible things can happen to you from this!" She brought me my coffee in bed and cried again the next morning. "You'll make a mess from your life. The men will steal the whites from your eyes if you let them. They'll make you for a living dead one."

"All right, all right already," I muttered.

"You'll make yourself cheap like dirt! I haven't suffered enough? You want to suffer now too?" She wept over my bed when it was barely light the following day. I leapt up and stormed to the bathroom, breathing noisily through clenched teeth, banging the door behind me.

But maybe she was right not to trust me. Maybe I was weak the way she'd been—an inherited weakness. I didn't know for sure. I'd almost succumbed to Carlos under the willow tree in Hollenbeck Park—I couldn't lie to myself about it. Maybe even to Falix Lieber too, there on the dirty floor of Fanny's furnished room. What would stop me from making the same mistakes she'd made? I'd even been tempted by the Silent Film Star's proposition in that place with the mirrors and fur bedspread. She'd never forgive herself if I ended up like her. I'd be her final tragedy.

She was outside the bathroom door, and I could hear her sniffing. "Shut up about it!" I yelled. I perched on the rim of the cold white bathtub and didn't leave until I heard her steps retreating. Then I made a beeline for my room and slammed the door behind me.

But I vowed to myself not to upset her anymore. I'd quit modeling. Yet if I quit, how would I get money for the plastic surgery to make my nose Hollywood quality? And if I couldn't have a nose job, I might as well give up the dream I'd lived with for so long, that she'd planted in me when I was seven years old.

Actually, she herself gave me tacit permission now to let the dream go. "Lilly, I beg you, be a good girl," she said, standing in back of me a few days later as I brushed my teeth.

"Okay. What's a good girl?" I asked her imploring reflection in the mirror, my toothpaste mouth grinning ironically.

"Be good in school, like you used to be."

Sure, brilliant. I'd flunked almost everything I'd taken in the spring semester.

"If you're good in school, you can become somebody. A secretary maybe. A bookkeeper. You won't have to work in a shop your whole life like me."

A secretary! A bookkeeper! So those were her paltry dreams for me now, no better than what Fanny thought I could do. She'd given up on me, on the dreaming we used to do together. I spat the toothpaste loudly into the sink. It was only when I slammed the door of my room yet again and paced the floor in a funk that a startling insight hit me: To her, a secretary or a bookkeeper was a high-class job. "That *Americanerin*"—she used to tell me about the woman who kept the books at Schneiderman's—"she makes so much money, and she dresses so beautiful that she's just as big a snob as the owner's wife." Or about Mrs. Frank, who'd been a secretary for Allstate Insurance before she married a salesman, my mother had remarked, "So educated! She graduated school and worked at such a nice job in a office." It was probably all the same to her—an actress, a bookkeeper, a secretary—any job in which you weren't imprisoned in a shop the way she'd been was a good job, a great job. She'd told me to be an actress when I was a little kid because I'd been too young to be a secretary or a bookkeeper, and *actress* was a good job that even a young girl might get. I just hadn't understood her simple job categories before.

But it was too late. Understanding couldn't free me from the yearning for the golden apple that had been my lifelong obsession. I couldn't settle for "a nice job in a office" because I knew the difference, even if my mother didn't.

So I stared at my nose in the mirror every chance I got. If I didn't have a three-way mirror or a hand mirror to hold up to a larger one, I cocked my head to the right, to the left, shooting my eyes in the opposite direction so I could get a glimpse of my profile. My nose wasn't getting any smaller. I pinched the bridge into a thinness, I lifted the nub into a ski jump, but it always bounced back to its grotesque shape. There was Pinocchio in the mirror, Jimmy Durante. There was W. C. Fields and Cyrano de Bergerac. "A Roman nose," I thought, recalling a dumb joke I'd heard at Geller's about some other poor girl. "Roamin' all over her face." I had to have that nose job.

How much had I managed to save from my months of modeling? I kept my loot in an old black sock in the back of my closet, behind a scatter of shoes. Now I pulled the wrinkled bills out and counted them, six twenties, twelve tens, seven fives. I'd squandered so much, now I didn't have nearly enough to pay for plastic surgery, which E. J. Smith had said could cost five hundred dollars. If I didn't go back to Andy's, it would take me forever to earn the difference as a salesgirl or a file clerk at $1.25 an hour—if I could even get such a job without experience.

"Why can't you meet a nice Jewish boy in high school and start to go out?" my aunt kept pestering me, and I'd laugh to myself, thinking of the slob disguises I wore to school. "Sweet sixteen is old enough to find a nice boy," she said now when I went to her place to fetch some old issues of the *Forward* for my mother. "You wait too long, you can't have babies no more. Like me." My first son I was supposed to call Avrom, after her father. A daughter should be Sarah, after her mother. I'd heard it a million times.

I stood on one foot, ready to fly out of there and away from her nagging. "I better go. I have a rehearsal."

"Wadda you have to go out to rehearsals for and come back late at night, all by yourself? It's *mishugas*, craziness. Mrs. Pinsky downstairs from me's daughter is only seventeen, and she's already engaged with a beautiful ring."

"Well, maybe I could find a nice boy and be engaged with a beautiful ring like Mrs.-Pinsky-downstairs-from-you's daughter if I weren't so ugly," I grumbled.

"Ugly? What are you talking? You're so *shayn gevacksen*, beautifully grown." She defended me against myself. "But you look too sad all the time. Smile and the boys will like you."

Smile and the boys will like me. She hadn't the tiniest inkling of who I was because she knew nothing about my life: the chicken dance, Falix, the nude modeling, my aching ambition. And what the hell did she know about what boys liked anyway? She couldn't find a husband until she was in her forties. "I have an ugly nose," I said. "All the girls at Fairfax High School with noses like mine got them bobbed last year."

"Wadda you mean? Bobbed like a hair bob?"

"Sort of. Plastic surgery." Now I sat down on her sofa, and she sat down next to me. I could tell she was interested, and if this was my chance, I had to take it. "A doctor can make your nose look small, like a *shiksa's*."

"It's not dangerous?" She leaned forward to listen. So I was right— even my aunt thought my nose was ugly.

"The girls that did it were back in school after about ten days."

"Then do it!" my aunt said, ever the practical woman.

I'd inherited that trait. "It takes a lot of money. Maybe two-fifty, three hundred dollars, but the girls at school told me about a very good doctor. It would make such a big difference in the way I look," I said. "Maybe with a different nose I'd find a nice boy."

I could hear Mr. Bergman rummaging through drawers in the kitchen. My aunt got up—to help him I thought—but she stood at the window with folded arms instead. "I didn't do good by you from the time you were small," she sighed. "I meant to do everything right, and nothing worked out."

I went to put my guilty arms around her. We stood together, not talking, just looking out the window at nothing, the stucco of the ugly apartment building next door. In my high heels I was practically a head taller than My Rae now. I kissed her hair. She smelled like matzoh ball soup and all the good things she used to cook for me.

"I should have taken you away to live with me when I married Mr. Bergman. Maybe if you'd had a good home when you were small you wouldn't look so sad now, but that Mary—she was always a selfish cat. She wouldn't let me do nothing. A no-good selfish cat!" Rae hissed with all the old fury.

Their unhappiness with each other, their tirades—through all the years nothing had changed. Yet, despite the vitriol, they were sisters, two limbs on a bare tree. They never talked about the shared root that

TOP: *Lil, Mother, and Albert: "When I invited him to come along with me and my mother to the Cocoanut Grove he did, because it was Dr. Nathan Friedman's favorite nightclub."*

BOTTOM: *Mother, Albert, Mr. Bergman, and Rae: "Though they were both married now, the men had come too late."*

had been all but blasted, but they couldn't forget it, and it bound them together, despite curses and thrown shoes and bitter recriminations. Though they were both married now, the men had come too late to matter; even if Albert and Mr. Bergman had been different, they couldn't have counted for much. The important people in their lives were each other and me.

"That selfish cat Mary wouldn't let me do what I wanted for you, but to me it was always first God, then you. What else am I still working for if not to help? I'll go tomorrow to the bank. I bet you Mrs. Pinsky's daughter with her small little nose had it fixed too."

That was what American girls did these days to get a boyfriend, my aunt must have figured.

The nose the plastic surgeon gave me wasn't the Marlene Dietrich nose I'd hoped for, but neither was it the big convex burden I'd been carrying around with me for so long. I called E. J. Smith's old agency to make an appointment for an interview as soon as the swelling went down and I could get a new publicity picture.

I'd expected secretaries and a suite of offices, but Mel Kaufman was alone behind a big metal desk. He was portly and pockmarked and gap-toothed, an ugly man surrounded by a wall of framed black-and-white beauties. When I told him on the phone that E. J. had given me his number, he was very friendly and invited me to "drop by when you're in the neighborhood," but when I walked through the door, he seemed brusque. "What can I do for you?" he asked. I'd brought several monologues to read for him and the photo that I'd just paid a Hollywood portrait studio thirty dollars to take.

I handed him the photo, and while he glanced at it I eyed the pictures on his wall. Mine still looked nothing like them, I realized with despair. How had I deceived myself so badly? The women all had blond hair and light skin and looked carefree, with big, open smiles. All-American girls, the girls next door, the sweethearts of Sigma Chi. I, Semitic-looking, dark, sad-looking, with plenty to hide—I was their diametrical opposite. Of course, plenty of male actors in Hollywood looked Semitic like me, and from what I could figure out, the producers and directors and agents were mostly Jewish. A lot of them even came from immigrant families as I did. But the pictures on Mel Kaufman's wall showed me what I should have known already. If you were a woman and hoped to act, you had to look like a lighthearted *shiksa* unless you were old enough to play Molly Goldberg.

"A *lantsman*, huh?" Mel Kaufman said, glancing again at my photo and then at me. He knew instantly—of course he did. I'd told him my name was Lil Foster. I'd gone through my aunt's hard-earned money and all my own, and still I couldn't pass.

I ignored his question as though I didn't understand it. Maybe if I could just get him to watch me act he'd see the talent I had, even though I didn't look like the women on his wall. "E. J. Smith thought you might let me read for you," I began in my low, confident-woman's voice. "I was the lead in *Night Must Fall* at Geller Theatre, and the play broke all records for audience attendance over the last five years."

"E. J., that old *pisher*, I hear he runs a stable now. Is that so?"

A stable? "I didn't even know he rode," I declared off-handedly.

Kaufman threw his head back and laughed as though I'd said something hilarious. "You're a funny girl, you know that? Look, I was just going out to lunch. Come and have something to eat." He didn't stop for an answer before he steered me out the door by my elbow.

"So are you a pony, or what?" he asked, zooming his red MG out of the crowded parking lot, turning sharply right on two wheels, careening down a small street as though we were escaping from a crime scene.

"A pony?" I laughed. What the hell was he talking about? "Not unless I've just grown two more legs."

"Let's see," he said, squeezing my kneecap. "Nope, feels like a *maydeleh's* leg to me." He didn't remove his fingers. What was I supposed to do? If he was really a powerful agent, as E. J. had said, I wanted him to like me. How else would I get an agent? But I couldn't let him keep his hand on my knee. I lifted it, a damp, heavy paw, and fixed a smile on my face. "Now, now," I said in what I hoped was a charming *shiksa* lilt, "we've only just met."

At Googie's, a Sunset Strip diner, Mel Kaufman asked the hostess for a table right in the middle of the room. He kept swiveling his head around and waving to people who waved or nodded back—men who wore big diamond rings on their pinkies, women who were slim and tall with flawless complexions and long, mascaraed lashes. "You see that girl. Sexy, huh? It's Mara Corday. I got her signed to *The Quiet Gun*." "Recognize that guy from *Mister Roberts*? William Henry, one of my boys." My head swiveled along with Mel Kaufman's. "How'd you like to read at Paramount Studio, next week?" he asked me between giant bites of tuna sandwich.

I put my own ham and cheese down on my plate and tried to swallow the wad that was in my mouth. So I had impressed him somehow. Though he hadn't even heard my monologues yet, he'd seen something in me that made him think I could audition at Paramount Studio. Was it really, finally, after a lifetime of hoping and dreaming, going to happen? "I'd like that very much," I told him, surprising myself by how suave my voice sounded although I was ready to soft-shoe on the ceiling.

I learned on the drive back to Mel's office (as wild as the drive to Googie's) that it was for Tom Saulus he'd arranged the audition. "I got you another reader," he said, introducing me to a powerfully built young man with an even profile and big white teeth who was lounging in Mel's chair now, black-sneakered feet folded on the metal desk, reading the green sports section of the *Herald*.

"How ya doin'?" Tom looked over the top of his paper and acknowledged me with a slight wave of a hammy hand.

"If the studio people like the scene, Tom'll get a screen test," Mel explained, handing me some pages from Odets's *Waiting for Lefty*, a play I already knew because I'd read it in the back row of my algebra class.

"By when do I have to have it memorized?" I asked them, ready to stay up all night if necessary.

Tom let his agent do the talking. He'd gone back to perusing the baseball scores.

"You just read it. You don't have to *memorize*," Mel answered, as though I'd asked a stupid question.

I was Florence in the three-minute scene we rehearsed the next day. I had five lines: "I know you're not, I know." "I know." "I got a lump in my throat, honey." "The park was nice." "Sid, I'll go with you." The rest of the speeches belonged to Tom, who kept his gaze in the middle distance as I fed him the lines. His acting was wooden and he used his hands like a robot, yet he was getting an audition at Paramount. Why? I was a Bernhardt compared to him, but Mel intended this to be Tom's audition, not mine. The dumb injustice of it!

Waiting at the bus stop in front of Mel's office, I decided that as soon as I got home I'd call and say he'd have to get someone else to feed Tom lines. But before I reached Stanley Avenue I changed my mind—after all, what did I have to lose? I'd have an opportunity to step on the same gravel where Gloria Swanson and Barbara Stanwyck and Shirley Booth had placed their glorious feet . . . and who knows what might happen?

"Who knows," Mel said as he drove me to the studio the next week, "you might catch their eye. Doesn't matter if you only have a few lines, they might like what they see. Stranger things have happened." I remembered the Lana Turner legend of my childhood. I would give it my all.

"Did they say anything?" I dared to ask Mel as we whizzed away from the Paramount lot. I held on to the seat with my fingernails. He was going to kill somebody one of these days.

"They'll call. Tom did a great job," he said. "So, what did you think of the inside of Paramount Studio?" This time his hand landed in my lap and his fingers darted between my legs. The paw stuck like a boulder when I grabbed it. "Hey, hey, you want me to have an accident?" he laughed, speeding up the car and pulling abruptly onto a side street. He stopped the MG in front of a house with closed shutters and turned the motor off.

"What are you doing?" I asked. Before I could make sense of what was happening, he'd unzipped his pants and pulled out his member. I snapped my head away, but I'd already seen it—a gargantuan dark rod. "Please take me back," I said, struggling to hold my voice steady. There was no movement in the unfamiliar street—no cars, no one in sight anywhere on the tree-shaded sidewalks or in the front yards bordered by picket fences.

"Don't worry, just give me your hand," he rasped. I fought to keep my hand away, balling it into a fist, yanking it from his grip while he fought to force me to touch the thing, to hold it. A serpentine monster. A deadly gun. In all my struggles—with Chuck, with Jake Mann, with Falix Lieber—I'd never seen one.

I rescued my fist, kept it balled like a street fighter's. "Dammit, take me back!"

"Hey, hey, how far you think you'll get in Hollywood?" He looked at me with a sincere expression, as if he was offering a bit of reasonable advice, but his round cheeks were splotched red. "Okay, just sit there," he said when I glared.

I edged my body close to the door. I could open it and get out and run. I wasn't trapped in the car. But then I'd have to admit it was all over, all my Hollywood dreams. And I didn't even know where to run. I had twenty cents in my pocket, and that wouldn't even get me a bus ride home from this distant neighborhood whose name I didn't even know. I turned my head away. I could hear his hand moving quickly up and down the ugly pole. I forced my eyes to keep staring straight ahead, but I still saw the movement peripherally. I turned back to him, ready to beg him to stop, careful to look only at his face, but I could still see all of him, see him grab a starched white handkerchief from his breast pocket, cover the hand that moved, close his eyes. I was glued there, my own eyes lidless. He shuddered and let out a big breath.

"Okay, let's go," he said seconds later with good cheer, tossing the wadded handkerchief over his seat, fumbling with the fly of his pants; the tires screeched as he tore out onto the street. When he pulled up in front of his office building he glanced over at me, and his lips spread in a friendly, gap-toothed grin. "I guess you don't know the game, huh?" he said.

"Go to hell, you bastard!" I snarled after I jumped free of the car. "I hope it falls off!"

I almost bumped into an elderly, blue-haired lady carrying an I. Magnin hatbox. She'd heard what I said and gave me a sidelong, horrified look as she scurried on.

. . .

I'm twenty-six maybe. Not sixteen. (Is it me or is it the pitiful, dark-haired creature that I've seen twice wandering around Hollywood Boulevard, looking as though she'd been hit in the head?) I'm wearing red circles of rouge on my cheeks and black circles of mascara around my eyes. My nylon stockings have huge tears that go from my shoes all the way up to my knees and beyond; the garters rolled on them three days earlier don't keep them from sagging. My stained skirt is practically as high as my pupik, *as my aunt used to say, my bellybutton. I cross the street and a truck swerves and honks, but I'm oblivious. I've walked up and down and around for hours, for days. I'm for sale, and no-body will buy. The furious driver circles the truck back and zooms toward me, but my mother appears and without a second's pause throws herself under its wheels.*

8 THE OPEN DOOR

THE GOLDEN APPLE would never be mine. I'd never get by the fearsome guardians at the gate because I'd never be a girl who could charm them like Doris Day, or make them silly with desire like Marilyn Monroe. How could I have believed that Lilly from Fanny's furnished room could win the golden apple? Girls like me were used for something else in Hollywood. And now I had no idea what to do with the rest of my life.

Then we moved because Albert had a fight with Mrs. Ostroff, the landlady. She told him what a slob he was when he refused to wrap the garbage in a sack before throwing it in the communal can. He shook his fist and yelled at her, "Go to hell!"

"I'm getting an eviction notice," she yelled back.

He found us a little court bungalow on Fountain Avenue, just a few blocks from Hollywood Boulevard. "It's more cheap too," he told my mother. "May an onion grow out of her nose."

I kept going to Geller's because I had nowhere else to go that summer, and if I stayed home my mother drove me crazy. Everything I did was an unsettling mystery to her.

"Some lady with a funny voice is on the telephone for you." She stood at my door looking aggravated one evening soon after the Mel Kaufman fiasco. "Choo Choo Sand."

"I don't know anybody by that name. What kind of funny voice?"

"I dunno. With an accent. Who do you know with an accent?"

Some stupid prankster from high school? I didn't need this now. I marched into the living room and grabbed the receiver. "Hello, who's this?"

"Who?" my agitated mother echoed, standing right behind me.

"The Queen of the Night." The melodramatic falsetto sounded familiar. "So is your name up in lights yet or was Miss Mary right?" it dropped two octaves to say. "Let's bury the knitting needle, Glenda. I want to see you."

Eddy. I hadn't heard from him in a year, not since he'd been insulting about Irene and laughed at me about Geller's. Why had he come back into my life?

Eddy came to pick me up with a young man he introduced as "Zack, my boyfriend," and when we parked on Western Avenue he told me we were going to a new place they'd just heard about, the Hearts and Spades. "It's a place where the guys like other guys," he said with a laugh. I'd heard words like *fairy* and *queer* because people used them at Geller's. I knew Eddy was like that, though I'd never before put a name to it, and now I also understood from the way he kept his hand on Zack's muscled thigh as he drove that they were lovers. For a brief second it felt strange to think about, but soon it made me feel sort of comfortable, though I couldn't have said how or why. Maybe it was because I knew Eddy's hand on Zack's thigh was about sex, yet it didn't trigger in me those disturbing images that sometimes crept through my brain like bogeymen stealing through my window — the Silent Film Star in that mirrored bedroom, Mel in his parked car.

The Hearts and Spades was dark and dank, and the alcohol fumes reeked even before we pushed open the heavy door. It was on Sunset Boulevard, but far east of Vine, in a neighborhood that had never been glamorous despite its proximity to the real thing. Eddy said to call him Herman Hermine because that's who his phony identification said he was, and he slipped me a tattered birth certificate that said *Arlene Knopfelmacher, born 1934*. I was to show it to the cocktail waitress if she asked my age because you couldn't drink in California until you were twenty-one. As I sipped at the Brandy Alexander that Eddy ordered for me I felt like an outlaw — and it was fun, like my double-agent act, the kid in high school and the grownup at Geller's.

Eddy's boyfriend was fun too. He looked like a tough, with a full beard, high-laced work boots, tight Levi's, and a battleship tattoo, yet he articulated his words precisely and his eyes were soft brown. He was in costume, I saw right away, and of course I understood the idea of costume very well. I liked him, and I also liked the people around us in the Hearts and Spades. They were mostly men, but I wasn't a rabbit among coyotes here. When we'd only been inside a few minutes, one of them came up to our table and said to me, "Can I tell you that you've got beautiful eyes?" But I knew he wasn't flirting. "Yoo hoo, Charlie," he soon called, waving to his friend who walked through the door.

Zack was quickly a happy drunk, and though I'd had only one Brandy Alexander, he and Eddy and I sat slouched with our arms around one another, giggling immoderately at the tales he told about his year on a navy ship. "Zack, the Belle of the Pacific," Eddy called his boyfriend, and we all toasted the navy. I was having a fine time. I couldn't even remember when I'd had such a fine time before. "Say, I know a bar where the gay girls go," Zack confided after another patriotic toast.

"She's straight, dodo." I saw Eddy nudge him in the ribs. "Ain't you?" He winked at me.

Gay girls. I'd seen them once at Venice Beach, where I'd gone with the Geller's gang. Simone and Stan had wanted to get lunch at a little Mexican restaurant up the boardwalk. "That's a gay bar," Stan had said as we passed a place with a big printed sign on the roof: LUCKY'S. "You know, they're *queers*," he'd added when we looked at him uncomprehendingly. A tan man in bermuda shorts had stood at the door of the place and called to a black poodle, "Come to poppa."

"Oh, Deb, she has to go potty," a pretty young woman had said, and then I'd looked again and saw that "poppa" was a woman too. *Queers.* I'd grabbed Stan's arm as we walked by.

Eddy drove through neighborhoods that got worse and worse: newspaper-littered sidewalks, boarded-up store windows, burnt-out abandoned automobiles. As we slowed down at the corner of 8th and Vermont, an elderly woman, wearing a red hat perched on her head in drunken lopsidedness, lurched across the street, barely missing us. Eddy parked in front of a place with a green lettered sign: THE OPEN DOOR. "Miss Thang, are you ready?" he asked as though presenting something fabulous, then led me in with an arm light around my waist, as though we were two girlfriends. Zack stumbled behind.

"I think we're the only guys here, loosely speaking," Zack slurred after a quick glance around, "except for him." He gestured with his head at a bespectacled man standing at the long bar who tugged nervously at his starched white collar, and Eddy whispered something in my ear.

"What?" I shouted above the din of the jukebox and voices.

"Fish queen," he shouted back.

"What?" I shouted again, still unable to make sense of the words, but Eddy had turned to the bartender to order three beers.

I looked around. What was Zack talking about? There seemed to be plenty of men — or at least boys — in the dim, smoky room. Most were dressed a little like the pachucos — duck pants with button-down long-sleeve shirts open at the raised collar, a patch of white T-shirt showing beneath, hair slicked back in a pomaded duck's ass.

Then I grabbed for Zack as I had for Stan at Venice Beach.

"Whoa . . . What's happening?" Zack laughed. "You okay?"

I'd been staring at the one my eye had selected as the handsomest of the boys, with dark curls that fell over his ivory forehead and gold cat's eyes with black lashes, and he winked when he caught me staring. His stance was a pose — one crisp pant leg forward, the palm of his right hand cupped over a cigarette that he brought to his lips from time to time, the fingers of his left hand holding a beer bottle by its neck — a tough guy pose calculated to look like James Dean, I thought, or Elvis Presley. Presley's "I Want You, I Need You, I Love You" blared on the jukebox. And then the boy transmogrified into a girl, which was when I grabbed Zack's arm. But now I let go.

"Yeah, I'm fine," I answered Zack. Suddenly I was more than fine. They were all girls, I saw now. A lot of the more feminine ones were decked out in capri pants and high heels, the uniform Simone had taught me to wear that signified sexy. I wasn't out of place here. Some of them stood with the boy-looking ones at the crowded bar, their arms around each other. Some couples sat together at tables and held hands.

One pair stared into each other's eyes as though no one else were around. The girl—the feminine one—had a face full of makeup and a hairdo of elaborate auburn curls and swirls, and the other one lifted a hand and let it rest gently on her friend's cheek. They kissed, right there in the crowded bar, and I watched. I liked it. I loved it.

"You're looking odd, Miss Chicklet. Shall we depart?" Eddy pulled at my collar.

"I'm never leaving! This is where I want to be," I laughed, and tears sprang to my eyes and rolled down my cheeks. Was it the turmoil I'd been through in the past months that made me so emotional, standing there on the packed floor of the Open Door? I don't know. But I felt as I had when I'd first glimpsed Irene hanging the picture of the tutued dancers and she'd turned her violet eyes on me. Though there was no one that night at the Open Door who overwhelmed me as she had, I was transported. It was as if I was looking through a brilliant prism that reflected all the parts of my life with absolute clarity and brought them together, wondrously, into one intelligible whole.

"Copy cat. Just because I told you I was gay, you want to be too." Eddy's words were teasing, but I could tell he wasn't happy with me. "You don't even know what it's all about," he said later, when he drove me home.

"Well, I'm gonna find out," I answered.

"He's just trying to protect you," Zack said from the back seat, where he lay stretched out. "It's a hard . . . hard life," he hiccupped.

All day long I'd replayed the images of the night before in my head. The cat's eyes of the ivory-skinned girl in boy's clothes who winked at me, the one who touched her friend's cheek, Elvis Presley's voice on the jukebox, "*Hold me close, hold me tight*"—that was the song they played over and over. "This is where I want to be," I'd told Eddy. Now I could think of nothing else, not even my resolve that I wouldn't upset my worried mother anymore. "Important rehearsal," I shouted to her as I was halfway out the door at eight o'clock the next evening.

The Open Door. I even loved its name. I swung open the door, and all eyes seemed to turn to me, but only for an instant, and then I was pulled into Presley and the beer fumes and the din.

"Hello again." The bespectacled man in the white starched shirt, the one Eddy had called a fish queen, grinned at me as though I were a friend.

"Hi." I moved away quickly and positioned myself on a stool at the opposite end. I hadn't come to the Open Door to meet a man.

"What'll you have?" the bartender asked when he noticed me, and I remembered what Eddy had ordered the night before. "Bottle of East-side beer," I told him. Suddenly it all felt dangerous—that strange man, those odd women. What if I got caught and they put me in jail or reform school for being in a bar? But I'd already ordered a beer. I'd go as soon as I finished it.

I sat for a long time, sipping, as alone as if I'd been in my bedroom. The gold-eyed one was there again, but she was with a beautiful light-skinned Negro girl. They sat at a table and snuggled into each other and never even glanced at me. But I had to stay. I wanted a lover, and I didn't know where else to find one. My lover could never be a man. Men had made themselves so unlovable in my life. I lit each new cigarette from the stub of the last one, puffing away. I sat until my seat hurt. I'd never have the courage to start talking to someone. Now I watched two people at the jukebox who were too busy to notice me. The dark-haired girl deposited a quarter and was punching numbers with an angry finger. She wore dangly rhinestone earrings, and her shiny satin blouse was pulled down over her shoulders and cut to expose high, creamy breasts. A beauty mark beside her chin looked as though it had been placed there with an eyebrow pencil, and it moved as she twitched her lips in a mutter. Then a tear furrowed down her cheek and dropped to stain the blouse.

"Don't you get up and walk away from me," snarled the woman who stood behind her. I could hear it through the din. This one was blond. In her left ear was a single small, hooped earring, and she wore a corduroy men's jacket that was too big for her. She talked out of one side of her mouth, like a gangster, though she had a patrician face—high cheek-bones, a narrow nose, a cleft in her pronounced chin. Outside the movies, I'd never seen anyone swagger and squint the way she did. Was she serious or was she acting James Cagney?

"It's over, Jan. I'm not putting up with your shit anymore," the one in high heels said with a sniff. She flung her patent leather purse over her shoulder in a wide and angry arc and wobbled out the door.

"Fucking slut," Jan hissed after her. "Don't you know it?" she asked in a loud voice, and I realized with a start that she was talking to me. She'd caught me looking. "That broad's a first-class bitch!" Then she was beside me, and I could smell the alcohol on her breath. "Hey, you're a cute little femme, you know that? What's your name?" Jan lifted her lips in a drunken bad-boy smile. I'd never seen such white, even teeth.

"Gigi," I said.

"Gigi. I like that. I'm Jan, the hottest butch in town. Ask anyone." She guffawed at her own braggadocio. "Ask Terri, that fucking slut."

I stared into my glass of beer. Should I get up and leave?

"Got a light?" Jan breathed at my neck. I handed her my matchbook. "I can get it off your cigarette," she said, "just like you've been doing. I've been watching you." She winked and lifted my fingers toward the cigarette clenched between her teeth. She bent her head and inhaled, and a whiff of the clean, lemony scent of her shampoo surprised me. "Don't pay attention to my bad talk," she said, exhaling a cloud. "I'm not usually like this, but Terri just pissed me off—whoops, sorry— provoked an extremely irritated response in me," Jan pronounced carefully and flashed her perfect bad-boy smile at me again. "May I sit?" She bowed like a young gentleman at a debutante ball, then straddled the barstool next to mine, pert and jolly. "I promise to behave. Lemme buy you a real drink." She whistled toward the bartender. "Scotch straight up for the lady—me too."

I kept meaning to leave, but as soon as I'd finished the first scotch, she ordered another round. She put her hand on the small of my back and let it rest there. I jumped as though she'd stabbed me with a needle when I felt her fingers on me, but I didn't try to shake them off. She'd hitchhiked with Terri from New Orleans to L.A., she said. They'd been together on and off for six months, but now they had broken up for good. Before Terri, she'd been Stormy's lover. Had I ever heard of Stormy? Stormy was the hottest stripper in New Orleans, owned her own club on Bourbon Street; everyone knew Stormy. There wasn't a butch within a hundred miles of New Orleans who wasn't dying to get into Stormy's pants, but she was very, very selective.

I found myself leaning into Jan's touch. Now she moved her hand to my thigh, and I remembered Mel Kaufman with a start, but this was different because she was a woman. I let her keep her hand there, and suddenly I was aware that it was hard to catch my breath.

"Why don't you come to my place?" Jan stared me down at midnight, her nostrils flaring, a look on her face that I couldn't quite read, a look like anger or a dare. "C'mon," she urged again, and I could see the golden flecks in her eyes.

"I've got to make a phone call," I said, and wobbled to the telephone booth in back, near the toilets. "This rehearsal will go on for another couple of hours," I told my mother when she answered the phone in a voice heavy with sleep. "Simone said I could stay at her place tonight." I was careful to enunciate clearly, like a sober person.

Jan lived on the third floor of a hotel that was a couple of blocks from the Open Door. TRANSIENTS WELCOME, the sign on the plate glass window said. $2.00 NIGHTLY $12.00 WEEKLY. HOT WATER TUBS SHOWERS.

She unlocked the door of her room and ushered me in with a mock bow. Then she shoved the door shut with a foot and pushed me to the wall, knocking the breath out of me, her hands tugging at the zipper of my capris, her mouth on my lips. My Jell-O legs wanted to sink to the floor, but the pressure of her body held me up. "Wait," I begged. "Wait a minute!"

She laughed a low and dirty laugh and whispered something that sounded like "I'm gonna make you cry Daddy." A button popped from my blouse under the pull of her rough fingers, and her teeth bit through my bra to my nipple. The pain shocked me for a second, and my reflex was to push at her, to hit her. But the pain gave way to desire, and I rode with it, opened to it, to whatever she wanted to do.

"Get on the bed," she ordered me, and she ripped away at the rest of my clothes, parted my legs, flicked and sank her tongue. I held on to a high cliff by my fingernails until I thought my fingers would break, until she tumbled me into space.

I drifted to sleep with the lemony scent of her hair in my nostrils, my own moans still in my ears, her fingers cupped hard around my breast. I hadn't slept beside anyone since I was a kid in my mother's bed, and here I was, held by a woman who talked liked James Cagney. It was scary, funky. I liked it.

During the night I'd keep waking up, excited and restless in the strange room. In the dark, I kept remembering the couple that was leaving the apartment next door when we arrived — a woman in a big blond wig and a huge man in a black leather jacket and leather pants who held her firmly at the waist. Jan was as still as a stone now, her back to me, and I pressed my cheek as hard as I dared against her firm flesh. I could still feel where she'd been on me and in me, and I kept thinking of the frightening, wild tumble that had been nothing like the sweet pulsings I used to feel in the dark when I thought of Irene. Then I'd fall asleep again for a little while.

"Hey, where'd you get a body like this?" Jan growled in a gravel voice the next morning. She'd awakened me by running her fingers over my thighs, my belly, my waist, and I watched her handsome face, then glanced at her strong skillful hand that was gentle now on my breast. I hadn't noticed the night before the two angry wounds on the back of her hand. Each was the size of a dime and looked as though the skin had been gouged with a dull knife.

The raw skin made my already queasy stomach lift. But I loved her hand and felt pity for it now. "How did you get hurt?" I asked.

"You really want to know?" She laughed. "This john said he'd give me five bucks if I could hold a lit cigarette to the back of my hand until he counted to three. I got *two* booboos there 'cause I ended up with ten bucks."

"No, come on, really." I didn't know who John was, but I was sure she was teasing or making light of an accident. "What really happened?" I wanted her to trust me enough to let me comfort her.

"That's what really happened, baby." She flashed me her perfect smile. "It was an easy ten bucks."

I called my mother from a Vermont Avenue phone booth on Sunday morning, when the streets were empty of anyone except addicts looking for their next fix and drunks for whom the night was still not over.

"Well, we've got to rehearse a lot because it's such a long play," I said. A hungry cat brushed up against my legs and meowed. "It's Shakespeare, *King Lear,*" I added. She'd heard of that one, the parent with the bad daughters—it was even a Yiddish movie.

"When are you coming home?" she cried.

I had to ignore the aggravation in her voice because there was no way I was going to leave Jan just then. "I've got to stay at Simone's for a few days. We start rehearsals early and go till late at night, and she lives just a few blocks from Geller's. You wouldn't want me to take the bus late at night, would you?"

"What are you going to do when school starts? You have to enroll in a new high school in September."

"I'll worry about that in September."

"You come home right now," she yelled. "You hear me?"

"I've got to go, Mom. Simone's waiting. Look, I'll call you tomorrow. There's nothing to worry about." I hung up without waiting for more. Jan was still in bed, and I just wanted to scamper back to her like a rabbit to a warren. I wanted to get out of my clothes again in that dark, secret room and curl into her arms.

Jan doesn't work. Here is our day: We stay in bed until the morning has passed, though I usually wake up by ten o'clock and snuggle closer to her, listening to her breathing and to the hotel sounds while she sleeps. Sometimes I hear the lady with the big blond wig screaming next door when her boyfriend beats her; sometimes I hear other voices coming from that room and the squeak of bedsprings. "She's a whore. Don't you know anything?" Jan says when I ask about the sounds.

Then about one o'clock Jan opens one eye and says, "Where's my coffee? You know I'm no good without coffee in the morning," and I get up and spoon instant Yuban into a glass and heat some water on the hot plate. Jan drinks propped up on two pillows, then puts the empty glass on the cigarette-burned avocado carpet, pulls me back into bed, makes love to me.

Now it's after three o'clock. "I'm hungry," she says, and either we dress and get a hamburger at a stand down the street, or I dress and she gives me a couple of dollars and sends me for ribs and sweet potato pie to a Negro takeout place a few blocks away. We eat sitting on the bed, listening to rhythm-and-blues and static on the Negro station that comes over a radio that's missing its tuning knob and can only be turned on and off. Later we pile the dirty paper plates and napkins and rib bones on top of the collection that's been accumulating on the floor since before I came into her life.

Then she gets up to take a bath, and I lie there still feeling all the things, old and new, she'd done to me on her bed that day. "Go get cleaned up," she tells me when she's finished in the bathroom, and I run the hot and cold water into the rusty tub while the pipes bang and hiss.

It's only about six now, too early to hit the bars, so we saunter down the street and go sit in Harry's Coffee Shoppe. A lot of people know Jan, and she says hi to all of them. "They're as crooked as corkscrews," she sometimes says, gloating about her cronies. Their talk goes something like this:

"Hey, where's Penny hangin' out these days?"

"Oh, man, they busted her ass."

"Oh, man, when's her case come up?"

"Don' know and don' give a fuck."

"Hey, you seen Barry around?"

"The fucker's dead, man. OD'd."

"Man, fuck that lyin' fucker, anyway."

How did Lilly come to be here? I sometimes wonder. Though I'm not really a part of it, I tell myself. It's like looking through a window, watching a drama unfold in the house next door, and I can't look away. "He's a hustler" or "she's a junky," Jan tells me after each one leaves. "He's an old fish queen," she says about a skinny bald man in a black suit and black tie.

"What's that?" I ask, remembering that Eddy had used those words too.

"It means he doesn't like to fuck. All he does is eat pussy," she says. "Doesn't mind paying for it too. He's a john. Good money." She flashes me her dazzling smile. "Terri did it more than once."

We never say anything of consequence to one another. There are so many things I can't tell her, like that I'm ten years younger than she is and not twenty-two, as I'd said I was; and there are probably a lot of things she doesn't tell me. But once, after we sit in Harry's for almost four hours and she chats with a long procession of pimps and prostitutes and addicts and johns, she says, "I don't know why I do this, I have a good education." I don't think to ask her what she means.

At Harry's we have something more to eat, another hamburger maybe or a bowl of soup. Now it's about nine or ten o'clock, so we saunter toward the Open Door or the If Club, across the street. Jan studies the streets to make sure they're safe. "The vice always travels in these unmarked cars," she instructs me, "but they're really dumb 'cause they never use anything but blue or maroon Fords, so you always know when they're around." One night we're a half block from the bars and we see a black wagon parked in front of the If Club. "Shit." She pulls at my arm and we reverse direction, walking quickly, almost running, for at least a few blocks. "It's a fucking raid," Jan says as she pants, holding her side. "Didn't you see the paddy wagon, the Black Mariah? Those asshole owners probably forgot the payoff this week." My heart shakes. If I'm caught in a raid, my mother and aunt will die and Jan will find out I'm a minor.

Most of the time we start at the Open Door, drink until I know I'll vomit if I have one more sniff of scotch, then I hold on to her arm because it's not easy to walk and we cross the street to the If Club, where Jan has another glass or two. When she looks at the femmes I worry, because I don't want to lose her now. "Mmm mmm mmm, watch the ass on that one," she tells me. "Great tits!" She points to another. I know she's only trying to get a rise out of me when she laughs her naughty-boy laugh.

Now it's two o'clock and the bars close, so we walk the mean streets back to the hotel. It helps to grab on to her waist beneath her corduroy jacket as we walk because I still have a hard time making my legs move. We climb the stairs, she slides the bolt into the lock on the door of her room, and knocks the breath out of me with a bruising kiss. She flips me onto her bed or the floor and makes love to me until I'm aching and the morning light seeps through the torn window shade, and then we sleep.

"Hey, baby, you better go get some other clothes," Jan said the next Sunday when I was getting ready to go to Mattie's Ribs for our lunch. "Your stockings have big rips up the back, and your blouse is a rag."

I'd safety-pinned the place where she'd torn the button off that first night, more than a week ago. Now I looked at myself in the mirror on the squeaking closet door, and a disheveled mess of a girl looked back at me. I'd have to go home and get some things, but I didn't want to leave Jan, even for a few hours. "Come with me," I wanted to say, but wouldn't my mother be horrified at her? Wouldn't she ask, "Is that a man or a lady?" And Jan would be even more horrified by my mother, with her Yiddish accent, and Albert, with the holes in his head.

"I'll wait for you at Harry's," Jan said over her shoulder, and was out the door.

I could see that the lights were burning in the house as though they'd been on all night. It was Albert who greeted me: "Lee-lee, where have you been? You didn't call your mother for three days." His gray eyebrows twitched and his eyes blinked like an insane cat's. "She's going crazy and taking me with her!" He grabbed at my shoulders as though he wanted to shake me, and I jumped back, astonished. He'd never before put a hand on me. "She didn't even go to bed last night," he hollered.

My mother heard him and ran to the door. "Louse! You gave me a heart attack," she howled, and swung at my face with her open hand, but the blow landed on my neck. "I called the police. They're looking all over for you."

The police! "Shut up," I bellowed at them both. "Don't you try to hit me, goddammit. Call them back right now and tell them I'm okay." I pushed her toward the phone. If the police came and asked questions, what would I tell them?

"What kind of girl disappears for a week?" Albert pulled me away from my mother.

"None of your damn business. You're not my father." I couldn't let them tell me how to live my life. "You don't know shit!"

"You lousy tramp!" He bared his rotting teeth, and I could smell his stale cigarette breath as he grabbed my shoulders now and shook me. I smacked his chest and broke free. "Go to hell!" I screamed.

"She's home, she's okay," I heard my mother sobbing to the police or Rae as I ran to my room and slammed the door. They weren't going to keep me from going back to Jan.

Though I lived with them for almost two more years, Albert and I didn't speak to each other again until I got married.

Jan broke our routine a couple of days later because she'd run out of money and said she knew this john of Terri's who sometimes hung out at the clubs in the late afternoon. "He'll let us borrow a few dollars if we can find him. Hank's his name, always wears a starched white shirt and these glasses with black frames." The fish queen I'd seen on my first visits to the Open Door.

Hank wasn't at the Open Door now, but there was a chance he'd be at the If Club, Jan said, and we jaywalked across the street, her hand steering the back of my neck. "Oh, shit, no," she hissed between clenched teeth, and a black and white car made a U-turn and pulled up in front of the If Club before we'd stepped onto the curb. "The fuzz, goddammit," she whispered.

A pudgy man in blue with a silver badge on his chest got out of the car. "Did you know jaywalking is against the law?" he asked, smiling.

"No, suh," Jan said, quick and polite, with a heavy southern accent. "I'm not from heah, suh. I hail from Lu-siana, only been in L.A. a couple months."

"I can give you both a ticket for this," he said, looking at me.

"Yes, sir, I'm sorry," I said, following Jan's lead.

"Well, we can't hold up traffic in the middle of the street. Step into the car, both of you," he said, and opened the back door. I could hear a woman dispatcher's voice, droning on the radio. Jan nudged me in, then got in herself, her face a blank despite the flush creeping up her neck. I was inside a police car, like a criminal, sitting where people who got sent to jail sat. For an instant I wondered if I'd faint. The officer drove around the block onto a residential street.

"Ah you goin' to book us, suh?" Jan's voice was high and almost feminine for the first time since I'd known her. "Book us" meant jail. Because of my stupid, dangerous ways, I was going to be arrested, and my mother really would have a heart attack. And Rae—I could hear her screaming in my ears: "Hitler didn't do enough? You had to kill us?"

"So what's the deal? You two together?" The police officer grinned affably.

"Yes, suh," Jan answered, but it wasn't her he wanted to talk to now.

"You go sit under that tree and shut up." He reached back and opened the door for Jan, and I watched, helplessly, as she marched over to a pine in front of a white stucco house and slouched against it. She looked at the sky, at her shoes, anywhere but at the police car with me inside.

Would he rape me? My ears rang. I'd heard Tommi and Roseann tell Jan such a story only a few nights before at Harry's. "This cop just picks us off the street when we're walking along, minding our business, and he tells me to get in back and Roseann has to get in front. Then you know what that fucking sonofabitch does?" Tommi said, pounding the table with her fist. "Makes her go down on him!" Pale Roseann bit her lip and kept shaking her head.

"So how come you don't like men?" the policeman asked me now, his tone curious, as if he were examining a lab specimen.

"I do, sir." I strove for a tone that was unoffended and unoffending.

"Then why are you with that dyke over there?"

"Oh, she's just a friend, sir."

"I bet," he chuckled. I could feel his eyes on me, though I was looking at my hands in my lap. "Do you work?"

What could I answer? If I told him I was a waitress or a clerk, he could check. "I'm a model." It wasn't illegal as long as he didn't know my age. "My real name's Arlene Knopflemacher, but I work under the name of Gigi Frost." I could give Andy's telephone number. Andy would say he was my agent.

"Well, Arlene or Gigi or whatever your name is," the police officer drawled, "that one over there"—he pointed toward Jan with a fat thumb—"she's bad news. And you better straighten up or you'll end up like her." He reached back and opened the door. He was letting me go! "Don't ever let me catch you jaywalking again or I'll take you in. You understand?" he said. Then he drove off as I shook, from relief first—I wasn't going to be arrested—and then rage.

"Fucking bastard, what right does he have?" I growled, the tough girl now, when Jan came back.

"What are you getting so upset about? It happens all the time," Jan snickered.

Hank was at the If Club and lent Jan five dollars. I knew he was smiling his sickly smile at me, trying to make eye contact, as he handed her a crumpled bill from his pocket. I looked down at the floor.

Two days later we were broke again.

"I've got to get out of this town," Jan sighed as though she were thinking out loud. She leaned against the propped pillows, wearing the T-shirt and boxer shorts in which she always lounged around the hotel room. She sipped loudly from the glass of coffee I'd brought to her. "I just can't make it in L.A. I'm calling Stormy—I'll tell her to send me bus money back to New Orleans."

I'd been lying on the bed next to her, but now I sat up. "No! What about us?" I cried.

She blinked at me, surprised, as if she'd momentarily forgotten I was there. "Oh, baby, I wish it didn't have to be this way. God, I hate to leave you. Don't you know that?" She furrowed her brow and looked morose. "We've been so great together. Hey, you know what we'd do if I had some real bread? You'd come with me." She smiled her beautiful smile and sounded little-boy excited now. "I'd get us a motorcycle, and we'd zoom off to New Orleans together. I can drive those suckers good, and you'd ride at my back. Wouldn't that be a kick?"

New Orleans. She'd told me about the fabulous gay bars and drag queens and Mardi Gras and how the police never bothered you there. In New Orleans, seventeen was the drinking age. One more year, and there I'd be able to go to bars with no hassle.

She tore me from my idyll: "Gigi, baby, we can have it," she cried, touching my cheek with a warm hand, gazing intently into my eyes. "We can have everything. Hey, you know how much money you can make us with that fantastic body of yours? You know how quick it would be?" I jumped from the bed as though she'd shoved me. "We'd have that cycle in no time." She talked rapidly, earnestly, as if it were a life-or-death matter. "Hey, Hank said he would give us twenty bucks, and that's just a start. You wouldn't even have to touch him. Terri did it all the time. Please, baby. Baby, please," Jan implored with eyes full of tears, her arms extended to me, "If you love me . . . if you love us . . . please."

I did love us. I did. I'd never felt as alive as I had the past weeks. And all I wanted now was to sink into her arms and stay there. But I'd given up my cherished dream to be an actress because I was afraid it would lead me to the very place she was now urging me to go. "Don't ask me to, Jan," I begged weakly.

"Don't be a dumb bitch!" She bounded up and raised a hand as though to slap me. I stared, mouth open, in disbelief. "Do you want to lose this?" she cried, dropping her hand. Then her face softened. "I'm sorry, baby. I didn't mean that . . . but you hurt me if you don't trust what I say. Baby, I want us to be together always," she whispered.

I backed away from her and sank into the room's one chair. Its knobby upholstery reeked with old odors of sweat and urine. Maybe I couldn't escape what Jan wanted me to do. I covered my face with my hands, and Jan was quiet. After a while I could hear her trimming her nails with the clipper she kept beside the bed. Maybe what Jan wanted me to do was my destiny. Wasn't it useless to fight your destiny? And if I did what she asked, we'd go to New Orleans together. New Orleans with Jan. But what about my mother, Rae?

"Jan," I finally looked up and said, "it's such heavy stuff. Give me a while." I went to sit beside her, to rest my head on her shoulder, but she shifted away. "Look, Jan," I said after long, silent minutes, "I haven't been home or called for days, and I've got to go." She leaned against the propped pillows and examined her nails. "I'll be back," I promised. She never looked at me as I threw on my clothes. I closed the door behind me softly.

The last time I'd called home, my mother had screamed at me to come back right away. "You've got to trust me," I told her calmly. "I'm grown up and I know what I'm doing." I gave her the rehearsal story again— *King Lear*. "I'll be home as soon as I can," I said, and hung up. But now, as the bus crawled west on Sunset Boulevard, I was wild with agitation, and when it finally stopped at Highland, I flew the blocks from the bus stop to the Fountain Avenue Court Bungalows—ignoring street lights, dodging cars, stumbling on curbs—as though Beelzebub and Banshee were at my heels. What if she were sick? How had I been so cruel and crazy?

It was Mr. Bergman who held open the screen door. He bent his round, bald head away from me. "Lilly, Lilly," he said, "I thought you were a good girl." I started to guffaw at his righteous pronouncement, but a sob escaped my lips instead. I could hear my aunt and mother sobbing too, as if someone had died. The second they saw me they pounced, they clutched at me, they wet my face with tears. "We're almost dead, both of us! You almost killed us!" they shrieked. They pulled at me, and I let myself be pulled, the three of us collapsing in one heap on the floor. "You're all we have in the world!" Rae hollered in my ear.

"I'm back! I'll be good!" I wept. I kissed at their wet cheeks. "I won't do it. Don't cry!" I struggled up from the tangle of us. I stumbled to the bathroom, locked the door, ran scalding water in the tub, threw off my dirty clothes, sank into water up to my nose. I didn't care how my skin reddened and hurt. I wanted it to hurt.

"You'll get sick if you stay in the bathtub so long! It weakens the heart!" my aunt yelled, banging on the door a half-hour later. I sat there doggedly for another few minutes before I got up and rubbed my skin dry with rough strokes of the towel. Then I bolted to my room and locked the door.

"Are you in there, Lilly?" my mother called.

When I said, "Yes. I have to sleep now," they didn't bother me anymore. But I was happy they were close by, in the next room.

I lay on top of my bed, too exhausted to cover myself, and closed my eyes. When I awoke it was dark, the middle of the night, and I missed Jan—the smell of her clean hair, her knowing hands. I imagined her holding me now. I felt her on top of me, her teeth on my neck. There was a recklessness in me that resonated mindlessly to what was savage in her. But I had to control it or I'd do something crazy. I'd known how to fight the men, because everything in my life had primed me for that struggle: I wouldn't be their rabbit. But a woman was more insidious for me. I wouldn't know how to keep resisting Jan, though she too was a coyote.

If I was too dumb to dash for my own sake, I told myself as I drifted off again to troubled sleep, I had to do it for my mother and My Rae. So I wouldn't be their worst and final tragedy.

9 GETTING THE GIFT OF WISDOM

ONCE THERE WAS *a young girl who went into the forest with a big basket to pick mushrooms because her sick mother said, "My poor child, we have nothing to eat and we're going to starve." Just as the girl was about to start she saw a fat, glossy fox lying under a tree. He was fast asleep because he'd stuffed so many mushrooms into his greedy belly.*

"I'm going to catch this fox and sell him for his fur," the young girl thought craftily, "and then I'll be able to buy a lot of good food for my mother and me." Quickly she threw her basket over him and sat on it, waiting for a hunter or somebody to come by and help her. Hours passed, but no one came.

Finally the fat fox woke up and realized his predicament. "Hey, lemme out," he called to the girl.

"No," she replied. "I know this isn't a very nice thing to do, but I can sell your fur for enough money to keep us going for a year. We're desperate at home, and I don't have a choice. I'm just waiting for a little help."

"Look," the fox said. "I can be a lot more valuable to you than what you can get for my fur. If you release me I'll give you the gift of wisdom — three profundities that'll keep you going, not just for a year, but for your whole life."

That sounded like an offer she couldn't refuse. What precious gems of wisdom would he bestow on her? "Okay, it's a deal," she said. "Tell, and then I'll let you free. I'm all ears."

"Number one," the fox began. "Never regret the past."

"Hmmm," the young girl thought, and she nodded without committing herself.

"Number two," he said. "Never be credulous."

That made some sense. "Got it," she said.

"And here's the last one: 'Never desire the impossible.'"

She sighed. Truth be told, she was pretty disappointed, but she stood up from the basket. "A bargain's a bargain," she thought, and let the fox slither out.

Then — quick as a fox—up the tree he shinnied. "Little fool," he taunted her from a high limb above her reach. "Don't you know I'm a magic fox with great powers? In exchange for my freedom, you could have asked for a castle; you could have demanded a hundred gold apples; you could have gotten two tickets to America from me. And instead all you got was those paltry maxims."

"You damn sly fox!" the young girl cried. "You tricked me! I'll capture you again, and this time I won't be so dumb!" The basket under her arm, she took the tree at a run and shinnied up, just as he'd done. But she fell and broke two arms and a leg.

The fox practically split his belly open laughing. "Boy, are you an idiot," he sputtered between guffaws. "Here I give you these important rules to live by, and right away you turn around and forget them. Remember, I told you 'never regret the past'? But immediately you regretted letting me go without asking me for more than I gave you. Remember I said 'never be credulous'? Silly child, have you ever heard of a fox who has a castle or gold apples or steamship tickets to America to give away? And what was the last thing I said? Remember? 'Never desire the impossible.' Girl, you have a lot to learn."

My mother's parents died without knowing of my entrance into the world, and of course I never knew my paternal grandparents. So there was no wise, white-bearded *zaydeh* or homey, kerchiefed *bubeh* to sit me down and tell me this shtetl fable that had been passed on, in one version or another, through the ages. If my mother remembered such tales, or any of the useful bits of wisdom from our ancestors' Book, she never told them to me. Maybe her first vision of the green lady's heaven-pointing torch burnt the old stories from her mind, or maybe they were crowded out by all the movies she saw and all the pop tunes she heard. In any case, her losses and her struggle for existence here in the promised land must have made all the old wisdom seem useless. So what she handed on to me were not those stories her people were supposed to live by but tragic stories of pogroms and other annihilations and sweatshops and a bad man. And she unwittingly gave me the antithesis of the fox's advice never to desire the impossible. What could she know, after all, about what was impossible or possible for her American child?

My aunt handed me another kind of story. When I was little and cried because I'd scratched myself in some childish game, My Rae always tried to comfort me by saying, "By the time your *chusen*, your bridegroom, comes, it won't show anymore." This was an early preface to the fabulous tale she told me through my growing-up years—that a Jewish prince would someday marry me, rescue me from life's harshness, and give me many children to make up for those our family had lost. And now that I was grown, the time had come, as far as Rae was concerned, for me to find the prince.

"I see so many girls with such fine Jewish boys, it's a heartache for me," Rae had said when my nose job didn't immediately yield a prince. "You're better looking than those girls. Why can't you find a nice Jewish boy?"

"I don't want a nice Jewish boy," I callously muttered through the new nose she'd helped pay for, and, because I still had hopes for a Hollywood career, I stuck that nose back into *The Complete Works of Eugene O'Neill.*

She would not give up. "Why do you want to make us miserable? Why do you want to make yourself miserable?" she would cry, begging me to attend to real business instead of acting lessons and play rehearsals. When I stopped going to Geller's, her hopes blossomed. "Sophie from the Litvisheh Verein's daughter just got engaged to a wonderful dentist," she told me.

"I'm only sixteen, Rae."

"When me and your mother goes you'll have nobody. Sweet sixteen's the right time to get engaged, especially a poor girl like you. You're better off married to a nice serious boy—a dentist, a doctor, an accountant." She'd mastered that American fable, all right.

Though I still hadn't a clue about how to maneuver in the world, I knew with certainty that the Jewish prince dream she tried to fill me full of was as much the antithesis of fox-advice as the dream of Hollywood stardom that my mother had planted in me. Yet how could I convince Rae she had to give it up? Not by telling her that except in fairy tales, Jewish dentists or doctors or accountants don't marry poor girls who have no father, whose mother had been crazy, and whose stepfather still was. Nor by explaining that though I was sweet sixteen, I was a woman who already had a considerable history in an era when princes' brides were supposed to have no history whatsoever. And certainly not by insisting that I had no interest in princes. She couldn't hear such things.

Nor did she, any more than my mother, have any real idea of either the limits or the possibilities of lives in America in the middle of the twentieth century. My mother and aunt had barely known thirty years earlier how to survive as immigrants, and their worlds never got much bigger than the shops they worked in or the homes they kept for their husbands. So what tools to help me flourish, what wisdom, could they possibly pass on to me? What besides the example of their failure? What coin that I could turn to good use?

Only the most valuable gem in the universe, much more precious than what the sly fox pretended to offer: the knowledge that I was deeply loved, that I was the most important being in the world to them, all that was left to them. And because I was the cherished remnant, I couldn't let myself be destroyed. My life was important, and I had to find a way to do something with it.

What false starts, what near-disasters, what lows and what highs I'd already known and would continue to know. I had no neatly wrapped fables or maxims from the past to live by (in that, I was actually lucky, though I didn't see it that way for a long time). I would have to start from scratch. I would have to create my own fables, my own dreams, unique ones that I could tailor to myself and live by here in America. Yet where would I get the wisdom to figure it all out?

If I'd spent my life in my mother's shtetl of Prael, the inflexible rules would have been drilled into me from birth: "Be a dutiful daughter." "Learn to cook and sew and take care of the house." "Get married and serve your husband and children." I couldn't have escaped my shtetl fate except perhaps for a short respite in Dvinsk, working for a tailor and sending money home to my parents in lieu of my daily services, until a marriage could be arranged for me.

And if Shtetl Lilly had had a rambunctious, striving spirit in her like American Lil's, the family patriarch would have straightened it out early with a callused heavy hand if gentle persuasion didn't do the trick—or failing that, the rabbi would have come to visit. Sitting her down on a stool, he would have lectured, with beard wagging, on what the sacred Book said about her obligations as a daughter of Israel. There wouldn't have been many decisions for Lilly of Prael to make in her narrow, little life, because the path was as inescapable as it was obvious.

But Prael had burned away in the Holocaust, and I was an American. For me, now, here, nothing felt obvious, and nothing yet was inescapable. I'd learned a few things so far: Mel Kaufman and company, for example, showed me what I couldn't do and where I couldn't go; Jan showed me that the coyote could be either gender. But who would show me what I *could* do, what doors I could open, what dreams I could invent to replace my worn-out dreams of stardom?

"When are you going to sign up for school?" my despairing mother asked after I'd been back from Jan's hotel room for a week.

I slept until ten or so every morning now, and when I woke I stayed in bed, staring at the squiggles and patches you could read like a Rorschach test that were made by the peeling lavender paint that covered the walls and ceiling. I didn't know what I'd do with myself if I left my room. If I wasn't going to be with Jan anymore or go back to Geller's or read plays or take modeling jobs, how could I pass the day and the long evening and the night?

"You have to register for Hollywood High School. Mrs. Marcus from next door told me. You hear me, Lilly? It's five blocks away. Sunset and Highland." Since I'd disappeared for days, my mother never talked to me anymore without the shrill edge of lamentation in her voice, as though she feared I'd already taken the inevitable next step after letting myself be photographed in the nude. There was nothing I could say now to reassure her. Hadn't I reassured her after the terrible discovery of the pictures? And right after that I vanished, didn't even call her. What good were my reassurances?

"In a week it starts. You need to sign up," my mother nagged.

All the previous year I'd waited for my sixteenth birthday so I could quit school. Now I was sixteen. Why should I go back? And yet if I didn't, what would I do with the rest of my life?

If no patriarch or rabbi is imposed on you, or even available to you, to whom do you turn in America for guidance?

I opened the Yellow Pages to Psychologists and with a steeled finger dialed a number.

When Dr. Sebastian Cushing heard that I was only sixteen and my family had no money, he told me about a counselor who was hired by the Rotary Club to talk to underprivileged youths in trouble.

When had I not been an underprivileged youth in trouble?

"But his clients are mostly male juvenile delinquents." Dr. Cushing oozed sympathy over the phone.

"That's okay, I'm a juvenile delinquent, even though I'm a girl," I told him truthfully, and scribbled Mr. Maurice Colwell's number on the yellow page.

The old stone edifice looked as though it had once housed studio glamour, but when you walked through the big oak door you were assaulted by the pungent odor of chlorine coming from a huge, enclosed swimming pool. The building was now the Hollywood YMCA, a shrine to male physical fitness, and Mr. Colwell's office was on the second floor.

I stood at the desk, feeling awkward and waiting to be acknowledged by the only female in sight, an elderly lady in a prim chignon who worked the switchboard. I could hear the gruff shouts of male camaraderie behind the closed gym doors and the dull bouncing of basketballs.

The switchboard lady directed me up the marble staircase and down a dark hall to Maurice Colwell's cubbyhole of an office.

"Come on in. Lillian, right? Come on in." His voice was jarringly robust. He rose and extended a big mitt of a hand, but he didn't move from behind a desk that was topped by a rat's nest of scattered books and piles of papers; torn, empty boxes of Kleenex and one full one; and a cane with a duck-bill handle on top of it all. He had a brownish crewcut, and he wore round, horn-rimmed glasses and a gray flannel suit with a navy tie, like a respectable Rotary Club type. "Babbitt," the guys at Geller's used to call men who looked like that.

"So, tell me, what's your story?" Mr. Colwell asked without ceremony, pointing me to a metal folding chair opposite his desk. He sat on one too, leaning forward, cupping his cheeks in his hands, his elbows balanced on a piece of the desk's disorder. He looked like an owl on a perch.

How could I begin to tell my life to a strange man in a depressing office while brawny jocks walked up and down the halls? I searched my head for bland words that would tide me over until I could get out of there.

"While you're thinking, let me tell you one," he began. "There was this *schnorrer*, you know what a *schnorrer* is, right?"

I remembered what my mother and Rae had said about Fanny. "Yeah, a person who acts like a beggar." This guy's name was Colwell?

"Right. He goes to a rich man and says, 'I'm hungry. Give me something to eat.' And the rich man says, 'What *chutzpah!*' Do I need to translate?"

"No, it's nerve . . . or daring . . . like, outrageous daring."

"Yeah. So the rich guy says, 'What *chutzpah*, a man like you, with the arms of an ox, what right do you have to go around begging?' And the *schnorrer* says, 'What should I do for the lousy few cents you'll give me, cut off my arms?'" Maurice Colwell grinned, and the gap between his front teeth looked wide enough for a cigarette to get lost in.

I laughed, more at his silly grin than at the joke, which I wasn't sure was really funny.

"Now let's see a little *chutzpah* from you," he said seriously. "What's your story?"

"How do you know '*chutzpah*,'" I asked.

"I'm an honorary Jew. My wife's Jewish," he said. "*Nu?*" and he leaned so far forward that the upper part of him was halfway across the desk.

I told him. What did I have to lose? About my nude modeling and the Open Door and how I kept my age a secret and about getting D's and F's at Fairfax High School and not wanting to go back to school, and then about how I'd failed my mother and made her get married — and here tears tumbled out, and he handed me the full Kleenex box — and why I gave up on my Hollywood dreams that I'd hoped and planned for since I was a little kid, and how I still thought sometimes about what it would be like to go to New Orleans with Jan on a motorcycle. I handed him my whole life.

"So, you really think you're a homosexual, huh?" he asked after two hours.

"I don't *think* I am. I am," I said. Did this guy in a Brooks Brothers straitjacket want to rescue me from being gay?

"Well, listen good. It doesn't matter if you're a polka-dotted baboon, you still gotta eat. And if you're a homosexual, you don't want to get married, right? So you gotta work to eat. And if you gotta work to eat," he intoned with Talmudic scholar logic, "it may as well be a good job that lets you eat good, right? So you better finish high school and get yourself into college. You don't want to go full-time now, I'll write you a letter, you take it to the principal, and he'll let you leave before lunch every day. Deal?"

He was right. Why hadn't it occurred to me? If I didn't want to get married, I'd have to work. If I couldn't work as a movie actress and didn't want to work like my poor mother at some miserable job that paid next to nothing, I had to go to school.

"So what do you like to do—when you're not carousing in bars or picking up sociopaths or risking your neck on motorcycles?" He blinked his owl eyes at me. I couldn't figure out if he was trying to moralize or be funny. What could I tell him about what I liked to do? Make love with Jan?

I fished in my memory: "I used to read plays all the time," I said.

"Good start." He stirred around in the mountain on his desk. "You'll love this, *A Tree Grows in Brooklyn*. It's a novel, a poor girl who becomes a writer, Irish Catholic—not like you but not that different. Read it and tell me next week what you think. This too, and these." He extricated a half-dozen dog-eared paperbacks from the debris and handed them to me.

"See you next week," he said, offering his mitt again in a handshake that swallowed up mine, "but in the meantime, think about this one, okay? There was a king two hundred years ago who hated Jews and he made this decree: 'Every Jew who steps foot in my kingdom has to say something about himself. If he lies he will be shot, and if he tells the truth he will be hanged. So one day this Jew comes—long black coat, sidelocks, the works—and the king's guards command him to tell something about himself. 'I'm going to be shot today,' he says. This really puzzles the guards (they all have *goyishe kups*)—what should they do with this guy? They go ask the king for direction, but he's puzzled too. '*If I shoot the Jew, it implies he told the truth,*' the king says to himself, '*but in that case my decree says he should be hanged, so how can I shoot him? But if I hang him, that implies he told a lie, and for a lie my decree says he should be shot, so how can I hang him?*' What can he do? He's gotta let the man go free." The gap-toothed grin. "Quick—what's the moral?"

I laughed inside. This guy really was funny. But I shrugged in answer to his question.

"The moral is," Maurice Colwell said, "you have to use your head in this world. Now, chew on it."

He pulled his cane from the pile and walked me down the hall with a bobbing limp, one foot encased in an elevated shoe that tried in vain to make up for the shortness of the leg. "Polio," he told me much later. "That's how I started reading. You stay in bed for a year or two, you discover a lot of things."

I hugged his books close to my chest and walked west on Sunset Boulevard, back to the Fountain Avenue Court Bungalows. Maurice Colwell was right—about almost everything, but mostly about my using my head. I'd stopped doing that. But now I would go back to school, and I'd figure out what I wanted to be and how to do it. I'd spent a good part of the last year in photographers' studios, dressed in feathers and harem pants and beachballs and nothing; I'd been in the Houdini whorehouse; I'd consorted with addicts and drunks; I'd been a regular in gay bars; I'd made love in a flophouse with a butch pimp. And now I needed to be an eleventh-grader. I had to bring this off. I had to get the high school diploma that Mr. Colwell—Maury, he told me to call him—said I needed if I was going to go to college and become somebody.

I found myself soaring in seven-league boots down Sunset Boulevard because I was suddenly higher than Jan's scotches had ever made me, though my mind was absolutely clear too, as though I'd ripped off layers of gauze. I could do something good, even if I couldn't be an actress. I remembered that I'd once wanted to be a lawyer, and Fanny had said that poor girls couldn't be lawyers. I'd ask Mr. Colwell—Maury—what he thought about it. He knew this country as my mother and Rae and Fanny never could.

Algebra II, History, English, Latin—my classes went from eight o'clock to twelve. I couldn't imagine now how I'd managed to mess up so badly at Fairfax. You just had to pay attention and turn in whatever the teacher said to turn in, and your homework came back marked with *A*'s, or at least *B*'s. It was easy.

Though I was done for the day before lunch and was free to leave, by the third week I didn't want to. The Speech Club met at noon. *"We are looking for new faces — debaters, oral interpreters, extemporaneous speakers,"* the flier had read. *"Help Hollywood High bring home the bacon from the Pepperdine regionals!"* Oral interpretation—that meant dramatic reading. I no longer had actress dreams, but I missed the craft I'd studied for so long. In one of the books Maury had given me, *USA* by John Dos Passos, I found "Body of an American," a piece about war horrors—what I'd felt in blood and bone since infancy.

I loved the familiar sweet calm and sharp focus I felt when I walked up to the front of the classroom at the Speech Club's second meeting. Lil disappeared into Dos Passos's angry ironist. I held the book in my hands, but I knew the lines by heart, and I modulated my trained voice to the nuance of every phrase. I loved the hush in the room and the look on the faces of the kids and on the face of Mr. Bell, the speech coach, too. "Wow!" I heard a boy whisper when I finished. Like Irene's "wow" all those years ago.

For a while they become my gang. I never before had a bunch of friends my own age, and I like the novel feeling—finally I'm something like a teenager. There is Ken, the boy who said "Wow!"—he's the son of a famous leftist lawyer and lives in a big house in the Hollywood Hills. That's where I learn that while money can buy a home like Simone's, to create one like Ken's you need culture and taste too. Ken lends me hardcover books with intact dust jackets—Dalton Trumbo and Upton Sinclair and Howard Fast—that he takes down from the floor-to-ceiling bookshelves in the rumpus room of his family's house. We sit on furniture that is shiny oak and rich brown suede, and he holds my hand and gazes at my face while he tells me with great passion about socialism and about the evils of McCarthy and how his father had defended blacklisted screenwriters and directors, and the brave and clever things they'd said in front of the House Un-American Activities Committee. There is Alice, who pirouettes through the school halls on fairy toes, who wants to learn to play the dulcimer so people will call her the Damsel with the Dulcimer, who declares everything to be "curiouser and curiouser" because she knows she looks like Alice in Wonderland, with her wide periwinkle eyes. There is Mario, who reads aloud to us from the paperback of Baudelaire's Flowers of Evil *that he carries in his back pocket, his full, red lips in an expressive pout, the bicep of his smooth, raised arm rippling as the book moves to the rhythm of the words. Ken is the heartthrob of all the cerebral girls in the Speech Club, but Mario is dubbed the sexiest boy in school by almost all the other girls and by Denny also, who calls me late at night to talk about the hidden content in any crumb—any word or gesture—that Mario deigns to pass in his direction.*

I lugged the giant trophy to the YMCA in a big paper sack, feeling foolish, but I needed to hear Maury tell me that I'd done something fine. I'd shown it to my mother first: Grand Prize in Oral Interpretation—Southern California Forensic League Regionals. "Kids from fifty high schools," I'd said. She put down the Morton's Kosher Salt that she'd been sprinkling on slabs of red brisket, wiped her hands on her apron, and lifted the gilt and wood Winged Victory gingerly. She moved her lips, trying valiantly to read and understand all the words on the base, and her smile was radiant. The way it was when she used to watch me performing with Irene's troupe. But what did she know?

"Extracurricular activities. Colleges love that stuff." Maury gratified me with the words, his owl eyes fluttering under his glasses. "Keep rackin' 'em up."

If he thought it worthwhile, it must be. I was itchy in anticipation of the next tournament—mostly because I wanted to win again and have another trophy to carry up the marble staircase of the Y and present for his approval. "Sixteen going on ten," I chastised myself, but I put myself to sleep many nights with the vision of how I'd walk through his door with another Winged Victory in my hands, and he'd say, "Ya dun good, kid! Keep it up."

"Let's see what you got in that bag," he never failed to say. Wise owl, he knew my need.

"I took a first at Occidental" or "I won the State in oral interp," I'd tell him, ashamed really by how much I relished his praise. "They're sending me to the nationals in Lexington, Kentucky!" I ran to tell him, the telling more delicious almost than the happening.

He talked and talked, for two hours or three every single week, sometimes twice a week. He was as generous with his pronouncements as he was with his time, and I accepted them both like a lost wayfarer, grateful for the beacon, the road map, the searchlight, that illuminated the way. He pointed me to plush swaths of open fields and made me intuit horizons far beyond the eye.

He lectured me: "There's no such thing really as class in America, not like in the old country. There, where you're born, you stay. Here, you can go up, you can go down. Nothing's etched in concrete, no Book of Peerage. Your parents can leave you a million, you shoot it up in heroin or some such crap in a year, and then you're nothing. Or you can be born nothing and you make yourself into something—a doctor, a lawyer, a college professor. You need brains and hard work, and it's yours. You know who Horatio Alger was? Rags to riches. It happens."

He educated me: "Do you know the greatest horror, the greatest threat to civilization? Not poverty, not ignorance. Injustice. That's what denies your basic humanity the most. That's the first thing a civilized society needs to spend its energies on—fighting injustice. Everything else falls into place when that's taken care of."

He answered my worries: "Yeah, so you're right, there aren't a lot of women doing big things. But so what? There's nothing they can't do, it's just more of a struggle for them to get to do it. Look, there have been women politicians, women scientists, women inventors, women lawyers. It's not against the law. We're not in the nineteenth century here. You just have to want it."

To this day his pronouncements, right or wrong, are etched on my psyche as much as shtetl wisdoms were etched on my aunt's. "If you're destined to drown"—she used to repeat the narrow fatalism she'd absorbed with Prael potatoes and cauliflowers—"you'll drown in a spoonful of water." She loved that one. Her other favorite was: "If something isn't the way you like it, you've got to like it the way it is."

How could I not have preferred Maury's messages of hope and righteousness and free will?

10 KICKED OUT

DENNY WORE DAZZLING SHIRTS that were sunflower yellow, parrot green, candy apple red. He was puckish and too pretty for a boy, and anyone who thought about it would have known that his eyebrows couldn't have been arched so high and perfect without the aid of tweezers. In speech tournaments he did Biff from *Death of a Salesman* in an exaggeratedly melodramatic voice that was pitched in an upper octave and made his interpretation unintentionally comical, but that didn't seem to matter much to him. Mario was the real reason he'd joined the Speech Club.

When he called one evening to ask if I thought Mario looked greater in his black T-shirt or his white one, I said, "I'm gay too."

"I knew it, I knew it in my bones!" he shrieked and cackled; he became my best friend at Hollywood High School. I had too much to hide from the other kids.

It was Denny who introduced me to the secret life that played itself out on Hollywood Boulevard, just a couple of blocks from our school. Most passersby never seemed to notice the young men who trekked up and down the boulevard from Highland to Vine in little knots, shouting merriments or imprecations to other little knots of young men. "She" or "Mary" or some such feminine signifier was how they usually referred to one another, and they talked in high voices about cruising and camping and queens and sailor's rosaries ("the buttons on a sailor's pants that queens pray over," as Destiny, the most fabulous queen of all and my buddy for about three months, defined it for me). A casual stroller might see a beautiful, elaborately made-up woman and think "a Hollywood starlet," but Denny introduced me to many of them, drag queens who walked the boulevard to hustle or to see how well they could pass. It was Denny also who clued me in to the gay cruising scene on the boulevard; and he took me to the Marlin Inn, a coffeehouse where underage gay boys without fake I.D.'s for the bars could hang out. Our favorite after-school stop was Coffee Dan's, a regular meeting place for the Hollywood gay crowd, where the straight patrons seldom noticed that the people in the next booth—billing and cooing or camping it up, sometimes wearing gobs of eye shadow and rouge—were all male.

Being an honorary member of the secret world of gay boys made me long for the freedoms they claimed for themselves. I'd never heard of lesbians cruising one another on the street, but I yearned to know what it would feel like to pass a strange woman on the boulevard, exchange a significant glance that would be invisible to the droves around us, and follow her (as gay boys followed one another), our blood tingling, around a corner. But if lesbians ever walked down those streets, I didn't recognize them, and I lived in celibacy through much of my junior year because I knew I had to stay out of the bars. Mostly I was okay since I had plans: I'd finish high school in a couple of years and go to a college I'd seen only a few blocks away from the Open Door, Los Angeles Junior College, and when classes were over every day I'd stop by for a beer and meet women there and have all the lovers I wanted. I'd know how not to get myself in trouble with a brutal woman like Jan. For the present, it was something at least to walk down the boulevard with the queens or hang out with them in the coffee shops.

Once in a while I "dated" gay men I met at the Marlin or Coffee Dan's. Wendell looked like a beefy young businessman and worked for the Southern California Gas Company. He asked me to front for him at a Christmas party. "You have to bring a wife or girlfriend to those things, so it would be a big favor to me," he said. "Tell them you're twenty, okay? And if they ask, say we've been going out for about a year."

I was happy to do it. "I've got a date," I told my aunt when Mr. Bergman drove her over to the Fountain Avenue Court Bungalows.

"He's twenty-three, has a very good job with the gas company." I waxed ecstatic. Maybe it would put a halt to her nagging for a while.

"Jewish?" she asked.

At the end of each semester I took my report cards to Maury because they were trophies too: I'd ended the eleventh grade with mostly *A*'s. He blinked owl eyes behind his thick glasses as he scrutinized the grades. "*Mazel tov, bubeleh!*" he shouted and pumped my hand as though I'd brought him *nachas*, gave him pleasure as if I were his own kid. "Colleges forgive a lousy freshman year if you can make grades like this. It shows you've matured. A collitch lady you'll be, und a lady bachelor und a lady master und a lady phudd. So, where will you apply?

"Los Angeles City College?" He scowled at me when I told him my plans. "Ridiculous! That's a junior college—two years only. With grades like this and those first-place speech trophies you can write your own ticket—UCLA, Berkeley, Columbia University. Don'tcha know there's a difference between those places and someplace like Los Angeles Junior College? There's a whole big world out there. How'd you like to be living in the heart of New York? That's where Columbia is. Don'tcha know that in New York they got more theaters, concerts, museums, lectures—more of everything worth doing and seeing than anyplace on the planet?" I didn't know. I only knew that was where I came from, and those memories weren't too terrific. But Maury's words propelled me to dream of New York as a fabulous possibility. Columbia University. Or I could stay in California and go to Berkeley. Or UCLA.

The first time I saw Nicky I thought she was a straight boy. I'd gone to the Marlin Inn to meet Denny, and she was sitting at a table with him and some other queens. Her gray wool man's shirt hung loose outside her jeans, and her auburn hair was buzzed and shorter by far than anyone's at the Marlin. You had to really look in order to notice the breasts under the shirt—not because they were so small but because the whole effect was so successfully male that your eyes could trick you into ignoring the soft swell beneath the shirtfront.

She was the first lesbian I'd met in Hollywood. "Won't you join us," she said with great formality and jumped to her feet. She relieved me of my books and almost bowed as she pulled out a chair. At first I wondered if she was making fun of me, but no, she was serious. She was Humphrey Bogart in *Casablanca*.

"Thank you, that's kind of you," I said. I knew how to be Ingrid Bergman too, so I let her settle me into the chair. Denny giggled. I threw him a look.

The second I took a cigarette out of my pack, there was a worn, gold-plated lighter waving in front of my nose, and when the waiter brought the coffee I'd ordered, Nicky insisted on paying, then got up to get me some apple pie and then a second cup of coffee. When I said I had to go, she asked if she could walk me home. "Sure," I said, because I missed the gay girls at the Open Door.

She talked and talked as we sauntered down Hollywood Boulevard, as though she'd had no one to talk to in a long time. I saw now that she was a great galumpf of a girl with puppy feet and puppy eyes that belied her efforts to pass as a sophisticated man. She'd come to L.A. with a magazine crew, she said, a boss and six young people. Her job was to go door-to-door with a basset hound look and a heart-wrenching tale, like "My mother and father died in a fire last month, and now I have nobody in the world except for a maiden aunt in Topeka, Kansas, and I'm trying to make enough money by selling magazines so I can take a bus back there and live with her. Won't you please help me?" "They're good magazines—and a lot cheaper than on the newsstands. People enjoy them once they get them," Nicky explained earnestly.

"You don't have to go in right away, do you?" she asked when we turned the corner onto Fountain Avenue. She was a character; I'd never met anyone like her. So I plopped down with her on the apartment house lawn next door to the Fountain Avenue Court Bungalows and listened for another half-hour as she poured out her life story, plucking nervously at blades of grass and dandelions. In six months she'd already been to Chicago, Des Moines, Cheyenne, Salt Lake City, Reno, and San Francisco. She pronounced the name of each city with pleasure, a world traveler who'd seen wonders. "And I've made a lot of money. I'm good at it," she said in a boy's clear voice. "The crew boss keeps the money on the books for you, and they pay all your hotel bills and stuff. Then, when you're ready to leave, you get your wad." *Waaad*, she pronounced it, making the word sound as though it meant *chest of gold doubloons.* Though she was a year or two older than I, I felt like a jaded woman in comparison. The whoppers she'd told in the service of the *Ladies' Home Journal* hadn't yet made her eyes look hard and savvy, and there was an ingenuous air about her. She'd been a carhop before she joined the magazine crew, a telephone operator before that. "But what I really do is write," she said.

Sometimes, when I got rave comments from an English teacher on an essay, I thought that I might like to become a writer. It seemed as exciting as being an actress—more exciting, really, because it took intellect. ("You put some squiggles on a paper, and miraculously your mind goes out to the minds of thousands of strangers. You'll never even see them, but you've taught them, you've touched them," Maury had said. "The greatest profession in the world," he called it.)

"I've got around fifty pages done," Nicky said now, and I listened, awed. "The book's actually about me, but I call her Blackie, a butch from St. Louis, eighteen years old, travels around the country, trying to make it on her own. I'm naming it 'Walk With the Wind.'" When Blackie is twelve, she wins a national short story contest for Catholic school girls, first prize, and the story, "Big Red," about a *Call of the Wild* kind of dog, is printed in a magazine that goes to all the Catholic schools. The nuns at her school say she'll be the next Graham Greene. But when she's sixteen her mother makes her go to work for the St. Louis telephone company, even though the principal nun pleads with the mother, says she'll get Blackie (Nicole, she's called then) scholarships to college. Nicole's mother is adamant; she went to school only until she was sixteen, and what was good enough for her should be good enough for her daughter. So Blackie begins a life of plugging wires into the phone company's main switchboard. "I'm a homosexual," she tells her mother when she's seventeen, because she's fallen in love with a girl at the phone company. That's when her mother kicks her out, won't even let her take clothes with her, just says, "I don't have a freak for a daughter."

"Did that really happen?" I asked, incredulous that there were mothers who would do that to their children.

Nicky cracked her knuckles, loud, first on her left hand and then on her right, before she answered, "That's just the way it happened. That was last year. I've been walking with the wind ever since."

"But . . . doesn't she yell at you to come home when you phone her?" I remembered my own telephone booth calls to my hysterical mother.

"I only phoned once, when I got fired from the carhop job for stealing 'cause the pay was so lousy and I had no money and no place to go. I said, 'Mom, it's me, it's Nicole. I wanna come home, Mom.' 'I don't know any Nicole,' she says and hangs up. Bitch, huh?" Nicky grinned, but I saw her lower lip quiver.

"Can't I come in for a few minutes?" she asked, clutching my schoolbooks to her chest when I said I really had to get home now.

She was nothing like Jan, and I'd never met anyone who wanted to be a writer before. "You better tuck your shirt in and put on some lipstick," I said, handing her a tube of Red Hot Peppermint that I fished from my purse.

She looked horrified for a flash, but she took the lipstick. "I don't have a mirror," she said. "Tell me if I'm doing it right."

My mother was playing gin rummy in the kitchen with Albert and didn't even notice her. "I got a friend from school," I shouted in my mother's direction, and Nicky and I slipped into my room. "Okay," I heard my mother say. Albert said nothing. I closed the door and pulled from my cache of books a bunch with garish covers that I'd found on the twenty-five-cent paperback rack at the drugstore—*Women's Barracks, Queer Affair, We Walk Alone, Odd Girl Out.* "Take them," I told Nicky. "They're about lesbians, but your story is a zillion times more interesting. I know you'll get it published." My ambition for her was growing like a beanstalk.

My mother did catch a glimpse of her a little while later, as she was leaving, but she didn't seem to notice that Nicky looked like a boy. There'd been no butches in the shtetl, or in the movies she'd seen, or in the shops where she'd worked. "She's so tall for a girl. I never saw such a tall girl" was all my mother said.

Nicky came again on Saturday and then on Sunday, and when the workweek started she came the minute she was free in the late afternoons. Maury told me I needed to fill out college applications and write my essay on why any college should be happy to get me. I'd already decided to apply to all the good colleges in Los Angeles—UCLA, USC, Pepperdine, Occidental—because I wouldn't be too far from my mother at any of them. Nicky stayed with me in my room as I strained over my work. Sometimes she wrote a bit of "Walk With the Wind" or she read one of my drama books or novels, her big frame stretched out on the floor near me as I sat at my little desk. "Can I read you this?" she'd ask from time to time. I didn't mind the interruptions because usually she read passages I liked too, and I thought her comments were so smart, better than mine. "You're the one who should be applying to colleges," I told her. It was cozy—her company, our shared tastes—and I found myself dreaming a little, about how she'd become a famous writer and I'd become . . . I didn't know what yet, something else good.

When she kissed me the first time, there in my room, it was a shy, kid's kiss, with soft, closed lips. "Don't you know how to kiss?" I teased, and I showed her, like an older woman. Somehow, though, the pieces didn't fit; it didn't seem at all . . . sexy. Still, I went out to the living room to tell my mother: "Nicole is staying over. She's helping me study for a test."

I turn the lock and put out the light after I hear my mother or Albert close the door to their room and two pairs of shoes drop on the floor. I take off all my clothes and throw them in a pile. I can see Nicky's shadow, her back to me, as she gets out of her shoes, socks, shirt, pants, and nothing more. She climbs into bed before I do, covers herself, and then she reaches out for me. I slip under the blanket and she caresses me everywhere. I'd longed for a lover, and now I've got one who is so sweet and bright and ardent. But something crucial is missing. Whatever it is lets my mind keep wandering to other things — the sound of my footsteps on the marble staircase that leads to Maury's office, the dark circles around my mother's eyes. And suddenly I know: It's not Nicky's fault that I'm not stirred deeply. Together we are two left shoes. What I really want is an older woman. An older woman. *Even the phrase excites me.*

Yet I didn't want her to leave. I really liked the way the gay boys on Hollywood Boulevard coupled us—we were Lil-and-Nicky. Sometimes on weekend evenings I'd put on my harlequin capris again and the high heels that she loved, and we'd strut down the boulevard, her arm a shawl round my shoulders. "It's okay," she assured me the first time. "Everyone thinks I'm a guy." I decided she was probably right, and I relaxed into the masquerading fun of it, the charm of fooling the tourists who thought we were like them. "You make a stunning couple, darlings," Destiny gushed. I liked even more the way she sat with me while I did my schoolwork, and how we talked about her finishing "Walk With the Wind" and selling it for a lot of money. We were discovering books together like *The Prophet* and Edna St. Vincent Millay's *Renascence*. She said the book she loved best was Walter Benton's love poem sequence *This Is My Beloved*, because the beloved's name was Lillian. She recited the Benton poem "Your Eyes" to me again and again in a rich, melodious voice, her intonations subtle and canny.

In about a month the magazine crew had milked all the neighborhoods in L.A., and Nicky's boss told them they were shoving on to San Diego. She ran to my house as soon as she found out. "Tell me to stay." She held my hand, peering into my eyes and pleading, like a Victorian suitor proposing.

"Yes, stay," I said. I'd be lonely again if she left.

I went with her to collect her clothes and money at the hotel where the magazine crew had lived, the Hotel Royal Astor, a building as grimy as the one I'd lived in with Jan. The glass front door had a crack running its length, as though someone had taken a crowbar to it, and the lobby was decorated by a single overstuffed chair that leaked straw guts. I followed Nicky up familiar-looking unlit stairs and down a smelly corridor.

The crew boss had a thin black mustache and a cocky tilt to his chin. He wore red suspenders and his hair was slicked, like a 1930s gangster. Without so much as a glance at Nicky, he kept putting things into a suitcase and muttered that she had fifty dollars coming.

Even from where I stood at the door I could see the deep flush that spread over her face and neck. "But what about all my money on the books?" she cried.

"Yeah, that's fifty dollars," he snapped, still not looking at her, pulling a ledger book out of a big box and throwing it on the unmade bed. "Look, here." He pointed with a blunt finger on the page, and

Nicky leaned down, craning to see. "Right here—hotel rent, food, clothes, spending money." He flipped the pages wildly. She kept shaking her head at the figures. "A doctor in October when you had the flu—look at how much that cost us." He stabbed his finger like a shiv on another page.

"But I've been working since July. I'm the one who sold more than anybody!" Nicky wailed. I stood with my back pressed up against the door, suddenly scared for her.

"Damn it, it's all there!" His voice rose, and he slammed the ledger shut and glared at her. "You made $1,265 since July, and the company spent $1,215 for your upkeep. Can't you read?"

"Hey now, look . . ." I squeaked and came up behind him.

"Who the shit are you?" He whirled around as though he hadn't seen me before and curled his lip as if regarding a cockroach. My stomach tumbled and I backed to the wall, but he waved me off with a flip of his hand and turned again to Nicky. "We owe you fifty bucks, and that's what I'm giving you," he said now in a tone of sweet reason.

"That's impossible," Nicky moaned.

"Fucking dyke!" The reasonable veneer vanished quickly, and he tossed the ledger on top of the box. "Wadda you gonna do, call the cops?" he drawled.

Nicky looked at the closed ledger. Her mouth worked, but nothing came out.

"Do you want the money or not?" he snarled a few minutes later, locking his suitcase with a key, then sticking the ledger back in the box. "I can't just stand here clapping my jaws with you. Look, you're quitting on us without notice. By rights I don't even have to give you the fifty dollars."

"Carl, don't do this," she begged. "You can't do this!" But he'd already thrown two twenties and a ten on the floor. He put the box under an arm, then grabbed his suitcase and slammed the door behind him.

Wendell says Nicky can crash on his sofa until she gets work. Every morning she stands on the corner of Fountain and Orange Grove avenues, waiting to walk me to school so we'll have a few minutes together. When I get to the corner, I al-

ways find her studying the Help Wanted—Women *section of the* Los Angeles Herald *and circling ads with a green pencil stub—salesgirl, countergirl, file clerk. Now her hair is longer, her shirt tucked in, and she wears my lipstick and eye shadow. "I'll find something today," she says every morning, her energy renewed. But at three o'clock she's waiting for me at Coffee Dan's, lipstick worn off, eye shadow smudged, shoulders drooping. By then she's answered every ad, trekked all over Los Angeles. "They just turn me away without even asking me anything."*

One place, a department store, doesn't turn her away immediately. A woman in the office gives her four pages of forms to fill out and a six-page test to take. The woman grades the test while Nicky sits there, then calls her over and says, "You got 100 percent! Goodness, we've never had anyone get 100 percent before!" She tells her to go to another room and wait for the interviewer, who emerges from his office a couple of hours later, takes one look at Nicky, and says, "We don't hire tomgirls here."

When Nicky related that last story to me and Wendell in a booth at Coffee Dan's, he tried to lift the pall by telling us about a new bar in North Hollywood—"mostly lesbians, very chi-chi. Let's go this Friday." He smiled. "It'll be my treat."

"No, I better not," I said. If the bar got raided, my Herculean labors at Hollywood High would have been for nothing.

But Nicky immediately shifted mood, as though the brutal insults she'd survived for the past weeks were dead and buried and she was ready for life again. "Oh, yes! Lil, please," she begged. "We've never been to a bar together. Please, I need some fun now."

The Club Laurel was nothing like the Open Door or the If Club. The neon marquee in front read:

"BEVERLY SHAW, SIR"
SONGS TAILORED TO YOUR TASTE
APPEARING NIGHTLY FOR YOUR LISTENING PLEASURE

A colored picture in the blue-draped window showed a woman, forty perhaps, perched on a piano bar in a short dark skirt, high-heeled shoes, black bow tie, white tailored jacket. Her long legs were crossed at the

LEFT: *Lil and Wendell: "Once in a while I 'dated' gay men . . . 'You have to bring a wife or girlfriend to those things.'"*

BOTTOM LEFT: *"Beverly Shaw, Sir"*

BOTTOM RIGHT: *Nicky (in the 1960s)*

knee, her lipsticked mouth was open in song, and she held a microphone in her hand as though she were romancing it. I stared. I hadn't seen anyone so gorgeous since I'd last laid eyes on Irene Sandman. But there was something more: The woman in the picture projected a kind of power — not masculine exactly, but certainly not at all feminine. I'd never seen anything like it before. I was mesmerized.

"Let's go in," Wendell nudged at my back, but I couldn't stop looking at the picture. Was this really a lesbian?

Once inside, I was sure Wendell had made a mistake — this couldn't be a lesbian bar. There were straight-looking couples sitting in the black upholstered booths and at the sleek white piano bar. There were a lot of women with other women too, but almost all of them wore tailored dresses and high heels and makeup, and to my untutored eye they all appeared to be executives or lawyers or journalists. "Are these people gay?" I whispered in Wendell's ear.

"I promise you," he laughed at my open-mouthed bumpkin look. "Maybe a few are straight tourists who like to watch the scene, but trust me, there's mostly gay girls here." I felt the way my mother must have at the Café de Paris when she'd sighed, "Take it all in." I was drunk — with Beverly Shaw, the elegance of the Club Laurel, the beautiful lesbians in beautiful clothes! I could see that Nicky too was having a fine time, her cheeks pink with pleasure, gazing in wonderment.

"*I love youuu, for sentimental reee-sons,*" Beverly Shaw sang. She sat on top of the piano bar, as in her picture, crooning a caress to the microphone. The songs were the ones my mother and I used to hear on "Your Hit Parade," and Beverly Shaw now seemed to be looking right at me as her lips formed each entrancing word. Her voice was low and sultry. The rest of the world dropped away as she held me in the palm of her splendid, manicured hand. I felt her to the root of my spine. I studied the tanned skin on her neck and felt my lips there, then at her breast. I would kiss her belly, worshipfully; I would go down farther to feast on all her secret places. I'd never done that to anyone before. To touch her like that, to taste her, to devour her — would that break open for me the secret of her magical force?

I tried to listen to her singing, to pay a little attention to Nicky and

Wendell, but my fantasies spun themselves out, beyond my control. After each number Nicky banged her hands together happily, like a kid watching a fabulous high-wire act. My eyes couldn't keep away from Beverly Shaw's legs.

"We'll take a little break now. Don't go 'way," Beverly Shaw said to the crowd.

"Never," I whispered to her myself. "Never." I'd had a glorious epiphany. This was the kind of woman I wanted for a lover—one who looked commanding, in control of life, nothing like Nicky or me. And more than that, this was the kind of woman I wanted to become.

"That's Mark!" Wendell broke into my reverie. I looked where he pointed—to a man I'd noticed earlier because he'd seemed as enthralled with Beverly Shaw as I, hanging on to her every note. I'd wondered if he was straight. He had black curly hair and wore a pearl-colored tie and a dark suit that I could tell was expensive, even across the distance of the piano bar. A gentleman—a real one, I'd thought. Now Wendell said he'd met him the summer before, in Mazatlán, at O'Brien's, a bar where Americans hung out. "And that's Alfredo, his boyfriend." I hadn't noticed earlier the slight boy with a wavy black pompadour and a lugubrious expression. Wendell got up and took me and Nicky with him. Mark turned when Wendell tapped him on the shoulder and rose to his feet. They hugged and laughed about meeting once again in a bar, this one a thousand miles from O'Brien's. Then Alfredo stood up, and he and Wendell shook hands formally, and Wendell introduced me and Nicky. "My buddies," he called us.

"Have you ever been to Mazatlán?" Mark turned to me with a bright smile.

"Hey, you two look alike," Nicky piped up from nowhere.

"Yeah, you could be brother and sister!" Wendell grinned.

Mark peered at me. "I'm not that pretty," he said.

When Beverly Shaw came back for her next set, I was torn about where to put my eyes. Mark and I really did look alike. It was like staring into a mirror and seeing an older, polished, masculine version of myself. We'd all moved to a booth, and Mark had ordered a bottle of Mumm's and paid the waitress with a twenty-dollar bill. "*Salud, l'chaim, à votre santé,*" he said, clicking my glass first. Alfredo didn't toast with us. When the champagne came, he got up and went to the men's room, but Mark seemed not to notice that he was gone.

I let Nicky stroke my fingers under the table until Mark offered me a cigarette. I freed my hand to take it from his pack of Kents. Nicky pulled out her lighter, but Mark had already struck a match, and I bent my head toward it awkwardly, feeling Nicky's pique without looking at her. "Bev really knows how to get a number across, like Marlene Dietrich, don't you think?" Mark whispered to me between "I Get a Kick out of You" and "Let Me Go, Lover." "Have you ever seen Dietrich in person? She was at the Palladium last month."

Alfredo never came back to the table. He was chatting animatedly with two men sitting at the bar. He waved an absent-minded good-bye when we passed with Mark, who said he'd walk us to Wendell's car. "I've got a couple of extra tickets for Rubinstein a week from Thursday," Mark said as Nicky and I were getting in. "Alfredo works Thursday nights, and I hate to go alone. Why don't you two come with me?"

"Well . . ." Nicky began and looked at me. I knew she wanted to say no.

"We'd love to," I said quickly, though I had no idea who Rubinstein was.

I was really worried about Nicky now. She was down to seven dollars and looking scared and haggard. "Why don't you go back to school?" I urged Maury's solution as we sat at Coffee Dan's over the coffees I'd bought us.

"With what money?" She shrugged.

"Well, you could get a part-time job to support yourself. Maybe after the first year you could even get a scholarship." But I knew as I said it that it couldn't work. In 1957 poor girls like us could seldom traverse the enormous distance to college. Even to dare the expedition you needed an owl to guide you, a tiger to protect you, and a faithful creature whispering, "No matter what, I love you." If you had all that you might make it, because it could give you power—maybe more than even a chest of gold doubloons could. Without all that, how could even gold doubloons get a girl across the scary terrain?

Nicky had nothing, not the creatures and not the gold. Something else had to be done. "Maybe it's the way you dress," I said, trying to sound as gentle as I could. "I mean, the fly-front pants, the man's shirt . . ."

"Okay," she said as she shredded her paper napkin into bits. "I'll do anything. What do you think I should do?" She sounded almost angry.

"Listen, maybe when you go job hunting, if you had a lady's suit to wear and high heels . . ." Denny knew a tall drag queen, Miss Latisha, who might lend her a skirt and pumps. "Borrow Wendell's jacket," I urged Nicky. That was the way Beverly Shaw dressed. I loved the idea.

Denny came to get me at the Speech Club meeting. He was sweating and panting, as though he'd run for blocks. "Gotta talk to you," he whispered. "It's Nicky!" I followed him into the hall, feeling my throat close in panic. It was something awful, I knew. And it was my fault, because she'd stayed in L.A. for me.

"Tell me!" I shook his shoulder.

"She said to get you . . ." He fought to catch his breath. "She's being arrested. Right now! Coffee Dan's."

We dashed all the way up Highland to the boulevard. When I flagged, Denny grabbed my hand and pulled. "Denny, why? Tell me," I kept shouting. "Tell me!" But he wouldn't stop to say what had happened.

Two police cars were parked in front of Coffee Dan's. Inside, a couple of policemen stood, their guns in holsters, chatting and laughing as though nobody's life was being changed. "Where's Nicky?" I cried to Denny. He shrugged and looked scared. The people in the booths and at the counter were craning their necks to stare at the policemen.

Nicky came out from the ladies' room just then, head bowed, wearing a black skirt, black pumps, Wendell's gray tweed jacket. A woman in a police matron's uniform walked behind her. When Nicky lifted her head, I could see that her face was a sickly white.

"God, they're taking her in," Denny breathed, but the police matron went to join the policemen, and Nicky saw us and ran to me. "Thank God you're here! Oh, Lil, it was so awful." Her eyes looked as though she'd been flogged, and I opened my arms to her in despair.

"You guys, go sit in that booth," whispered Sandra, the plump waitress who knew us, pointing to a table in the back. Denny held Nicky's hand to lead her and Nicky held mine, and we walked in a line that way to the booth, with curious and hostile eyes following us.

The ugly story poured out of Nicky in heaves. She'd gone looking for work all dressed up. She went everywhere, but there was nothing. Finally she decided just to sit in Coffee Dan's and wait for me. "This fat cop comes up out of nowhere. He's swinging a bat in his hand. Right in front of me he stands and says, 'Do you have three articles of men's clothing on you.' I swear, I didn't even know what the hell he was talking about. 'Three articles of men's clothing,' he says again. 'Don't you know there's a law against masquerading?'" Denny looked as puzzled as I was. "Don't you get it?" Nicky cried. "He thought I was a guy dressed like a woman. He says he's taking me in. 'I'm a girl,' I tell him. 'I'm a girl!' But he doesn't believe me. 'I swear I'm a girl!' I keep saying, and finally he says, 'Okay, I'm callin' a police matron, but if you're tryin' to make a fool of me, I'll see to it they throw away the key.' That SOB made me stand up against the wall until this broad arrives, and she takes me to the ladies' room, makes me open my blouse and take down my underpants . . . feels me up everywhere. Oh, Lil!"

"It's okay, Nicky. You'll be okay," Denny said, hugging her to his chest, patting her back as if she were a kid who'd had a bad dream. "Lil loves you, I love you."

She broke from him and clutched my hand now with both of hers, as though she were going under. Beneath the harsh lighting her skin looked like a dead person's, and I could see that her hair was matted with sweat. I clutched back and kept saying, "You're okay, it's okay now!" though I knew it wasn't.

In the booth across from us was a man in a powder-blue polo shirt with his family. His wife wore rhinestone-framed glasses, and their three stair-step little blond girls had matching yellow barrettes in their hair. "I'm as innocent as cabbage," their round faces all proclaimed. They didn't notice us for a while, but then the woman peered through her glasses at Nicky. She must have recognized her as the one the matron had carted off, because, almost in a reflex action, she threw an arm protectively around the daughters on either side of her, like someone warding off evil or a plague.

"Cunt," I sniggered impotently toward Denny. "What's she looking at?"

Nicky was too upset even to notice. I knew she was still back in the ladies' room with the matron who'd made her undress and touched her where she'd never even let a lover touch her. "I'm so ashamed, Lil, so ashamed," she kept saying. And I was so ashamed for her, so angry too about the injustices she'd suffered over and over—her mother first of all, then Carl, the department store interviewer, now the police.

But I was also horrified by Nicky. Why did things always go wrong for her? With all her smartness, why did she always fall prey to the beasts of the world who could tear lone females to pieces with no more conscience than a pack of wolves picking over the bones of a lamb? The kinds of cruelty they inflicted on Nicky were different from those they wanted to inflict on me, but both were deadly. What my time with her was teaching me all over again was that I absolutely had to figure out how a female could arrange her life so the beasts couldn't turn her into carrion.

11 A JEWISH PRINCE

THE BLACK DRESS, one of those Simone had given me, with a drape that began at one shoulder and gathered in low folds at the bosom, leaving the other shoulder naked, was what I put on. Nicky said she didn't want to go, and I knew she didn't want me to either, but I'd never been to a live concert before. There were so many things to make her unhappy now, and my going to hear Rubinstein was just another one. At the start of the week, she'd gotten a job on the lipstick assembly line at Max Factor of Hollywood; she had to stand on her feet and mix vats for $1.25 an hour. By the end of her eight-hour shift, she was splotched orange and red and pink and plum from her hair to her soles. She washed, she scrubbed, but always traces remained on her skin, and strange chemical odors exuded from every pore. Nothing could get rid of them. When she pulled me close, I couldn't help wincing. "I know I smell loathsome. I'm sorry," she said, but she kissed me anyway, and I let her because I felt guilty, though I couldn't have said about what.

The lobby of the Philharmonic Auditorium was a mass of ermines and mink stoles and tuxedoes and dinner jackets. I felt as though I'd walked onto the set of a wonderfully sophisticated movie and become part of it. Wasn't that Robert Mitchum over there? Ruth Hussey? And the air was softly fragrant with perfumes, not like Emir, which I recognized now as being cheap in its crude assault on the olfactory nerves. No, these perfumes played lightly with the senses. They made you want to draw closer. They seduced you by their subtle complexity.

"I'd say we make as elegant a couple as anyone here," Mark whispered out of the side of his mouth and grinned as though he were enjoying himself hugely. We stood in the lobby bar, daiquiris in hand. He was even more good-looking than I'd remembered, with his black curls tumbling over his forehead and his dark eyes. I liked the audacity, the *chutzpah*, of his red bow tie and the matching red lining of the black cape he wore over a black tuxedo. Before the buzzer rang, he ordered a second daiquiri and tossed it off, then offered me his arm. We walked to our seats down a red-carpeted aisle. I loved our masquerade. Here we were, passing as a straight couple among all these worldly concertgoers. It was a delicious secret between us.

My own secrets I didn't share with him. What would he think if he knew everything about me?

In our second-row seats I copied Mark, applauding spiritedly when two men followed the orchestra onto the stage. "The short one's Rubinstein," Mark whispered. "Artur" was the first name of the dapper little man with crinkly gray hair who now took his seat on the piano bench with a flourish, tossing the swallowtails of his coat out behind him, his bearing straight as a rapier; already I was enchanted by the diminutive, charming figure. "Brahms's D-minor Concerto," Mark whispered in my ear. I nodded and let myself be transported, at first by Rubinstein's look of intense pleasure at what he was producing, and then, slowly, by the flow and the passion of the music. I found myself living inside each note as it sounded, bouncing rapturously with the pianist when he hit the great chords along with the orchestra, pulling deep into myself in the soulful measures when he closed his eyes. I'd never known that sound could be as sensual as touch. How deprived I'd been. At a pause I joined with great energy the smattering of claps around me, puzzled that there wasn't thunderous applause. "Don't they like him?" I whispered to Mark.

"Generally, you don't applaud between the pauses, 'movements' they're called," he whispered back.

He told me more about being a child psychologist at Children's Hospital as we watched the waiters at Lawry's bustle about, carving after-theater prime ribs on big silver carts. He'd gotten a Ph.D. in psychology at Claremont Men's College, had been working at the hospital for three years, lived with Genghis and Khan, his two Siamese cats, in the Los Feliz Hills. Alone.

"But Alfredo?" I sat far back in the red-upholstered booth, sipping at a glass of velvety burgundy that Mark had ordered.

"Oh, I put him through the Otis Art Institute. We still do things together, but now he's working for a hotshot designer and wants to live on his own." Mark ran a light finger absent-mindedly around the rim of his glass. "The truth is, we had two great years and then a lousy one. You get 'em young and worshipful, show 'em the world, and then they change." He shaped his lips to look comically rueful. "He says he doesn't need a papa anymore. He's twenty-three and thinks I'm an old man. Do I look like an old man to you?" Mark laughed.

"Of course not. How old are you?" As soon as the question left my mouth, I worried that now he'd ask the same of me.

"Thirty-four. And you?"

I'd take the risk. I wanted a friendship with him in which I didn't have to hide everything. "'Bout half that." I spilled the words out quickly.

"That's terrific," he said with a laugh. "I love it! You handle yourself like a mature woman. So you live with your parents? I thought you and Nicky lived together."

"I live with my mother and stepfather. They're a bit unusual." I'd risk more, but how much? "They speak mostly Yiddish," I began.

"You're Jewish!" Mark exclaimed. "Well, we have that in common. I was adopted by gentiles, but I'm a Jew through my mother. See?" He took off his bow tie and opened his shirt collar, exposing a gold Star of David that hung in the dense, curly hairs on his chest.

"Come to dinner on Saturday," Mark said when he dropped me off in front of the Fountain Avenue Court Bungalows.

"Nicky too?" My guilt had kicked in . . . and besides, I'd never been to a man's house alone.

"Play hooky," he laughed. "I'll pick you up at seven." It would be okay, I told myself, like with Eddy or Denny or Wendell.

. . .

"I have a date tonight with a Jewish doctor," I called my aunt to announce on Saturday afternoon. Albert heard "doctor" all the way from the living room, where I stood at the telephone, to the kitchen table, where he sat playing cards. "A doctor?" he asked my mother, pronouncing the word with reverence, as was his wont. "What kind of doctor?" As I dressed that evening, I could hear him again telling my mother, who still hadn't figured out what her husband did for a living, about "my boss, Dr. Nathan Friedman, the world-famous pathologist."

"Put on a nice dress before Mark gets here," I'd begged my mother, but Albert and I still weren't talking, so I couldn't make sartorial requests of him. He'd gotten sloppy-looking; his shirts and pants didn't fit anymore because of my mother's heavy cooking, and he wore a grease-stained hat that he never took off until he went to bed at night. I hated the thought of Mark's seeing him. Albert was sitting at the kitchen table with his solitaire deck when Mark rang the bell, and just as I was about to whisper to my mother to please close the kitchen door, Albert jumped up and closed it himself.

Mark wore gray wool pants and an off-white cable-knit ski sweater, a bold design with a black stripe that started at the shoulders and ran down the sleeves. I thought he looked stunningly handsome. "This is Dr. Mark Letson," I said, introducing him to my mother.

He smiled charmingly. "I noticed your beautiful mezuzah," he said, touching with respectful fingers the silver-plated object on the inside doorpost. "From Israel?"

My mother had put on lipstick and high heels for the occasion, but now I noticed the inch of gray and brown roots that peeked out from her dyed black hair. Why hadn't I asked her to go to the beauty parlor?

She was at my heels when I went to my room to get a jacket. "Lilly, such a handsome gentleman!" she squealed and clasped her hands and looked as though I'd presented her with a mink coat. "Drive careful with Lilly," she instructed Mark as we were leaving.

"What a sweet lady," he said, holding open the door of his white convertible for me. "I can see you're really loved."

A cedar-scented fire crackled in the fireplace, and Mark had prepared a pitcher of martinis for us. "Let me show you my sanctum," he offered. I followed him about, a long-stemmed glass in hand, the stuffed green olive sloshing in gin and vermouth. Genghis and Khan shadowed us, winding their tan and brown bodies around my feet whenever we stopped and brushing against my legs. "They like you." Mark smiled. "They're not always that friendly to strangers."

The five rooms of the house overflowed with objects—big vases that looked as if they were made of lapis and jade, small elephants of crystal. "This is Quan Yin, goddess of mercy," he said, lifting from a marble shelf a two-foot statue that was carved entirely of ivory and caressing it with gentle fingers. "I picked her up in Hong Kong." Lithographs crowded the walls—Chagall, Kollwitz, Miró—Mark mentioned names I'd never heard before. An open armoire contained nothing but neatly arranged record albums—Classical, Opera, Cabaret Music, Broadway Musicals, he'd labeled the collections. What would it be like to live in the midst of all this, I wondered, letting the fantasy carry me to some not-too-distant time when I, a psychologist like him maybe . . . a lawyer or writer . . . could dwell with such fascinating objects, such artifacts of beauty and fine taste.

We dined at a white-linen-covered table lit with white candles in bright silver candlesticks. Mark served paella in celadon dishes and sangria that he poured from a cut-crystal pitcher. "Bolero" alternated with Marlene Dietrich's throaty tones and Yma Sumac's eerie chanting about virgin maidens, and Mark told me about saffron and Seville oranges and the Spanish Civil War and the evils of Franco. I listened to all of it scarcely daring to breathe, searching my brain for appropriate comments. "Sounds like the Spanish Civil War was a prologue to World War Two," I said.

"Exactly." He beamed, like a teacher with an A student. "The fascists saw what Franco could get away with, and then there was no stopping them."

Mark calls every evening. I grapple with physics homework, bored, wishing my high school career at an end, and the phone rings. I hope it's Mark. I'm flattered that someone like him thinks I'm interesting enough to bother with. My mother knocks at my door. "It's Mark." She pronounces his name with reverence.

I don't say much in our telephone conversations, but he loves to tell stories, to teach. He has all the knowledge in the universe to share, and he's discovered what a willing pupil I am, how awed I am by the range of what he knows, his passions, his convictions.

He comes to take me to dinner; to a coffeehouse just opened on the Sunset Strip, where beatniks go; to the Huntington Theater to see Long Day's Journey into Night. *At a late supper I tell him I did a scene from* Anna Christie *when I studied at Geller's. He draws me out, wants to hear all about my life, listens, nods sagely at everything, even the stories about the Silent Film Star, about Jan. His eyes tear when I tell him about my mother's dead brother and sisters, her stories of the shtetl, our life in East L.A. "Obsessive-compulsive." He gives me a free psychological evaluation of my mother's past anguish. We go to the Club Laurel again, and though I still want to put my lips on Beverly Shaw's belly and slowly travel south, I like sitting next to Mark while she sings to us. Do people think we're straight tourists?*

We shake hands warmly, fervently, at the end of every evening. "This was wonderful, I had a terrific time," we tell each other. Sometimes he pecks my cheek with chaste lips.

We are great friends, two homosexuals. We just love to be together. If we pass for a straight couple to a blind, hostile world, so much the better.

Albert and I still do not talk, but I know what will bring a bit of peace and respect to my mother: "Dad"—I force myself to utter strange words I have never used before—"this is Dr. Mark Letson. Mark, my father," and Mark offers a friendly, professional hand. Albert glows; I feel I have done a mitzvah, *a good deed. Of course Mark knows already that this man is my mother's husband and not my real father, that I have no father. "No, not a prefrontal lobotomy," he assures me and laughs. "Trepanning, it's called. They did it a lot in primitive medicine—drilled a hole in the skull to relieve pressure on the brain."*

What doesn't Mark know?

"Yes, I'm still going out with the Jewish doctor," I tell my aunt. "He's wonderful," I gush. "Tall, dark, and handsome!"—an American expression she knows. "What are his intentions?" my aunt asks.

We sped down Sunset Boulevard to the Sea Lion in Malibu one evening. I was telling Mark about how unhappy Nicky was at Max Factor's, what a good writer she was, how she was wasting her talent. "How's Alfredo?" I asked him next.

"He's out of my life," Mark said, lips tight, "for good now. His idea."

I was surprised by how I felt. As though my pockets were filled with secret rubies.

The tables at the Sea Lion were lit by soft candlelight. The waves washed against the illuminated rocks below, then crashed on the windows with a scary, delightful roar. "You have to try the sand dabs," Mark said over our martinis. "They're the best in the world." He ordered for me. "And a bottle of Paul Masson chablis, very cold, please.

"Passion and domesticity don't go together," Mark opined as the waiter collected our salad plates. He signaled the waiter to remove the empty bottle from the ice bucket and ordered a second. "I lived with Raymond for six years, Alfredo for three. I don't know what the solution is." Mark frowned. "But I know that for me it just doesn't work."

I agreed with him. I couldn't imagine living with Jan . . . certainly not with Nicky.

"My aunt asked the other day what your intentions were," I told him over the Baked Alaska. He could see from my expression that I thought it amusing, the way we were fooling the world. Nobody around us could guess the gay things we said together.

"Honorable, tell her." His warm brown eyes were twinkling.

In between school and going out with Mark I studied for the Scholastic Aptitude Test. Maury Colwell had said that much depended on it, and I still took his tenets seriously, even though my powerful need for his approval seemed to have dissolved in Mark's sunny friendship, and I seldom saw him now.

Some evenings, Nicky came to sit with me as I studied. "You could go to Cal at Berkeley. I hear that's a great school," she fantasized, "and we could live on a houseboat in Sausalito. I know I could really write there."

I turned my eyes up at her. "With what money?" I said. "Sweetie, I'm studying synonyms and antonyms," and I scrutinized the page again.

She pushed her chair back with a clatter and stood over me. "Look at this." It was a small pocket calendar that she tossed right on top of my SAT booklet. "The check marks are for all the evenings you spent with me, and the *x*'s are for all the evenings you spent with him . . . that I know about." She flipped weeks, stabbed at days. "Look at it. Practically no check marks. Full of *x*'s!" Her voice was high and grating. "If you have to study so much, how can you always be running around with that faggot?"

I closed the calendar, closed my SAT booklet, put them down on the floor at my feet, stared at Nicky calmly. "I'll probably marry Mark," I told her.

She looked at me as if I'd uttered gobbledygook. "But you're both gay!" she finally exclaimed.

"It would be a front marriage," I ad-libbed. I knew from the gay boys that front marriages were common in Hollywood with gay movie stars. "Look, my mother's upset because I said I'd move out when I go to college," I told Nicky. "The only way she'd accept my moving is if I get married."

It was partly true. I hadn't yet discussed moving with my mother, but I knew already what she would say if I said I needed to live in a college dorm. How could she even comprehend the idea of college? She would cry and beg me not to leave. I'd be trapped. I'd never be able to go away to college. But if I married a Jewish doctor—that she'd understand—and I could go to USC or UCLA while I lived with Mark. I couldn't imagine a future for myself if I didn't find a way to get out now.

"But what about me?" Nicky cried.

"What about you? I'd still see you. We'd still be like we are now. This is just . . ."

She flung open the door with such force that it banged against the wall and books tumbled from a shelf. She stormed out. I didn't see her again for seventeen years.

Mark called while I could still hear Nicky's heavy steps thundering down the walk, while I was still wrestling with the impulse to chase after her and say I was sorry. I sat on the plastic-covered orange chair in the living room while I talked to him, and I could see my mother at the kitchen table, picking up the gin rummy cards Albert had dealt. My hand that held the phone was shaking. "I guess it's over between me and Nicky," I told Mark. "I said the nuttiest thing, and it really upset her." I whispered so my mother and Albert wouldn't hear.

"What?" Mark sounded concerned.

"I don't know why I said it," I laughed self-consciously. "I told her you and I are getting married."

There was a long pause at the other end of the wire. Then Mark said, "Let's."

I'd led him there, but why? How could I marry a man? Except for Maury Colwell, my experiences with men had been grievous. I'd call Mark back. I grabbed at the phone. I'd never even felt close to one of them; they were as alien to me as apes. Suddenly I couldn't remember his number. I'd tell him that the comedy routine we just did was as funny as George Burns and Gracie Allen. We'd both laugh.

No. Why should I? Marrying him would solve lots of problems, and it wouldn't be at all the way it had been with other men. First of all, we were both gay; it would be a front marriage, plain and simple. And second, Mark had none of the bad features of other men. And he had all the good ones: He knew things that were a mystery to me; he knew how to maneuver in the world. In fact, his good points were so numerous that I wondered what I had to offer a man like that. Maybe he thought that as a child psychologist he needed a wife so that people would think he was heterosexual. Okay with me! I could help him just as he was helping me with my mother and aunt. And he'd said he thought that passion and domesticity don't go together. That must mean he didn't want to live with a man again, so we could be companions forever.

"He proposed!" I sprang in the air as though catapulted from a sling, as though joy had made me wild. "He proposed!" I cried again, unsure myself whether the joy was contrived for my mother's sake or real.

Albert and my mother jumped up from the kitchen table and came running, both of them. "You'll move away?" My mother paled. "Lilly, no! When? You're so young."

"*Mazel tov*," Albert shouted, forgetting forever the time he called me a tramp and we grappled with each other. He extended a hand of forgiveness and congratulations to his daughter who was going to marry a doctor.

Three days later I left the house in the morning as though I were going to school and waited for Mark to pick me up on the corner. "We'll go to Tijuana. They don't have age restrictions there." He'd planned it out very practically. "In L.A. your mother would have to come with us or we couldn't get a license."

"What a lark," I thought as we drove out of L.A., and my heart sang. But my mood turned as heavy and gray as the lowering sky before long. What was I doing? As we zoomed past oil rigs near Long Beach, I realized it was already too late to stop.

It was Rae I called afterward, collect, from a Texaco station near the San Diego border while the attendant pumped gas into Mark's car. Rain hit the glass phone booth in great slashing splotches, and I shivered in the damp wind and the dark. "I just married the doctor," I told Rae, weeping real tears into the phone, wiping my nose furtively on the sleeve of my jacket. "Call my mother and tell her."

"*A dank Gott*," Rae cried, "the best thing! Now finally you'll have a good home."

We drove through the rain looking for the El Cortez Hotel, and Mark said softly, contemplatively now, as though he'd been thinking about it for a long time, "Ours is the kind of relationship where we reach out to each other with one hand and to other people with the other."

I nodded. "*Il va sans dire*," I answered, showing off a phrase he'd taught me. He turned to me and we grinned in complicity.

"They've got a good restaurant downstairs at the El Cortez," Mark said.

I'd learn how to drive and he'd get me a car, he told me over the oysters. "From my house it's an easy jaunt to USC or UCLA." In a few months, when I graduated from high school, we'd go to Mexico together for the summer. He'd show me Mazatlán and Guadalajara and Acapulco. His supervisor at the hospital had told him about a summer lectureship he might apply for, in psychology, at the University of Mexico. Would I like to live in Mexico City for six weeks?

"Should I get a room with twin beds?" Mark asked after dinner.

"Nope. I promise not to bite in the middle of the night . . . or give you any fright," I said solemnly, and we giggled like teenagers because I'd had two margaritas and Mark had had three, and we'd finished a whole bottle of Chianti with dinner. Now I felt buoyant again. I couldn't even remember what had upset me so much when I called Rae. We sipped Kahlua over ice for a nightcap; then I waited in the lobby while he arranged for the room, and we followed the red-suited bellhop to the elevator, holding each other about the waist.

I stripped to my panties and bra and slipped between cold sheets. Mark switched off the bed lamp before he undressed. A beam of light from the corridor shone under the door, and I watched his white shorts moving about in the semidarkness as he folded his jacket, tie, shirt, and then his pants over the arms of a chair, then placed his shoes and socks beside it. I couldn't stop the shivers, and a swarm of nameless emotions buzzed in me. He climbed into bed, still wearing his shorts.

"Goodnight, Lil." He turned toward me, and I felt his lips soft on my cheek; I kissed him back the same way. Now my nervousness dissolved. I was safe with my dear, dear friend. I'd been almost certain I would be.

We both lay on our backs. When our fingers touched by chance, we clasped hands and lay with them lightly intertwined. "You're very dear to me, Lil. I want to take such good care of you," Mark crooned in the darkness, and my breath caught. No man had ever taken care of me. I couldn't even imagine what that meant. "You'll be as safe with me, my dear one, as in your mother's arms," he said, and I drifted off into sweet sleep.

I awoke to light and a whiff of cinnamony Mexican hot chocolate. Mark was dressed. He'd gone down and brought back a large pot and two mugs from the restaurant, and we lounged together luxuriously, sipping the still-steaming brew. I pulled the blanket up to my chin for warmth, and he kicked off his shoes and sprawled on top of the covers, reaching over from time to time to refill our empty cups from the big silver pot he'd placed on the nightstand. How pleasant this all was. He told me about his travels in Mexico, about the weirdly shaped giant rock formations off the coast of Mazatlán. "We'll see them this summer. You get the best view from O'Brien's. Fabulous!" Later he got up and stood at the window, looking to see if it was still raining. I watched the back of his head. I loved the way his curly hair came to a *V* in the little hollow at his neck, making him look so vulnerable, like a kid almost. I was jolted: I did love this man I'd just married.

"I think it's going to clear," he said hopefully.

In the hotel room I'd felt snug and at ease, but once in the car, heading north in another driving rain, I was beset with anxieties again. I imagined my mother weeping like an abandoned child. I was gripped by images of doom—my mother withering away, paralyzed by a stroke, choking and blue-faced with apoplexy, because I'd deserted her, left her alone with Albert in that sham of a marriage I'd tricked her into. I said nothing to Mark. How could he understand?

Off the L.A. coast, Mark headed east on Sunset Boulevard. On Highland Avenue a fire engine shrieked and gained on us, its red ogre eyes whirling. Mark pulled over, and the fire engine turned in front of us, toward Fountain, on the way to some terrible disaster. What if it were my mother? I saw our bungalow in flames, Mommy inside, trapped.

"I've got to make a phone call," I begged Mark when we were at Sunset and Vermont. I couldn't tell him to turn around and drive back to the Fountain Avenue Court Bungalows. He'd think I was crazy. "Can you stop at the next gas station? Please?"

"We'll be home in just fifteen minutes," he said reasonably. "Don't you want to wait?"

"Please, please." My voice cracked with urgency, and he looked at me, puzzled, but he pulled into the first gas station with a telephone sign. I couldn't help it. I couldn't wait another minute.

"When am I going to see you?" my mother cried. "Lilly, why did you run away? Are you going to have a baby?" It was half horror and half hope that I heard in her voice.

The Jewish wedding was Rae's idea. She'd planned for years how it had to be when I got married. "You're all we have left in the world. No more family but you," she said to persuade me to let her stage a wedding when I called her the next day from my new home.

"Sure," I answered magnanimously. Actually, I was feeling quite a bit like a success by now. Against all odds, I'd given her the fabled Jewish prince. I'd really done it! And my mother was happy, too. We lived only a few miles away, and I promised to bring my husband to the Fountain Avenue Court Bungalows for Friday dinners. She was ecstatic about the prospect. She'd be making Sabbath dinners for her married daughter and her handsome son-in-law who was a doctor. It was almost as good as if I'd become a movie star.

"Is it okay?" I asked Mark anxiously later. "The wedding? The dinners?"

"Why not? We're partners in crime," he said and laughed.

He was joking of course, but it hit me like a lash: I'm cheating them. The whole point had been to get them to believe this was a real marriage, and it wasn't. I made no answer to his quip; instead I busied myself hanging my clothes on the side of the bedroom closet he'd cleared for me. But the sting of it—*crime*—wouldn't let go of me.

But maybe it wasn't cheating. Mark and I did love each other—not the way my mother and aunt thought, but still it was love. In a way it was even the kind of love Rae had always said she wanted for me: someone who would take care of me. Wasn't that exactly what Mark had said he'd do—take good care of me? They'd even used the same words, though I wasn't really sure what either of them meant. I still hoped to go to college to become someone who could take care of herself. But what was important now, it seemed to me, was that Mark's intentions truly were what my aunt had hoped. So we weren't really cheating after all. I took comfort in the logic. "Done!" I emerged from the closet and went to sit at Mark's side, content again with the wisdom of my marriage.

. . .

Mark invited to the wedding an older couple he'd never mentioned before, Gilbert Pollack, a bony, stooped dentist he knew from the hospital, and his wife, Vera, a plump, matronly lady who fawned over Mark, straightening his tuxedo jacket, adjusting his curls around his white yarmulke, as though he were her kid. They were the ones who said they'd take him out for a drink while my mother fussed with my veil in the dressing room of the Litvisheh Verein Hall. "He's so nervous, like a boy. Look, his face is as white as his yarmulke." Vera's laugh was high and tinkly. "We'll get him out of your hair and bring him back in plenty of time to walk down the aisle." I glanced at my husband. He really did look scared. We smiled wistfully and waved fingers at each other as his friends led him off.

While Rae tacked up a dart that had unraveled at the waist of my white dress, my mother brought me a 7-Up so I wouldn't get thirsty while I was under the *chupa*, the marriage canopy. Albert came in with his solitaire deck, which he kept in the jacket pocket of his stiff new suit, and he told me I looked very nice and that my mother was so proud of me. I got up and kissed his cheek and said I was happy he had come to my wedding. Then he sat at a dressing table, where he played a couple of games away from the crowd, and out he went again. I could hear a din of voices, mostly Yiddish, coming from the hall. A song began in a screeching voice that wavered up and down, and then a few steadier voices joined in and a smattering of palms beat time on the tables. "*Shpilt oyf a chasene tantz, Greyt un das chupa kledyl*," they sang in Yiddish —"Play the wedding dance, Prepare the wedding dress, Toward him you'll go like a princess when he returns from battlefields and oceans." I could see how proud Rae was that her friends and neighbors were singing a bridal song for me. She virtually strutted on her short legs, in her long shiny dress, and I wanted to cry because I'd made her so happy. My mother, her eyes bright, sat close to me and along with the singing voices that came from the hall she sang-talked, the way she had when I was a child.

After a while the singing stopped, and I could hear only the drone of chatter. It was almost six o'clock, when the wedding was supposed to begin. But Mark wasn't back yet. My mother left me and went to peer out the darkening window.

As the room grew dimmer with the setting sun, my aunt's face changed. Her mouth became tight. She looked at her watch every few seconds and then got up and stood at the dressing room door, where she could see who was and who wasn't in the hall. Mr. Bergman came in, his daughter and granddaughter behind him. He snapped on a light, and I heard the concerned *buzz-buzz* of his whispers to Rae and hers back to him.

"Congratulations," said Diane, the granddaughter who was about my age, but she looked at me as though we'd just learned I had terminal brain cancer.

"Thanks," I answered in a too-loud voice.

At six-thirty the rabbi came to ask my aunt when he could begin.

My mother moaned.

"*Vus fur a finsterer nacht*, what kind of dark night is this?" my aunt said, groaning.

Did Gilbert have an accident? Maybe Mark was in the hospital. "Stop it!" I yelled at my mother and aunt. "They're just caught in the traffic. What are you carrying on about?" Had he changed his mind? Maybe he'd taken one look at the funny wedding guests, in their ill-fitting fancy clothes and terrible accents, and decided he wasn't going to get mixed up in such a family.

Mark returned about six forty-five, his eyes unfocused, his mouth slack. Gilbert's arm was around his waist, keeping him upright, and Vera's hand was at his shoulder, steering him through the dressing room door. I wanted to hide my husband, spirit him off, so my mother and Rae wouldn't see him this way.

"*Oy*, God in heaven," my mother shrieked and grasped the windowsill.

"Coffee," Gilbert mouthed to me. He and Vera maneuvered Mark to a chair and helped him sag onto it.

My aunt shoved Gilbert and Vera aside and pounced on Mark. "What's going on?" the foghorn blared. "How you can disappear like that, with the rabbi waiting, and Lilly, your wife?"

"Rae, stop it, please," I implored, trying to pull her away. She stood planted, breathing hard, glaring at him, but said nothing more. I rushed to get coffee from the big samovar in the hall. "Leave him alone!" I shouted over my shoulder.

I galloped back with the steaming black brew, ignoring the curious eyes of the wedding guests, and I placed it to Mark's lips. "It's okay, just drink, drink," I encouraged him.

"Red-dy," Mark slurred now. "I'm in fine father . . . feather. Look!" and he rose to his feet, shrugging off Vera's steadying hand. He swayed toward me, arm extended. "'s get married," he said.

"*Oy, Gott!*" my mother shrieked again.

"What kind of lousy friends are you to go get him drunk!" my aunt hollered in Vera's face. "Skunks!"

"Stop!" I shouted at my aunt. "It's okay now. We're starting." There was nothing for it but to go ahead. I turned to Mark, keeping my voice steady: "Can you walk?" I took his arm with a steely hand, ready to hold him up if necessary.

Mr. Bergman, Rae, Mark, Lil, Mother, and Albert: "No one could mistake Mark for sober."

"Yep." His mouth pursed in concentration and he put a foot forward.

"He had a lot, but he didn't seem drunk until he stood up," Gilbert lamented to the air.

I was supposed to walk to the canopy holding Mr. Bergman's arm, and Mark was supposed to be standing there to greet me. But I couldn't be concerned with such formalities now. I guided my husband down the aisle. We passed Denny first, in his powder-blue tuxedo and pink ruffled shirt. He blinked with astonishment. As Mark and I stumbled in tandem I caught quick glimpses of other faces. They mirrored Denny's. Nobody could mistake Mark for sober.

When the sour-faced rabbi saw us coming, he jumped to his feet and took his place under the blue and white velvet canopy. Would we make it there? Without Mark's falling down? The walk seemed interminable. The rabbi waited, his expression blank, for us to halt in front of him. Finally he uttered the few words that would make us man and wife under the law of ancient Israel. That done, he placed the wrapped glass near Mark's shoe and told him he must smash it. Mark lifted his foot gingerly and crunched. Then he screwed up his face and bawled like a baby.

"*Mazel tov!*" the guests shouted dutifully, as though nothing at all unusual had happened, and there was a patter of applause.

12 A MARRIED WOMAN

Our life together is a dream and a nightmare.

Mark takes me to San Francisco, a long weekend—to Aïda at the opera, to Anastasia at the Curran Theater, to the Top of the Mark and the penthouse restaurant at the top of the Sir Francis Drake. In between he expounds—on Maria Callas, Ingmar Bergman, Rosa Parks, the 1957 Civil Rights Act. He's eloquent, ardent, and I eat it all up, along with the caviar on toast points, the tournedos, the crème brulée. We visit all the gay places, Gordon's, the Paper Doll, the Black Cat. "That cute one with the curly blond hair, over at the bar, he's cruising you," I say to Mark. "There's a Barbara Stanwyck look-alike in the booth behind you, and she's sizing you up," he leans across the table to whisper. He smiles at the cute blond; I turn around and, with my eyes, flirt in the direction of Barbara Stanwyck. But Mark and I go back to our hotel together, slightly tipsy and very contented, holding each other around the waist.

When we're home, Mark sometimes cooks for us—bouillabaisse, quiche lorraine, osso bucco—succulent dishes I'd never even heard of before; and I'm his awed little sous-chef, chopping, dicing, cracking eggs. Often we go out, to the Ginza where I learn to eat with chopsticks, to La Chic Parisienne where he orders for both of us because only he can read the menu. We have cocktails and wines and liqueurs, and by the time we get home it's ten o'clock or eleven. That's when I begin my homework—Latin, trig, physics, advanced comp. I get four or five hours' sleep most nights, and, though I know they're lying on their pillows in a corner of the kitchen, sometimes I see Genghis and Khan slinking around the living room as I sit on the white leather couch and study. Sleep deprivation makes me hallucinate, but I don't care because we had a marvelous evening.

When I take the SAT, early on a Saturday morning after four hours of sleep, I see Genghis and Khan parading up and down the aisles of the auditorium, and I put my pencil down to watch them. "Time!" the monitor calls, and I'm horrified.

One Saturday we went back to the Sea Lion. We giggled all the way home about an officious waiter with a red toupee who began every sentence, "Well, my dear sir and madam," and we stumbled through the front door together, still silly, leaning against each other for strength. Then Mark stood upright and looked at me seriously. "Oh, my dear Lil," he said. "I'm so happy you're here," and we held each other tightly.

"I love you," I told him.

"I know you do," Mark said, still holding me, and then after what seemed to be a long time, "but only like your brother, I guess."

I never had a brother. I wouldn't know what it felt like. "No," I answered slowly, my hand on his cheek now. "Like you're really my husband." That night we made love.

I'm not at all frightened or repelled as I always thought I would be with a man, nor is it as it was with Jan, nor as I'd lived it so intensely in my imagination with Beverly Shaw. No volcanoes erupt. I feel no overwhelming lust in him or for him, but I love to hold him afterward, and I love the smell of his men's cologne and his shampoo and the feel of his strong back under my hands and his tight, muscled buttocks. When I'm sitting up late with my homework and he's gone to bed, I'm tantalized by the urge to wrap around him so that we are like two spoons, or to curl my fingers in the lush black hairs of his chest. I never loved a man before, and it feels bizarre. But how could I not love Mark? Mornings when I wake up before he does I study his face—his long, thick lashes, the strong cleft in his chin, the delicate pink of his lips. I touch his cheek, gently, so he won't awaken. I love his face. This is the face I adore, *I tell myself.*

But Mark drinks. He can drink and drink and still be fine, just as in the days before the wedding. Then he has the one sip that makes too many, and in a fingersnap "fine" slips into dead drunk. Nowadays he's not as careful as he used to be to stop short of that one sip.

If we're in a restaurant, I sometimes have to wrestle him before I can grab the car key from his tight fist and sit on it or drop it down my blouse; but I don't know how to drive. "Please call a cab!" I beg the waiter by mouthed words and urgent looks, please help me lead my husband out and settle him into the waiting taxi. If the waiter takes his arm, he'll pretend for a few minutes to be less drunk than he is and make himself stay on his feet. I can't handle his dead weight by myself. I hate the wobbly-legged, slack-jawed creature that's taken over Mark.

If that one sip too many comes when we're at home, it's worse. From the cupboard Mark grabs each and every wineglass, martini glass, whiskey sour glass—every vessel that will break—and he hurls them one by one against the kitchen wall, possessed, sobbing as though his heart has shattered into shards along with the crystal.

"Stop!" I cry the first time. I try to restrain his pitching hand, and he pulls back and slugs me in the eye by accident. I'm too baffled and scared to try again. When the glass smashing starts, I skitter to the bathroom and lock the door; I sit on the edge of the bathtub, rocking myself, until it's done. Who is this stranger going crazy outside the door? Then when the noise stops, I dart out and slip soundlessly into bed, but I can't close my eyes. I stare into the darkness, apprehensive. When I feel his side of the mattress sagging, I turn to the wall.

In the morning the other Mark is back. He sweeps all the bits of crystal into a dustpan and deposits them in the kitchen garbage pail. "Guess I really acted out last night. Sorry," he says, sheepish, after a while.

"Mark, what happened? Tell me why," I implore.

Instead of answering, he drives to Beverly Hills to buy more glasses from which we'll have our wine and cocktails until the next time he has one sip too many and snaps again.

What's the cause of the terrible anguish that pours out with such violence when he's drunk? He will not tell me.

"I don't understand," I said wearily one morning as he swept up shards after another Saturday explosion. Still Mark said nothing.

But later, when I sat with *The Aeneid* on my lap, straining to concentrate on my translation of Dido's speech, Mark slouched in the white leather armchair across from me and said, as though continuing a dialogue, "Did I ever tell you when I found out I was adopted? I was eighteen—the day I was leaving for the navy—and that bitch who called herself my mother all my life says to me, 'I have to tell you that you weren't born into this family.' Just like that!" He grabbed a Kent out of the pack on the coffee table, struck a match, inhaled with fury. "Just before I have to go off to fight a war. Can you imagine that?"

"Oh, Mark," I cried, forcing aside the anger I'd felt all day. I closed Virgil, went to perch on the arm of his chair, to kiss the top of his head and nuzzle him to my chest. He sat, still weighted with outrage. "Do you know anything about your real parents?" I asked, feeling the pain with him now as vividly as if his adoptive mother's betrayal had happened that morning.

"Only that my mother was a Jew, a whore," he said, his mouth working as it had the night before when the cocktail shaker hit the wall.

I was accepted only at UCLA, with a small scholarship, just enough to pay for books and the $108 tuition. Nothing would be left over, not even for lunches on campus. I was disappointed but not worried yet, because Maury Colwell had told me that Hollywood High would probably give me a good alma mater scholarship since I'd been a public speaking star for two years. June 14, 1958—I sat in white cap and gown, nervous but hopeful, under the hot sun at the Hollywood Bowl, where the school held its graduation ceremony: Before we filed up to the stage to get our diplomas, the vice principal called out the names of one scholarship recipient after another, more than a dozen of them, and each one leapt up to energetic applause as he announced through the microphone what they'd done for the school. Their accomplishments boomed out to the audience of five or six hundred and echoed on the thousands of vacant seats beyond. My name was not called.

"You're married already. Why do you want to go to college?" Miss Brooks, my advanced composition teacher, had said when I'd told her weeks before that I'd been admitted to UCLA. Was she serious? I could see no trace of teasing on her thin lips.

Angry tears had stung my eyes, as though she'd accused me of wrongdoing. "What does my being married have to do with whether I go to college?" I'd managed to say. Early in the semester she'd given me an A+ on my essay on *Jude the Obscure;* she said it wasn't a grade she gave lightly, that I ought to be an English major in college. But probably, when it had been time to decide who'd get the alma mater scholarships, all the teachers thought what Miss Brooks said: I was a married woman now, and married women had no reason to go to college.

It's okay, I told myself there at the Hollywood Bowl. I'd be a UCLA student in the fall anyway. Though I couldn't bear to ask Mark for spending money, I wouldn't have to worry about room and board at least, and I could get a part-time job. It would be fine.

We left for Mexico the next week, after we took Genghis and Khan to the Pollacks and most of my clothes and Mark's books and records and some miscellaneous boxes to my old room at the Fountain Avenue Court Bungalows. ("So far away! She's never been so far away!" my mother cried to Mark.)

"Why can't we just leave everything here?" I'd asked him the night before, puzzled when he began wrapping crystal brandy snifters in old newspapers and said we had to store whatever we weren't taking to Mexico.

"It's silly to pay rent while we're gone," he said. "We'll find a new place when we get back."

"But . . . don't you own this house?" As I pulled glasses from the shelf along with him, I searched my mind, confused now, trying to remember why I'd thought the house belonged to him.

"No, of course not. I've been renting."

"Well . . . but the furniture . . ."

"The place came furnished," he said a little impatiently, as though I'd missed the obvious.

I never asked about the jade and lapis vases and all the lithographs, or the crystal elephant or the ivory statue; but after we left the house in the Los Feliz Hills that June I never saw them again.

It was night when we arrived at the little Mazatlán airport. To a dark, squat man standing beside a taxi Mark spoke in Spanish, giving the address of the apartment he'd rented. Cigarette dangling from his lips, the man piled our suitcases into the trunk and opened the back door for us, never making eye contact with me. Then he sped us down long, bumpy stretches of unlit road in the rattling automobile, passing clusters of dilapidated little houses and stray mongrels who barked at our tires and chased us till we were gone from their village. The heavy, humid air wafted through the open window, its smell foreign and exciting; but it made me feel lonely too. I reached for Mark's hand in the dark, and he let me hold it.

Then lights loomed up before us and, soon, lively avenues. "*Aqui, aqui,*" Mark said, directing the driver down a narrow street. The car slowed and then stopped in front of a two-story building with a red, white, and blue BEBE PEPSI sign in the window of a little store on the ground floor.

When I stepped from the taxi my heel squished on something. I looked down. Swarms of huge cockroaches, each the size of a finger—the street was black with them. I shuddered and jumped back into the car.

"It's okay," Mark said. "They come out after the night rains."

"Yuk, disgusting!"

"Oh, Lil, c'mon. They'll be gone in the morning." He extended a hand to extract me from the back seat. "You just have to watch where you put your feet," he said distractedly, paying the driver who'd deposited our luggage on top of the ubiquitous cockroaches.

The apartment smelled of disinfectant and was furnished with only a lumpy bed and a scarred dresser and nightstand in one room, a mismatched couch and chair in another. The kitchen was bare. But the place seemed clean enough, and when we lay down on the bed I could smell the lavender soap with which the sheets had been washed. The sound of voices crooning to guitars drifted up from the street.

"Mariachis. I love them. They play at a restaurant down the street," Mark whispered from his pillow. "We heard them every night the last time I stayed here."

I snuggled into him, my lips on his neck, listening to the mellifluous Spanish. Yes, I loved the sound of the mariachis too. I wouldn't think about anything but being here with Mark, seeing Mexico with him. It would be fine. It would be wonderful. My husband was already asleep, breathing softly and regularly. I tamped down the free-floating anxieties that kept trying to erupt deep inside me. Finally I too relaxed into sleep.

The cockroaches were gone in the morning, just as Mark had said, and the beach, where the water was bathtub warm and picture blue, was only a couple of blocks away. At a little café from which you could see the still-empty beach, we had breakfast—rich black coffee and bolillos with pale yellow butter. Then Mark rolled up his white linen trouser legs, and we held our sandals in our hands and strolled down by the water. With my free hand I took his arm, but he kept it hanging limply at his side, so I soon let go. Maybe people didn't walk arm-in-arm on Mexican beaches.

"Look who's back!" A hefty redheaded woman in an off-the-shoulder orange sundress shouted a greeting to Mark from behind the bar when we later walked into O'Brien's. "It's Señor Doctor Mark! Where's Alfredo—and where's . . . what's his name?" she asked him.

"And where are the snows of yesteryear?" He grinned. She came around the bar to hug him, but he didn't introduce me. "That's Lucille O'Brien, a real busybody," he whispered to me when she busied herself with another customer. "But she's a big success, ex-pats love this place."

"Coco loco": he told me the name of the new drink—a green coconut with a hole on top, half the milk still in it mixed with ice and tequila. When you finished drinking, you spooned out the soft, sweet meat. We sipped at them on the verandah of O'Brien's while we gazed at the dark rock formations in the ocean. The water was emerald now. The rocks looked like little volcanoes, jutting out right in front of O'Brien's, just as Mark had described them months earlier.

Coco loco, an Irish-American woman who ran a bar on the Mazatlán beach, ex-pats, the blue and emerald waters and fantastically shaped rocks: I was swept up in the romance of the moment. *What a path I'd traveled from a furnished room in East L.A.*, I marveled as I sipped.

From the next table, a tanned blond boy in a white T-shirt grinned at us. A big straw sombrero dangled by a cord around his neck and made him look like a kid at Knott's Berry Farm, waiting to have his picture snapped. "Where you from?" he asked Mark pleasantly. He'd already ordered a second round of coco locos for us and now rose to pull a roll of bills as big as my fist from a back pocket to pay for the drinks the waitress deposited on our table. His arms were knotted with muscles that looked grossly exaggerated on his short frame. "I heard Lucille say you just got here. Welcome." He saluted us with his raised glass. He said his name was Stefano, from Newark, New Jersey (though I thought his accent sounded more like Dallas, Texas), lived in Mazatlán now, before that Oaxaca, and before that Cuernavaca. "Haven't been back to the States in seven years," he drawled.

Later Mark ordered another round of coco locos for all three of us. "Oh, no, no more for me." I laughed and hopped up. "Can't we get some lunch?" I'd be quick and clever; I had to keep Mark from the one more sip that made a mess of things.

Stefano walked out with us and led us to a little outdoor market down the beach where, he said, you could sit at a table on the sand and order unpeeled shrimp that had been in the ocean thirty minutes earlier. While we ate, he stopped some strolling mariachis and asked them to play "Bésame Mucho." He pushed his own plate of shrimp and shells aside and sang along with the mariachis, his arms extended and palms turned upward, as though imploring an imaginary lover to kiss him a lot.

Somehow, much later, we ended up at O'Brien's again, the three of us sitting on the verandah as the sun dropped slowly into the wine-dark sea and left the sky streaked with orange and red. Mark ordered beers — Dos Equis, he called them. I wasn't too upset because I'd never seen anyone get drunk on beer. Stefano talked on and on, about traveling all over Mexico on an old burro strapped with ten saddlebags, working for the Mexican government in some capacity he wasn't at liberty to divulge, winning the bantamweight wrestling championship in Guadalajara over Antonio Cardoza by a dumb-luck knockout. He'd spin a tale, we'd make a few comments, and then there'd be silence for ten or fifteen minutes. In the dim light we'd watch seagulls and pelicans circle round and round the weird rocks, where they'd finally roost for the night. Then Stefano would launch into another tale. He didn't demand much response, and Mark seemed amused by the theatrics of the stories he spun. With his blond hair bleached white by the sun, a toothy boyish grin, a child's red pouty lips, he didn't look much older than I. I rather liked him and thought he was interesting and droll. But finally I wished he'd leave so that Mark and I could walk together on the beach again, in the twilight.

Only when the stars twinkled so close above O'Brien's that it seemed if I held my arm up I'd be touching them, did I notice that Mark had disappeared. In the silence I'd looked over to tell him about the stars, and his chair was empty. Stefano was still sitting there, on the other side of the vacant chair. "Where'd my husband go?" I asked him, laughing at my oblivion.

"Probably to the loo." Stefano shrugged. "I've been watching the stars."

We both returned to our lonesome pursuit until it felt as if a long time had passed. "Would you mind looking in the men's room? Maybe he's ill or something," I finally asked, feeling a little prick of dread. What would I do if something happened to Mark in this foreign place?

Stefano returned a few minutes later, shaking his head. Mark wasn't in the men's room. "He probably just took a little walk," Stefano drawled, and gave my hand a quick pat. "Nothing to worry about."

But I couldn't help it. I had no money with me, and I wasn't even sure I could find the way back to the new apartment.

"Maybe he felt sick and went home," Stefano offered. "Would you like me to go with you and see?" His eyes were gentle, but what would I do if Mark wasn't there?

I hurried with Stefano down brightly lit busy streets, feeling the insistent gaze of men who stood about in little groups. "Looky *chiquita*," one leered into my face and moved to touch me. "Vamoos," Stefano hissed at him, and the man started in surprise, as though he hadn't noticed that I was with someone. We wandered up and down the maze of strange streets as I tried frantically to remember which way Mark and I had walked that morning, but nothing looked familiar. Suddenly the red, white, and blue BEBE PEPSI sign on the building where we'd slept the night before loomed up miraculously.

Stefano bounded up the stairs behind me. I didn't even have a key. "Mark," he shouted as he banged on the locked door.

"Mark, please open up!" I wailed to the silence, and we waited.

"We'll find him. Just come with me." Stefan led me firmly by the elbow. I let myself be steered because I didn't know what else to do. What had happened to my husband? Down in the street again, Stefano cupped his hands and whistled to a passing taxi.

"I don't have any money," I cried.

"Nothing to worry about," Stefano said, opening the taxi door for me with a gallant flourish, then sliding in himself and directing the driver in Spanish. With the fall of night the air had turned heavy, and suddenly rain gushed down in sheets, flooding the street in minutes.

What should I do? I looked over at the stranger sitting beside me now in the dark cab as we rattled and sloshed down muddy roads. I had no idea where he was taking me. "Don't worry. We're gonna find him," Stefano said again. He sat forward in his seat, tense and focused on the adventure of finding a missing husband for a girl who'd just arrived in a country where she didn't speak the language. What if Mark was dead? No, I was sure he wasn't, but where had he gone?

The taxi driver bumped down the dark road I recognized from the night before. "*A la derecha*," Stefano cried. The driver made a sharp right onto a dirt hill. In the distance you could see light from a lone house. The windshield wipers moved in a mad staccato as the taxi slowed.

"Stay here," Stefano yelled, barely waiting for the car to stop in front of the house, lifting the sombrero to his head and jumping into the rain. From behind the closed window, I could hear his loud pounding on the door. By the porch light I saw the voluminous blond hairdo and the purple lipstick of the woman who answered, and behind her, other women and a couple of men who came and went in a shadowy room. The woman at the door shook her head at Stefano and laughed, pointing into the distance.

He raced back to the taxi, his T-shirt wet and transparent and the sombrero dripping rain onto the seat. "Not there," he said breathlessly, and fired off another order to the taxi driver. We sailed into the downpour again.

We must have stopped at six or seven houses at least before the night was over. It didn't take me long to figure out that Stefano thought

Mark had gotten drunk and gone to find a whore. I knew that was impossible; but I didn't know how to tell Stefano that I understood what those places were that the taxi drove us to and that I'd bet my life that Mark wouldn't be looking for female prostitutes.

It was almost light again when Stefano told the taxi driver to take us back to the apartment building. Stefano's tragic-looking eyes, his mouth clamped soberly shut, upset me even more than I was already, but I had to get my mind clear. I knew I had to make a plan in case Mark never returned. First, I'd get Stefano to help me call the police. But what if they couldn't find him? What if he didn't want to be found? I'd borrow money from Stefano to call Rae. She'd telegraph enough for a plane ticket. There'd be no way to keep her from seeing what a terrible mess my marriage was and she'd be hysterical, but how else could I get back to safety? I would have to call her.

Stefano sat with me on the steps. "Mark will turn up," he said, but there was no conviction in his voice, and then he said nothing more. He just kept shaking his head as if the worst had already happened to my husband. It had stopped raining and it wasn't cold, but my teeth chattered as though I were in mortal terror, and I was exhausted.

At about six in the morning, when the dark streaks had disappeared from the sky and the sun had risen, Mark turned up. He walked nonchalantly up the steps, seeming not even to notice Stefano's flabbergasted expression or my murderous stare. He opened the apartment door and I fell in, with Stefano behind me, both of us speechless. He'd been riding around in a taxi, he explained. He'd watched the sun rise with the taxi driver, "and then I told him to take me home, but I didn't have enough money to pay him." His face looked as innocent as a seven-year-old's. *Idiot!* I wanted to scream. My fingers itched for crystal glasses to throw against the wall, to throw at his head. "So I gave the man my watch and my Star of David," Mark said, shrugging.

I flew at him with open claws. "You miserable son of a bitch! You fucking drunk!" A torrent poured out of me, all the hurt and anger I'd been bottling since the wedding fiasco; I couldn't stop. "You goddam faggot!" I shrieked. Mark clutched at my flying hands, protecting his face.

"Hey, hey, hey," Stefano cried, pulling me off my husband, trying to calm us both. "She's been really worried, man. How could you do something so dumb?" I slammed the bedroom door behind me.

I threw my clothes on the floor and sank into the bed, longing for some kind of magic to transport me to my mother's bungalow, to my old room. Yet I couldn't go home, I realized soberly. If I left Mark now I'd be back where I started; I'd never be able to break away from my mother. How could I go to college?

A while later I felt Mark get into bed. I turned away from him, furious still.

"Stefano's sleeping on the couch," he said.

"Go to hell," I muttered. Then I must have fallen asleep.

When I was awakened by a light, caressing hand on my pubes, I fought through a sleepy miasma to make sense of things. It couldn't be Mark's hand—his back was turned to me.

Fear seized me. I jumped from under the covers. Stefano was kneeling on the floor by my bed, a compact bundle of pink flesh and muscle, a pleading look on his face.

"Goddam it! Mark!" I screamed, flinging my pillow at the naked, kneeling form, grabbing a butt-filled ashtray to throw. "Help!"

Mark was on his feet in a second, trying to grasp what was going on, then seeing Stefano, who'd risen and covered his genitals with both hands. "You'd better go," Mark said in a voice I thought maddeningly calm. Stefano looked disoriented, like a kid who'd expected a hug and gotten a slap; then he went, quickly and quietly. I heard him gathering his clothes in the living room, and I clutched the ashtray until the door closed behind him.

"It's your fault! You called me a faggot in front of him," Mark sneered. "What did you expect, damn you? He probably thought we both wanted it!" He pulled his pillow off the bed and stormed out of the room. I heard him plop on the couch Stefano had vacated.

I was furious with Mark for days. I couldn't stop thinking about how he'd left me at O'Brien's, disappeared without a word, how I'd been sick with worry, not just for myself but for him too. My mind kept going back to it, as to images of a gory accident. But in between those thoughts I remembered the times in Los Angeles when we'd first met. What had happened to the Mark who'd taught me about Rubinstein and the Spanish Civil War? How charming he'd been with my mother and Albert in the beginning. How perfect the first night together in San Diego had been. Didn't we love each other still? I shouldn't have called him a faggot . . . and because I did poor Stefano was misled and it all ended so badly. So much was going wrong between Mark and me.

And there was something else, something awful I couldn't stop thinking about: Where had he been if not with a man? A prostitute probably, a hustler, who'd demanded jewelry because Mark didn't have enough cash to pay him. I was mired in dark, convoluted feelings—disgust, but rejection also, and jealousy too. *Il va sans dire*, I'd said so brightly at the beginning when Mark had reminded me that of course we'd be intimate with other people. But that was before he and I had become lovers. Once we'd drifted into that surprising territory, the rules had changed. Or had they? I was jealous that Mark still wanted men, but wasn't I stirred still by women? Where was my apex of desire? I saw Beverly Shaw's competent, manicured hand as she held the microphone, the way her skirt had hiked over her shapely, nylon-covered legs when she'd crossed them. The vision ignited in me all over again the fantasy of my lips between her thighs. Mark's lovemaking had never excited me like that, so why was I bothered that his apex of desire was not me? It was a contradiction I couldn't make sense of.

We were polite to each other now, but I knew I could never trust him to act with consideration for me, and he'd stopped trusting me too. Something had broken that day for both of us. One morning about a week later, waiting for the waitress to seat us in the café where we'd been getting our breakfasts, we saw Stefano's white-blond head bent over a cup of coffee at a corner table, and Mark and I quickly backed out. We didn't say a word to each other, about Stefano or anything else, as we walked through the streets looking for another restaurant, though I knew we were both reliving the whole episode. It was after we were seated in a new café that Mark said, so low I almost didn't hear him, "The danger of a Jew marrying a non-Jew is that when they get mad at you they call you a kike."

"That makes no sense. We're both Jewish," I said, though I knew what he was alluding to.

"You called me a faggot," he persisted softly, and tears sprang into his eyes.

I reached for his hand, but he pulled away. "Mark, I'm like a faggot too," I reminded him.

"Are you?" he snickered.

"Yes," I said with conviction, "I am."

We never make love anymore. Mark never approaches me that way, and even if I didn't feel ambivalent about it, I wouldn't know what to do to seduce him. What am I to him? I don't know anymore. What place do I have in his life or he in mine? Sometimes I feel that I'm living someone else's life and I have to leave and find my own. But how?

For now I'm trapped here, and I'm always scared and suspicious. I ask him for some money, to keep in my purse for emergencies, and without comment he gives me a little roll of pesos. I feel like a child, to have to ask for money, and I hate it, but what if he disappears on me again? He'll get drunk; he'll find a pretty boy; and I'll be stranded in the middle of nowhere. Now I'm always watching where he looks.

José, the boy behind the counter at the little store with the BEBE PEPSI *sign, has apple cheeks and café-au-lait skin that makes his green eyes greener and his white teeth whiter. He's about fifteen or sixteen, and every morning when we go downstairs Mark says to him jovially, "Señor José, como se va?" The boy is all smiles for Mark.*

One day Mark makes a stack of half a dozen shirts that have just come back, starched and neatly folded, from the laundry down the street. "What are you doing?" I ask.

"I'm taking them down to José," he says casually. "The poor kid dresses in rags."

When I looked out the living room window one morning, on the peaked roof across the street sat two blue-black vultures. They perched, one on each side of the peak, their wings extended, their fingered tips long and hideous. The next time I looked there were four—two on each side. I promised myself I wouldn't look out that window again. Whenever I passed near it, I averted my eyes, fighting the impulse to look, forcing myself to gaze anywhere but there. But one day I looked: The quickest of glances showed me that now there were six—three on each side, their grotesque beaks pointing precisely in the direction of our building. They had come for me. I was seized by certainty—they were just waiting a couple of weeks, for my eighteenth birthday.

I ran to the bedroom, where Mark was dressing, and threw my arms around him, buried my cheek feverishly in the pelt of his chest. "We've got to get out of here!" I cried. I told him how the vultures were multiplying.

For an instant he held my arms as though to peel me off, then seemed to change his mind and patted my back instead, like someone soothing a sick child. "But I've paid the rent until July nineteenth," he said gently.

That would be one day after my birthday. "Please," I begged, dropping to my knees. I had to convince him. "The nineteenth is too late," I cried. "We have to leave now. Please, Mark!"

And we did. "Okay," he'd said, amazingly, and we rushed to throw our clothes into suitcases as if we were heeding a hurricane warning. Then we ran into the street and he waved a taxi down. I didn't look back to see how many vultures were on the roof now. We caught a bus to Mexico City that very day.

On the bus I was suddenly embarrassed by my "acting out," as Mark called hysterical scene-making, but he held my hand as we rumbled south. "We'll be in Mexico City in just a few hours," he assured me, his voice low and soothing, a kind doctor. "Everything will be all right."

Mark leaves in the midmorning, and most evenings he comes back around eight or nine o'clock, tired out but exhilarated still by his heady day. "Dr. Sanchez says the field is wide open for psychologists in Mexico," he tells me, or "Dr. Cordova was really funny today. She said they'd erect a monument to me if I help them set up a department of psychology." He's in love with his work, with the campus, with his colleagues. To me they're phantoms; he introduces me to no one, and I never even set foot on the university grounds.

What do I with my days? Mark gives me a little money to wander around Mexico City, and though I still hate to take it from him, I do. I walk and walk, all day long, and when I'm tired I stop in a café and have something to eat and watch the passersby. I feel fine, though a tiny bit shaky still, as though I've recuperated from a high fever. Mexico City is beautiful, as I imagine Paris would be, grand old buildings and shop windows with lovely clothes, perfumes, flowers, jewelry. One day I stop to watch a procession of young men, hundreds of them, winding down a main boulevard, shouting with gusto, waving arms and placards. A trio passes close, the man in the middle grasping a hand-lettered sign that says 5 CENTAVOS, the two on either side holding a miniature open coffin, all three bawling great crocodile tears.

"What's going on?" I ask the balding man beside me who's been trying to pick me up in Spanish and English. "University of Mexico students, señorita," he tells me. "They are protesting because the bus fare has been raised from five centavos to seven. Very bad for poor people." I turn back to watch. I love their faces, so alive with passion and humor.

I'm a wanderer alone in a foreign city, and I don't dislike it. I have plenty of time to dream and to figure out my life. I can't be someone's wife. That would be a false me, no matter what the circumstances were. Everyone is rushing somewhere, to business, to romantic trysts, to change the world, and I love to mill in the crowds, to pretend to rush along with them. Of course I have nowhere to go yet, but I understand how important it is: You absolutely must have somewhere to go in life. That I've always known. I just forgot for a while.

Dr. Cordova asked him to stay until December, Mark said. He ran a hand through his tangled curls, pouring himself a cup of the hot chocolate he'd made on the hot plate in our little apartment. "It's a really attractive offer. I've decided I don't want to go back to Children's Hospital anyway."

"But I thought we were going back next week." I took my toast from the toaster and busied myself looking for a plate. *Would he try to keep me here? UCLA started in two weeks; I'd promised my mother we'd be back for the High Holidays.*

"Lil, look." I turned to look at him and our eyes connected, but only for an instant before he looked away. "You go back now. It's just a few months, and I'll join you in December." He looked at me again and smiled sweetly. I smiled back sweetly.

"I'm going to have to ask you a big favor," Mark said, rinsing his cup, his back to me. "Would you mind taking the bus? It costs a fraction of the plane, and I'm really strapped. They won't pay me until the session is over. It only takes three or four days."

He came to the bus station and waited with me, handed my suitcase to the driver, kissed my cheek. "I really love you a lot," he said. "Do you know that?"

"I love you too," I told him, my lips touching his stubbly cheek, but I doubt either of us meant it.

I'm happy to be on the bus. I wave good-bye to him from my window, and he smiles and waves and smiles. I breathe easier when we pull out of the station. I'm the only one on the bus who isn't Mexican, and I'm the only female who's alone, but I know I'll be all right. I can take care of myself. I don't want it any other way. I never really truly believed it could be any other way. We ride for long stretches of city, then green, then desert, then small villages and more desert, through places whose names I'd never heard before and would probably never hear again. I look out the window, watching the bus gobble the miles of road. I'm going toward Los Angeles, toward my mother and Rae and UCLA and my future.

The bus makes several stops a day so that the passengers can get food. In a little restaurant, in a town whose name I never learn, the waitress is a young girl who looks like Prince Valiant—smooth black hair that comes down below her ears, long smooth bangs. She wears a boy's checked shirt and boy's pants. All the time I'd been in Mexico I hadn't seen a single female in pants. Her black eyes are handsome and intelligent. I can see how efficient she is, how focused on her tasks, what a hard worker. I wish she could get on the bus with me, that we'd travel in the same direction—to Los Angeles, to UCLA—and we'd both become . . . what? Lawyers? Psychologists maybe. Do I imagine that when she gives me my check our eyes lock? "Thank you very much," she says in English, with only a trace of an accent. I watch her from my seat at the window until the bus pulls onto the road that will take me back to Los Angeles.

LILLIAN

13 HIGHER EDUCATION

I WENT BACK to the Fountain Avenue Court Bungalows because for the time being I had nowhere else to go. My mother pressed me to her breast, kissed my face with loud smacks, carried on as though I'd been gone for decades.

"Mom, I'm tired," I pleaded. "All I want to do now is take a hot bath." My white cotton dress was gray from five days on dusty Mexican roads, and my hair was a mess of wiry tangles.

"All by yourself he lets you go? On a dangerous bus from Mexico?" My aunt was waiting there too, just as I'd feared, an angry little warrior with balled fists on plump hips.

"He's a *paskudnyak*, a bad one," my mother cried.

"Look, he's coming back in December. They're keeping his old job for him at Children's Hospital," I improvised over the din of running bath water. "Mark's helping set up a very important department of psychology at the University of Mexico. He's like a hero down there." I shooed them out of the bathroom and locked myself in. If they knew it was permanently over between me and Mark, they'd try to trap me again. "I had to get back now to start UCLA, and I'm going to live in a dorm near campus," I shouted without stopping for breath. "When he returns, we're renting this beautiful house in Malibu." I closed my eyes, sank down in the water to my nose, and stayed there.

I delayed getting out until my skin was prunelike, but they were both still standing in the hallway when I opened the door, my mother looking tragic, my aunt glowering as if she wanted to yank Mark's thick black curls out of his scalp. The hardest part came next.

"Rae, look," I said. "He hasn't gotten paid yet. Could you lend me the money for a dorm room?"

"What do you mean, dorm room?" my mother said. "You stay here till he comes back. You have your own room and everything here."

"No way, no way! I need to live near the campus. I can't get to UCLA from here without wasting precious hours on the bus every day."

"Why do you have to go to college when you have a husband?" my mother yelled.

"What kind of a husband is that? A carrot should grow from his ear!" Rae shook her fist at my absent husband and grabbed her purse. "Come to the Bank of America with me," she said.

*My spirits are leaden one minute, soaring the next. My marriage has failed, but isn't a wonderful new chapter of my life about to begin? With my scholarship money I buy my schoolbooks. Introduction to Humanities —*The Oresteia, The Odyssey, The Divine Comedy, Don Quixote, Hamlet, Paradise Lost, Madame Bovary, *books about the failures and triumphs of men, things I'd never even thought about before, words set down hundreds of years ago, so vivid they could be happening today: The miracle of it, I think, worshipful even of the printed pages, to me like sacred text. Elementary French — the heavy, grainy-green cover feels significant with promise: I'll learn to understand people who speak no English, to read their ideas; someday I'll even go to France. Introduction to Psychology — I'll know what Mark knows; this is the first step. I daydream of a Dr. Faderman whose astuteness and wisdom will cure the obsessive, the agoraphobic, the compulsive, the paranoid. The books will be my key to a new life. Nothing will be impossible — they will make me a new person, the person I want to be.*

I have a week before classes start. I line the books up neatly on the shelf in my room at Rudi Hall, then I take them down, one by one, and pore over them, ravenous. I am a college student. A UCLA scholar. I've escaped from furnished rooms in the Bronx and East L.A., from nude modeling jobs and the Open Door, from all the forces that have worked to keep me down — the bastard who was my father, Fanny who'd told me what a poor girl couldn't do, Mr. Mann and Falix and Carlos and Jan—all of them. Already I feel like a success.

As we'd stood in line together at the Bank of America I told my aunt: "Of course Mark is sending me money for food. He just didn't have enough this month for a whole semester's dorm rent." But how would I eat? Now, just before the start of classes, I found thumbtacked to a wall of the common room at Rudi Hall a printed sign that said JOBS and under it handwritten white index cards: Baby Sitter Wanted, Part-time File Clerk, Student Library Assistant.

I spent four hours a day during the first week of classes wheeling loaded carts up and down the stacks of the UCLA library, searching for Dewey decimal numbers, putting books back on the shelves, envying students with the leisure to sit and actually read those books in the beautiful, old wood-paneled, high-ceilinged room. At the end of the week, I stood in line at an office in the bowels of the library in order to pick up a little brown pay envelope. Inside I found a check for $23.25.

It wasn't a decision I struggled over. Being exploited as a student library assistant wasn't much more pleasant than being exploited as a pinup model, and the pay was a lot worse for a lot more hours. Why shouldn't I use all the gifts I had, every one of them, to get where I needed to go? "Andy," I cried into the first public telephone I could find, "it's Gigi Frost. Remember me? I'd like to come back to work."

"Hey, the hourglass girl who doesn't own a bra." Andy laughed. "So what happened? Your boyfriend run off and leave you?"

"Something like that," I said. "Say, look, can I work on weekends in group shoots?" Four hours on Saturdays, four hours on Sundays, and I'd go back to the dorm with forty dollars in my pocket. It felt different to me now than it had two years earlier: I wasn't worried anymore about the photographers and where they might tempt me to go. Now I knew where I was going. Now I was sure I wouldn't let anything stop me from getting there. If I quit the library job and modeled on the weekend, I'd have twelve extra hours a week in which to study.

. . .

I loved my cubbyhole of a dorm room—the good, strong reading lamp, the scarred old desk and sturdy chair that nameless other students had used in the past. Before long, the nooks of the room were crammed with volumes that I read for pleasure in my idle time: Muriel Rukeyser, James Baldwin, Upton Sinclair. I could brew a strong cup of coffee on the hot plate I kept in my room (against the rules), slouch luxuriously with my stockinged feet on the desk, forget everything bad and sad—my worries about what my mother wanted from me, what Rae wanted from me—and feast on a book.

I loved the campus too—the rolling greenery and the grand old buildings, even the drab auditoriums that were the freshman class-rooms. I sat in the great rooms, stunned all over again by the wonder of it: Lilly from East L.A. at one of the best universities in the world. When a student to my right or left looked bored I was puzzled, offended even. The classrooms were to me sacred places those first weeks, holier by far than any synagogue.

Yet my reverence was often mixed with something else—something in which I perversely reveled, an angry resolve. Someone like me wasn't supposed to be the beneficiary of the knowledge being dispensed here —but they'd have to pass it on to me! They couldn't deny me.

On Saturdays and Sundays, I spent the four hours in Andy's studio and left with plenty of money in my pocket for the week's meals. And before that, on Friday evenings, I took two buses across town early enough to watch my mother kerchief her head to light the Sabbath can-dles and say the Hebrew prayers she'd never said at Fanny's because she hadn't been the lady of the house there. Then I'd eat the Sabbath dinner with her and Albert before I took another bus to go and drink tea and be stuffed with cinnamon *rugelach* by Rae. "A young girl doesn't travel alone on the bus late at night," my aunt would grumble over my per-functory protests when I rose to leave about nine o'clock, and Mr. Bergman would help her turn the plastic-covered, flowered-print couch into a snug bed for me until Saturday morning. It was a simple comfort to be near my mother and Rae, to know that even though they didn't have the slightest notion of what it meant to be a UCLA student and could not share my new world, they loved me and would love me no matter what. And it was another comfort to know that before too many hours I'd be leaving them to return to that world they knew nothing about, where I was learning to find my own way. So I had everything I needed to keep me going.

But sometimes I was lonely. I was close to no one except my mother and Rae. I never heard from Mark again. He just disappeared in Mexico City, and our months together seemed now like another life. What had we been to each other?

When I poured the champale into the long-stemmed cocktail glass the waitress placed in front of me, the old fear shook my hand. Would I be kicked out of UCLA if I were caught in a raid? But Beverly Shaw came to perch on the bar in her tailored white suit and high-heeled shoes, and she winked right at me—she remembered me after all that time! Every nerve of me sat rapt in voluptuous attention.

It was only at the end of the set, when she whispered, "Don't go 'way" into the mike and slinked off, that I glanced over at the woman in a black turtleneck who sat at the long bar. Her eyes were large—gray, I later saw—and her dark hair curled softly around her forehead and ears. She was alone. I watched her for a long time. She looked nothing like the intimidatingly majestic Beverly Shaw. There was something vulnerable in the set of her thin shoulders, her pale, pale skin. She was Mark's age perhaps, maybe a couple of years younger. Who did she remind me of? I picked over the silver screen images still lodged in my mind: Sylvia Sidney, the Jewish actress with fragile, heartbreaking beauty, the one my mother had loved so much.

I wouldn't hesitate. But how to do it? Not like Jan, no. Like William Holden, maybe. "I'd like to send that woman at the end of the bar a champale," I told the cocktail waitress with all the suavity I could muster, plunking down on her tray two dollars of Andy's money. Then I stared at the dark curls until she looked over at me and stared back, but only for a moment before she lowered her eyes shyly—and that made me braver. I stared at her, unblinking.

The waitress placed a glass and a Champale bottle in front of her, nodding in my direction and whispering something. The woman raised her eyes again to me, and I held my own glass up, smiling boldly, sexily I hoped, despite the crazy tattoo pounding in my ears. I would do this— what I'd never done before. I watched her neat breasts move under her sweater as she shifted her body to face the bar. She sipped at her drink with eyes lowered again, then glanced up. Our eyes locked.

"My name is Lillian," I said in an actress-sultry voice when I went to stand next to her at the bar. Her perfume was lightly spiced, not at all like the dark, heavy musk I'd loved before.

"Door," I thought she said. "My name is Door."

"Excuse me?"

"D-apostrophe-O-R. It's French. It means 'of gold.' Sabina's my first name, but I like D'Or better." As she spoke I noticed her small, well-shaped ears, her delicate chin. And Beverly Shaw disappeared forever from my head. It was no longer Beverly Shaw I desired—it was to *be* her. How would Beverly Shaw pick up Sabina D'Or? What would she say? How would she make love to a woman?

"The way you looked at me . . . ," Sabina D'Or said later in her car. She'd offered to drive me home when I told her I'd taken a taxi to the Club Laurel. That was after I placed my hand on the small of her back and drew my head close to hers as we laughed together about a big woman in an ermine stole who'd asked the bartender in a baritone voice where the men's room was. Then I ordered another round of champale, and my hand dropped to D'Or's knee. She batted her gray eyes at me in surprise, but she didn't try to pry my clutching fingers off.

"What about the way I looked at you?" I kept my voice low, seductive. I had to sound sure, though I wasn't sure of anything just now.

"So unabashed," she smiled wryly. She seemed less fragile than she'd looked at a distance.

How would I do this? An ocean roared in my ears. I'd ask her to come in. We'd sneak into my room—probably all the girls would be gone anyway on a Saturday night, and nobody would even know she was there. And then . . . I'd do the things to her that Jan had done to me. Could I make her believe I knew what I was doing when my fingers were so icy cold? I pushed them furtively under my thighs to warm them up.

. . .

When I awoke that morning she was still pressed next to me, breathing softly, there in my narrow dorm bed, an exotic, disturbing intrusion into my nun's life. How splendid I'd felt the night before, felt still. I relived it, silently, with D'Or nestled beside me in sleep: how I'd filled my mouth with her breasts, sucking on nipples that were pale brown, pronounced, unlike mine—like my mother's really, just as I remembered them from when I was a kid. How I'd tasted her everywhere—her neck, her belly, her smooth and crinkly hairs. Finally her juices on my tongue. The unaccustomed feel and smell of it, like seaweed, had been startling to me at first, then quickly delicious. I'd swum in the sea of her; I'd made her moan. I had really done it—brought another woman to pleasure! Now I pressed her to me tenderly. This was what I wanted. I kissed her gently, trying not to wake her. Yes, this . . . for my whole life. How hadn't I known it before?

Later we strolled down Gayley Avenue to Westwood Village for brunch, our arms and fingers brushing, barely touching. Walking in broad daylight, I was back in bed with her, in the dark, mysterious night, tasting her everywhere.

"How much we say in silence." D'Or broke my reverie. "I'm so aware of you, and that means you're aware too—I know you are, or I wouldn't feel it so strongly."

"Oh, yes," I whispered fervently. I'd never seen a woman so lovely, so graceful in movement, so musical in voice. And she'd let me make love to her, and would again! The mere thought of it telegraphed sweet sensations to my groin.

She lived in San Francisco, she said over our French toast and coffee in a booth at Colby's Diner. She'd come back to L.A. to visit her parents for a few weeks, then her father had gotten sick. That was months earlier; now he was in the hospital. "It's awful." Her gray eyes clouded, and her beautiful mouth trembled. "My mother says I upset them so much that I gave my father a cancer. Can you imagine? My father gets cancer and they blame me!"

I covered her hand with mine, not to seduce now but to sympathize, and our knees pressed together under the table. "You're an island of rationality because you *listen* to me," D'Or cried. "They won't listen— they never have."

As we got up to leave she looked under our table, behind the seats of our booth, under the table again. "What did you lose, D'Or?" I asked, looking under the table with her.

"Can I help you find something, miss?" the waitress asked.

"No, nothing, it's all right," she said quickly but kept looking.

D'Or is an artist, she tells me, a writer, though she hasn't yet written much. When I say I'm a psychology major she merely nods, and I sense that she thinks psychology is a lesser pursuit, that she's a bit disappointed. I long to impress her. "Artistic types are naturally different," she says of herself. "You're like that too. I felt it in the way you stared at me that first night . . . the wonderful inappropriateness of it. It signifies the creative spirit."

D'Or loves words like maverick, iconoclast, mad genius, self-defined original. *How can I be those things for her?*

She lies naked on my dorm bed after I've made love to her. "Ours is a mystical connection, rarefied, nebulous," she murmurs, "beyond the sexual, far beyond good and interesting companionship."

"Yes." I fall to my knees and devour her hands with kisses. "Oh, yes!"

"Pageboy, my page." She sits up to anoint my head with a beloved hand. Her breasts gleam in the semidarkness, the brown nipples pronounced, erect. I kneel at her feet. I'm a page in livery, a boy in the service of my queen. "My Rosenkavalier," she sometimes calls me.

My dorm room was on the ground floor, with a screenless window that overlooked an alley. During the school week, D'Or would scratch at the glass at about ten o'clock in the evening. I'd drop my book and pen and slide the window open so she could climb into the room and hurl herself wordlessly into my arms. Moments later, never loosening our barnacle grip on each other, we'd collapse onto the bed and unglue only long enough for me to pull at her clothes, to fling them on the floor.

In the morning I'd leave her in bed—though to separate from her, even briefly, felt as painful as pulling off a limb—and I'd go to my classes, galloping always so that I wouldn't be late; I'd waited until the last possible minute to go. When the sound of voices stopped in the dorm, by midmorning usually, she'd leave too and go to the hospital and sit with her father.

To explain my absences on Saturdays and Sundays, I told her that I was a bathing suit model. She didn't ask for details.

Then her father was put on a respirator in Cedars of Lebanon's intensive care unit. "The doctor thinks it won't be more than a few weeks," D'Or sighed, sagging onto my bed, a delicate, sweet wraith. I sank down beside her, kissed her, nestled her head on my breast, held her.

We both jumped when the phone rang. "It could be for me," D'Or cried as I reached for it.

"I need to speak to Shirley Ann Goldstein." It was a woman with a New York accent.

"I think you have the wrong number," I said, ready to hang up.

"Is it for me?" D'Or grabbed the black receiver from my hand. "When?" she shrieked. Her face crumpled like a little girl's before she sank again onto my bed, and I took her back into my arms.

To be near her I went to the funeral, a Jewish funeral at Mount Sinai Memorial Park. She didn't introduce me to her weeping, red-nosed mother or any of the other black-clad, prosperous-looking mourners. In the cold marble chapel I lost myself in the crowd, but I never stopped watching her. She sat in the front row, hemmed in between her stiff, stern-faced brother and another man. The rabbi talked about Isaac Goldstein—a good Jew, a generous contributor to the Etz Jacob Synagogue, the founder of the Goldenrod dress shops of Beverly Hills, Brentwood, and Palm Springs. D'Or kept her head down, and her shoulders shook. Then we all filed out into the April winds and made our way up a little grassy hill, her mother and brother and the other relatives, then the friends and business acquaintances. But D'Or walked alone, trailing behind them all, and I trailed behind her. She wore black pants, her black turtleneck sweater, a black leather jacket that flapped noisily in the wind. How utterly alone she looked. I loved her more tenderly than ever, and I stood as close to her as I dared while we watched Mr. Goldstein being lowered into the ground.

For weeks D'Or lives hidden in my dorm room and I sneak enough food in for us both. When I'm in class or the library, I can't stop worrying about her. Her plaintive voice sounds in my ears over my professors' lectures. Her pale, satiny skin slides incessantly between my eyes and the pages I read. It's nothing short of a miracle that I manage to end the spring semester clutching three A's and two B's.

"Compulsive disorder." D'Or used the words for the first time the day we were supposed to meet for lunch at Colby's Diner and she didn't show up. I almost missed my afternoon Experimental Psych final, because I waited for more than an hour and then ran to the dorm to look for her.

"I can't help it." She shrugged casually, but I saw torment in her face.

"What happens?" I asked, my fear mixing with determination. *She's like my mother used to be! But this time I won't fail.*

"I count things—books, pencils, shoes . . ." In halting sentences she told me the extent of it. She kept things—like newspapers and magazines. She couldn't throw them away until she'd read every word. And she had to scrub her hands often, very often. And she had a horrible fear of losing things, couldn't leave a place without searching thoroughly to make sure she'd left nothing behind.

I will love her enough to cure her! She will love me enough to be cured, I thought.

"Come back with me to San Francisco," D'Or whispered that evening when I held her on my bed. "I kept my apartment there."

"Your job too?" I murmured, my lips on her curls. If leaving her for a few hours felt like severing a limb, how could I part with her forever?

"My father . . . used to send me . . ." When she pronounced *father* I could feel her thin shoulders shudder in a noiseless sob. ". . . a hundred and fifty dollars a month."

A hundred and fifty dollars a month. Couldn't I earn that much in San Francisco while I went to college, to Berkeley?

"Mark and I are going to live in San Francisco," I told my mother and Rae. "He's getting a good job there in a few months, at a big hospital. I'll stay with a friend of his until he can join me." I ended the tale with a tone of finality. What could they say anyway? I was nineteen and a married woman.

"Come back to live on Fountain Avenue," my mother pleaded. "You got some college already. You'll get a good job."

"What kind of husband . . . a no-good *schicker*, a drunk, who leaves you alone," said Rae. "A thunder should strike him. A fire should burn him!"

In the living room of D'Or's apartment on Washington Street in San Francisco were innumerable brown paper sacks, bulging from the sides but folded over neatly at the top and lined up precisely against the walls. The bed was there too. In the dining room was a plastic-topped red table with two chairs and a refrigerator. The kitchen was empty except for an ancient and long-unused gas stove and balls of dust that had gathered in the corners. D'Or asked me not to go into the two bedrooms, though much later I peeked. They had nothing in them but more brown sacks lining the walls and yellowed newspapers stacked in high piles.

But the apartment was filled with the wonderful music she played on her phonograph — *Der Rosenkavalier, The Magic Flute, La Bohème, Tristan und Isolde*. From the dining room window you could see the gleaming white city and the Bay Bridge and an expanse of water that changed with the hours from battleship gray to sapphire. All summer long the front rooms were flooded with sunshine. In this magical place, with a beautiful woman who needed me and belonged to me, how could I not be flooded with hope?

She let me see her writing that first night as we sat together on the dining room floor. The first story she showed me was about a fey young girl with an arcane smile who disguises herself as a boy in red velvet knickers and a golden cap and runs around London in the 1890s with Oscar Wilde and Aubrey Beardsley. D'Or's prose was rich, dark, delicately jeweled, filigreed in twisting images. I read on and on, enchanted. *Brilliant*, I thought with a shiver, *This wonderful woman is absolutely brilliant*. When I finished, I placed the neatly typed pages in a little pile on the floor, marveling still, impatient to begin the next story. "No!" D'Or cried, snatching the desecrated pages up from the scuffed hardwood, clutching them to her breast.

"Oh, God, sorry!" I uttered, chagrined at my gross indelicacy. I made sure to keep the pages of the second story on my lap. That one was about a sadistic mother who joins forces with her cold, ambitious son to torment the daughter of the family, a girl who is sensitive, delicate, imaginative, and is failed even by the father she loves who is always away on business. The mother and brother were caricatures of cruelty and the plot was thin, but in this story too there was such craft and polish in her style. "Let me read more," I begged.

"That's all I've written. Writing requires a certain frame of mind I seldom have the luxury to enjoy. Can't you see why from 'The Mother'?" she cried, grabbing me by the shoulders, peering into my eyes as though she had to be certain I understood and believed her. "Can you imagine a sensitive child who is always the scapegoat, living with people who care about nothing but making money and Golden-rod?" Her lovely lips sneered at the corporate name, and I nodded in sympathy.

"There's such a resonance between us," D'Or murmured one mellow morning of that first week, after we'd made love on the dining room floor. We could hear the cable cars clanging down the hill every few minutes. "Don't you feel it?"

"Yes, oh yes," I murmured. "It's so . . . ineffable . . . so rarefied."

"That's it!" she laughed, delighted, I knew, that her words were now in my mouth.

With her father's death, she got no more money from her family. How would we eat and pay the rent—seventy-five dollars a month? What kind of job could I get? I spent the second week in San Francisco walking into one North Beach nightclub after another, asking for the manager, saying I'd had experience in L.A.—as a waitress, hat check girl, cigarette girl. Would they call the places I said I'd worked and ask for a reference?

D'Or's lips curled as though she'd swallowed something foul when I told her that the owner of Big Al's Hotsy Totsy Club said he'd hire me as a waitress but only if I would also be the Bubble Bath Girl. "It's so tawdry!" She shuddered.

"I guess we could both get little jobs," I offered reluctantly, remembering the $1.25 an hour I'd earned at the library. "What have you worked at before?" I asked.

She batted her big, light eyes for an uncomfortable minute. "I've worked at election polling places," she said finally. "You know," she added when I looked blank, "checking to see that people are registered, and then giving them a ballot." But there wouldn't be another election for more than a year, I calculated. "My father was sending me money for a long time," she sniffed, and her eyes welled up.

Of course she can't hold down a regular job with her compulsive disorder. I have to take care of her. I want to! "D'Or, if I took the job at the Hotsy Totsy Club it would just be a source of income," I argued. "There's no sexual component in that kind of thing." We agreed, finally, that I'd work there only until school started in September. We'd save up a nest egg.

"But . . . you won't make it blatantly vulgar, will you?" she said at the Buena Vista over Irish whiskeys that we'd paid for with the last twenty-dollar bill I'd earned at Andy's. "It needs to be aesthetically pleasing," she lectured me. "Try for delicacy . . . and grace." Her enthusiasm for the project waxed. "You can do it with balletic insinuations, with refinement."

"Yes," I said, nodding to everything she said. "Yes, I will."

"Be subtle," she said, "be classy!"

On the walls of Big Al's Hotsy Totsy Club were murals—Prohibition gangsters holding machine guns with one hand and blond molls in minks with the other and, in the background, Keystone Kops with googly eyes and giant phallic batons. The gangsters all had the face of the nightclub's owner—Big Al, as we waitresses were supposed to call him. We dressed in knee-length jazz-age red shifts with black fringe that shimmied when we moved. As soon as the nightclub filled with customers, a siren would go off as though the Prohibition police were about to burst through the door, but it was only my signal to put my tray down, pass my last order on to another waitress, and run upstairs and change into a pink see-through negligee with a black faux-fur collar and cuffs. Underneath I wore only glittering silver pasties over my nipples and a pink patch of material, a G-string, around my pubes. Downstairs, the colored bubbles were already popping out of a machine and up through a gleaming white lion's claw bathtub in the middle of a little stage. As I walked down the stairs, I struggled to imagine refined ways of removing a see-through negligee onstage and stepping naked into a bathtub without water. I was supposed to saunter on to the tune of "Night Train," test the nonexistent bathwater with a provocatively graceful bare toe, disrobe, then slide into the bubbles and cavort charmingly for five minutes until the police siren went off again and the whole place was dark enough for me to scamper out of the tub and out of sight. A tardy pattering of applause usually followed me. For this I was paid an extra five dollars a night, which meant that, working Wednesday through Saturday, I could take back to Washington Street about a hundred dollars a week—no small sum in 1959.

I tear out of Big Al's after my last bath and run to hop a bus. Then, if I'm lucky, I make the transfer to the final cable car of the night; if not, I have to spend money on a cab that will take me up the hills. I love it when I make the cable car: I jump off at Washington and Jones and look up to our window on the third floor. She's in bed, I know, warm with sleep, and in two minutes my arms will be holding her, and her mouth will taste like bread fresh from the oven. If I felt stupid or exploited that evening or my feet or my head hurt, I've forgotten it by now. I bound up the celestial pathway of stairs.

By the close of summer, though, I was loathing the end of the afternoon, when I'd have to put mascara and rouge on my face, change from blue jeans to my sheath and high heels, and gird myself for the long trip to North Beach and the inanity of the noisy patrons to whom I carried drinks, people who could be titillated by fake gangsters in a fake speakeasy and a girl taking a fake bubble bath.

Without the Hotsy Totsy Club, would I have loved school so intensely, been so grateful for it? I perused the catalogue, craving almost every course that was offered—Cultural Anthropology, Hebrew Literature, Pottery Making, Criminal Law. Once the semester started, I felt cheated because I couldn't be part of student life outside class. Berkeley students were surrounding City Hall in San Francisco, shaking righteous fists at white-haired old men who subpoenaed public school teachers and sat in the hearings of the House Un-American Activities Committee, ruining careers and lives. I remembered the marchers in Mexico City whose absorption in the cause of preventing a two-centavo bus fare hike I'd envied, and I yearned to join the students in San Francisco. But I was taking Zoology and Sociology and Abnormal Psychology and French 3 and fake bubble baths four nights a week, riding at least eight different public conveyances most days, and living with D'Or. When was there time to fight against the HUAC and the San Francisco police, who washed the students off the steps of City Hall with fire hoses?

Yet I had to acknowledge that something else would keep me from joining Students for Civil Liberties, the protest organizers, even if I'd had the leisure: Wouldn't they be horrified if they really knew me? I couldn't tell those sons and daughters of the upper and middle classes about Gigi Frost, the Bubble Bath Girl. They'd never comprehend my life with D'Or in our sack- and newspaper-filled apartment, how I longed to rescue her from her sickness, my sorrow that so far I wasn't making a bit of difference. She still spent ten minutes looking under restaurant tables for invisible objects as I waited, embarrassed, at the exit; her hands were still raw and blistered from the fifty scrubbings with harsh soap and hot water to which she subjected them every day; the mysterious stuffed sacks and the newspaper stacks doubled, quadrupled, sextupled. Who among those radical kids could understand my life?

And who could understand the way I loved D'Or and how I loved to make love to her? I saw no other lesbians on the Berkeley campus, not even a single gay man. I was the only homosexual there—I was sure of it—though one of the personality tests all the entering students had to take the week before the start of classes had asked, "Have you ever kissed a person of the same sex?" and "Are you attracted to those of the same sex?" I answered no to all such questions. How dumb they were to think I'd fall for a shabby little trick like that. I'd be kicked out of Berkeley if they knew about my life, that was clear to me. So I kept my own counsel and talked only in class.

. . .

DER LILI YOU NO YOU AR DERER TO ME THEN THE EYS FROM MY HED. WY DO YOU LEV US LIK THAT AND GO TO SAN FRANSISCO. HOW DO YOU LIV. HOW DO YOU MAK A LIVNG. YOR NO GOOD HUZBAN DUZ NOT COM. I NO IT. PLEZ COM BAK TO LA. YOU CAN GET A DIVORS AND MARY A GOOD MAN. I WIL HELP YOU. COM BAK RIT AWAY. YOR LOVNG ANT THAT LOVS YOU MOR THEN THE MOON IN THE SKI.

It was the first letter I'd ever received from Rae. How excruciating it must have been for her to sound out the words and write them down in an alphabet she barely knew. I laughed at the letter's drollness, but I held the paper to my lips, and my eyes filled with tears.

No, I couldn't do what she asked. How could I leave D'Or? And if I returned to L.A., my mother would make me live with her and Albert again; I wouldn't be able to resist her pleas. All my elaborate schemes would have been for nothing. No, there was no way I'd go home again.

Dear Rae,

I've already started college at Berkeley and I can't leave. Please do not worry about me. I'm living with a good friend, and I have a job in the school library. I'll come to visit you and my mother this winter, when the semester is over.

DER LILI DU NOT WORK IN A LIBARY AND GO TO COLEDG AT THE SAM TIM. YOU WIL MAK YOURSELF SIK. YOUR HELT IS VERY INPORTANT. I WIL SEND YOU MONY EVRY MONT TIL YOU FINISH THE YER. THEN YOU COM BAK. I WIL HELP THE DIVORS. I WIL SEND YOU 150 DOLARS. WHAT DO I WORK FOR. YOUR LOVNG ANT. YOUR MUDER LOVS YOU TO.

Twice a month, a money order for seventy-five dollars arrived on Washington Street along with a phonetic note admonishing me to take care of my health, come home soon, and get a divorce. Now I could devote the four evenings a week I'd spent at the Hotsy Totsy Club to schoolwork and D'Or. A hundred and fifty dollars a month paid the rent, our food bills, and my transportation back and forth across the bay. If I skipped a few lunches, on a Sunday we could even take a bus across the Golden Gate Bridge to Sausalito, where we'd sit puffing on Turkish cigarettes and gaze at the city across the whitecapped bay.

"Creature" was D'Or's pet name for me now, "my glowering, brown-eyed creature." We both wore black turtlenecks; and I had a black leather jacket just like hers, which I'd bought when I was working at the Hotsy Totsy. "We're Gemini twins," D'Or said, glowing. "But why do you always look so sad?"

Did I look sad? When I was with her I didn't feel sad. "Get into the moment," she'd say with zest over glasses of mead at the Glad Hand Bar, which sat at the end of a dock that poked out over the bay in Sausalito. And I did, I thought, I did get into the moment.

"But you still look like you're carrying the weight of the world," she complained over quiche. "Take pleasure in this divine wine, this superb food, this fantastic view. Let's be sybarites," she urged. "What do you worry about so much?"

Doing well in school so that I can someday make a living without depending on my body's curves. Whether Rae's $150 will last until the end of the month. Whether the sacks and stacks will crowd us out of the apartment. How I can keep my aunt from trying to marry me off again once I get a divorce. How I left my mother to bear her miserable, lonely life alone.

"Nothing," I told D'Or. "I don' worry about nothin'." I grinned like a circus clown. "Let's have another mead."

That winter I drove to L.A. with a girl from my French class who wanted someone to share gas expenses on her way to Pasadena. She dropped me off in front of the Fountain Avenue Court Bungalows, and there was my mother. I saw her before she saw me. She was pacing up and down the sidewalk, her wild hair gray for three or four inches past the scalp, then a fading, strawlike brown. She looked lost in some aching thought, distraught, as in the bad days of my childhood. How could she have become such an old woman in the seven months I'd been gone? "So long," she cried when she saw me, and her hug was the familiar old breath-stopping pounce and octopus grip from which I had to break loose. "So many terrible months without seeing you!"

"Leelee." Albert swung open the screen door. "Since twelve o'clock your mother is driving me crazy. She thought you got killed."

"Mom, I told you I wouldn't leave until nine o'clock, and it takes about eight hours to get here."

"She's been walking in and out the house, up and down the sidewalk, the whole afternoon."

"I forgot you told me nine o'clock," my mother said.

How strange it feels to be sleeping in my old room. I'm not at all the same person I was before I left to get married. My spirits lift at the realization: I know where I need to go now. I really do, though I haven't quite mapped out the way.

But my mother has nowhere to go. Her life has been frozen, and I can't escape seeing it. Albert goes off to work with Dr. Friedman and the corpses every day, and what does my mother do? She sits in the little living room and watches television. The soap operas are her favorites—As the World Turns, All My Children, The Days of Our Lives. The tortured look around her eyes and mouth goes away when she watches other people's problems, stories about men who betray, children who disappoint. She shakes her head in commiseration at some other poor woman's troubles. "American children, what do they care about the aggravation they give?" she says when a soap opera actress shrieks her maternal grief.

Sometimes the soaps are about happy lovers, and then my mother gets the look in her eyes that I remember. It's the look she used to have after the Charles Boyer movies we watched together, when she still dreamed that Moishe would love her again. What does she have to dream about now? She's given up on dreams. She's had an aborted life, my poor mother. Nothing worked out for her. Not even me.

About four o'clock she turns off the TV and starts making supper. She wants me to sit in the kitchen to be near her. "Talk to me while I'm cooking," she says. "Who do I have to talk to?"

But she never asks about my life, and I don't know what to tell her. "School's good. I made the dean's list last semester," I say. I know she's not really listening. She wouldn't know what a dean's list was even if she were.

When she talks, it's always a tirade of her grievances: "What kind of man is Albert? All he wants is supper and to play cards. He's the crazy one, and he has the nerve to say I'm crazy." She chops the onions for the chopped liver and brushes away a tear. "I didn't live to feel one whole good day in my life," my mother sighs as she cuts the carrots that she'll cook with the chicken. "That cholerya Rae, what kind of sister? She dragged me to this lousy Los Angeles, and now she lives with Mr. Bergman and that's all she knows! I can go to hell." She beats the matzoh ball mixture as though it were her sister's head. "What kind of daughter do I have? I see you once in nine months; you never call. I hardly get a letter. What do I have in the whole world?"

It's the same thing over and over. My mother is a broken record of suffering. She's been crippled by all the terrible things that have happened to her, and there's nothing I can do to help. My impotence feels unbearable to me.

"How come you want to run away so soon?" she sniffs when the two weeks are up. She hangs on to me in the street until Michelle's old green Nash pulls up and I break away from my mother's grip of death.

I hated the soporific statistics lectures and the silly white mice experiments that were a prominent feature of the psychology major at Berkeley, so the reading I did for my literature class was like eating a juicy sour pickle when you've had a long diet of cream of wheat. *"For he on honeydew hath fed, And drunk the milk of Paradise." "During the whole of a dull, dark and soundless day . . ."* Words on the page could do for me what D'Or said opera did for her: They could be luscious, harrowing, stirring. Mere written words could transport you to another world. I was high with the realization of it. *"O! Let me have thee whole, —all—all—be mine! . . . Withhold no atom's atom or I die."*

"If you like literature so much, why don't you major in English?" D'Or suggested when I asked her to turn the phonograph off so I could read to her Keats's yearning lines to his mistress. D'Or had majored in English at Berkeley, which she'd attended for four years, though she wasn't sure she'd actually graduated.

I laid my book down. "How do you make a living with an English major," I asked, a rhetorical question. But she stared at me with the same look I'd seen when I asked her what jobs she'd had. "There's more to life than making a living," she instructed me soberly before setting the needle back on Papageno and Papagena's duet.

"Yeah, but who's going to pay our bills?" I said above the music, trying to keep exasperation out of my voice.

"The bills will get paid one way or another," she said patiently over Papagena's bliss. "What's important in life? Beauty. Subtlety. Nuance — the things of art." She pronounced the words reverently. "The rest is bourgeois. Unworthy of the artist's sensibility."

"But an artist's sensibility is a luxury." No, I couldn't keep my voice down! "Before you can have luxuries, you need to attend to practicalities."

She lifted up the record needle; Papagena screeched and fell silent. "You sound like my brother," she snickered. "All my life I've had to argue with people like that. Why can't you understand what I'm saying? I want to be classless. The artist is always classless."

"But I can't be classless!" I wanted to shake her. Why didn't she understand me? "If I don't become somebody, you know what choices I have? I can work in a garment factory or I can use my body to make a living."

"There are always other possibilities."

"Like what?"

Her nostrils flared at my obtuseness. "I want you to be a natural aristocrat, just as I am. That's what I thought I saw in you when we met. The natural aristocrat has nothing to strive for. The natural aristocrat lives in essences, in sensibilities. I never knew anybody to study as much as you do," she suddenly cried, accusingly. "You're so disciplined . . . and organized!" She said it in the tone someone else might have used to exclaim "You're a scoundrel . . . a thief!"

14 HOW I BECAME
A BURLESQUE QUEEN

WHEN I WROTE TO MY MOTHER and aunt near the end of my sophomore year to say I was going to stay in San Francisco until I graduated, Rae wrote back:

> I CANT SEND YOU MONY NO MOR TIL YOU COM BAK TO LA LIK YOU SED. WHY YOU DONT GET A DIVORS LIK YOU SED. WHY YOU WANT TO RUON YOUR LIF. TAK CAR ON YOUR HELT. YOUR HELT IS VERY INPORTANT.

If my aunt stopped sending me money, how would we live? I might get summer work as a salesgirl or a waitress, but what would I do when school started again?

"I got a job!" D'Or announced when she returned to the apartment one afternoon while I was studying for finals. "I start tomorrow." She'd be going from house to house to take the census. For one month.

I couldn't go back to Big Al's Hotsy Totsy Club because I'd quit without notice. Anyway, when school started again, I'd hate to give up all those hours every week to serving drinks and taking phony bubble baths when I needed the time to study. I was changing my major to English, and I had to make up the literature classes I'd missed as a psych major. I'd decided I really wanted to be a writer, and because I knew that writers didn't always make a living, I would get a Ph.D. and become an English professor too. That way I'd be sure to have a salary, and I'd be teaching the works of other writers that I loved.

But I couldn't think too much about long-range plans now; I had to think about how D'Or and I would get by when the San Francisco census was done.

"Girls wanted 21–28 for burlesque chorus. Some dancing. $55/wk." The ad was in the HELP WANTED—WOMEN section of the *San Francisco Examiner*. Why shouldn't I? Here, in San Francisco, away from my mother and Rae, why shouldn't I use whatever I could if it would get me where I needed to go? Why shouldn't I turn to coin whatever gifts I had to make up for the patrimony I would never have?

I'd see what a burlesque chorus did before I applied for the job, I decided. The President Follies was a faded old theater palace on McAllister Street, with big black letters on a cracked marquis that announced: TWO WEEKS ONLY THE FAN-TASTIC MISS BRANDY DEVINE. The redheaded woman in the booth looked suspicious. "Just for you?" Her orange lips pursed. She hesitated, then took my money and shoved a ticket at me.

In the chorus were about a dozen girls, and each time they came out on the stage they wore a different costume—shocking-pink harem pants with see-through bras; satiny black Apache-dancer dresses with a slit all the way to the bellybutton; pleated schoolgirl skirts so short that white panties winked at the slightest move; and, for the finale, pastel muslin gowns, debutante style, that broke away with one brisk pull. No matter what they were wearing, the point was to shed one piece of clothing after another. From my seat at the back of the big, musty-smelling theater I could observe the sparse audience—mostly middle-aged men alone; a couple of clusters of frat boy types; a few opposite-sex couples.

About the time the schoolgirls were wiggling out of their middy blouses, a stoop-shouldered man in a hat he never took off plunked himself down across the aisle from me and opened a newspaper on his lap. The schoolgirls shook their butts at the audience in a mock exercise until the little pleated skirts dropped to the floor. I could hear the man's newspaper rustling in a steady rhythm, and I fought the impulse to gag, to bolt. No, I wouldn't let him scare me off. Now the schoolgirls kicked high in time to drum rolls, pulled at the breakaway white panties, which came off in their hands, and, finally, faced the audience, bumping-and-grinding Lolitas, twirling panties in an arc above their heads, clad now only in G-strings and pasties that twinkled in the footlights. "Umff," the man softly cried.

But from the stage, with the footlights shining up at you, you probably couldn't see past the first rows. You'd just do your thing and you wouldn't have to think about who was in the audience. You'd be onstage for a total of only twenty or twenty-five minutes during the whole show, and the rest of the time you could be sitting in the dressing room, doing your homework, reading Shelley and George Eliot and Theodore Dreiser.

There were other acts at the President Follies as well. There was a comic, Buddy LaRue, with a bulbous bright red nose, who honked on a horn in the pocket of his baggy clown pants after the punch line of each fatuous sex joke. And there were three or four "regular features" with names like Boston's Blond Bombshell Miss Bathsheba, the Sexy Sultry Satana, and the Electrifying Electra (who, with a dexterous toe, triggered some motor in the drum on which she did her gyrations, causing a gush of wind to send her long, black hair flying straight up in the air). All these acts led up to the two-week star, "the Fan-tastic Miss Brandy Devine," who had a white-blond Veronica Lake hairdo and danced around with a huge fan. Every time she opened it, another piece of clothing would drift to the floor, then she'd close it again so the audience could have a look at what she was exposing now. Miss Devine had long legs and well-formed buttocks, but her breasts and hips were boyishly flat. How much did she make? I wondered. More than fifty-five dollars a week, I was certain. And she had to come out onstage only once. I knew I couldn't dance like her—in fact, I couldn't dance at all—but didn't I have a better body? And wasn't that the main point?

"You'll go in, ask for the manager, say you're my agent." I'd thought it all through. "Tell him that I've worked everywhere—New York, Chicago, L.A. How'll he know I didn't? Tell him you can bring me to town for three weeks at, say, $500 a week. Look, you'll show him my magazine pictures. The *King* cover looks as if I do a sword act. We'll get me a sword I can dance around with. And there's one where I look like a belly dancer."

"It's sordid." D'Or grimaced over a carton of chop suey that I'd brought back for our dinner.

"Then how will we live?" I asked, trying hard to be patient. Her census job would be over at the end of the week. She balanced a single bean sprout between her wooden chopsticks and didn't answer. "Hey, what the hell happened to the iconoclastic, classless, self-defined original?" I snorted.

"What?" D'Or asked.

Now I was too upset to eat. I put my cardboard container down on the red table and went to stand at the front window and stare at the city beneath us. Didn't she care about us? I would rather die than leave her and go back to Los Angeles, but how could I be a student at Berkeley and make enough money to stay with her? Why the hell couldn't she get real work and take care of us until I graduated? *No. D'Or can't do what she can't do*, I lectured myself. *It's cruel to demand it.*

That night, as she held her hands under the bathtub jet, scrubbing them with Lava until little drops of blood oozed from a palm, I told her, "I know how we'll do it. Listen. When I've finished as the main feature at $500 a week, you'll go in and tell them I want to stay in San Francisco and that I'm willing to take half the pay to be one of their regular features. If they hire me permanently at $250 a week, we'll be getting about five times what the chorus girls make, and I'll have loads of study time between my acts. There's no other solution. Let's work on this together," I begged.

"Okay . . . okay," she finally said, though her lip was raised in disgust.

But in the morning she was in high spirits. "We'll do it right," D'Or declared. My name would be Mink Frost, we decided together over our coffee, and my style would be cool and sophisticated. The Most Beautiful Body in Burlesque, my tag would be. I'd wear the rhinestone necklace and earrings I still had from the Simone days, and we'd find some fake fur that we could cut up into a mink stole. I'd do a classy under-a-streetlamp act. With my first paycheck, we'd get a dressmaker to cut me a fake-mink bikini that I'd wear under my gowns. We were laughing now. Inventing Mink Frost. It was an adventure. "Nothing sordid," we recited together in punchy fun. I remembered Marlene Dietrich images

"In my college briefcase, she carried my girlie magazine pictures."

—seductively cold and commanding, sophisticated, mysterious. It would be a role no harder for me to play than that of Blanche DuBois or Anna Christie. We hurried to a Thrifty Drug six blocks away and bought some cans of silver and gold spray. Then, on the dining room floor, we laid out a tight, white backless dress I'd once had made with my modeling money, and—craftswomen, businesswomen—we squirted the canned glitter all over it. My first costume. It looked pretty good by the time we finished.

The next day we decked D'Or out—my high heels, a French beret I used to pose in, her black trenchcoat. We studied the effect together in the long bathroom mirror, delighted at how much like a real agent she looked. In my college briefcase, she carried my girlie magazine pictures.

She came back in an hour, breezing through the door, beaming with accomplishment. "I got you two weeks at $250 a week." She laughed. "I thought $500 sounded like a lot, so I didn't even ask, but he went for the $250 easily. Now do it with class," she admonished me once again. "I saw some peroxided blonde on the stage, bumping her pelvis on the curtain as if she was having sex with it. Disgusting."

. . .

It happens as I hoped. After my two weeks as the main feature, D'Or goes back to Mr. Chelton, the manager, and says I'll stay on at half the pay, $125 a week. He thinks he's getting a bargain. "Be a vamp, not a tramp," D'Or instructs me for the hundredth time.

I work seven days a week — two shows on Monday through Friday evening, four on Saturday, three on Sunday — seventeen altogether. I do my act once each show, and I also appear in a half-time chorus number and the finale. The rest of the time I can sit in the dressing room and read novels and poetry. I don't say much to the other girls, and they probably think I'm very odd. "How come you're reading all the time?" Electra asks.

"I dunno. I just like it," I say. How can I tell them that I'm a college student? Better to say nothing.

One day Bathsheba presents a quandary to us. She can buy this fantastic Chevy convertible — white leather upholstery, low mileage, practically brand new. The guy who lives next door to her will let her have it for five hundred bucks. "A real bargain," she sighs and picks absent-mindedly at the tomato-red polish on her nails.

"So get it," the new feature, Gilda the Golden Goddess, tells her, slipping into her sequined gold gown.

"I don't have five hundred bucks," says Bathsheba, brooding, as she stirs herself to take off her street clothes. "But there's this guy who's been coming around to the stage door all week. You probably seen him — wears a nice suit and tie and everything. He says he'll give me the money if I go with him just one time."

"Well, then what's the problem?" Satana asks, zipping the black satin she'll unzip onstage in a few minutes.

Aren't they afraid of getting pregnant? How do you even find someone who'll do an abortion? My mother had two abortions. And look how she ended up.

"I never did that before," Bathsheba says and stares down at the floor.

I put my book down on the dressing table and look at Bathsheba. Don't do it, is what I want to say, but she's already told us that on the eighty-five dollars a week she gets, she'd never be able to buy a convertible, and she'd die for one.

Three days later Bathsheba says she got the pink slip on the car.

. . .

One night on my dressing room table there's a vase holding a dozen yellow roses. "Dear Mink," the note says, "If you will have dinner with me at the Mark Hopkins, I guarantee you will not regret it. Your admirer, John D." There's a telephone number at the bottom. Don't the patrons understand that Mink Frost is a stage illusion, that I'm an actress and not the under-a-streetlamp vamp they see onstage? I'm repelled. I lift the note by a corner and drop it in the dressing room wastebasket. The yellow roses I give to Greta, a former stripper who choreographs the chorus numbers and loves flowers. Another night I'm getting into my street clothes after the last show, and Greta comes to say there's a man waiting for me at the stage door. By now I'm a master of disguise. I wipe off my makeup, the scarf I wear around my neck becomes my babushka, I rub a bit of powder on my black coat to make it look soiled. Mink Frost has disappeared. I'm the cleaning lady. That's the way I leave the theater from that night on.

But none of this is really scary, not the way it was when I was a model four years earlier, because I'm getting a college degree now. I know my life at the President Follies is only temporary . . . that, really, I'm safe.

D'Or's washing-searching-counting-collecting got worse instead of better. "If you loved me more you'd stop that shit," I yelled at her one day in the spring of my junior year. "I'm working myself to death—fifteen units a semester at Berkeley, seven days a week at the President Follies, and I don't ask you to do a goddam thing but get over your sickness!" Sometimes I daydreamed a D'Or who was perfectly well. *"You rescued me from dragons and devils,"* she'd exclaim in the fantasy in which I became Mary Marvel again. *"You brought me so much happiness that I don't need to do those things now."* Then I'd hear the gush of water in the bathtub, where she always washed her hands because it made a stronger stream than the little faucet on the sink did.

We hardly ever made love anymore. Instead we fought, a lot, about anything.

One Sunday, before the three o'clock matinee at the President, we went to brunch at a place on Powell Street. Then, despite a San Francisco drizzle, we strolled arm-in-arm and stopped to press our noses on the shop windows around Union Square, and I felt lighthearted, being away from the manacle of the dressing room for a few precious hours. In a toy shop window was a stuffed bear that D'Or cooed over in a child's voice: "Oh, oh, just like the one I wanted when I was a little girl! They'd never buy it for me."

Monday, after classes, I skipped the usual quick dinner I got at the Berkeley cafeteria before hopping the buses that would take me to the President in time for the seven o'clock show. I headed straight to Union Square. But the teddy bear was gone from the window.

"They're on order," the salesgirl said. "Try us in ten days."

I traipsed through the streets, a knight seeking a treasure for my lady love, until at last, thirty minutes before I absolutely had to get into my costume, I found it. Not a little bear like the one in the window, but a huge bear, a beautiful bear, with rich brown fur and a green satin ribbon and two tinkly little silver bells around its neck, a bear I too would have lusted after when I was a kid. The cashier put it in a big pink box with a white bow. Then I balanced the box in one hand, my briefcase stuffed with books and homework in the other, and dashed down Geary to the President. I felt silly but happy too, and as Mink Frost bumped and grinded and peeled off layers under the footlights, I saw myself handing D'Or the healing gift.

After the second show I rebalanced my load and hurried through the dark streets to hop the bus that took me down Market and then the cable car that took me up Powell. At Jones I jumped off and looked up at our window the way I used to when I first came to San Francisco to be with D'Or. The old feelings I'd almost forgotten came back with a wild rush. *She's up there, my beloved,* I told myself now, *and soon I'll be holding her in my arms and kissing her.* "You remembered!" *she'll exclaim, her eyes overflowing with love.*

I've been too hard on her, I thought, shamed now by my ongoing pettiness. *If I can't be sympathetic to her problems, who in the whole world can?*

I bounded up the three flights feeling just a bit foolish. I was carrying a teddy bear to a thirty-five-year-old woman. Yet, why shouldn't we do such things for each other? What did years matter between lovers? Lovers could do anything—they could take away the hurts of childhood. *Here you are, little girl,* I'd whisper as I gave her the present.

She did say "You remembered!" when she opened the pink box, and then she put the gift down and hugged me. But I'd seen something fleeting in her eyes when she'd pushed the tissue paper aside and glimpsed the fur. What?

"Well," I laughed. "Do you really like it?"

"Yes," she exclaimed, then her lips pursed analytically. "I love it, because it came from you . . . but . . . it's not exactly . . . Do you really want me to say it?" Her voice was little-girl high.

"Yes. What?" She paused for a long time, as though considering whether to come out with it. "What?" I asked, impatient now.

"It's not . . . Oh," she squeaked, "it's not like the one I wanted when I was a kid. The one I always wanted was a little panda bear—they're black and white, just like the one in the Union Square window. They're small and you can cuddle them," she said wistfully.

I tore the brown thing from her arms. "Forget it!" What would I do with the absurd object? "It was dumb of me," I snarled. I hid my childish grief in anger; then the anger became more real than grief, and my fingers itched to pull the bear's head off, to rip the phony fur to pieces. I hated it!

"No, no. I love this bear. Really," D'Or cried.

And I hated that grating little-girl voice! She tried to retrieve the stuffed animal from my arms, and I wrested it back from her. "I don't want you to have it now," I yelled, pushing open the side window that overlooked the alley. I hated her too. "You've reduced us both to infants!" I pushed at her grasping hands, hugged the ridiculous thing to my chest, then flung it out the window with all the force my arm could muster. It rebounded against the neighboring building, then somersaulted silently.

"No!" she screamed, as though it were a person. We both peered down in horror. By the light of a window on the first floor we could see it, splayed on the ground in a puddle of water, a dead child, a pathetic, broken thing.

"Why did you do that?" D'Or cried.

I slept on the bare dining room floor that night, my black coat my blanket. The next morning I left earlier than usual to catch my cable car and the three buses to the Berkeley campus.

. . .

But we didn't always fight. San Francisco was gloriously warm and sunny the summer after my junior year. I stayed on at the President Follies, but since I wasn't in school, from Monday through Friday I was free until the evening. Our favorite thing was to go to Tiburon and sit in some isolated spot near the water, gazing at the blue bay, chatting and dreaming about how someday we'd travel and see the Bay of Naples and the Bay of Rio, and all the other magnificent bays in the world, how we'd write books together and support ourselves as authors. We loved to drink mai tais at Tiburon Tommy's that summer and wander around the green hills of Marin, our hands linked until someone approached. We'd jump apart, and when they passed we'd laugh and link hands again. At those times we were in love once more. I'd forget about our fights and how often after a rage I'd feel sickened, contrite, trapped; how I'd look down to the alley from the side window to see on the ground, not the brown bear, but a dead D'Or or a dead Lillian; how often I'd be sure that our life together would end in homicide or suicide.

Our knockdown drag-out fight came near the end of the fall semester. "I read this really fascinating article in the *Examiner* today," D'Or said as I was getting ready for bed after the Saturday midnight show at the President. "Are you too tired to listen? It's pretty long."

"Yeah, I'm exhausted." But I could tell she really wanted to share it with me.

"That's okay. I'll just summarize. Listen to this: Dr. Steven Donnelly, a Cornell professor, studied a hundred women who were employed as exotic dancers—like you. He looked at their families, economic background, everything." She was excited, as though she'd finally discovered the key to a giant puzzle.

"Um-hmm." I flopped onto the unmade bed.

"Can you guess the primary thing they had in common?" D'Or asked, a ninth-grade teacher administering a quiz.

"Not a clue." I felt my stomach tighten. I had so little in common with the girls with whom I worked. I liked them because they worked hard for their bit of money, and they were always sweet to me, even though we didn't say much to one another because my "nose was always in a book," as Celestial Celeste had remarked the other day. But I was as different from them as a raven from a salmon.

"The Cornell professor found that all the women in his study came from the lower socioeconomic classes and were rejected by their fathers," D'Or enunciated, standing over my prone body. "*Every* one of them had those things in common," she squealed.

I sat up in bed, yanking the covers tight around me. "Look, I'm working at the President, not because I was rejected by my fucking father, but because somebody's got to pay the rent and buy the fucking food around here." I felt my face contort. How ugly I felt, how ugly she made me feel. "And as long as I'm going to school, there's no other job I can get that will let me do that and have time left for study," I yelled.

D'Or still hovered above me. "The point is," she said in the cool voice of a detached observer, "you wouldn't have been able to conceive of such employment if you'd had a normal relationship with a father and if—"

"What the shit does that mean?" She was telling me I was a victim. I'd struggled so hard not to be that, to exercise control over my life. I bounded out of bed, grabbed her shoulders, shook her. "Did you have a normal relationship with your father? You're crippled, damn you!" I raged into her face. "At least I function in the world. I may be a bastard and low class, but who's supporting the Daughter Goldenrod, you bitch? Who?"

"I'm just explaining why you're so willing to take your clothes off in front of strange men." She shrugged me off with maddening calm. "There's never anything wrong with the truth, Lillian."

"You go to hell with your truth!" I leapt at her again, claws extended, ready to throttle. She dodged and I tripped, and my head met the wall with a dull thud. "Go to hell," I muttered, ashamed, disgusted, wrapping my arms around myself like a straitjacket. She would drive me to distraction, to deadly violence. I went to stare out the window. *I will either jump or push her,* I thought again. *What a blessing it would be, what a satisfaction!* The splayed brown bear was still down there. I could see it, nothing but a desiccated heap of rag after all these months. If I didn't get out soon, that would be one of us.

· · ·

But then, before long, I'd watch how a beam of sun played with her hair as she sat at the red table. Or I'd think about the way her black leather jacket had flapped in the wind at her father's funeral. Or some poem or piece of prose would move me to tears, and she'd let me read it to her. "Yes! I love that, yes!" she'd cry. Her gray eyes were beautiful to me again, and I'd forget, for a while, how she made me feel ugly and common, how she made me feel like committing mayhem.

That's the way three years passed on Washington Street.

In the late winter Mara Karrara came to the President Follies. I'd never heard of her, but people who knew about burlesque knew her name. Mr. Chelton rented two huge searchlights to stand in front of the theater and send great beams to the sky that were visible for miles around. For the first time since I'd been at the President, the theater was packed for almost every show. Bathsheba, who'd watched the first crowd come in, reported, "Everybody dressed up fancy today, no guys carrying newspapers for their laps."

"The Queen of South American Burlesque" was Mara Karrara's tag. She was a honey blond, with gleaming honey tones to her skin and a bearing that was regal despite her petite stature and voluptuous, pear-shaped breasts. Mara was a real dancer, with all the balletic skill and class that D'Or had once pretended I could put into my poor little numbers. Her costumes were extraordinary too—huge headdresses of exotic green and gold feathers, jeweled lamé capes, extravagant gowns of heavy satin. Toward the end of her act, when she had already rid herself of cape and gown and headdress and shaken out her honeyed tresses, she paused before the audience in only her golden skin and the patch of pink G-string; then she reached into a gigantic basket of colorful wax fruits on stage-left. Out came a live green snake, long and fat and penile, with which she danced an intricately choreographed ballet of love. Word got around that Chelton was paying her two thousand dollars a week and that she'd earned her entire salary on the first weekend.

"You know what she does when she gets out on that runway?" Satana sneered. "She takes a picture. That's how come they like her so much."

I knew what *take a picture* was supposed to mean, but I'd never seen it: The stripper pushes her G-string aside, pulls her labia open, and exposes her clitoris to the audience. "My boyfriend saw the show and he told me," Satana insisted when I said, "Why would someone with such a great act do that?" I'd watched Mara from the wings whenever I could —she really was an artist—though of course I couldn't see the end of the runway from the wings. But I decided the *take a picture* story was born out of jealousy, because Satana had also whined the night before, "What's so great about that Mara Karrara for her to get two thousand bucks a week and us to get peanuts?"

"You are very nice," Mara said when I nervously complimented her on her act. "Very nice." Her deep-red lips smiled vivaciously, and she molded her hands to suggest breasts and waist and hips. Our eyes connected, then she winked a long wink. She traveled with a man—"my manager," she called him when I dared to ask if Sergio, a stomachy gentleman with thinning gray hair who looked like an insurance salesman, was her husband. "He make my costume, teach me the dances, everything," she said, straightening with competent fingers a twisted shoulder strap on my new red gown, then patting my bare shoulder.

"That Mara Karrara gets two thousand a week, can you imagine?" I exclaimed to D'Or. I just wanted to hear myself say Mara's name out loud. Her bright smile kept playing itself over in my head. I kept feeling her long fingers as they smoothed my gown strap.

"I've never heard of a woman making that much money." D'Or's eyes grew wide at the munificent sum. "Does she really have anything you don't have?"

"Nah." I laughed. "Only that she's beautiful, she knows how to dance, she has incredible costumes, a fantastic act, a manager who knows what he's doing."

"Couldn't her manager train you?" D'Or asked.

"Why would he do that?" I shrugged.

But why not? I hadn't thought about it before. Maybe he would take me on. If I was going to be a stripper, even for a little while more, why shouldn't I try to be a star? What couldn't D'Or and I do with that kind of money? "Hmm, maybe it couldn't hurt to try," I said.

We became almost giddy about the scheme. With Mara and Sergio, I'd get into big-time burlesque, travel the fancy circuit—Las Vegas, Rio, Paris, places like that. I'd spend a year or two at it, earn a real nest egg for us. I wasn't even twenty-two. I had plenty of time to go to graduate school.

"You'd be able to afford Harvard or Yale," D'Or said, serious now. "I'd move east with you if you wanted an Ivy League," she promised.

The more I thought about the idea, the better it seemed. I sat in my Milton seminar the next day, figuring out the details as a student droned his paper on "Eve's Impaired Judgment." If I earned a lot of money now, I wouldn't have to work in graduate school, and maybe if I felt less pressure, D'Or and I wouldn't have so many fights. I did love her. Whenever I'd been certain that it was over, that we were finished, I'd see a gesture of her hand, an angle of her head, or she'd say something like "Oh, Creature, what would I do without you?" and I'd feel the love well up all over again. I couldn't leave her, but neither could I go to graduate school and keep living with her and fighting with her and working as much as I had been.

"Okay," I told D'Or that evening, "here's the plan. You go ask them. You'll say you're my manager. Go ahead and tell them I'm a college student and that I can join them in June, when I've finished school." What if I did it for just one year? Say I made only half of what Mara got—I'd come out with around fifty thousand dollars. It would see us through graduate school and years after if we were even a little careful.

Sergio watched my act from the wings after D'Or talked to him. I sensed how his serious eyes were trained on me, following me, like someone evaluating a business proposition, but when I glanced back and saw him in the shadows he had a tiny smile. The next morning, before I left for school, he called D'Or to say that both he and Mara would like it if I joined them. They'd be in Toledo, Ohio, in June, and I could meet them there.

That evening Mara invited me into her dressing room, and I watched her in the mirror as she placed the huge feathered cap on her head. I'd travel with them, she said. Sergio would make costumes for me, she would teach me dances like hers, we would have a very wonderful time. We smiled at each other in the mirror. "Very wonderful," she repeated. Then she turned to hug me, her green and gold feathers brushing against my cheek, and she hurried out to take her place in the wings before her music started up.

Now, when I was drifting off to sleep at night, I saw Mara's golden skin; I saw it in my dreams too, and when I awoke in the morning. I was discomfited by my fantasies, and suddenly I was badly confused. Was I going with them to make money for graduate school and for D'Or and me or was it because of Mara? My head rested on a pillow only millimeters from D'Or's. What kept my perfidious thoughts from slithering out of my skull into hers? I wondered guiltily.

Then Mara's two weeks were over. "In Toledo!" Sergio wore the same smile I'd seen when he stood in the wings, and when I gave him my hand to shake, he squeezed it in a damp paw. We would meet on June 22, a week after I graduated. Sergio held the theater door open for Mara. She made him stand there at the door while she put her arms around me, and we hugged much longer than casual friends would. When I turned my lips to her silken cheek they brushed by chance near her mouth, and I felt her fingers tighten on my back. The look she gave me when we finally pulled apart was charged, sexual. It couldn't have been anything else. But Sergio must have seen. In fact, it felt as though she'd wanted him to see. When I glanced at him, he was again smiling that mysterious little smile.

Were they lovers? I wondered about it all the time now.

And what would they expect of me? The question popped into my head days later, and I couldn't get it out. She'd looked at me like that, knowing that he was watching. What kind of deal did they have between them? What if he wanted me too? What if that was their deal? Something was sure to happen between Mara and me, but what if he wanted to be a part of it too—and she wanted him to be a part of it? I'd be alone with them both in a strange city. Anything could happen. Anything. Did she really *take a picture* on the runway?

. . .

The questions hung over me like a bogeyman's threat. I think it was Dr. Jackson who kept me from getting the answers. Dr. Jackson was an elderly man with a great shock of white hair that fell over his forehead, dressed always in the conservative tweeds that were practically requisite for Berkeley professors in the early 1960s. All semester he'd made Victorian England come alive for me, and he'd made me understand that literature wasn't just gripping characters or striking images or musical language. "Dickens, Kingsley, Disraeli—they entertained, but they also seduced their smug middle-class readers into caring about social problems that were right under their noses, though they couldn't see them without the help of art." That was Dr. Jackson's lecture the week after Mara and Sergio left San Francisco. "We mustn't denigrate other kinds of artistic goals; but theirs—to alleviate social injustice through art—that's the artist's most noble undertaking." The class applauded, though lectures were never applauded at Berkeley except at semester's end. Maybe because what Professor Jackson said made me remember how I felt standing on the street in Mexico City, watching the student demonstration, and how I felt about the HUAC protests, and how I loved the things Maury used to say about justice; or maybe it was because I was on an emotional edge over Mara and Sergio—whatever the reason, I sat there, intensely moved, not applauding but crying. Tears streamed down my cheeks, and though I felt like a fool I couldn't stop them. I swiped at my face with the back of my hand. I was giving up the possibility of doing fine things . . . for what? To go to Toledo, Ohio, and be a stripper—and who knew what else? I couldn't do it . . . not even for a year, not for money, nor love of D'Or, nor the fascination of Mara. I wouldn't! Sitting there, runny-nosed, in the auditorium, I felt I'd been rescued from a hot fire just in time. It had almost gotten me . . . that thing that had always awaited me . . . just when I thought I was completely safe. But Dr. Jackson plucked me out at the eleventh hour.

"I'm going to graduate school right away," I told D'Or that night. "I can't go touring. If I work as a stripper, I won't be able to stop after a year."

"But . . . what will we do?"

"I'll figure it out," I said, though I had no idea how.

. . .

I'd written to my mother and Rae to say I wouldn't be visiting during Easter break, because when I asked Chelton for time off he'd grumped, "If you're leavin' all the time, whadda I need you for?"

A week later, I got to my Chaucer class early and settled into the empty room with an open text before me. " 'This child I am comanded for to take,'—And spak namoore, but out the child he hente Despitously," I read, and the fourteenth-century English in my head was suddenly mixed with words in a Yiddish accent—my mother and Rae's Yiddish accent—so real, it was as if they were standing in the hall.

"The lady said Wheel Building, upstairs, thirty-three." That was my aunt's unmistakable voice.

"Maybe we're not in Wheel Building. There's no thirty-three here." My mother's voice.

"Excuse me, we're looking for Lilly Faderman, in Wheel Building," the foghorn blared.

"Well, this is Wheeler *Hall*. There's no thirty-three upstairs, but room two thirty-three is right there," a young man's voice said politely.

I closed my book. *This is what comes of always working, no rest, fighting all the time with D'Or. You hallucinate, like the times you saw Genghis and Khan slinking around the living room at Mark's when they were asleep in the kitchen.* I drifted out to the hall as though in a dream.

But there they were. In the flesh! In their sweet flesh. My mother was wearing a new woolen suit and patent leather high heels, and I could tell she'd been to the beauty parlor because her hair was all brown now and in shiny waves. Her mouth was bright with lipstick. My aunt wore a purple coat and a green hat with a veil, such as nobody had worn for ten or fifteen years, and on her feet were her orthopedic shoes, a hole cut out on the left one for her bunion. They both looked so beautiful to me, even when Rae yelled at the top of her voice, "Lilly! Mary, look, she's here!" and my mother jumped on me and wept, "Lilly! We haven't seen you for so long! When are you coming home?" and everyone who passed stared at them and me and tittered.

I gulped down the sob that would betray my pretend composure. "Shhh," I whispered, "classes go on here. We have to be quiet. Soon," I promised my mother, my finger to my lips, my heart full with the miracle of these two old ladies, my treasure, standing right there in Wheeler

Hall. "I graduate in June, and then I'm coming back for good. Soon." I kissed them with my mother's style of loud, smacking kisses. To hell with the tittering students.

"Don't work no more. You'll make yourself sick with work and school. That's what we came to tell you," my aunt said, ignoring my *shhh*. "I'll send money till you graduate. Only stop working," she roared in the second-floor hall of Wheeler.

I finally got the whole story: D'Or had attended Berkeley from 1949 to 1953. At the end of the four years she went to the graduation ceremony, just sat in the audience. "I thought it was my right," she said.

"But you didn't graduate?" I tried to get it straight.

"I don't know. I just went for four years and got mostly *A*'s, but I don't think I finished everything."

"Let's order your transcripts and see," I said.

She'd gotten three incompletes in English classes and lacked one course for her foreign language requirement.

I applied to graduate school at UCLA, just barely under the deadline. Though I'd failed to change D'Or's life, I had to change my own. "If I'm accepted at UCLA I'm going," I told her the next week, chomping on one of the corned beef sandwiches I'd brought back from David's, avoiding those gray eyes that had made me forget iron resolves a hundred times before.

"You know I'm not going back to Los Angeles," D'Or cried. "You know I can't live near my mother and brother."

"Let's worry about that later," I said quickly. I'd made a plan. "For now we'll worry about your college degree."

"Why? I haven't done schoolwork for ten years!" She was dismissing the idea. I couldn't let her.

"Look, D'Or, I'll help you write the papers to make up your English incompletes." I'd do anything. I had to.

"I wouldn't even know where to begin," she said, and shook her head.

"Okay, okay, look . . . *I'll* write them. You just convince them to let you into a French class, even though it's late in the semester." I gave her my best encouraging smile. "You're a great saleswoman, D'Or: You convinced Chelton and Sergio about me."

The next day I waited for her outside the dean's office. She emerged smiling triumphantly. The dean would let her enroll late in a French reading class. "But it meets four days a week," she cried seconds later, a mountain of impossibility on her frail shoulders. "How am I going to come here for classes four days a week?"

"Present," I answered each day when the teaching assistant went down the list in the rollbook and at the end called "Shirley Ann Goldstein." Miss Goldstein earned a B in French.

"D'Or, we have to talk." The night after my last final I stood behind her as she held her hands under the bathtub faucet. "D'Or, I've got to find my way, because unless I do I'm nothing. And I can't find my way by going off to be a stripper with Mara."

She whirled to face me, holding her dripping hands up like a surgeon after a scrub. "But that was your idea!" she shrieked. "It's not fair of you to imply that I was the one who wanted you to be a stripper!"

"You're right, D'Or, of course you're right." I couldn't blame her for it. But now, finally, I wanted out. I had to get out. "It was my idea, but I can't keep doing stuff like that. I want my life to be different, but I've been so exhausted for the last years, with work and school and everything else, that I haven't been able to think clearly."

"So you *are* blaming me." She glared at me as she rubbed her hands brutally on a clean white towel that was soon dotted with drops of blood. "You're making me your scapegoat, just like my mother and brother always do!"

It would explode. We'd have another knockdown drag-out fight, I'd feel guilty for my rage and I'd apologize, and we'd be right back at the beginning. I couldn't let it happen again. I had to make her see, once and for all. "D'Or, look at me." She wouldn't face me, though I followed at her heels. "D'Or, I need to find out what I can do in the world, and—it's like what you once told me about your writing—that kind of discovery takes a certain frame of mind that I don't have yet. For now, I need to travel alone."

Finally she looked. Her smile was bitter. "After everything you promised," she sneered.

"I know. I failed," I said. "D'Or, I'm sorry. I'm really sorry I'm not Mary Marvel."

I was accepted in the English graduate program at UCLA, and D'Or and I graduated from Berkeley at the same time. The day her diploma arrived in the mail, I got on a Greyhound bus and headed back, toward my mother and aunt.

Lillian, 1962,
UC Berkeley

15 MEN II

I RECITED THE LESSONS of the past three years as the bus lumbered south in the night, through Tracy, Stockton, Merced, Bakersfield, and the teenage girl in a baseball cap sitting next to me cracked her gum and puffed on mentholated cigarettes and stared into space. *Here's what I know that I didn't know before I went to San Francisco: (1) I can't rescue women like D'Or (any more than I could rescue my mother), and I've got to give up that Mary Marvel fantasy. Point to think about: If love with a woman is so full of wrenching extremes—such unreal ecstatic highs, such too-real murderous lows—do I really want to be a lesbian? Do I have a choice? (2) There's a bogeyman lurking in wait for me out there (I'd smelled his breath on Mara and Sergio), and if I don't stop placing my naked self in full view, one of these days he'll surely pounce and drag me off to the fate prepared for girls like me. Point to think about: How will I get the money for graduate school if I don't work as a nude model or a stripper? How will I even get through the summer? (3) I'm in love with poetry and fiction. Point to think about: What do poetry and fiction have to do with the noble causes that stir me, with what Maury once called* justice? *Should I live in a high tower? Can I?*

It was number 2 that I had to deal with immediately. Back in my old room on Fountain Avenue, I spread the *Los Angeles Herald* out on the bed and scanned the HELP WANTED —WOMEN section. The pickings were slim in the summer of 1962 for a young female with a B.A. from Berkeley in English. I could be a telephone operator; I could sell magazines door-to-door (as Nicky had, without even a high school diploma);

I could be an ad-taker; I could be a desk clerk at the Ambassador Hotel or a hostess at Googie's restaurant. I had to take something and fast. I had to get my own apartment before my mother got too used to my living with her again and I felt trapped. I went to work for the *Hollywood Advertiser,* a throwaway newspaper with a dozen pages of "Apartment for rent" and "Used dishwasher for sale" ads.

With my first two weeks' salary I moved out of Fountain Avenue and rented a little apartment at 420 North Curson—but before I knew it, my mother and Albert moved into 401 North Curson and Rae and Mr. Bergman were occupying 404 North Curson. My living alone was pretty much over before it had really begun.

I have given up the sex trades for good. Now I am a member of the legitimate labor force, from eight to five, with a half-hour off for a sack lunch gobbled on a couch in the ladies' room and two fifteen-minute cigarette breaks puffed away on the same couch. We sit in narrow cubicles made of thin gray board, just high enough to block each of us off from her neighbors. We wear wire headsets that clamp at one ear and reach around to our lips. Every few minutes an operator at the main switchboard buzzes one of us and we click on, ready to write down the ad dictated by a new disembodied voice. Our pens are always leaking, and by the end of the day our stiff fingers are purple with ink, our faces streaked with it, our skirts splotched with it. "No talking!" The clean-fingered, clean-skirted supervisor appears at my elbow, shaking her head as if at a naughty kindergartner, when I lean around my cubicle's partition to ask Judy, who'd complained at our cigarette break of bleeding right through her Kotex, how she was feeling. At five, we drag ourselves to the bus stops for the sardine ride home in the rush-hour buses. At seven the next morning we are back at the bus stops.

But this is a good job, I understand. I don't have to stand on my feet all day. The place is air-conditioned. I endure nothing like my mother's sweatshop labors, and I earn twice what she did. Yet how soul-eating, how dismal. This is work the way most young working women in America experience it—if they're lucky. The alternative to such drudgery is finding a man who would take all the wage-earning upon himself.

I must do well in graduate school. I must.

. . .

To step on the UCLA campus after three inkstained months at the *Hollywood Advertiser* was like filling yourself to the eyeballs with fresh water after a long desert trek, feeling your cheek cool after a burning fever, romping in gold-poppied meadows after a dark imprisonment. I'd made it back to the green haven. I could spend my days contemplating Donne's wit and Swinburne's word-music. Bliss.

But I was terrified. I watched my fellow students out of the corner of my eye that first day, and I sensed they watched me too. Did we all think *they* had made a mistake by letting us into this heavenly sanctum and that soon we'd be found out, sent packing back to places like the *Hollywood Advertiser*, where we belonged? Every afternoon I took the bus right home after classes, shut myself into my apartment, and read and read and read. I was certain they'd never before let anyone as stupid, as slow-witted, as ignorant as I into graduate school. Am I really going to be able to do this? I devoured everything on the reading list, all the critical sources I could find in the library. How much sleep did I need? Could I make it on six hours a night? Five?

"Why do you want more school? The head uses up the blood you need to have babies," Rae declared. But she bought yards of heavy blue silk and soft brown wool and crisp beige linen. She was working at Roth LeCover now, the factory that supplied I. Magnin's, and she paid the cutter to cut the lovely materials into patterns "like what the millionaires buy." She ordered me to stand statue-still while she drew hemlines below my knees with blue chalk or to turn round and round in small steps on her living room floor while she pulled pins from between her lips and stuck them here and there in the material with which she'd draped me. For the next weeks, whenever I climbed the stairs to her apartment, I could hear her sewing machine *whrrr, whrrr,* just as it had when she'd lived with us in the Bronx. She made me millionaires' clothes to wear to UCLA. With her help, I fooled them about that too: They never guessed I was poor as well as dumb.

She also paid my rent until I got a teaching assistantship. By November, the money I'd saved from my months at the *Hollywood Advertiser* was almost gone. I had sixty-three dollars to my name, and the landlady was coming to collect her seventy dollars in a couple of weeks.

I actually thought about calling Andy. ("Gigi Frost. Remember me?" I'd say. "The boyfriend dumped you again, huh?" he'd answer. *And the bogeyman would leer from behind his shoulder.*) Instead, I applied for a weekend position—countergirl at Schwab's. "No, no," Rae protested when I told her. "You'll make yourself sick with school and work together." Though she didn't want me to get a Ph.D. (she didn't even know what a Ph.D. was), on the first of every month she slipped into my hand a used envelope with a canceled stamp that now contained crisp green bills— three twenties and a ten.

"When are you getting the divorce like you said, and then we'll go to the *shadchen*, the matchmaker?" my aunt demanded.

"Okay, okay, I'll get a Jewish divorce," I told her. I was drowning in obligation and love. The next Sunday Mr. Bergman drove us to a white stucco duplex on Pico Boulevard; Rae rang a loud buzzer at the door.

"You'll feel a lot better, Lilly, you'll see," Mr. Bergman said as we stood waiting. He patted my back for courage, as though he were delivering me for a medical procedure. I patted his.

The door opened a crack, then wider. I could smell burnt toast. The rabbi had small watery eyes and a yellowed beard. "Come inside, come in," he said with a heavy accent, and led us slowly up creaky stairs into a room where the windows were covered by dark shades. One bare bulb, hanging from the ceiling, made a stark, unpleasant light. "Here you stand"—he motioned Rae and Mr. Bergman off to the wall. Me he took by the arm to the center of the room, under the bulb. On top of my head he settled a square of wrinkled lace kerchief that he'd drawn like a magician from the pocket of his black alpaca coat. Then he sat at a Formica table and with a fountain pen scratched words on a long sheet of paper. "Deserted?" he asked in the wavery voice of the very old, then shook his head *yes* in answer to his own question and wrote it down. "Your name?"

"Liebe." Rae moved to his elbow, gave him my name in Yiddish, watched him write it.

"Husband?" the rabbi asked.

"Mark. I don't know the name in Jewish," my aunt muttered with distaste; "Lesson," she mispronounced my husband's last name. When she was done, she went back to stand beside Mr. Bergman. They watched, hushed, with strained faces, ready to witness a life-saving operation.

The rabbi presented me with the paper on which he'd written, folded now into a square. Then with his bony fingers he clasped my hands and squeezed them together, the paper in between, breathing through his mouth as though it were difficult labor. His eyes seemed filled with tears. I felt bizarre, disoriented, outraged too. I'd been kidnapped into a quasi-medieval ghetto—I, a UCLA graduate student. I pushed the feelings down. Since I'd come, I would do it right; I would follow the ritual as he directed. With bent head, I paced slowly to the door, the paper still between my hands. ("You, Liebe Faderman," he entoned, "got the *gett*, the divorce, in your own two hands, and you are free to leave from your husband's life.") Next I was to retrace my steps and hand him the paper. He took it from me as though he'd never seen it before, unfolded it, read it aloud in Hebrew, then mumbled an incantation that he ordered me to repeat. "She is a free woman!" he told my aunt and Mr. Bergman triumphantly.

"*A dank Gott!*" Rae cried. I was halfway down the stairs already because I knew what she was going to say next.

Supper I eat across the street, with my mother and Albert. "It gives me so much pleasure to make you something nice," my mother says almost every evening those first months, hovering over me with solicitude. I'm the prodigal daughter, home at last, sitting down at the oilcloth-covered kitchen table that groans with food. Sometimes in the afternoons I'm in my apartment, writing a paper or reading the week's assignments, and I hear the creak of the wooden wheels of the shopping cart she pushes down the sidewalk. She's coming back from the stores on Fairfax Avenue, where she went to forage for my sake. Now she will spend the next hours cooking for my sake. I go to the window and look down on her bent form, her thickened shoulders, as she crosses the street. I remember myself as a little girl reaching for my beautiful mother's arm. "Mother and daughter," she'd say. I want to run into the street and take her arm again.

But the euphoria between us doesn't last. After a few months of suppers, I'm not the long-lost-daughter-returned anymore. Yet my mother needs me there. She pulls out from her trunk of miseries all the old, worn complaints and drapes herself in them for me to witness. From my trunk of miseries I pull the old, worn pity and guilt. Except sometimes I refuse to don them. Instead I explode. Every word she says is an irritant now, like D'Or's words at the end.

"You know what the lady next door told me?" She didn't wait for me to ask what. "That I shouldn't let you go to college because soon you'll think you're better than me and you won't want anything to do with me no more." This, as I sat down at the table and she deposited a plate of chopped liver with eggs and onions in front of my nose.

I shoved it with an angry hand (harder than I'd intended), and it crashed to the floor, a mess of crockery and goop. *Let me go to college? What had she ever done to let me go to college?* "What did you ever give me in my life?" I leaped to my feet, glaring. "What kind of lousy childhood did you give me?" tumbled from my mouth.

She stared at the bits of plate and food on the floor, then at me, baffled. "What was missing from your childhood?" she cried. "What do other children have that you didn't have?"

She was serious, my crazy mother—she really didn't know! How could I begin to spill it out? The dance of the two beheaded chickens, Fanny's filthy furnished room, my filthy tangled hair, filthy Falix. I opened my mouth, then clamped it shut. There was no point. I stooped and gathered the pieces of crockery in my hand, then swiped at the floor with a wet rag. Albert came in, reeking from the cigarette he'd just smoked on the porch, and drew his chair up to the table, waiting to be served.

Every day my mother summons her energy and tries to give whatever she has to give by the food she prepares—and every evening I must eat every bite, the waterlogged lettuce with cucumbers and carrots and tomatoes and "scunions" (as she calls scallions), the leaden matzoh balls suspended between gobs of grease, a half-boiled chicken with green beans that are gray from too much cooking, and mashed potatoes that float in loose and lumpy gravy, then a great mound of apple strudel that laps over the perimeter of the cracked saucer on which she serves it to me. Albert chews noisily, smacks his lips, says nothing, and my mother looks at me hungrily, her knife and fork sitting on her plate. What does she want from me? It's me she eats instead of her food. She devours me. Every inch of me.

"I can't eat the dessert," I say. "I've had enough." *My mother is making me fat. What if I flunk out of graduate school and have to go back to modeling to support myself?*

"I try to make nice things for you and you don't even appreciate," *my mother complains loudly.* "You come and eat supper, and then right away you disappear."

"I've got to study, dammit! Let me live my life," *I scream at her, and throw my paper napkin down on the table.*

"Shaddup, the two of you, and let me eat in peace," *Albert says, spewing food in all directions from his full mouth.*

"Where are you going?" *she yells after me.*

"Home!" *I slam the apartment door and stomp up the block, my heels clicking furiously on the concrete. All she knows how to do is stuff me, complain, stuff me, complain. Never once does she ask me about how I'm doing in school, my ambitions, who's in my life, whether I'm lonely. Nothing. I'm too upset now to go home and study. My feet head toward Fairfax Avenue. There I go to Canter's, where I can find a decent cup of coffee and calm down.*

I made a friend in the English Department, Paula Huffermann, a thick-set woman of thirty with a mezzo-rich speaking voice that sounded her brightness, and with frowzy hair and rumpled dress as untidy as that of Alice's White Queen. Paula invited me to her book-cluttered rabbit warren of an apartment in Santa Monica to study with her for our History of the English Language exam. She lived with Tsatska, a lugubrious mongrel whose long white fur had turned pinkish because of some disease. "My main companion," she called Tsatska, who placed a big woolly head on her lap as we sat cross-legged on the floor, sipping tea from old jelly jars before we settled down to work.

What Paula really wanted, she confided as her fingers absent-mindedly stroked Tsatska's discolored coat, was a man who was a good lover, who'd be a comfortable hubby and give her four kids and a sprawling house on a ranch in Wyoming. "But since I can't seem to get those things," she said, "I'm getting a Ph.D. so I can teach instead."

"I'll choose a Ph.D. and a professor's job over a husband and a farm any day," I ventured.

"Oh, we'll get the Ph.D., all right; they won't stop us from that. But they won't let us become real professors," she added. I looked at her blankly. "Well, how many women do you see on the UCLA faculty?" she asked.

I hadn't really thought about it. I'd noticed that at least half the graduate students in the department were women, so I took it for granted that there were jobs for us when we graduated. But Paula was right, I realized now. How could I have missed what was so obvious? Out of an English faculty of sixty at UCLA, only two were female, Florence Ridley and Ada Nesbitt. At Berkeley I hadn't had a single woman professor. Who would hire me after I got my degree?

"Of course, who knows, maybe you'll get lucky like Ridley or Nesbitt." Paula shrugged her plump shoulders and spread her History of the English Language notes on her generous lap. "But neither of them is married," she added. "Is that a life?"

The job situation couldn't be as bad as she was making it sound. Ridley and Nesbitt were proof that women could get fine positions—I just needed to find out how. "Harvard, something like that," Paula said when I asked if she knew where they'd gotten their Ph.D.'s. "Rich Episcopal daddies," she said with a shrug, "like we ain't got. I expect if the man with a hoe doesn't come along, I'll be working at a junior college. They hire women for that, or maybe a good private girls' school. Don't frown like that, my dear," she said. "It's just the way it is."

We studied late into the night, calling out for pizza about ten o'clock, oblivious to our lusterless futures and slaphappy as junior high school girls by midnight. "Why don't you stay over?" she asked around two o'clock, and she made up a Murphy bed, which came down from the wall. Tsatska jumped up to join me, landing on my belly, panting in my face, around 4 A.M. I wasn't sleeping anyway because I kept thinking about Paula's saying, "We'll get the Ph.D., but they won't let us do much with it."

We studied again in the morning, then she drove me back to my apartment. I was about to flop on the couch to review my notes again when, through the open window, I heard my mother and Rae. "If she's still not up there, something terrible happened," Rae said, and I realized with a start that I hadn't told them I'd be staying at Paula's overnight.

"*Oy, Gott*, what should we do?" my mother cried.

I ran to the window, but not before my aunt said, "If anything happened, we'll kill ourselves, both together. Okay?"

"Yes, okay!" my mother agreed.

In the middle of my second year at UCLA, Mr. Bergman, that gentle soul, died. He was eighty-three. "Mendel!" my aunt shrieked over his open coffin, and the other mourners sighed their pity for her widow's grief. She gripped the black rim of the big lacquered box where Mr. Bergman lay, as though woe had made her too weak to stand on her own feet, and her blue eyes were long lakes of tears. It was the first time I'd ever heard her call him by his Yiddish name. "Don't leave, Mendel," she sobbed.

After the funeral his oldest daughter, Rosalie, invited all the mourners back to her house, where a big spread of cold cuts and bottles of sweet heavy wine were waiting in the dining room. "Papa said we shouldn't neglect you when he was gone," Rosalie said to my aunt, placing a bejeweled hand on her shoulder, "and we won't."

My aunt nodded politely.

I'd been standing at her side. "That's so nice," I whispered to her after Rosalie turned to talk to someone else.

But the next day, when Rosalie called to say she was inviting Rae to lunch on Sunday and all Mr. Bergman's children and grandchildren would be there and Rosalie's husband would be happy to drive from Brentwood to pick her up, my aunt refused to go. I'd brought a stack of books to Rae's apartment so I could keep her company while I studied, and I sat across the kitchen table from her as she spoke to Rosalie on the phone. When I gathered what the call was about, I signaled her to tell Rosalie *yes*, but she shook her head vehemently *no*. "What do I have to do with them?" she mumbled when she hung up. "Let them live and be well, but I don't need them."

"But they're family to you," I urged.

"I don't need to make believe I have them for family," she declared, waving a hand that dismissed them to eternity. She was still wearing mourning black, but her funeral-day fragility had vanished. She took the upright vacuum cleaner from the little hall closet and busied herself with house-cleaning. "I only have two people in my family now. God willing, someday I'll have more," she bellowed over her shoulder toward the table where I sat.

That night, as I gathered my books to leave, my aunt said, "Stay. I'll make up for you the couch in the living room, like we used to. To keep me company," she added. I looked up, surprised. She'd beseeched me plenty through the years, but always for something that was supposed to be for my own good. This was different: She was asking for something for herself.

"Sure," I said. How lonely the little apartment must have felt now. She'd lived with Mr. Bergman for fifteen years.

She brought sheets and blankets from a closet and we put them on the couch. Then she plopped onto the green armchair, and I stood gazing at her with tender feeling, waiting for her to open her heart to me. "If you need to study some more, go ahead. I won't stop you," she said. "You can lay in bed and study. That way you'll rest more."

"We can talk if you like. I'd rather."

She pursed her lips together and said nothing.

"Do you remember how Mr. Bergman used to leave my mother five dollars for me when you came to visit on Dundas Street?" I said, smiling.

"Study, study. I know you have to study." She popped up and went to the kitchen, eluding me. She wanted my presence, but it was clear she wasn't going to let sentiment make her vulnerable. I sat on the chair she'd left and kept my book closed at my side. I didn't want to study now. I felt cheated of what I'd hoped was a chance to show my love for her.

Minutes later, she returned with a tray. "What is, is, and what isn't, isn't. We can only ask God for what's possible," she said, placing a plate of macaroons on my knees and a glass of warm milk on the little table near my chair. "Now is the present and tomorrow is the future," she added. I sighed, resigned. I would get nothing out of my aunt except cookies, milk, and *bon mots* that were either simple-minded and signified nothing or quite beyond my ability to decipher. "The past is past and we got to forget it," she concluded.

Though I'd been earning a decent salary as a teaching assistant since the start of the school year and could easily afford the rent, I gave up my apartment at the end of the month and moved in with my aunt. "She's lonely," I told my frowning mother. ("I'm lonesome too," she grumped, as I knew she would. "Why can't you move in with me?"). I slept in Mr. Bergman's old bed, three feet from Rae's. The first nights, as she breathed emphatically in sleep, I lay there on my side for a long while, watching in the dark the small hump of her form under her bedcovers, thinking how I would have luxuriated in this proximity to My Rae when I was a kid; how she'd been my only model of sanity, a sturdy anchor against the terrible waves of my mother's craziness.

My adviser, Professor Bradford Booth, is a veritable Mr. Samuel Pickwick — bald head, rimless circular spectacles, middle-age paunch; like Pickwick too, eloquent, gentlemanly, decent. "There's no point in waiting," he encourages me as we stand outside Rolfe Hall. "I think you have reason to be confident." The round spectacles twinkle in the Southern California sunlight. I'm ready to take the exams that can give me a master's degree and advance me to candidacy for a doctorate.

Now, except for the three hours on Wednesday evening that I spend in his Victorian Literature seminar and the hour from nine to ten on Monday, Wednesday, and Friday mornings that I spend teaching my freshman English class, I'm a prisoner in the green armchair, barricaded with big volumes of thin pages and small print. I have read them all, practically memorized them, thought and thought about all the possible questions I might be asked — "Why was the eighteenth century called 'the Age of Reason'?" "How might Thomas Grey be considered a forerunner to romanticism?" (What if I fail?) *"What explains the rise of the naturalist school of literature in the late nineteenth century?"* (Strippers don't get Ph.D.'s, habitués of the Open Door don't get Ph.D.'s, Fanny said that girls who live in furnished rooms don't get Ph.D.'s. Bastard daughters certainly don't get Ph.D.'s.) *"Discuss the influence of Walter Pater on the fin de siècle Decadents."*

I study day and night. I don't get up from the green chair. "What if I fail?"

I ask aloud to no one in particular. Rae brings me coffee with milk and sugar, Russian rye bread smeared thick with sweet butter. "So you should have energy," she says.

"More coffee, please," I call to her in the kitchen an hour later, and soon I can hear the kettle whistling, and soon she comes with a cup of coffee in one hand, a plate of buttered Russian rye in the other. "What if I fail?" I cry again.

"You won't fail. You won't fail," she says, though she has no idea what it is I must not fail.

It becomes a joke between us. "What if I fail?" I sing the self-mocking lament now. "You won't fail, you won't fail," she sings back, placing the cup in my hand, balancing the plate of buttered bread on the arm of my chair. I take a sip and a nibble and then return to formulating my explanation of James Joyce's use of Homer.

They sent me to await their verdict in the hall—Professors Booth, Durham, Longeuil, and Jorgensen. I paced, swallowed big drafts of water from a hall fountain, paced some more. The "what if I fail?" song played itself again, but the wonderful loud bellow of Rae's recitative drowned out its puny squeak. Then Bradford Booth, wearing a dignified Pickwickian smile, came out of the room where I'd answered their questions for two hours. "Phil Durham said it was the best oral he'd ever heard," he said, pumping my sweaty palm.

"I'm Master Lilly!" I called first my mother and then Rae to announce it.

"Master means a boy," my mother remembered from her moviegoing days.

"*Mazel tov,*" my aunt said, and then without stopping for new breath: "In two months you're twenty-four years old. Let that be enough studying already."

Paula and I call each other most evenings. I want to hear what she thinks of my ideas for a dissertation topic: "How about 'The Problem of Anti-Semitism in the Victorian Novel'?" Professor Booth wants me to do my dissertation on Benjamin Farjeon, a minor author in the Sadleir Collection, which he'd helped UCLA acquire. "I don't have to stay in Victorian lit. How about Langston Hughes?"

"Do you know what Ridley did her dissertation on? Chaucer. Nesbitt? Dickens." Paula cautions practicality. Then she goes on to subjects that interest her more. What do I suppose Bill Dowdy meant when he said she didn't have to bring the Coventry Patmore book he wanted to borrow to school because he lived only a few blocks away. "Do you think he wants to come over to my place? Or wants me to take the book over to his place? Do you think he's got a girlfriend? Don't you think a guy like that has them waiting in the wings?"

"I don't know," I say.

"A guy like that probably doesn't go for one whole day without getting propositioned by some woman. Don't you think?"

"You're probably right," I say.

"Do you know how long it's been since I got laid?" She sighs.

Sometimes in the evenings we go to Mario's for a pizza and split a bottle of cheap red between us. Then Paula makes me laugh and laugh by telling droll scatological stories in her musical voice about the billions of men who got away. One Friday evening we weave out of Mario's holding each other tight around the waist, guffawing still about her last brief boyfriend, Solomon Schlong. "I swear, that's his name," she shrieks, and our laughing fits begin again.

"Oh, Paula, I love you," I say with a sigh between hiccups. (I don't mean it at all the way I'd said it to D'Or, about whom Paula knows nothing.)

She jumps away with such an exaggerated leap that I think she's clowning. "Now that's one weird place I've never gone," she declares. "I'd rather be dead than that desperate."

Paula set me up with a blind date, someone she'd met in a café in Westwood Village and had had coffee with a few times. "I'd grab him myself in a jiffy, but he already told me he likes me like a sister. A philosophy major," she said. "Jerry Proben. An Adonis."

Jerry came to pick me up at my aunt's apartment and drive me to Malibu one bright afternoon. He rolled up his white trousers, and we took off our shoes and strolled near the water's edge. He really was handsome, I thought—bronze skin, big shoulders and arms, and slim hips. I could see the glistening dark hairs on his legs, little drops of water and grains of sand clinging to them.

Later we sat against a big rock as the sun dropped into the ocean. By then I'd already decided I'd go through with it. Jerry's lips touched mine tentatively, and I kissed him back hard. He seemed startled for an instant before he gripped my shoulders and locked his mouth to mine. "Should I not have kissed you back so hard?" I dared to tease later as we drove down a dark Pacific Coast Highway looking for a restaurant.

"Oh . . . Well, I guess you don't usually expect a woman to be so . . . there."

"Do you want me to be more coy?" I asked, laughing, but really a bit confused. How were women supposed to be with men? I didn't know.

"No, no, not coy," Jerry answered.

What if I got pregnant? I worried. What would be worse for my mother and aunt: if I never had a baby or if I had one out of wedlock? I wasn't sure, but anyway I couldn't take a chance with my academic career. I called Paula because I didn't know anyone else to call. "Do you know a doctor who'll give me a diaphragm?" I asked her.

There was a long, eloquent pause. "Do you know how lucky you are?" Paula sighed and then put the receiver down to get her doctor's number.

Jerry is almost thirty but still lives with his parents because his father had a stroke two years before, and Jerry must help shower and dress and undress him. For these services his mother gives him one hundred dollars a month. Every Saturday night he picks me up and we go to a Chinese or a Mexican restaurant for dinner. I tell him about my dissertation problems, and he tells me about Heraclitus and Gorgias and pre-Socratic paradoxes, on which he might do his master's thesis. When the check comes Jerry takes it, adds ten percent for a tip, then calculates a fifty-fifty split. "Right down the middle" or "I'll pay the extra penny," he announces. If there's an Ingmar Bergman film or an Antonioni or Buñuel or Fellini we go to the movies first. Usually we go directly to a motel, either the Cozy Cottage or the Alpine Village or the Ocean Breeze. They all cost six dollars. I fish out three from my purse, and Jerry receives the bills in his palm. The rooms always have creaky doors and squeaky bedsprings and smell of stale cigarette smoke.

When the door closes behind us, Jerry always seems uneasy, removed for the moment, almost as if he's waiting for some distant voice to make a pronounce-

ment; yet in minutes he's all there—direct, potent, agile. I don't mind making love with him. In fact, I like it. Sex is sex, I realize. Mammals are programmed to respond to the stimulation of certain nerve endings. It's only natural. And he's a good lover: He knows a woman's body as though he's studied it like a puzzle in logic, and he doesn't stop until he brings about the desired response. You can't fault Jerry for technique.

But when it's over for him, he rolls off me, sits up in bed, breathes deeply, and exhales a great gust, as though he's recovering from an athletic feat. He has poured all his prowess and potency into the game, and now he needs to rest. He closes his eyes.

Where has he gone in his head? I don't know, and it makes me uneasy that I don't know. Though he's there, right next to me on the jumbled sheets, in his head he seems to be somewhere else. I reach out to him, throw an arm around his waist, place my cheek on his chest, but he seems oblivious. Soon I roll back and drift off into myself.

Jerry gives me a lot of time to think during our year and a half together in postcoital beds. I think about everything—Jan. D'Or. Whether I'll find a job after I get my Ph.D. Love (he never says that word to me, and I never say it either). I think about the history of the English language—I spend quite a bit of time thinking about that: Old English derives from the dialects of the Germanic inhabitants of Britain during the fifth to the eleventh centuries, *Dr. Matthews lectured. Jerry is mute, maybe asleep, as still as death now. I think about the German vocabulary I'm learning because I have to pass another language exam before I begin my dissertation:* fugen (transitive verb): to join, to connect. *Jerry slips down on the bed, hugs the pillow, curls farther away from me. I think about myself and Jerry, our lovemaking. We fuck well, I think.* Fuge, Fuck. They were probably the same word in the eleventh century. To join, to connect. *Jerry and I fuck beautifully—but we do not connect.* Something is missing, something . . . ineffable. *I laugh at myself for using D'Or's word. But it's true that something is missing. His male rhythms are not mine: He fucks, then withdraws, then disappears into his head. I think about the* tap, tap, tap *of the shoes of the man who looked like Charles Boyer when he left me standing on the sidewalk with my mother. I'm not your father, he said as he withdrew and disappeared. I don't know where they go when they disappear.*

. . .

I moved out of Rae's apartment and away from Curson Avenue into a bachelor apartment near campus. I'd been promoted to teaching associate, and in the summer I would be working for the Upward Bound Project, tutoring underachieving East L.A. high school kids to prepare them for college. I could afford my own place; and if Jerry and I didn't have to go a motel all the time, if I could try to cook dinners for him and we could spend the whole night together and wake up to each other in the morning, couldn't we learn to connect? We wouldn't have such compartmentalized meetings that ended in athletic, predictable sex acts and then good-bye.

My mother was surprisingly calm about my move. "I don't get to see you that much anyway. You're either eating by her or going out with him."

"It's not good for a young girl to live alone," Rae protested when I told her about the apartment.

"Well, maybe I won't be alone for long. Maybe Jerry and I will get married soon."

I spied a smile playing around my aunt's lips, as though she could already see the pram with the infant inside sitting in her living room.

"I know you're all busy with Adonis," Paula said the week I moved into my new apartment, "but you can spare a friend just one Saturday. Remember, I'm the one who found him for you. I want you to come to my little dinner party, just you, my sister who'll be here from Philly, and an old college roommate of mine." But the next morning she called to say that the sister's nine-year-old son had woken up with tonsillitis and a fever of 104 and she'd canceled her trip to California. "Come to dinner anyway. My old roommate is still coming, and honestly, I don't know what I'd do with her alone. She's nice, but her enthusiasms are incredibly exhausting. A confirmed old maid schoolteacher to boot." Paula said it with pointed aversion. "Do a buddy a favor."

Binky was a big woman with the look of a young Gertrude Stein, except that her eyes were a light blue and her auburn hair was tipped with gold and was thick and glossy. "Kennedy hair" was how I came to think of it.

We sat on the folding chairs at the kitchen table while Paula pushed books and papers into a scattered heap that rested where her sister's place setting would have been. Then, as Tsatska nosed her legs, Paula dished up the overcooked spaghetti and the iceberg lettuce she'd pinked with French dressing.

My first impression of Binky was her bluster, but I sensed a bashfulness too. "Superbrain!" she called Paula in a booming voice when Paula remarked that Professor Cohen had told her to send her seminar paper on the Bergsonian concept of time in *Tristram Shandy* to *PMLA*. I watched her while she and Paula talked about old times, and once in a while I caught her glancing at me shyly. I thought her handsome.

"What do you do?" I asked when Paula went to dish out the ice cream she'd bought for dessert.

"I teach at Marshall High. The only public school in the city that's proven integration can work." She took flame instantly with the subject. "I see a hundred and fifty kids every day in my classes—black, white, yellow, brown, red—you name it. And they love each other. No gang fights. No Watts riots. No white flight, thank God." Her broad smile flashed a mouthful of strong, straight Kennedy teeth. "I teach creative writing, and they turn in fabulous stuff. Fabulous! To hell with those people who say that Mexican kids can't write, that Negro kids are lousy students. I see every day how great it can be."

Paula reached over Binky to deposit a dish of watery chocolate ice cream on my plastic placemat and flash me a doleful look that said: "What did I tell you?"

"I teach American lit too, and I don't have to struggle to make them read." Binky was unmindful of her hostess now. She waved her long, slim hands about with unexpected grace as she talked. On the finger where most women her age sported a wedding ring she wore a handsome jade stone set in heavy gold. "They love it because I give them stuff that has something to do with their lives—Richard Wright, Langston Hughes, James Baldwin. To hell with the usual curriculum! We need more voices, different voices, in the classroom. All the teachers could do it if they weren't such lazy sons-of-bitches." Then, as though she were embarrassed that she'd said too much, she looked down at her hands, now spread quietly before her on the table. "They're my kiddos and I love 'em," she added softly.

I looked at her hands too. I couldn't take my eyes off them. They were truly beautiful hands. "I like those writers also," I murmured. "Do you know Countee Cullen? 'We shall not always plant while others reap The golden increment of bursting fruit."

"Countee Cullen! I love Countee Cullen! 'Not always countenance, abject and mute, That lesser men should hold their brothers cheap.'"

"Ralph Ellison?" I laughed, enchanted.

"Ellison! That man's my God. That man has written one of the most important American novels of the century!"

"Yes, oh, yes," I agreed as silent Paula got up to take the dishes to the sink.

"Can I give you a lift?" Binky asked at the end of the evening when I stood at Paula's door waiting for her to find where she'd placed my purse and sweater.

Later, in Binky's car, we sat in front of my new apartment, both of us speaking lines we knew by heart from Gwendolyn Brooks, Claude McKay, Jean Toomer, correcting each other in fevered enthusiasm or reciting in perfect harmony. "I guess I'd better go," I finally said when I saw the illuminated hands of her car clock show 1 A.M.

"This evening has been a gift to me. An absolute gift," Binky said. Her voice was as passionate as when she'd recited the poems we both loved.

"Me too," I said, meaning it. I dared to rest my hand on her arm before I opened the car door. "Hey, come to dinner. Tomorrow. You'll be my first dinner guest in the new apartment."

"Oh, I'd love that!" I felt her fleeting touch on my shoulder as I slipped out of the car.

"Bye." I turned around to wave, and she was watching me, waving back.

We touched no more than we had the night before, that Sunday evening over the tomato omelette I served with a bottle of straw-colored chablis. We talked mostly about the books we loved. She told a funny story about a disgruntled colleague who had reported her to the principal: "She's neglecting to teach the patriotic classics that have made America the superpower it is," Binky mocked the man's pompous voice. We said very little that was personal. She mentioned only that she lived alone; I never said anything about the women I'd been with or about Jerry either.

But when she was getting ready to leave we stood together on the landing, not speaking, and I heard my heart sounding in my ears, pounding as it hadn't since I first laid eyes on D'Or. *Was it happening all over again?* I had to swallow hard before I could say, "May I call you tomorrow?"

"Please, *please* do," she answered, and we stood there, looking at each other, not saying anything more for a full minute before she lowered her head and walked down the stairs.

I hurried back into the apartment and leaned on the big window, a knee on the low sill, watching by the light of the streetlamp as she got into her car, watching her sit there and not move for a long time, her arms draped around the steering wheel.

I tried to make my mind go blank, but I felt as though I were jumping out of my skin all night long. "Please, *please* do." She'd said the second *please* breathily. I could see her well-shaped lips as she said it, *pleeeze*.

16 PROFESSOR FADERMAN

BINKY HAS HER OWN *apartment, but most afternoons she comes directly to my place when she's finished with her day at Marshall High School. I hear her footsteps on the stairs, and my heart begins its delirious gigue. She knocks, and I put down my Benjamin Farjeon notes and my pen and take a deep breath before I fling open the door. We clasp each other and kiss and grasp and gulp and gasp as though we've been tortured by a separation of months.*

Most nights, after a short dinner and long hours of love, we fall asleep in each other's arms, and at 6:45 A.M. we're awakened by a love song on the little clock-radio she has given me that sits on the table beside my bed. Binky pulls away slowly, tiny millimeter by tiny millimeter. "It's as excruciating as chopping off an arm, a leg," we groan to each other every morning about our disjoining.

The bed is bereft of her warm skin and sweet flesh, but I lie there, eyes closed, engrossed by love images from the night before, imagining her beside me still. Then, to my sleepy delight she appears again, as in a dream, smart now in her teacher's uniform—a tailored dress, high-heeled shoes, seamed nylons, her gold-tipped Kennedy hair neatly coiffed. In her hands she's holding two steaming cups of coffee. She sits on the edge of the bed while we sip and intertwine fingers and fill ourselves with last looks to carry us through the long day. Always, before she leaves, the radio disc jockey announces: "Comin' up—my favorite start-the-mornin'-right song," and the singer croons, "Sunny, yesterday my life was filled with rain. Sunny, you smiled at me and really eased the pain." I set my coffee cup on the floor and nestle my head in Binky's lap. The song is about

Binky, who most certainly, as the words say, is my sunshine, my rock, my sweet, complete desire. She tells me I'm all those things for her too. "I can't remember living before I met you," she says.

She leaves for the day, and I take my place at my desk, where I concoct with renewed vigor one sentence after another about Farjeon's stylistic shifts. I'm determined to finish this academic exercise quickly so that I can go on to more gratifying work.

I had only the vaguest idea of what such work might be, but Binky was at the center of that too. She asked me to spend the day at her school, "to see what I do that the UCLA English and Education profs turn their academic noses up at." I was awed by what she did, how the students loved her, trusted her. "My little United Nations," she called them. Four kids from her first-period American literature class—one Negro, one Oriental, one Mexican, one Jew—showed up in her room during morning break, lunch break, afternoon break.

"We're just hanging out," one of them said with a shrug when I asked, amused, if they had another class with her that day.

"We just like to shoot the bull with Miss B.," another confessed.

They looked at her—all of them—as though they were in love. They sat on the desks or on the floor near her, munched sandwiches or apples, and she gave them her attention, her little bit of free time, her wisdom. The "bull" was mostly literary because she'd made books come alive for them, opened a universe of ideas, told them to ponder what other teachers told them to take for granted, and they caught fire with what they learned from her. Long before Ivy League scholars thought of it, she taught them to question the canon that was sacrosanct in all American schools. "How come everyone has to read *The Autobiography of Benjamin Franklin*, but you don't get to read *Black Boy* unless you're in Miss B.'s class?" Arthay asked. "Wright can write circles around Franklin," Ian said. "The Japanese and Chinese have been in America for more than a hundred years. How come nobody tells us about Oriental writers?" Lloyd asked. "How come there's no Mexican writers like James Baldwin?" Rafael wanted to know.

And I caught fire too with those novel ideas. "They're right," I said over the pizza Binky and I shared in Westwood Village. "In eight years of university courses, I've read just about nothing but white men, as though they're the only ones who ever said anything important about the human experience."

"I'd give anything to find good Oriental writers and Mexican writers and let them speak for themselves in my American lit classes," Binky said.

"Wouldn't that be a wonderful idea for a book? It could be poems and stories by writers of all colors." No book like that existed, but why shouldn't it? "Binky, why couldn't we do it—together? Just as soon as I finish my dissertation?"

"God!" she shouted. The pizza-dough thrower behind the counter shifted his eyes to us and missed his catch. "Let's do it," she cried.

"By all means, I have absolute confidence," Professor Booth told me in the fall of 1966 when I asked if he thought I was far enough along on my dissertation to begin my job search. "Absolute confidence," he repeated, smiling his cordial Pickwickian smile. He ruffled through a little stack on his desk and pulled out several fliers to hand me: job announcements, I saw with a tremulous glance, for the 1967–68 academic year. "I'll pass on to you whatever else comes up that's suitable," he said helpfully, holding his office door open with a slight bow as I left. Would somebody actually give me a job as a college professor?

I stood outside his door and perused the announcements. There were four—Wilberforce College, Michigan State University, a small, regional campus of Purdue, and Fresno State College. I'd have to go to Xenia, Ohio, or East Lansing, Michigan, or Westville, Indiana, or some godforsaken town in the San Joaquin Valley of California if I wanted to be a professor. My cheeks burned as if they had been slapped. A Ph.D. would open great things to me, Maury had promised. Had I walked through a forest only to pick up a crooked stick? I'd have to live alone in some far-flung alien place where there was a college that would hire me. How could I leave Binky when I'd just found her, and my mother and Rae?

Paula was the last person I wanted to see at that moment, but she spotted me near Professor Booth's door and dogged me down the stairs of Rolfe Hall. "So, is Booth recommending you for the Berkeley job? There's one at Columbia too. Dr. Nix is recommending Ron Hommes for both," she said with a smirk.

"Ron's dissertation is on Henry James, so the position must be for someone in American lit." I stopped to drink water at the hall fountain; I took slow sips, straightened up, bent down for more sips, but she wasn't going to leave. "I do Victorian lit," I mumbled to the faucet. Her snicker made me enormously despondent.

"You know Lois Damer? She's Nix's student too." Paula trailed me from the building, hopping around a crunch of students to keep up with me. "Her dissertation's on Edith Wharton. You know the job he's recommending her for?" she asked with a meaningful sniff. "Long Beach State." Finally she left to go off to the stacks, to labor the rest of the day and far into the night on her George Eliot dissertation.

I wandered around the UCLA campus. Soon I'd be cast out of this paradise of brilliant sunshine and brilliant scholars — to what?

"Hotbox of the nation," Professor Booth said pleasantly when I told him a month later that I would have an interview at the Modern Language Association Convention for the job at Fresno State. I'd barely heard of Fresno before I saw the job announcement. It was farm country, about two hundred miles from L.A. and the coast. How do people breathe away from oceans? I'd lived only on coasts.

"So you think I shouldn't even bother with the interview?" I asked hopefully.

"Oh, I didn't say that." Professor Booth's smile was placid.

Of my few possibilities, it was only Wilberforce, a Negro college, that seemed at all interesting, although it was in Xenia, Ohio. "We're vaguely connected to Antioch College," the urbane Negro professor who interviewed me at the MLA Convention said. "Seven miles north, and another thousand miles below the stairs." He smiled ruefully. I imagined myself at Wilberforce, a political firebrand, fighting the good fight against presidents, deans, whomever, to help rescue the college from its second-class status.

But how would I teach, how would I write, if all my time were spent in political battles? I had to figure out what I really wanted to do with the Ph.D. that I'd been struggling so hard to get.

I go to his office with a contract in hand. "Well, I guess I'm off to Fresno State College," I tell a jolly Mr. Pickwick.

"Fresno State," he chortles. "A girl who did the best graduate oral exam in the history of the UCLA English Department? A girl like that doesn't end up at Fresno State College. You're going to UC Berkeley: They're hiring you, sight unseen, on the basis of my glowing recommendation."

I'm speechless. I'm going to be a professor at UC Berkeley! I sink to the floor in a delirium of groveling obeisance. Professor Booth lifts me with gentle, paternal hands. "There, there," he sings, "no thanks necessary. It's only what you deserve." From his desk he takes a magnum of Veuve Cliquot — "Enjoy with Binky, your woman lover." He beams and then, with a fatherly wink, he pins a giant gold medal on my lapel.

I went to my adviser's office with the contract in hand. "I've been offered a job as assistant professor at Fresno State College," I said. The contract had been sitting in my desk for two weeks, and whenever I'd opened the drawer and came upon it inadvertently I was plunged into a dark funk. Fresno.

"Wonderful!" He smiled benevolently. "Is it a tenure track job?"

No one had ever told me what "tenure track" meant, and I wasn't really sure, but the contract did contain those words. "Yes," I answered.

"That's superb," he said, pumping my hand in hearty congratulations.

"So you think I should take it?" I asked, desperate still for rescue, as he walked me to the door.

"Oh, by all means, by all means," Professor Booth averred, bowing slightly as he ushered me out.

So Paula was right after all. That year and the next there was a boom in college hiring. The men who got Ph.D.'s from the English Department were offered jobs at places like Cambridge University, the University of Pennsylvania, Tulane, the University of Massachusetts, the University of Texas at Austin. There they would teach one or two classes a semester and have research assistants and Ph.D. students working with them. The women, if they were lucky enough to get jobs at all, were hired at places like California State College at Northridge and California State College at Hayward, where they would teach four classes a semester to undergraduates and a few master's students, and they would do their research during the summer—if they could muster the energy and motivation to do it at all.

I wrote the conclusion to my dissertation in early March and passed my defense two weeks later. I was Dr. Faderman; I had finished my studies at UCLA. But the Fresno State contract still sat in my desk drawer, a fearsome monster in hiding—out of sight, but never out of mind. *You should be grateful to be offered a job as assistant professor,* I told myself. *Professor Faderman*—wasn't that what I'd worked for all these years? But one afternoon, before Binky got home, I peered into the full-length mirror on the back of the bathroom door and I stripped naked. The young woman who stared back was five years older than Mink Frost, but the waist was still small, the breasts still firm. Weren't there nightclubs that hired exotic dancers all up and down the Sunset Strip? Was it really better to leave everything I loved and go to the desert of Fresno for a mediocre academic career? In the name of what silly vanity did I need to be a professor when I knew other ways to make a living?

I dashed to the desk, still naked, fumbled frantically, tossed the jumbled contents to the floor. Where was it? Had I thrown it out without thinking? My blood froze. There—it was under my *Bleak House* paper on which Booth had written two years before: "Shrewd and splendid insights." I pulled it from the mess and scribbled my name and the date in triplicate, then sealed the envelope along with my fate.

I'd put a white linen cloth on the table and lit white candles. "How beautiful," Binky said, and we smiled feebly at each other, then pushed the food around our plates in funereal silence. I put my fork down, sipped ice water, watched the flicker of the candles and the shadow her bent head made on the wall. Maybe in the morning I'd call the Fresno State English Department. "I sent you something in error," I might say.

"Could you please return the envelope unopened." Who cares if they thought I was crazy? I'd never have to see them.

"Can you really bear to give this up?" Binky bit her lip, blew her nose.

I pushed my dish to the side. In two months it would be our one-year anniversary. I'd been happy—happier with her than I'd ever been in my life. How could I leave to go to Fresno?

"I'm going with you," she said suddenly. Her strong chin was tilted upward, an Amazon ready for superhuman efforts. "I've made up my mind!"

"Fresno is two hundred miles from the nearest bagel or Ingmar Bergman movie or major library," I laughed mirthlessly. "The Fresno temperature gets up to a hundred and ten degrees in the summer. Paula gave me the full report. The tule fog socks the city in for months in the winter."

"I'm going. That's all there is to it. We'll do the book there, just as we planned, and you'll publish your way back to L.A. They must have heating and air conditioning in Fresno. It's still civilization. I'm going with you."

I put off telling my mother and Rae until the last minute because I couldn't bear their wailing on top of my own. "It could be a lot worse," I said from the same green chair on which I'd studied for my orals that had gone so spectacularly well because of the million cups of coffee and slices of buttered rye bread my aunt had kept me fueled with. "I could be off to Michigan or Ohio right now instead of Fresno, which is less than four hours away by car. I'll be back to visit every few weeks," I promised above my aunt's warnings about the ogre-filled world, the tragedy of the unwed, the ticking clock in my womb. "Sarah, after your grandmother," she reminded me irrelevantly. "Avrom, after your grandfather. You're almost twenty-seven years old!"

Then I planted a kiss on my mother's cheek and slipped from her grip.

Driving north on Highway 99, it was already a lot worse than we'd imagined—the flat yellow land that stretched in unrelieved dullness as far as the eye could see; the thick, choking smell of cow dung and urine every few miles; the heat that wrapped around you like a rough, binding blanket and made your skin prickly and your lungs heavy. The car zoomed toward Fresno, relentless, inexorable. Binky and I held hands, two prisoners headed to the gallows. We had nothing to say to each other.

I look out on small seas of blondness, broken by only a few darker heads — occasional Mexican or Armenian students. I teach Victorian literature but — much more exciting to me — I teach a seminar in which I use the material that Binky and I are gathering for our book.

"Who won the Armenian beauty contest?" a raucous young voice says in the hall.

"I dunno," his buddy answers.

"No one!" Guffaw, guffaw, guffaw.

I storm out of my office, ready to put that dumb jock in his place with a withering stare, but there's only a knot of slight, cherub-faced blond boys standing there.

They really need me here, *I think.*

In all my classes they listen quietly, obediently, used to professorial lectures from the podium — but from men. I am the only woman in the department. "How come?" I asked a colleague, my lips curved in a pleasant smile that said *I'm not challenging, just curious,* when I encountered him in the mailroom at the end of my first week. "Oh, there were a lot of women in the department when I came here in 1959, because that's who was hired during the war, but we got rid of them." I must have looked startled. "Oh, because they didn't have Ph.D.'s," he explained. "We upgraded." *How will I be Professor Faderman if "professor" is a dark-suited, starched-collared middle-aged man?*

But I am an actress. Just as I once played stripper, now I can play professor.

On April 4, 1968, the day Martin Luther King, Jr., was killed, Binky and I signed a contract with Scott, Foresman to publish our book. For the rest of that week we moved between the glow of our achievement and the multiple shocks of external events — first the tragedy of King's death and then riots in Los Angeles, Washington, D.C., New York, Chicago — in every city of any size. The sky filled with flame and smoke, as though the whole country, the whole world, were on fire. America was falling apart. How insignificant it was that we were passionate about our work and were going to publish a pioneering college text on multiethnic American literature.

"But it's what we can do," we told each other. "We can't stop the riots or bring racial justice to America, but we can make a step toward integrating what's taught in literature classes."

"It's obvious why I'm dedicated to this stuff, but how come you are?" I asked Binky one evening as we sat side by side writing our section introductions.

"I can't remember when I haven't been," she said. "Maybe it was because I grew up in South Pasadena. They used to have a covenant about not selling to anyone but white Christians. Even when I was a kid I thought that was disgusting. Or maybe it's being gay and seeing through different eyes because of it. I don't know. It all seems connected somehow."

"We'll have fiction and poetry by writers of all colors — good works that have been neglected or forgotten — and we'll let the writers speak for themselves." "They'll show what's unique about their lives but also the similarities that blast through racial and ethnic differences." "They'll show that literary study has to be integrated just as society does, that white men don't have a monopoly on eloquence." We went on and on. We'd already gathered gems by Toshio Mori and Hisaye Yamamoto, Phillis Wheatley and Ossie Davis, Americo Paredes and Piri Thomas, N. Scott Momaday and Emerson Blackhorse Mitchell. Now we mined for more in the Fresno libraries, and when we ran out there, we trekked back to Los Angeles to search neighborhood libraries and the bowels of the UCLA library, which held forgotten books and magazines and newspapers.

My classes are over at 4 P.M. on Thursday, and we hurry down to Los Angeles for a long weekend of research. At night we'll sleep on a bed that pulls down from the wall in my mother's cramped, undusted living room. As always, she's been waiting for our car to turn the corner hours before it could possibly happen, pacing the sidewalk, her face grief-stricken, as though she's already mourning the loss of her only child in a fiery auto accident. When I step from the car, she pounces on me and weeps because I've returned from the dead. Nothing changes. It's as if no time has passed.

Binky views it all with equanimity, as though everyone has a crazy mother and a stepfather with holes in his head who rises from his chair to declaim about the fabulous power of his boss, Dr. Nathan Friedman. "When he walks down the corridors of Cedars of Lebanon Hospital, the interns shiver in their shoes," Albert declares with waving arms. He includes Binky in his audience, though sometimes he calls her Bessy — which is better than my mother, who doesn't call her anything except, to me on the telephone, "the shiksa you live with." "Binky, Binky, Binky," I remind her. Binky, my good, generous love, acts as though she doesn't even notice. ("My family's worse," she says when I ask if she wouldn't rather we stay with her mother, a widow now, living still in the big pink house in South Pasadena that Binky drives me past. "She hated my teaching at Marshall—she hated the Negro kids because she knew how much I loved them.")

The instant Binky excuses herself to go to the bathroom, my mother stands over me to say "Mrs. Sokolov's daughter and the new baby came to visit her yesterday. Her third grandchild." She sighs a huge sigh that says nu? *"Such a cute little baby," she remarks later, when Binky goes out to get our suitcase. "Some people have all the luck." She hasn't been one of the lucky ones, she wants me to know.*

Before long my aunt arrives, wearing an old blue dress and green sweater, hugging a heavy paper sack that comes up to her eyes. "I know you're too busy to see me, go in good health. But take this back with you to Fresno."

"Rae, I'm not going back for three days," I protest.

"I'm afraid I'll forget."

The sack is smelly and ripping at a damp spot. It's bulging with fruit— plums, peaches, honeydew, apricots, cherries, all of it squishy, overripe, leaking. I know that the moment my aunt heard I was coming, she ran to Fairfax Avenue to shop, and the fruit has been sitting in her kitchen ever since, for a week at least, ripening and rotting. "Rae, Fresno is the fruit capital of the world." I struggle to keep my voice calm, but I'm losing the battle. "I can buy all the fruit I want there."

"But you don't," she grumps. She turns to Binky to say "Make her take it." Then she cries, "I forgot something," and runs out the door. She returns a few

minutes later carrying a pink cardboard box that's freckled with gray grease spots. CANTER'S BAKERY is printed on it, and she opens the cover for me to look, though I already know what's inside: butter cookies, two dozen at least, crumbly and stale and dotted with cherries that glow and look as if they've been injected with red dye, also purchased the hour my aunt heard I was coming to Los Angeles. "Put it in the car now so you won't forget," she tells Binky, who takes the box. The charm of her wonderful Kennedy smile is lost on my aunt.

Friday and Saturday we close the libraries, then rush to Malibu, to the ocean, where the breeze is soft, where we wait like condemned women for one more look at the bittersweet sight of the gold sun kissing the water before it merges with it and leaves glorious silver streaks behind in the sky. "We'll come back to L.A., won't we?" Binky says wistfully.

"Are you that miserable in Fresno?" I ask.

"No." She shrugs, but I know she is.

(And I know too, though I don't want to think about it, that despite how much we love each other, her misery sometimes saps her energy. "Let's just cuddle," she often says now when I try to make love to her.)

On Sunday we must drive back to Fresno, as my aunt knows, and she watches from her living room window, starting at dawn probably. When she sees us come out of my mother's building, she hurries down her stairs. Before we can open the car doors, she is standing in front of us. "Watch how you drive with so many maniacs on the road," she says, giving her ritual admonishment to Binky.

"Oh, I will, don't worry about a thing," Binky patiently assures my aunt.

"Bayg arup dos kepele, *bend down the little head,*" Rae orders me now, and I do it (though my head hasn't been little for twenty years). She spreads her fingers over my crown and mutters words in Hebrew that I don't understand as she blesses me. I feel the pressure of her blessing hand all the way up Highway 99.

These are the ways my mother and aunt show me that though I live two hundred miles away, they have not forgotten.

"How many college students would you say there are in this country? Millions, right?" Binky sat at the kitchen table and worked figures with a green pen. "Let's say the book sells only fifty thousand copies—and maybe a quarter of the students who read it go on to teach high school English."

"Yeah . . . and let's say, modestly, that only half of them use material they've gotten from our book in their classes." I peered over her shoulder, helped divide and multiply. "Let's say they use it for only five years —and each teacher has three hundred students a year. That means our research will have touched—" We scrutinized the numbers together. Could it really be?

"Nine million kids!" we cried, hugging each in our double passion. *Maybe this will make up for how much she misses her students at Marshall.*

My days were full—with the book, of course, and with teaching twelve units of Victorian literature and American ethnic literature, with department meetings and committee meetings, with advising students, grading papers, trying to make friendly small-talk with the men in my department so they wouldn't notice what an anomaly I was. But once we finished the book and sent the manuscript off to the publisher, Binky's days were mostly empty. When I came home, never before five or six o'clock, I'd find her sitting in half-darkness on the brown La-Z-Boy, still in her plaid bathrobe, bare legs flung out on the footrest, staring glassy-eyed into space or thumbing through *Time* or the *Atlantic*. A half-full cup of cold coffee flecked with spoiled milk and the bread-crust remains of a sandwich would be on the end table.

"Postpartum blues?" I tried to joke one day.

"There didn't seem any point in getting dressed," she said apologetically (but with a hint of something else, something new, in an undertone). "There's no place much to go here, is there?"

"The book will be out soon." I knelt beside her and rested my head on her lap. "And when that happens, I'll get a job in L.A. We'll get back there, I promise."

"I know," she said, patting my hair distractedly.

But what if I couldn't get a job in Los Angeles and we were stuck in Fresno forever? Didn't most of the men in my department have wives? What did they do all day? "Isn't there anyone interesting in the neighborhood to talk to?" I asked.

She stood up. "They're housewives. Fresno housewives, and I feel like I'm becoming one too. I have a profession, remember?"

I jumped to my feet, ready to rumble as I used to with D'Or. But this was Binky. What sour note was creeping between us?

"Binky, I want to get out of Fresno too," I told her evenly. "Look, I'll write to Long Beach State . . . L.A. State also." Paula had been hired at a new state college that just opened in southwest Los Angeles, Dominguez Hills; maybe she could help. "I'll write there too. As soon as the book is out, I'll write to them all."

"Yes, please, please!" *Pleeeze* was how she said it. How miserable she looked.

The next semester she got a job teaching a freshman composition course at Fresno State, but that made things even worse. I couldn't risk my colleagues' figuring out that I was a lesbian, so when Binky and I ran into each other in the department office we'd become secret agents, cocking heads and batting eyes to signal which one of us ought to leave so that no one would intuit we were lovers. On top of that, part-timers received the munificent sum of two hundred dollars a month per class. "Peon labor," Binky called it when, after taxes, her check came to $183.

Even worse, part-timers were virtually invisible to the professoriate. "Listen to this: I'm reaching into my mailbox to pick up my students' papers and this pompous ass comes in." Over the salad I'd made, Binky screwed up her mouth and fluttered her eyelids to mimic him. "And he says to me, like I was *trespassing*, for God's sake, 'May I help you?'" She struck the table so hard that the flatware bounced. "You're a professor here. You get to be important! But what do I get to be?"

The next year she got a job teaching in a Catholic high school. The pay was about two-thirds what she would have made in Los Angeles, and the students were spoiled and sheltered. They were bored by what Arthay and Rafael and the rest of them had loved.

What did raise Binky's spirits a bit was that she'd been discovered by the neighborhood kids—a set of towheaded, front-toothless boy twins from across the street and a couple of little Chinese girls from next door who often wore matching red dresses that came just above their matching, knobby knees. The twins showed up whenever the sisters did, though they never talked among themselves. It was as though the boys and the girls didn't know one another outside our house. It was Binky who brought them together—the Pied Piper of the neighborhood. "Binky," they all called her, as though she was a kid too. "Binky, can we come in and play?" they'd shout at the door and scamper up the steps, the tousled towheads on one side and the smooth black heads on the other, and soon they'd all be dashing around together, hilarious, in some scary-fun game of hide-and-seek or Frankenstein's monster that Binky devised, or she'd race them to the kitchen and they'd pull open the drawer where she kept the Tootsie Rolls and Milky Ways and they'd all —Binky too—be shrieking with candied laughter. She put immense energy into the kids, and they loved her. They threw their arms around her and nuzzled their heads on her chest like puppies when they heard their mothers calling them home; they left little bunches of daisies or dandelions at the door for her or crayon stick figures that they'd drawn at school and signed "i luv you."

"You'd make a terrific parent," I told her one evening, and out of nowhere tears pooled in my eyes. No, not nowhere. My mother's envy of Mrs. Sokolov, my aunt's nagging about my aging womb. They buzzed in my head and preyed on my peace as they never had before. I was almost twenty-nine.

"Are you crazy?" Binky laughed. "Look, most of my childhood was stolen from me because I had to take care of my brother and sister while my parents were doing business all over the country." She shuddered as if parenthood were *her* bogeyman. "I did enough mothering to last a lifetime by the time I was fifteen."

The editor's note that came with our authors' copies said: "Many advance orders. Congrats!" The cover of the book was perfect: shades of brown and beige in the background, and in the foreground an elderly, angry-looking Mexican or American Indian, his index finger held up as if punctuating the message: "Shut up and listen. I'm speaking now." We planted copies all over the house so that we would come upon them unexpectedly, and our delight—we published a book together!—would be renewed over and over again. Binky was merry. "Is this how a man and woman feel when they look at the baby they made together?" she laughed.

But the book didn't help me get another job. "Bad timing," Paula said sympathetically when I called to ask if she'd recommend me for a position at Dominguez Hills State College. "When I came aboard, last September, four people were hired in the department, but this year we're not hiring anyone."

"We're cutting back," the chair at Long Beach State College wrote in answer to my letter, and at Los Angeles State College I was told that the department was overstaffed and the days of big expansion were gone.

I was lucky to have a tenure track job anywhere. Within a year or two, most new Ph.D.'s in English were getting hired only for temporary lectureships or part-time work, or they were going back to school for degrees in business, or they were driving cabs.

For those of us who did have teaching jobs, it was, as Dickens wrote, the best of times and the worst of times, an age of wisdom and an age of foolishness. It was an era when campuses around America erupted in fury—against the draft, institutional racism, organized paternalism—and Fresno State was only a little tardy in catching fire. By the end of the fall 1969 semester, large segments of the student body and faculty were smoldering. After our president, Fredrick Ness, quit under pressure, almost all the blacks who'd been hired to teach in a newly formed Ethnic Studies Program were fired by the new administration for "lacking proper academic credentials," and many of the untenured left-leaning white activists weren't rehired. Maybe I continued to be safe because my own brand of activism was too academic to be threatening to our new acting president, Karl Falk, who'd been the head of a local bank before he was pressed into service as CEO of FSC. (Or maybe I was safe because those in power thought I was the department secretary.)

In any case, it was the campus dramas of the next semester that taught me once and for all what kind of activist I was. It was not the kind I'd envisioned twelve years earlier in Mexico City. Fresno State students staged a boycott of classes that February after the acting president had gutted the new Economic Opportunities Program for poor students, dismissed more minority faculty, and begun to dismantle the School of Arts and Sciences, which he believed to be a hotbed of leftists. The huge crowd of students and faculty at a morning rally bristled with anger and testosterone. I believe I was the only woman professor there. (Most of the women faculty taught in areas such as nursing, home economics, and women's physical education—disciplines not noted for their radicalism.) Banners that read "ARE YOU GOING TO STAND BY AND GET FALKED?" were everywhere. On the lawn in front of the administration building, Chicano students were camped in a hunger strike because the new La Raza program had been completely destroyed by the administration.

The rally organizers had pledged nonviolence, but it couldn't last long. Agriculture students in cowboy hats ragged the striking Chicanos, and a free-for-all followed, with flying fists and cheers and blood and girls huddled off to the side. The bloodshed made the mood ugly. A bearded, tie-dyed young man next to me cupped his hands to his mouth and howled, "Fuck Falk!" and a knot of students picked it up and made it a chant. The speakers on the platform punctuated their seething words with raised fists, and hoarse cheers went up all around, as though the fists were smashing the enemy's noggin. The crowd turned into a roaring, multiheaded monster. To me it felt like mass hysteria, like a football crowd, like the Nazis. I was surrounded by it—male voices screaming "Fuck Falk!" and cheering mindlessly. I felt it in my gut. They were the radicals I liked rather than the reactionaries I hated, but it didn't matter. The frenzy triggered in me primal anguish, like a racial memory—the violence used on those who belonged to me. I hurried back to my office as though pursued by a pack, and I locked the door against that part of human nature that filled me with fear and loathing.

I'd learned something about myself that was surprising and even disappointing—but immutable. Demonstrations frightened me. I was terrified of their resemblance to the acres of hypnotized spirits who had thrust up their arms in *sieg heil* ecstasy. That's okay, I assured myself later. My activism would be my scholarship. I'd do more books. I'd work for the causes that stirred me deeply through my editing and writing and teaching.

. . .

At home, a dull discontent settled on our lives like the dust on our furniture. Nothing could blow the monotony of it away except occasional outbreaks of rage, different only in substance from the ones I'd had with D'Or; they would leave us both shaken and unsure. The first major storm was over my student Omar Salinas, a sweet-faced, fragile man of twenty-nine, a poet who wrote magical realism long before García Márquez became popular in the United States. He called himself Omar the Crazy Gypsy and spent many hours in my office complaining about his rejection slips from magazines. "I know great Chicano writers all over the U.S.," he told me one day, "and no one is publishing them."

We'd used his poems in our book, but it hadn't been easy to find other good Chicano writers. If he was right, what a treasure a textbook of Chicano literature would be to the Chicano Studies classes that were being established now at many colleges. There wasn't yet a single such book.

"We could do a collection of their work!" I exclaimed, more excited than I'd been about anything in a long time. "Let's you and I do it together. What do you think?"

He laughed. "That there are two crazy gypsies in this room if you believe we can get it published." But he agreed to do the book with me.

Two or three weeks later, as we were dressing for work, I told Binky about it. I'd been afraid to tell her earlier. "I have an idea for another book." I tried to make it sound offhand. "It'll be an anthology of Chicano literature. *From the Barrio*, we're calling it."

"What a great idea! Let's do it." Binky grinned now.

I busied myself putting on my nylons, fastening my garter belt. "I think it's important that I do it with someone . . . with a Chicano . . . with Omar Salinas." I stumbled over the words, but I had to say it all. I didn't dare look at her; I didn't have to. I could feel her shock, then her indignation.

"While you do that, what am I going to do?" she finally asked, her voice low and cold. Half naked still, I hurried my skirt on, my blouse, my jacket. "What am I supposed to do in this hellhole I came to because of you—because of us?" she shouted now.

"I don't know," I said, my head bent over jacket buttons. But I did know that I couldn't do *From the Barrio* with her—I needed to do it with Omar, who could teach me the things I needed to know about his culture. But there was more that I didn't want to have to say: I needed to be free to develop my work in every way. How could that happen if we always had to work in tandem?

"You don't know? Well, I don't know either," she said tonelessly.

"Why can't you do your own book?" I snapped at her as I grabbed my briefcase.

"What am I doing here"—she stood on the threshold and snapped back—"teaching in a school I hate? I left Marshall High to come here." Then she slammed the door behind me so hard, I could feel the vibrations on the wooden stairs as I descended.

I drove a few blocks and then had to pull over because I'd narrowly missed a kid on a bicycle. I just sat in the parked car near an open field, my forehead against the steering wheel. I'd once said she was my sun; she'd said she hadn't lived before she met me.

That evening Binky was waiting for me at the door, dressed as she used to when she taught at Marshall. I couldn't remember when I'd last seen her look so lovely. "If you want to do books, fine, you can do them in L.A. Look, I've really thought about it." She was almost cheery. "I'll get my teaching job back at Marshall, and you can work on your projects. You said you wanted to write a book on the Harlem Renaissance. Do it. Do the book with Omar too. Only I want to go back to L.A."

So did I. Of course. Though I liked teaching, loved getting young people to open up to ideas, I hated being the only woman professor in a department of thirty-one dark-suited men. I hated having to hide my woman lover. I hated having to live in a town so alien to my urban Jewishness. "But what about money?"

"It's my turn to support us. I'm offering you the leisure to write." She looked soft and loving now. "Write for both of us," she said. It had been so long since she'd looked at me that way. "Let's not lose the wonderful things we have. I came with you three years ago, now come with me."

. . .

We drove to Los Angeles at Easter break to look for a house. Perhaps because it was springtime, the San Joaquin Valley, which had always seemed so deadly dull to me, was suddenly vibrant with fertile swaths of rich green fields, trees lush with fragrant pink and white blossoms, and big, open sky with rolling clouds. (*How beautiful*, I thought, with a quick prick of regret that this would be my last spring in the valley. *How had I not noticed before?*) We'd buy a house in L.A. instead of renting, we decided, because home ownership would be a symbol of the permanence of our love. We'd figured the finances and we could do it: I'd saved about five thousand dollars from my salary, which would be enough for a down payment, and the mortgage we'd pay with Binky's salary. "We'll find a place with an office. When I leave for work every morning you can go in there to write, and it'll be like having a regular job." Binky gripped the wheel and kept her eyes on the road as she recited the plans.

But what if I couldn't do it? What if I gave up my job and then found I couldn't write? I'd have nothing.

Suddenly the image of what I needed loomed over my head like the bubble in a cartoon: "Okay, we'll live in L.A., I'll write. But I also want to have a baby now" came out of my mouth. Binky laughed as though I'd told a joke. "I mean it. I'll write, but I want to get pregnant too. I'll be thirty years old this summer. If I don't do it now, when will I ever do it?"

She glanced at me and saw I meant it. "What are you talking about?" she cried. "You never said that before—that you wanted a baby."

I'd never been sure before, but now the logic and the imperative of it were absolutely clear. Of course I had to have a child. I was a remnant, all that was left of my mother's family. I remembered an image from a Steinbeck novel, about a turtle that struggles through the hazards of field and highway and barely makes it to the other side. Somewhere along its journey, an oat seed lodges in its shell, and on the other side the seed falls out and into the earth. *My mother is the turtle and I am the seed, and I've got to come to fruition. This gift of leisure that Binky wants to give me comes at just the right time. I must have a baby.*

"You'll make a wonderful other mother," I said, sure of it all now. "Kids love you and you love them. A baby is what we really need in our lives," I implored.

"The kids that I love go home after a couple of hours." Binky took her eyes from the road to stare at me as though she suspected my sanity. "How do you plan to get pregnant?" She laughed hollowly.

I hadn't thought that far ahead. "There are choices," I said. "We could find some gay guy . . . or I could go to a doctor for artificial insemination."

She seemed to consider it for a long while. I watched her as we drove. Her expression was mummy-rigid. "No," she said finally. "This is crazy. One reason I'm a lesbian is that I never wanted to have children."

"But I'll be the one to have the child. Binky, please," I implored again. "We'll be a family that way—forever."

She drove for at least half an hour more before she shook her head and sighed, then said in a whisper I could barely hear, "Give me a few days to think about it."

17 HOW I BECAME
A COLLEGE ADMINISTRATOR

WE FOUND THE HOUSE and the feminist movement on the same day.

In the lollipop-red Mercedes of Dottie Dorey, the real estate agent, we rode up and down the hills of Laurel Canyon, a funky enclave of artists and struggling actors. Before there were jets to whisk the rich off to Rio or the Riviera for a week, the Canyon was where the silent film stars built twenty-room vacation cottages, Dottie Dorey said, and she pointed out the ruins of dirty pink or moldy gray mansions still visible behind overgrown masses of trees. In between such bits of history, she chatted about her girlfriend in New York, a set designer, who was coming to Los Angeles to live with her.

"That must make you happy," I said.

"Oh, positively gay." She grinned, and with the uttered secret word we relaxed into sociability. "We'll have you to dinner as soon as Betty gets here. You'll like our crowd," she said, and turned her head half-circle to wink at me in the back seat. How good it felt to be back in civilization again. In Fresno we'd been so constricted, we'd been in hiding —the only lesbians in town. But here, in Los Angeles, we could breathe. Binky and I would have friends together. We'd make a real life.

The house Dotty showed us on Lookout Mountain Drive had four rooms rather than twenty, and one of them looked makeshift and bohemian, protruding at an odd angle as though it just growed, like Topsy. From its big window you had a view of the backyard, which was thick with blossoming trees as pretty as a stage set, but they were real—fragrant citrus flowers, I discovered when I stepped out. And beyond the trees was a lopsided little one-room cottage that would be mine, a room of my own where I could go every day to write. It was only the third house we'd looked at, but after a ten-minute tour Binky and I huddled together in a corner of the bedroom for a few quivering seconds. We emerged ready to make our bid—$37,000. "I'm coming back to Los Angeles to live!" I told my delighted mother that evening when we arrived to spend the night.

As though the house weren't enough to set me and Binky reeling, after my mother and Albert went to bed and Binky to her shower, I lounged on the Murphy bed and flipped through the magazine we'd brought from Fresno. "Women's Lib: The War on 'Sexism'" was the title of the cover article. I'd been hearing words like *women's liberation* and *sexism* over the past year or two, but somehow I'd paid them little mind—until I saw them in that March 1970 *Newsweek*. Now I was riveted. Here was my story, not in exact detail but the gist of it: Whatever had angered me about men, about women's place in the world, had angered other women too, had made them unhappy with their lot and suspicious that the fault lay not with them but with forces beyond them. So it wasn't just my peculiar personal history, I realized. Thousands of other women were feeling the very same thing—millions, maybe. I read the long article again, caught up totally in the heady rhetoric of the feminists whom the reporter had interviewed. I felt transported—like the night I first stepped inside the Open Door. "Binky, you've got to read this! Hurry," I said, laughing and pounding on the bathroom door. "We're missing the revolution!"

Driving north on 99 after Easter break I felt positively wired with plans: I'd finish the semester and we'd move to Los Angeles, and I'd set up shop in the cottage in back of our new house. First I'd finish my work on *From the Barrio* and then I'd write—about women authors, women characters . . . everything about women. Had anyone ever done it before? I'd dedicate my life to it—to that and to the family Binky and I would make. She hadn't returned to the subject of the baby yet, but I'd told her, right after we'd signed the papers Dottie had given us, about how my mother was the turtle and I was the single oat seed that had managed to plant itself on this side of the road. Binky nodded slowly, as if she were really listening. I'd write while I was pregnant and while the child was growing up too. What better job for a mother, to be able to stay home and still be productive?

I was keen to announce my departure to Gene, the department chairman. "I'm leaving," I would say, just like that. Had anyone but my students even noticed I'd been there? Had the tenured faculty even bothered to look at my great teaching evaluations? I piled up grievances — not a word of congratulations from the department when Binky's and my book came out. "And in case you haven't noticed," I'd say, "seventy percent of our majors are female, and you won't have a single woman professor in the department when I leave."

Yet my feelings weren't quite so simple. I thought of Gene's rugged face that showed the moral blows he'd suffered at the hands of Falk and his henchmen — three radical professors fired, an attempt to hire another young man rebuffed because he was a political activist. The other men in the department had been egging Gene on, as though not only academic freedom was at stake — as though it were a monumental battle between the forces of good and evil, and I knew that he, a World War II combat veteran, would continue to fight to the death. "Our warrior," Earl Lyon, a crusty professor of about seventy, had called Gene in a department meeting, and the others had nodded solemnly or grunted their agreement. They were a tribe of warriors, young and old. And Gene stood there, slim-hipped and handsome, a warrior king, looking at that instant, there in the meeting room with the streaked blackboard behind him, as though he envisioned himself leaping from the pages of the *Beowulf* text he taught and set to slay the Grendel monsters with his fists. I felt bad about the fired professors, bad about him. Yet what had the overblown warrior tactics of the department to do with me? If I were in his place, I'd try to find a subtler way, I thought. How would a woman do it?

The day I returned from Easter break, I found a message from Gene in my department mailbox, asking me to come by at eleven. How had he known I wanted to see him? In the mild early spring sunshine, on the way from my Victorian seminar to his office, I looked around the campus as though I were seeing the Spanish red tile roofs and the freshly leafed-out trees that shadowed them for the last time. I had only six weeks to go before I'd retreat to my little cottage once and for all. That was what I wanted, but now that I knew it was going to happen, the thought of it seemed bittersweet. I wouldn't be a college professor anymore.

"This is my last semester," I said when Gene closed the door to his office.

"What? You don't want to leave now." He peered at me darkly. "We've just been notified that you were promoted to associate professor." I opened my mouth to speak but nothing came. "Yours was one of the few promotions that went through this year. Don't quit now. At least think about it," he said. *Associate Professor. How many twenty-nine-year-old women were there—in the whole country—who were associate professors?* "Incidentally, you won't be the only woman in the department anymore," he added. "They let us hire because we lost people, so we're getting someone who just finished her Ph.D. at Stanford and two women in creative writing."

Back in my own office, I sank into a chair. It was as if I'd worked myself up to perform a demanding physical feat—every sinew was ready—and then I didn't perform it after all. I felt limp. I had to figure things out. What if I stayed? Just for one more year. I could teach the material I was going to write about. I could call my course Women's Liberation in Literature.

Yet Binky and I had already plunked down our deposit for the wonderful house. What if I got a Tuesday–Thursday teaching schedule? I could fly to Los Angeles after my last class on Thursdays and fly back on Tuesdays. Five nights a week I'd be with Binky in our home. Why not? As associate professor, my salary would go up by about twenty-five percent, which would more than pay for the airfare and a little apartment I'd rent near campus.

And the baby?

I'd do it for just one year; then I'd return to the original plan.

But what if I weren't allowed to teach Women's Liberation in Literature? I'd go to Gene's office now and say, *I'll stay if I can teach a feminist class.* It would be like rolling dice: If he said *yes,* I'd stay; *no,* and I'd be off to L.A. Either way would be fine.

"Why not?" He shrugged. "We've never had such a class." How simple he made it. "Here's something else you might be interested in," he said, handing me a memo that he pulled from a file. It was a call for semester-long classes that would go out to the Fresno community over television. "Why not do it as a television class also?" he suggested.

"But we just bought a house," Binky cried. She looked at me now as if I really were insane. "I thought that was what you wanted."

"I do. I do. But it'll be just for one year. Love, listen to me, we'll be together five nights a week." I went over the whole litany again. The promotion. Women's Liberation in Literature. The television program. Everything except what I didn't want to say out loud because I was scared to admit it even to myself—that if our L.A. plans didn't work, I'd have stopped being a professor, and who would I be? "It's only for a year," I promised again.

Tuesday mornings at seven-twenty, Binky drops me off at the Los Angeles airport on her way to Marshall High School, and I race to catch the seven-forty puddle-jumper to Fresno—fifty minutes in the sky (where I keep checking my watch as I finish grading papers or review the class notes I'd written over the weekend; if we land late, I'm sunk), then another race out of the plane and through the terminal to the old clunker Plymouth that I keep at the Fresno airport parking lot (silent supplications to the god of heaps to make it start), and a zoom down Clinton Avenue, burning amber lights all the way to the college, where I dodge through a quad jammed with sauntering students, bound up the steps of San Ramon two at a time, and tear down the corridor to arrive, shaky-limbed, at my office door, no more than a minute or so late for my 9 A.M. office hour if I'm lucky.

Every hour is packed—I teach American Ethnic Writing, Victorian Literature, Women's Liberation in Literature. On Tuesday nights I go to one of the Fresno television stations and record Women's Liberation in Literature in front of a camera, modulating my voice the way Irene showed me almost twenty years

'If a female is aggressive she is called bitchy, but if a male is aggressive he is a go-getter.'

'Think how our (women's) history would be different if there had been a Judith Shakespeare instead of William.'

By Linda Koch

Dr. Lillian Faderman is living proof that the "weaker sex" need not be weak in the profession.

At 30, Dr. Faderman is the youngest department head at Fresno State College and first woman chairman of the English Department. She was elected to the post by her 34 fellow professors, only four of them women.

As a model for other women, Dr. Faderman is not content "to be." She stresses the verb "to become." "Historically, women have not been allowed to 'become.' We have been predefined like blacks and chicanos," she explained.

"Our history has been hidden from us. What happens throughout history is that without models, the pattern perpetuates itself. The greatest injustice, I think, is the predefinition."

Lillian Faderman did not let predefinition deter her. The only child of a "very poor family" reared in East Los Angeles, Dr. Faderman was graduated from the University of California at Berkeley with a bachelor's degree and from UC at Los Angeles with her master's and doctorate degrees. At 26 she began teaching at FSC, marking two firsts: the first and only woman in the department four years ago and the first and only woman to receive tenure.

The petite, intense professor attributes the approval of her chairmanship by the administration — in light of recent controversies in the department — because, "I'm not flamboyant."

If flamboyancy is not the word to describe Dr. Faderman, dedication is. Her dedication goes further than wanting to do a good job "for students, the department, the administration and the community." It also includes a commitment to emphasize "teaching rather than publishing," and a desire that the college represent the community.

"I am interested not only in hiring women faculty," she explained, "but that our hiring reflects the community. We are homogeneous now. Where are the blacks and chicanos?"

"And I don't just want warm bodies, but quality on the faculty."

Dr. Faderman said her first obligation is to the department, "which means the community." Secondly, she is concerned about the lack of women, Negro and chicano instructors. Although she is a woman's libber, Dr. Faderman disassociates herself from the more radical members of the movement.

She is not pessimistic: "Things will get better," she said.

"Women have not had the tradition that men have had. There could not have been a Marlowe if there were not a Shakespeare. And there could not have been a Shakespeare had there not been a Chaucer.

"Think how 'our' history would be different if there had been a 'Judith Shakespeare' instead of a William. But society would not have allowed a Judith to publish. At that time men also played the roles of women on stage.

"Blacks and chicanos were predefined and forced into roles just as women were. And if women have been petty, it's because they have had to be. It a female is aggressive she is called bitchy, but if a male is aggressive he is a go-getter.

"TV has perpetuated the stereotyping, the predefinition. The only way to stop it is have people to protest."

To give woman her proper place in history, Dr. Faderman teaches a course called Women's Liberation in Literature, also taught Saturday mornings on KMJ-TV. Ingrid Saltebury, one of the four women English instructors, teaches a course called Women Authors.

Dr. Faderman's course focuses on women in the 19th century — authors George Eliot (a female who used a male pseudonym), Charlotte Bronte and Virginia Woolf — giving women an historical perspective.

She is herself an author. "Speaking For Ourselves," co-authored with Barbara —

See Faderman Page W2

Women's Activities

THE FRESNO BEE   Sunday, May 23, 1971   Page W1

High Kicks For All Guild Picnic

Colorfully clad cancan dancers will provide part of the entertainment at the annual All Guild Picnic of the Valley Children's Hospital and Guidance Clinic Wednesday. Showing off their choreographic skills are, from left, Mmes. Leon Anderson, Jack Schmoor, John Van Curen and David Castellucci, members of the Tenaya Guild of Chowchilla. The picnic will begin with a social hour at 11 a.m. in the Harold Parichan garden. Lunch will follow. Prizes will be given for the most unusual hats and the best decorated tables. Reservations, at $3.75 a person, may be made with Mrs. Genoey Arthur at the hospital. Mrs. G. L. McKean is the picnic chairman.

Bee Photo by Gene Rose

Porterville Man Strikes A Blow For Male Chauvinism

PORTERVILLE — Joseph Manfrini, a retired investments analyst, is a male chauvinist who wants woman to get out of "the gutter, the jungle of mud, sweat and tears and back on her pedestal."

Irked because the formerly all-male Commonwealth Club of California is admitting women to its membership, Manfrini has angrily submitted his resignation to the 14,000-member group.

"The purpose of this club is to defeat public issues," he said in a telephone interview. "Let the women get their own club. Most of the men would say the same thing I'm saying after they had the fourth martini.

"But these guys are a bunch of babies . . . they're afraid . . . they're scared rats afraid of their own wives. But after that fourth martini they suddenly become big powerful he-men.

"Besides, the decision to let women in the club was not voted on democratically. It was strong-armed and high-handed through by management who took the power unto themselves."

'If those gals had a date or two they wouldn't be waving flags; they'd be making love or thinking about it.'

'The Commonwealth Club is like the Boy Scouts, the YMCA, the men's latrine. Women don't belong there.'

Manfrini, 64, says he is a happily married man who "even loves my mother-in-law."

And he adds, "I was even idiot enough to love my school teachers. I loved one so much that I stayed in the eighth-grade four years."

Manfrini likens the Commonwealth Club to Boy Scouts or the YMCA: "When I was a boy I joined the Boy Scouts. As I got older I joined the YMCA and when in the Army I became an officer and used the men's latrine.

"The Commonwealth Club is like the Boy Scouts, the YMCA, the men's —

See Manfrini Page W2

The Fresno Bee, *May 23, 1971*

earlier, using body language like an actress, words like a scholar, zeal like a preacher. When I'm not teaching or holding office hours or going to department meetings or working with Omar on From the Barrio *(we now have a contract with Harper and Row), I go back to my apartment across the street from campus and wander about the stuffy rooms like a small stone rolling around in a big, dark box. Why am I in Fresno when I want to be home, lounging in the Topsy room or writing in the garden cottage? I'm exhausted, but I can't rest. I miss Binky.*

But when I get off the puddle-jumper in Los Angeles at eleven on Thursday

How I Became a College Administrator   311

evenings, we hug each other and fall into silence. It's as if the week apart has made us shy with each other, as if we have to get acquainted all over again. But we've known each other for years, so the sweet buzz of beginnings is no longer there, and most weeks we even seem to forget to make love or we just don't get around to it. I love her, but are we still lovers? Maybe that doesn't matter so much because aren't we family for each other?—family I'm still hoping will grow.

There were now four women and twenty-eight men in the department. Ingrid was a young poet who inspired from the male faculty the chivalry I had already learned to suspect because they saw the woman before they saw the colleague. They addressed her in gentle voices, they almost bowed when they held doors open for her—and they didn't renew her contract. But that year she gave a seminar on women poets. Here we were, in the fall of 1970, on a little campus in the middle of the agribusiness capital of the world, and two women professors were teaching feminist courses in the English Department. In the Art Department there was a visiting professor, Judy Gerowitz (who became Judy Chicago before the year was over), who taught courses in feminist art. Three of us at Fresno State College—what a happy irony, we agreed. It couldn't happen at a place like UCLA or Berkeley, where the faculty was hidebound. It certainly *wasn't* happening there.

The excitement was palpable in my Women's Liberation in Literature course. "You know how students complain that their courses aren't relevant to their lives?" a young woman in jeans came to my office to say. "This one is so relevant that night and day I can't get it out of my head." A bespectacled older woman student stopped by my table in the cafeteria to tell me "This class is making me question all the things that used to make me say 'That's the way life is and you can't do anything about it.'"

We were conspirators, Ingrid and I told each other, teaching dangerous, revolutionary ideas. "Are we getting away with this because we're beneath their notice?" we marveled, "or maybe the guys just don't understand what *feminist* means." What we were doing really was dangerous and revolutionary—it was impossible to teach Women in Literature or Women in Art in 1970 and not be fiercely political. In later years our passion came to seem excessive, but in 1970 it felt exactly right. For me, it was about helping my students see the barely masked hatred, the stereotypes and mindless pusillanimity, in the images of women that some of the most revered male writers had concocted, and it was about discovering with my students neglected female genius. It was all angry-making stuff, for them and for me. What did it signal if not a call for a cataclysmic upheaval in thinking about literature? And, by an extension that the class couldn't ignore, how could that not lead to an upheaval in how you thought about the male-female relationships in your own life? If the class was successful, the student who finished it in December would not be the same being as the one who began it in September. Ingrid's and Judy's classes were at least as political. But to the higher administration, revolutionaries were people with Adam's apples and beards. We were blissfully safe.

My department wasn't. That winter, in the presence of newspaper and television reporters, our chairman accused the administration of placing student spies in the classes of radical professors. The dean of the school was not going to be upstaged for drama. He ordered the campus police to lock up the department files, bolt the door of the English office, and keep Gene out. A uniformed guard with a gun was stationed on the roof of San Ramon. Fresno State College made the national news.

"This place is a laughingstock. Everyone is nuts," I groaned to Binky over the phone. "Except for my students, it's torture to be here."

"Well, you'll teach one more semester, and then you'll never have to go back," she said.

Dottie invited us often to parties in Manhattan Beach, where she and Betty had a circle of friends who were nothing like the women I'd known at the Open Door. Some were film editors or set designers; most were teachers, social workers, nurses, real estate agents—serious members of the few professions that had been open to females ten or twenty years before, when these women first set out on their own. There were some gay men too in the circle—"honorary lesbians," Dottie called them. Roger, my favorite, was Japanese, with a long, thin face and a lithe dancer's body, like the kimonoed figures in ancient art prints. He loved to camp—to throw a lace armchair doily on his head, grab me by the arm, and strut me through the genial knots that were chatting and sipping beer from frosted mugs on Dottie's bougainvillea-covered patio. "We're getting married," he announced with prissy lips.

"Nope, I've already been there," I laughed.

He ignored my demurral. "Guess which one's the bride." He tossed his head and primped for his audience.

He'll never be my bride . . . but he's hit a nerve, I realized. *Why didn't I think of it before? If I get pregnant without being married, how will my mother bear it? She'll think some man has destroyed my life the way Moishe destroyed hers. She'll be sick with worry and shame, and so will my aunt.*

But what if I told them I was getting married . . . to someone in Fresno . . . who was leaving right away to take a job back east . . . in Pittsburgh, Pennsylvania, say . . . and that I had to stay in California for my own job? Then, when Binky and I traveled in the summers with our baby, I could tell them that I was going east, to visit my husband in Pittsburgh.

"Take a picture with me, Roger." It wouldn't work if you had a family who knew the world, who might hop a plane across the country to introduce themselves to the absent groom—but my mother and aunt had probably never even heard of Pittsburgh. "You'll never have to meet them," I told Roger. "Just lend me your image to show them."

"Haven't you noticed I'm Japanese?" He frowned.

He's right. Why throw the complication of race into it? "Will you wear these?" I pulled a pair of sunglasses from my purse. Around my ring finger we wrapped a gold cigar band lifted from a Cubano that Thomas, his movie-extra boyfriend, smoked. I plucked one of Dottie's daisies, and when Roger and I sat close together on the lawn, I held it up in my left hand so that the camera could not miss the wedding ring. He circled me with his arm, and Dottie snapped the picture.

It's the one I find after Rae is gone, fourteen years later, in a little falling-apart album she'd kept in the top drawer of her dresser and filled with photos of me, from my birth to her death.

After Gene's removal as chairman, the English Department became a protectorate, chafing under the uneasy jurisdiction of the same hated

RIGHT: *Dr. Faderman, spring 1967, UCLA*

BELOW: *Roger and Lil: "You'll never have to meet them. Just lend me your image to show them."*

dean who'd stationed the armed guard on the roof of San Ramon. Three months later, he assembled us in the department meeting room — grim citizens of a defeated little country. His head swiveled on an Ichabod Crane neck as he eyeballed us from left to right and back again. "You have two choices," he barked. "You can nominate a chairman who'll be acceptable to me and our new president, Dr. Baxter, or we can find a chairman from the outside and bring him in." White knuckles showed on the fists of the men around me, but they were silent. I too said nothing. I'd be turning in my resignation anyway, right after spring break, and then I'd get on with my life—with the baby, with the books I'd write. Sometimes, when I waited for Binky to pull the car out of our garage on Tuesday mornings, I'd look longingly at the little cottage in the back. I would put a cradle in there so that when I went to my desk every morning, I'd be able to take my baby with me. I'd rock her with one hand and write with the other.

"Okay, I'm announcing my resignation as soon as I get in," I promised Binky when she dropped me off at the L.A. airport the Tuesday after Easter 1971. I flew up the stairs of San Ramon as usual, but instead of going to my office I went to find the white-haired senior professor who was acting as the liaison between the dean and the department. "Russ, this is my last semester," I said as he reached for the mail in his box.

Russ turned around, blinking. "You're kidding," he said. "I was just talking to some other people in the department. We think you'd be our best shot for chairman."

I touched the cold wall behind me for balance. *Binky glared with ice blue eyes. "You promised," she hissed. "No, you gonif! You liar, no," my mother and Rae hollered.* But in the entire college there was only one woman chair of an academic department. I'd complained about it in my classes, and here was my chance to begin to change it. How many women were there in the whole country who might be handed such an opportunity?

After three-thirty I began calling Binky, dialing the number in Los Angeles every fifteen minutes. I could see the black telephone on the desk in the Topsy room. In my head I could hear the ring, how it bounced off the walls in our empty house. I'd tell her how I'd found out that day that Judy Chicago was leaving and that Ingrid's contract hadn't been renewed. If I got elected chairman—"chair," I'd call it—I'd make the department replace Ingrid with another woman who could teach feminist classes. Where was Binky? She said she always went home right after school, to a lonely house.

She finally answered the phone around ten o'clock. "You said just one year. You promised," she said when I told her. She sounded as glacial as she had in my imagination that morning in the mailroom.

"Binky, listen to me. Who'll teach the women's courses?" I recited all the reasons I had to stay. "The term's only three years, and I'll leave after two. By that time the department won't need me anymore."

"I need you," she said, unmoved. "I need you to live with me. Here. Seven days a week. Where you said you wanted to be."

But as chair I could defuse the terrible tensions—no warrior tactics, no press conferences about student spies in English classes. The department needed a calm style of leadership now, and there weren't many men who could bring it to them. I'd be quietly revolutionary by serving the cause of women. I'd make sure to fill every position with women; I'd promote a new curriculum that would include neglected women authors; through the prestige of the chair I'd fight for women's rights all over campus. No one else could do the things I would do.

I'd call Binky again when she was calmer, in the morning, and I'd tell her that if the department elected me, I had to stay—but for two years and no more.

The election was held the next day. Someone nominated a young man to run against me. The dean and Russ counted the ballots; Russ came to my office to tell me: I won by a vote of 28–4.

Despite the photos in the national news that made Fresno State look like an eastern European satellite, the department was inundated with job applications that spring because there was a glut of new Ph.D.'s on the market. We had only one position available, and I had to make it count. I practiced my spiel in front of the mirror in the women's bathroom until I could say it in a voice that was forceful and calm. "We've lost Ingrid, so I think it's only right that we replace her with another person who can teach women-in-literature classes," I told the department. "Judith Rosenthal." I picked a dossier from the top of the pile. "She looks great." I handed the file to Russ for him to pass around the room, then folded my hands on my lap so no one would see them trembling.

The vote to hire her was unanimous. I retreated to my office and sat there, amazed. How easy it had been — perhaps because the time was right, perhaps because women's liberation had already invaded their homes through their wives and daughters. The reason didn't matter. Clearly they were going to give me a chance — to give women a chance.

Before the semester was over, it seemed that the whole campus wanted to give women a chance — through me, since my election as chair had made me the salient female academic. I was elected vice president of the faculty union — United Professors of California — and then the college representative to the statewide Academic Senate that was made up of the faculty leaders of all eighteen campuses in the California State College system. "Those three positions together make her the most powerful professor on campus," I overheard one male colleague matter-of-factly tell his officemate as I walked down the corridor. I loved it — suddenly these guys were thinking that a woman was the most powerful professor on campus.

Every Saturday afternoon I go back to Curson Avenue to visit first my mother and then my aunt. Sometimes when I get close to their street I hear a distant siren — an ambulance maybe, or a fire engine or police car. Los Angeles is a city of millions. But I'm certain the siren is speeding toward them. My mother has had a heart attack, Rae has been killed by a mugger, Curson Avenue has been leveled to rubble like a shtetl in a pogrom. They are dead, and they have died before I could present to them a Sarah or an Avrom, before I could assure them that Hitler hadn't done his job completely, that they hadn't lived in vain, that we would reach into another generation.

Sometimes when I sit with Rae on her living room sofa and we haven't spoken for some minutes, I see her eyes grow heavy, her head nod, and then she is very still in seated sleep. But what if it's not sleep? What if I've waited too long? "Rae?" I stand before her, bend my head to her face, nudge her as gently as my fright permits. "Wake up, My Rae."

"Just two years, I swear it," I promised as Binky drove me to the airport the first day of the fall semester, when I officially became chair of the English Department.

"Okay," she said with a sigh, "two years."

On the campus I found that mementos still remained of the past, such as the wrecked Ethnic Studies program, but the big storms had subsided. A new dean and a new vice president for Academic Affairs were already in place, working on repairing the wreckage. The ambiance of the campus had changed too. The bearded and fiery radicalism of the last years had shifted the perimeter of what was radical. The rhetoric of the radicals would make my soft-spoken message seem tame, I realized. For what I needed to do, the times couldn't be better. "The college needs an affirmative action policy," I could say in a reasonable tone of voice. "We need an interdisciplinary women's studies program." I could make those things sound as though they weren't much, as though what I was asking for wouldn't bring upheavals to the academy that were even more revolutionary than the demands of the boycotters and protesters and marchers of the last few years.

Phyllis Irwin was about forty, with prematurely silver hair and blue eyes that seemed familiar though I knew we'd never before met. "I'm a horsewoman," she'd said, and told me she owned a ranch. Maybe that was why it took me so long to realize it was Rae's blue eyes that hers reminded me of. The idea made me laugh out loud: Rae as a cowgirl.

She was about Rae's height too, or maybe just two or three inches taller, and a lot trimmer; and she was a music professor and a pianist, and now assistant vice president for Academic Affairs. She called herself Scotch Irish and lived with Muffy, a silver schnauzer. No, Phyllis and My Rae were nothing alike, of course not. But the more I got to know her, the more it *felt* as if they were. Maybe she reminded me of Rae because they were both small and feisty.

Phyllis had called early in the fall semester to invite me to lunch. "I have you to thank for my new position," she'd drawled over the phone in a Texas twang. "I wouldn't have applied, but when I heard they made you chair of English I thought, 'Yeah, maybe things are finally going to change around here.'"

"We've got to push for more women and minority faculty," we'd said before our conversation was over.

"Right! At the least, fifty percent of new hires have got to be women and minorities."

"Right! We've got to get the college to set goals in that direction."

How fantastic, to have someone I could talk to about such things, an ally—two women administrators in a college, collaborating on behalf of women. Had that ever before happened in the history of the world? *I'll call Binky this evening, tell her how our sacrifice is already paying off.* "And we've got to get more courses about women in the curriculum," Phyllis and I agreed before we hung up.

Over lunch in the crowded faculty cafeteria we seemed to have less to talk about. "I first saw you about four years ago," she finally said. "Actually, it was right here. At this very table. I even remember what you were wearing." She laughed and looked down at her coffee cup as she said it. "A flared blue skirt with a white silk blouse. You were with someone . . . a tall woman with light hair."

Binky. "Yes, my roommate." I didn't know this person. I wanted to work with her, but I'd have to be careful about what I told her.

She called again a week later. "The vice president said we ought to write an affirmative action faculty policy together and present it at the academic senate." We whooped. We'd change the campus.

We had dinner together, usually at her place, every night that I wasn't in L.A. We talked mostly about what we'd do for women on campus. "I'm so happy you're here. I hate to eat alone," she said one evening. She was standing near the sink, wrapping bacon slices around thick filets. She looked up at me, then quickly back at the steaks. I began to say "Me too," but I stopped myself and said nothing. I didn't stay long after we ate. I slipped out the door, into the black night, and drove back to my apartment at fifty miles an hour, though the posted speed limit was thirty. The rooms were dark and mausoleum-still. I switched on a light in the kitchen; then, so lonely for a voice, I picked up the wall phone and started to dial my number in Los Angeles. Halfway through I hung up. I dialed Phyllis's number, but I replaced the receiver after one ring. I sat at the table and stared into space.

One night, in Los Angeles, in the bed I share with Binky, I dream about Phyllis. She's invited me to lunch at her ranch, and I lean against the kitchen counter, watching while she shucks oysters. Outside the window two white horses stand gleaming in the sunshine—a mare and her baby. The colt nuzzles and nurses while its mother licks at its fur in voluptuous content. Now Phyllis is slicing apples, and from where I stand I can smell their freshness and sweetness. I know if I do it, some great change will happen—there'll be no going back—but I can't stop myself: I put my arms around her, draw her to me. Her mouth tastes like fresh apples.

I jumped awake as though I'd been slapped. In the darkness I could see Binky's head, inches from mine, and I turned over guiltily and closed my eyes again, but my sleep was over.

"The vice president said we ought to plan a women's studies program together," Phyllis came by my office to say at the beginning of the next week. "He's making it part of my assignment." I remembered with a rush of heat to my face how she looked in my dream, bent over the apples.

Sheila, my secretary, buzzed me and said, "Uhh, line 2." She sounded confused.

"Who is it?" I asked.

"Wouldn't give a name or say what they wanted . . ."

The voice on line 2 was unfamiliar, boyish, but I was sure it belonged to a woman. "Lil?" it said.

No one had called me *Lil* in ten years. *Lil* had absolutely no connection to *Lillian*. "Who's this?" I demanded.

"Remember Nicky?" She laughed.

"Just a minute," I said quickly. I jumped up to close my office door. Sheila didn't need to overhear my conversation with somebody from another life.

"You're easy to find," the voice said when I returned to the phone. "This is only the fourth call I had to make."

"So, have you written your novel?" That I said in a loud and friendly voice, just in case Sheila was listening through the door.

"Been busy doing other things. Remember what you once told me about Jan?" I jumped again and pressed at the door, to make certain it was closed. "That's the way my life has been." She wanted to tell me all about it—the women she'd lived off, the clothes and jewelry they'd bought her, the opium she'd tried, the crystal she'd been addicted to.

She sounded jolly, flippant. I listened, nervous, but morbidly fascinated as well. *I've got to hang up*, I kept thinking. "Now I'm a madam," she laughed and spun another story about the house she managed in San Francisco.

Why had she called to tell me this? And what did I have to say to her now, this creature from another universe? "You're not what you think you are, Nicky," I told her. I felt foolish as soon as I uttered it.

"I'd better be what I think I am. Otherwise what's it all for? Besides, I've had a damn good time, Lil."

"So why are you calling?" I forced a laugh.

"I just wanted to hear your voice. Lil, can I call you from time to time?" she asked softly.

Suddenly I saw her as though it had been fifteen days instead of fifteen years and she was still that big galumpf of a girl who was so bright and naive and unlucky. And if there'd been no owl, no tiger, no weeping, clinging creature crying in my wilderness years before, wouldn't the bogeyman have pounced and carried me away as he had her?

"Lil?" she repeated when I didn't answer right away.

I went to the faculty senate with my nails biting into my palms, but there was almost no resistance to the proposal Phyllis and I had drawn up to establish a women's studies program at Fresno State College. When the senate president called for a vote, it was adopted by a large majority. Two faculty slots would be set aside for instructors, who would teach the introductory courses. The rest of the program would be interdisciplinary.

Phyllis and I kept plotting. We'd get the college to allow the Intro to Women's Studies class to satisfy a General Education requirement, along with Intro to Ethnic Studies. We holed up in the assistant vice president's office and planned more strategies. We continued to plan in the evening, as I watched her feed the horses, and as we sat with Muffy on the ditch bank and looked at the sunset, and as I helped her make dinner.

"Think of all the years we wasted when we were both on campus and didn't know each other," Phyllis said when she walked me to the car at the end of another evening spent devising strategies. Everything was quiet in the warm spring night except for the sounds of crickets in the grass and frogs in the ditch and the banging of my heart.

I had to prevent myself from putting my arms around her as I had in my dream. I told her about Binky instead. "I don't go to L.A. every weekend just because I miss bagels in Fresno," I began.

"Well, I guessed," she said, "years ago, when I saw you two together. I came here with someone too. She left a couple of years ago to get a doctorate at the University of Arizona."

"Then she'll be back in another year or two?"

"It's never the same river twice," Phyllis said.

Marshall High School also wasn't what it had been to Binky five years earlier, when I'd watched her share her literary passions with a rainbow of adoring kids. "No more United Nations," she sighed to me over the phone one evening. "This kid called me a *white honky bitch* today," she cried another evening.

"Oh, Binky, oh God, I'm sorry." I knew how the words must have hurt her. "I wish I could be home to take you in my arms."

"Well, you're not," she snapped. "You're two hundred miles away."

And you've still never said anything about the baby, though it's been two years since you asked for time to think about it, I wanted to snap back. (But that was unfair, I knew. I couldn't have a baby right now anyway.) "Love, the semester is almost over. Let's have a wonderful summer together," I said instead. "We'll go somewhere romantic . . . the most romantic place we can think of." We had to learn how to be together again, how to touch again. We occupied the same house every weekend and slept in the same bed, but we were exhausted from our separate weeks and preoccupied with tensions we didn't share. "I love you," I cried now over the phone.

I think it was in Montego Bay that I really understood how you always take yourself with you, no matter where you go. If it's not working for two people at home, it won't work while they're sipping piña colada on a sandy beach. We'd already left Kingston because it was too hot. Or too noisy. Or too crowded. Because we weren't having a good time.

Now we drove the length of Jamaica in a rented car, squabbling absurdly all the way about whether the window should be down or the air conditioner should be on, whether to have our big meal at lunch or at dinner, whether to spend four days at Montego Bay or a week. When we fought, there in Jamaica where we'd come to learn how to be in love again, I felt defeated. Even Fresno would be better than this, I thought, remembering Phyllis's kitchen where you could look out the window and see Arabians grazing in high grass.

It was night when we arrived at Montego Bay, and the blue-black sky I saw from our balcony looked as though someone had taken an ice pick to the heavens and pricked out thousands of tiny silver holes. I could hear the soft lapping of the warm waters, and I could hear Binky unpacking in our room, hanging things up, opening and closing drawers. An aroma of gardenias wafted up from some secret bush below. Finally Binky came to stand beside me on the balcony and look up at the stars. I moved to put my arm around her and she let me, though there was nothing yielding in her posture. "That was a long drive," she said after a minute. "Guess I'll turn in."

"Okay." I dropped my arm. *Let her turn in. Twelve days in Jamaica, and we'd never once made love.* I stood on the balcony, enveloped in humid air that was as sensual as touch. Between the brief lulls in the lapping of the water, I could hear somebody on a far beach playing a drum, an insistent calypso beat. Then in the darkness tears rolled down my cheeks, down my chin. *You want too much out of life,* I chastised myself. *You want more than anyone can get—work of consequence, a home, a baby, a lover. You haven't changed a bit from your seven-year-old self—the spring of '48, the train to Los Angeles, a suitcase bulging with gigantic wants.* Now I pressed against the moon-cooled railing, leaned as far over as I could to glimpse the source of the heady gardenia smell, wished like a moonstruck adolescent for a lover to be standing there with me. Maybe so much wanting was wrong, but I couldn't stop no matter how I tried.

We left Montego Bay after four days. Perhaps things would be better in Ocho Rios. But the drive seemed interminable, and we had almost nothing to say to each other. Better than fighting, I thought glumly. From the road right outside the town, Binky spotted a small, nondescript hotel and pulled into its empty parking lot. "I'm too tired to look further," she said, overruling my perfunctory protest. *It doesn't really matter*, I thought. *A romantic hotel would be a mockery anyway.*

The room was as dismal and anonymous as if it had been a Motel 6. I hung my clothes on the wire hangers, wondering if it were possible to change our airline tickets for an earlier return. When the phone rang, I thought it must be a wrong number.

"Well, eureka!" It was Phyllis's voice, as if my thinking of her on the way to Montego Bay had conjured her up. *Like Rae and my mother in Wheeler Hall.* "How did you know we were here?" I cried as I shot a guilty glance at Binky.

"They don't have that many hotels in Jamaica." She sounded girlish, breathless. "I was ready to phone them all. Terrier persistence. I get it from Muffy."

Binky was staring. What was she thinking of this strange call?

"Hey, I'm calling on official business," Phyllis laughed. "From the vice president's office. Are you sitting down?" She paused only for a second. "Your dean resigned today."

"Jim Light?" Why did I need to know that in the middle of Jamaica?

"Yep. He's been offered a provost position in New York. And . . . the vice president told me to find you." She paused, and I struggled to make sense of what she was saying. "To find you and ask if you'd accept the position of acting dean of the School of Humanities for next year."

"What happened?" Binky saw the panic on my face. "What's wrong?"

"Can I have a day to think about it?" I managed to say into the receiver. But as soon as I said it I knew there was nothing to think about. There was no way I could turn down the offer. There had never been a woman academic dean at the college.

"Oh, we also found out today that our name change was approved. We're now California State University, Fresno. You'll be a *university* dean. Oh, and I've been checking your mail like you asked me to. Harper and Row sent the galleys for *From the Barrio*. They look great!"

"You just have to be important, don't you?" Binky said when I told her about the deanship. "Do what you want. It wouldn't make any difference what I said anyway." She pulled her bathing suit from the drawer she'd placed it in minutes before. "I'm going to the beach," she said over her shoulder.

We should part. Now, I thought, as we bumped through dense clouds back to California. But we'd loved each other, hadn't we? Binky was leaning her head against the window of the plane with her eyes closed, an expression of infinite sadness on her mouth. I stared now at the face I'd found so handsome — the strong nose, the fine cheekbones. I felt sadness too, for her, for us . . . for those times when she said she couldn't remember living before she met me, the way I'd grab her in my arms at the door when she came home from school, how excited and hopeful we were when we got the contract for our book . . .

Twice a month the nine academic deans sat around a long table in a formal chamber and discussed administrative matters with the vice president for Academic Affairs and the assistant vice president, Phyllis. The vice president's secretary sat at his side and kept her head bent over the steno pad on which she took lightning shorthand. The deans were almost all cut from the same pattern, with dark suits and somber ties, bald or balding heads, and a bearing that announced *I'm engaged in serious business here.*

"How are you supposed to *look* if you're a woman and thirty-two years old and have just been made a dean?" I asked Phyllis lightly, though the question really troubled me. It seemed important not to call attention even before I opened my mouth to how different I was from almost everyone else in the room. There were no models of women deans for me to emulate, no real-life images to show me how to make sure the appearance of the messenger wouldn't distract from the message. Where could I look?

Only to the movies of my childhood. How would Joan Crawford or Barbara Stanwyck be dressed to play a lady executive? Severe suit, button-down shirt, no-frills hairdo. That would be my costume. The visual effect I strove for wasn't mannish exactly, but neither was it womanly, since *woman dean* was an oxymoron in 1972.

But no costume could blind the other deans to the fact that a woman had been placed in their midst. They were always gentlemanly, but every time I spoke they seemed to flinch, as though from a tiny electric shock. "If there were just one other woman dean," I complained to Phyllis.

Yet my work as head of the School of Humanities came easily to me. I knew what needed to be done and I liked doing it. I'd heal old wounds and create trust between the departments and the dean's office. I'd be the faculty's advocate to the administration. If my style in dean's meetings was neuter-gendered, the style I strove for when acting for the school was decidedly female, maternal, a bit of a tiger mother. I'll never know if my school finally got long-delayed promotions and badly needed positions because of my approach or because the times had changed and the school's radical stance no longer seemed threatening to a punitive administrative hierarchy; but I know the faculty was happier than they'd been in a long time.

Binky drops me off at the L.A. airport on Monday mornings instead of Tuesday and picks me up on Friday evenings because, as an administrator, I have to be on campus five days a week. "Dottie said that not even for a million bucks would she fight the madhouse traffic at the L.A. airport to pick someone up," Binky says, laughing, one Friday as we sit in a jam of cars and honking horns on the Santa Monica Freeway. "She tells all her friends to take a taxi."

"What are you saying?" I ask Binky.

"Nothing." She laughs again. "You're not just a friend, are you?"

*But I feel more and more like a stranger in the Laurel Canyon house that's mine now only on weekends, and not even then really. I wander through the rooms, getting acquainted all over again with the space. When I wake up in the middle of the night and head for the bathroom, I bump my nose on a wall because I've gone in the direction of my bathroom in Fresno. Nothing is familiar here anymore. Every Friday night I find towers of new books piled atop the old ones on the little coffee table and scattered in a great heap on the narrow shelf above the bed and stacked on the floor beside the toilet—*Introduction to Zen Buddhism; Zen Mind, Beginner's Mind; Tibetan Buddhism. *Once in a while I pick one up, peruse a few pages, try in vain to* *track, then shut it again. The words are so far from the world that interests me right now.*

"Sometimes people grow in different directions," Binky tells me after one of our petty squabbles.

I didn't realize until I was awaiting the president's decision how much I wanted the permanent deanship. The Dean Selection Committee had read through hundreds of applications and chosen five finalists. "You're our top choice," a committee member told me off the record. If I could become a dean at thirty-two, couldn't I become a college president at forty? How many women college presidents were there in the world? I'd grab the golden apple, I decided, not just for myself—for other women too. I'd be the model for them that I'd craved for myself. In Fresno that week I could think of nothing else.

That weekend it rained in Los Angeles, and I spent most of it sitting in the Topsy room, gazing out at the sheets of rain that knocked blossoms off the citrus trees and seemed strong enough to pierce the cheap wood and thin asphalt roof of the garden cottage. It looked frail and neglected now.

On the last evening, Binky came to sit beside me in the dim light of the Topsy room. We'd hardly spoken all weekend, but now we held each other. "What are we going to do about us?" she said in a little voice.

"We're in a mess," I said, and we both smiled sadly. *I should let her get on with her own life, I should get on with mine.*

"You know I want you to be happy," Binky said now. "I want you to have a baby if that's what it takes." The rain pelted the roof of our house, then lightning cracked. "I love you," she said above the angry rumble of thunder that followed.

Sitting in the airport, waiting for my Monday morning plane, I felt like an ant on those 33⅓ records Eddy used to speed up to 45. How would I ever be able to think my way clear? I made plans all over again as the little prop plane bumped through the clouds. If I didn't get the deanship, it would be a sign that I'd been headed in the wrong direction. Fine. I'd quit, and Binky and I would live together and I'd write and have the baby. But even as I told myself how it would be, I couldn't believe it would happen. She'd said she'd be an aunt to my baby. I couldn't imagine her being what Rae had been to me. I knew that wasn't the kind of aunt she meant.

And . . . Phyllis. I'd miss her. A ripple of old sadness and loss stirred in me. Rae walking down the steps of Fanny's porch, into Mr. Bergman's waiting car. A rip in my heart.

Later that day the vice president showed up in my office and sat across from me in a swivel chair, smiling kindly. I sensed what he was going to tell me. President Baxter had decided, the vice president said, that considering the difficult history of the school, he needed to appoint an older person as dean. He'd chosen a man from a Texas university who'd been in administration for twenty years.

Only for an instant did I feel that the golden apple had been torn from my hand. *I'll definitely quit and go back to Los Angeles*, I thought, relieved now that the path I would take was clearly marked. The minute the vice president left my office, I'd call Binky at Marshall High. "I'm coming home," I'd say when she got on the phone.

"But now the good news," the vice president went on. "First of all, Dr. Baxter has approved an early promotion for you to full professor as thanks for the fine work you did as acting dean. And secondly"—he grinned—"I'd like to offer you the assistant academic vice president slot. You'd be in charge of innovative programs and the Experimental College and anything else that seems useful and interesting to you."

"But . . . Phyllis?"

"Oh, she'll stay on, of course. I'll have two assistant vice presidents."

What odd fate was it that yanked me back each time I started wriggling free from where I thought I didn't want to be? And now here was a new pulley. If I were the director of the Experimental College, I'd be able to bring courses into the curriculum that would be inconceivable at most universities, and as a full professor I'd have nothing to lose. A new area of study was just emerging out of an infant gay rights movement. I'd be in the best position in the country to help make gay culture and identity—what had been despised by so many and so central in my own life—a part of academic discourse. The Ivy Leagues, Berkeley, UCLA—it would be decades before they could do it, but as director of the Experimental College, I could bring gay studies classes to California State University, Fresno.

I dreaded calling Binky. I postponed it until I returned home to my apartment after dinner with Phyllis at the ranch. Would she hang up on me?

"Good for you. Congratulations," she said when I told her the news. She didn't sound upset or angry in the least. "There's a Buddhist monastery at Mount Shasta I want to visit," she said without a pause. "Do you think you'd like to come with me for a couple of weeks this summer?"

18 SHEAVES OF OATS

To ME IT WAS LIKE visiting a distant culture to see the orange-robed monks and hear their chanting, which went on for hours. Interesting; but if I couldn't find in myself what Charlotte Brontë called an "organ of veneration" that would let me practice the religion of my mother and aunt and their slaughtered family, there was certainly nothing in the droned mantras I couldn't understand that had the power to draw me in. Binky, though, was ecstatic—about the Mount Shasta monastery, about Buddhism, about the changes she felt inside herself. She'd found a new passion. "The wise man thinks, 'Here is suffering. Here is the cause of suffering. Here is the path that leads to the cessation of suffering.'" She quoted the monks with the same conviction my ancestors must have had when they quoted the tablets. For the weeks that remained of the summer, we drove north through the cool, wet green of Oregon and Washington and into Victoria, and as she talked on and on I thought about what I might do as assistant vice president for Academic Affairs in charge of Innovative Instruction. Sometimes I thought about how Binky and I were at an impasse, how there was nowhere for us to go together, that I couldn't blame her for her new passion. And sometimes I thought about Phyllis's hands on Zahita, the Arabian she liked best to ride, or the way her hands looked as they played Mozart's D Minor Concerto.

When I returned to campus that fall, the vice president was gone. The rumor was, he'd had battles with the president over tenure issues, so when he was offered a job as chancellor at the Denver campus of the University of Colorado, he took it. The president replaced him with a business professor who'd been about to retire, a garrulous Polonius who wore bright white shoes in all seasons and didn't have a clue about how to be a vice president except to do the president's bidding. It was pretty clear that he'd never be my mentor, as I'd hoped his predecessor might, but he was affable enough, even though he didn't seem to know that the Experimental College existed. This left me free to be as experimental as I wished: to organize cluster courses in new areas, such as conflict resolution, courses that ignored discipline boundaries—and courses in my major interest, gay studies.

I went down the short list of gay and lesbian professors I knew, but though the Stonewall riots had occurred four years earlier in New York, word of them hadn't yet reached Fresno. "Would you consider teaching a gay studies course in the Experimental College?" I asked. "I wouldn't even know where to begin to look for material," one said. "What does 'gay' have to do with 'studies'?" said another. "Are you kidding?" a third said.

"Please don't use that word on campus," one woman hissed into the receiver before she hung up on me.

"Why can't you do it?" Phyllis asked when I complained over lunch in the cafeteria, my voice barely above a whisper when I used the *G* word.

I looked at her, this orderly, quietly dignified little woman. "Everyone knows what good friends we are," I laughed. "If I come out, they'll suspect you too. Doesn't that bother you?"

"No," she said flatly.

"Well . . ." I was about to say *I wouldn't even know where to begin to look for material*, yet that wasn't true. I knew how to do research. What was there to stop me from learning how to teach gay studies?

Nicky called again that fall. She'd tracked me down in the assistant vice president's office, but I didn't even jump up to close the door this time, not even when she said, "I've been in jail, Lil." I listened to her boy's voice telling me the latest chapter in the bad novel that was her life.

"The house got raided"—she laughed—"and we all got busted. I got carted off in a paddy wagon together with the hookers. It was no big deal. Really. Except for the lousy jail food and the lumpy pads you had to sleep on. The guys who owned the house sprung us loose after a few days. Now they want to set up in the Tenderloin and keep me as the manager. What do you think?"

Why was she calling me again? "I already told you what I think. That you're not what you believe you are. That you have to stop." But what did I know about her now, really? Red ogre eyes whirled in my head. She wasn't still the eighteen-year-old with puppy feet whom I'd taught how to kiss, who liked to read *This Is My Beloved* because the beloved's name was Lillian. But if she was calling, it must be because she wanted me to tell her something. "Nicky, you have to stop," I repeated.

"To do what?" She laughed again, though I sensed she was really listening.

"Nicky, you wouldn't be talking to me right now if what you've been into weren't wearing thin. Isn't that right? Let me help you get into college. You can do a lot with a diploma." The Maury solution again. But it was all I knew . . . and why shouldn't it work for her as it had for me?

"I'm up shit creek, Lil. We used to be in the same boat," she laughed.

"Well, I found the oars. Let me paddle you out too." The red ogre eyes whirled again, but I clicked them off. How else could she escape from her ongoing melodrama?

In November the Fresno fog settles in for a long gray sleep, and the whole San Joaquin Valley seems somnolent and still. For days sometimes you can't even see the stoplights in town until you're almost on top of them. Most evenings after work I drove at a crawl to Phyllis's ranch, and then at nine or nine-thirty back to my apartment in town. But one night after we'd said good-bye, I opened her front door and saw that the porch light had its own little envelope of haze around it, illuminating nothing. I couldn't even make out the three steps that led from the porch to the paved walkway.

"How can you drive through that?" Phyllis said over my shoulder.

The heavy white blanket of the fog was palpable even at the door. How would I avoid the ditch bank that bordered the ranch? "Look, this place has four bedrooms," Phyllis said. "Stay."

I came back to the bright light of the living room, chilled from my thirty seconds in the cold. "I've got an apple liqueur, Calvados," she said, and went to get it.

Our fingers touched when I reached for the snifter. We looked at each other, saying nothing, though my mind was gyrating like a fly-wheel. *If I do this, what will happen to Binky? If I do this, nothing will be the same again.* Then the whirl stopped, and I put the snifter down on the coffee table, deliberately, carefully. I drew her into my arms.

"Ohhh," we breathed together, as if we'd found some vital thing we'd mislaid years before.

And that night—as Radclyffe Hall wrote—we were not divided.

"What do you eat for breakfast?" Phyllis asked the first morning as I drifted into wakefulness and worry, and then delight. How lovely, how giving, she'd been.

She was dressed in her ranch uniform, blue jeans and the blue sweatshirt that picked up the blue of her eyes, and she'd already been out to feed the horses. She sat on my side of the bed and placed her fingers on my bare shoulder. "What do you eat for breakfast?" she asked again.

I rose to my knees and pulled the blue sweatshirt over her head. "No breakfast this morning," I said.

On Friday evenings Phyllis drives me to the airport, parks the car as far as possible from the high aluminum lamp posts, and we hold each other for a few frantic minutes before I must break loose and run to catch the small plane that will take me to Los Angeles and Binky, who is waiting at the other end. There Binky and I hug, and I marvel that Phyllis doesn't show on my face. Should I say it? But we've been together for seven years. How can I find the words to tell her?

On Monday mornings Phyllis is waiting again, to drive me to my office, to drive me later to the ranch, to have dinner and breakfast with me, to make love with me. How can I leave her on Friday afternoon? I'm a juggler with a clown's

mask, and soon the balls will come banging down on my head. I'm Lilly on the
run, age eight, bounding from Mommy to My Rae to Mommy to My Rae.

One Monday in February, all the flights to Fresno were canceled. "Pea soup fog," the clerk at the United Airlines desk said brightly. "Fresno's been shut down since Saturday. I don't think we'll be landing anything there today."

"Oh, no, I've got important meetings today," I wailed.

"Well, I can get you on the nine forty-five to Merced," the clerk offered. "That'll get you closer." But Merced was an hour away from Fresno, and if the fog was that bad, I probably couldn't get a taxi to take me in.

Phyllis had just gotten to her office when I called, and when the plane landed in Merced, she was waiting at the gate. How many times already had I seen that neat form and silver hair waiting for me at an airport gate or looking after me as I was leaving? I drew her into my arms now, and we gripped each other as though I'd just returned from Mesopotamia.

Twenty miles out of Merced patches of blue were breaking through the gray sky, and a silvery perimeter peeped around a great cumulous cloud. *I shouldn't have bothered her to make this long drive,* I thought, embarrassed now. *The L.A. plane will probably land in Fresno before we get there.* "I'm gonna make you an offer you can't refuse," Phyllis broke the quiet to say. "I've been thinking about it for a long while, and on this morning's drive, though I couldn't see the road clearly, I saw everything I'm about to say like I was peering through crystal." She recited the lines as though she'd been rehearsing them all the way to Merced. I watched the firm grip of her hands on the wheel and braced myself. It would be an ultimatum. How would I answer it?

"I've heard you talk for almost three years about how you want a baby and how you're worried that if you keep putting it off it'll be too late." She slowed the car, looked at me squarely, reached for my hand before she looked back at the road. "I'm proposing. I know I'll make a good other mother. Live with me and have the baby and we'll raise it together."

I gasped as though I'd been socked in the diaphragm.

By the time we reached the campus, the sky was a clear and cloud-less blue such as I'd seen in Fresno only on days in late spring.

I open my purse and there's a small packet of seeds inside, though I don't re-member buying them. The picture on the envelope shows graceful sheaves of some sort of grain. I'm a city girl who can't tell one grain from another, but the sheaves look golden. Lovely. So desirable. More precious by far than golden ap-ples. "We must get the seeds in the ground immediately," I rush to tell Binky.

She's reading a big book, and I strain to see the title. The Influence of Zen on American Literature, *I make out the words on the cover. Or does it say* Zen and the Art of Archery? *Or* Zen and the Art of Motorcycle Maintenance? *No matter. I can barely see the top of Binky's head, which now she raises so that her eyes are visible. "Go plant them," she says sweetly, and waves her hand toward the back of the house, toward the bare little square of land in front of the empty Writing Cottage. "There's* plenty *of room to plant whatever* you *want there." She gestures expansively with both hands. Then the hands disappear and she lowers her eyes and then her head again, and I can see nothing but* The Upanishads. *Binky has vanished.*

"But who'll help me harvest?" I shout toward the book.

"They're oat sheaves," Phyllis whispers in the wind.

I wanted to say it at the L.A. airport, but the words wouldn't come. Nor would they come on the way to Dottie's house for dinner, where I pushed the food around on my plate and pretended to listen to Betty's funny Hollywood stories and felt my cheeks stiffen from the phony lit-tle smile I kept plastered on my face. As Binky slept, I stared into the dark for a hundred lonely years and then watched the gray light slowly fill our bedroom. I could see her long, graceful hands, thrown over her head now, palms up, in peaceful surrender to sleep. She stirred; I crept noiselessly from the bed, like a thief. I'd take a shower first.

Binky was still in bed when I returned, her face to the wall now. I'd already gotten my clothes on. Though she didn't move and her breath was regular, I knew she wasn't sleeping.

"Binky," I bent to whisper, and she turned over and stared at me. "We have to talk."

She sat up quickly. "Don't tell me. They've made you president! Right?" She laughed without mirth.

"I'm having an affair with Phyllis Irwin."

Her eyes widened, then narrowed. For an instant I wished I could take back my words. Then I didn't. "Get out," she said evenly. She leaped from the bed, towered over me. "You've never really lived here anyway," she yelled, "so now get out!"

From the Topsy room I called Yellow Cab. Binky slammed the bedroom door behind her when she heard me on the phone. As I waited, alone, I looked out the window to the backyard, to the abandoned, rickety cottage in which I never wrote a single word.

The taxi drove me to the Greyhound bus station in Hollywood, where, for the third time in my life, I bought a one-way ticket. Then I leaned against a wall, staring into space for a couple of hours, until a canned voice announced over a loudspeaker: "The Bakersfield–Fresno bus will depart in fifteen minutes."

The very pregnant blond woman next to me on the bus tried to scoot over when I sat down, and we both smiled at how little space she could make. Then she closed her eyes and kept them shut through most of the trip, which was fine because I needed time to think.

How could two people who start out in such easy tandem pull so far apart? Once we'd finished our book, nothing between us had gone right, but what we'd shared the first couple of years had seemed so wonderful that it kept us hobbled together for the next five or six, even when we knew that it wasn't working, that we'd be better off going in opposite directions. Finally we were like ball-and-chain convicts—snarling, resentful, but stuck with each other. I was sick about it now. The tiresome discord we'd made ourselves live through. Maybe I wasn't cut out for love relationships.

The bus crawled over the mountains and zoomed toward the Valley and the pregnant woman dozed, her fingers laced over her aquamarine polyester stretch pants, sheltering her belly protectively. She wore no ring on her left hand, and whatever she was dreaming made a little smile play around her lips. Her face looked young and relaxed in sleep. What had been so shameful and brutally hard for a woman in 1940 seemed a lot simpler in the 1970s.

By the time the bus left Bakersfield I'd made a plan. I'd find a doctor who did artificial insemination. Then I'd send my mother the picture that Roger and I had taken at Dottie's party three years earlier. I'd make a copy for Rae. *He's gotten a job as a sociology professor in Pittsburgh, but we're in love, so we got married,* I'd tell them, because although the world had changed, they hadn't. Then I'd buy a house, a nest for me and my baby, and I'd hire a girl to care for her while I worked. If the young woman next to me could take a six-hour bus trip though she looked ready to deliver momentarily, why couldn't I sit behind a desk until the last minute? They couldn't fire me. I was a tenured full professor. And in this day and age they'd be ashamed to fire a pregnant lady anyhow.

The fertility specialist I found was a thin-lipped, serious man. On his office wall was a large portrait of a smiling wife and three teenage daughters, all with sleek, long blond hair. "If you want a child, why don't you just get married?" he asked as I sat opposite him in his office, but he seemed more curious than disapproving.

I'd rehearsed the right answer the week before as the bus was pulling into Fresno. Now I looked Dr. Rich directly in the eye—a guileless professional woman who had no inkling about men, who unwittingly scared off all potential suitors—and I answered with unadorned fact: "If you're thirty-three years old and have a Ph.D. and you're an assistant vice president at a university, it's not easy to find a husband."

Dr. Rich understood what men liked and didn't like in 1974. "Yes, I see," he nodded, then ushered me into the examination room. My feet in stirrups, nervous and vulnerable, I stared at the ceiling while he probed my body. *What if I've waited too long? I would be the end of the line.* I was a prisoner, helpless in a matter that was life-or-death to me now, awaiting the judge's verdict. *Would the verdict be death?*

"Everything looks fine," Dr. Rich finally said from between my feet, "but since you're already thirty-three, I think we'll do an endometrial biopsy to be sure you're ovulating regularly. And if you're not, we'll help nature along a little by giving you a fertility drug, Clomid."

His promise drew the air from my lungs. I was doing it. It would happen!

"We'll need to chart your temperature," he said after I'd dressed in an ecstasy of relief. *I hadn't waited too long!* "And when we have it all figured out we'll do the insemination three times—at the start of your cycle, then in the middle, then at the end." *They would live, into the next generation.*

Phyllis presented me with two new state-of-the-art thermometers, "in case one breaks," she said. Every morning before I left the bed she brought me one, waited by my side, scrutinized the numbers, passed the thermometer back to me to scrutinize, and we noted on the chart the minute variations from 97.8 to 98.9, that secret code to longed-for treasure.

"I match the sperm donor's profile with the patient's," Dr. Rich explained at my cycle's beginning the next month. "For you I've got a donor from the East with a medical degree, mesomorphic type, light complexion, Jewish," he said, reading from a file after comparing its number with the one on a small tube he took from a small refrigerator. "Hold this while I get things ready," he said, his thin lips forming his only smile of our brief association.

Inside the tube he'd handed me was white viscous fluid. I held the cold glass in my palm carefully, lovingly, overwhelmed with gratitude to it, to what the mesomorphic, light-complected, Jewish doctor from the East was giving me.

My feet in the stirrups again, I started when I felt Dr. Rich insert something cold and metallic in me. I stared up at the ceiling and held my breath. "It's best to keep still for a few minutes," he advised before leaving me alone in the room.

I knew for certain I was pregnant several weeks later as I sat in a meeting of the deans and the vice president and a sharp ray of heat radiated from my nipple outward to my breast, like a bright white star. I glanced over at Phyllis, who'd been watching me from the other side of the room. My face must have revealed that something had happened, because now I could see it on her face, as though she'd felt it in her breast too.

"Come live with me on the ranch now," Phyllis said when we left Dr. Rich's office. The tests confirmed what I already knew. The wonder of it! "Come, please," she said again, pulling me back from my euphoria.

Live with her. How could I live with her? Three times I'd tried to make a life with someone, and each time it had ended in my boarding a Greyhound bus alone. "We'll be a family," she said.

"I can't," I told her gently. I couldn't spend the energy I'd need for my child on another love affair that would last a few years and then fail. "If it doesn't work, it would hurt not just you and me but the baby too." She was loving and present and ardent, but so had Mark been in the beginning. So had D'Or and Binky been. What I felt now for her, I had once felt for them too. *Oh, where do they go, lost loves and lost passions? Into what forlorn graveyard do they sink?* "I can't," I said again.

"I'm really grateful for everything you've done," I told her when she dropped me off at my apartment, and I kissed her cheek. "I hope you know that."

"I'm not going to stop," she said, smiling.

I closed the apartment door behind me and laced my fingers around my belly, protecting what was inside. I was going to have a baby! I'd done it. For myself and for them. I'd be like that woman on the bus from L.A., alone, with the baby inside her, strong.

"I'm looking for a three-bedroom house in a good school district," I called a real estate agent to say. Phyllis and I could see each other from time to time, but mostly I'd be a mother and an assistant vice president for Academic Affairs.

I bought a house in a manicured area of Fresno, with a graceful backyard that looked like a park designed by a Japanese landscape architect. Behind a discreet fence was a small orchard of gigantic oranges and bright yellow globes of grapefruit. Inside the house you could fit ten of Fanny's furnished rooms. Maybe twenty. Property in Fresno cost a fraction of what it did in Los Angeles.

"Lilly, a palace!" my mother exclaimed at my dwelling, worthy in her mind of Duke Boyer.

"Dr. Leelee, where do you get so much money to buy such a house?" Albert asked, his ingenuous old eyes big beneath his horn-rimmed glasses.

"All alone with a baby coming, in so many rooms," Rae complained, wandering through the maze of my mansion. "You're not afraid?"

"A baby! A baby!" my mother said for the hundredth time. "Albert, you hear? Lilly's going to have a baby!"

"*Mazel tov!*" he shouted again.

"*Mazel tov!*" Rae shouted too. "When is your husband coming back?"

I took them to Phyllis's ranch for dinner so they'd see what nice friends I had in Fresno, so they'd know that the baby and I wouldn't be all alone, even if "Roger" never returned. Just as I steered my car onto her long gravel driveway, Phyllis came from the barn in her jodhpurs. Rae, sitting beside me, peered over the big mauve plastic purse she held on her lap. "*Oy!*" She adjusted her glasses. "She looks just like that Binky. Where do you get them?"

"Like Binky?" I laughed. Phyllis was six inches shorter and forty pounds lighter than Binky. Then I understood. Of course. All gentiles looked alike to my aunt. "No, My Rae, my darling. She looks just like you," I said.

My aunt spanked my fingers. "Don't be silly," she cackled. "I don't look like a *shiksa.*"

But Phyllis spoke Viennese phrases to them that sounded like Yiddish. She cooked a salmon so that Albert wouldn't have to eat anything *trayf,* unkosher. She popped up to fill water glasses and coffee cups the instant they were emptied. She was charming, darling.

"Oh, I forgot something," I announced after I settled Rae and my mother and Albert into my car at the end of the evening. I ran back to thank Phyllis in private, to kiss her and tell her I'd miss her terribly that night.

"Such a nice lady," my mother said on the drive back to my home.

"The *shiksa* doesn't worry to live all alone in such a big house?" my aunt asked.

Nicky called again, when I was about five months pregnant. "Did you mean it?" she said, as though we'd talked just the day before.

"Mean what?"

"About school. About what I am."

"I meant it." She wouldn't be calling me if she had anyone else to call, I knew. "You'll breeze through the high school equivalency exam," I told her. "Then we'll get you into Fresno State. Come, Nicky. Now I can help you."

"I already shipped my stuff," she said.

"Okay," I told her. "I'm not going anywhere."

She came, wearing jeans and a sweatshirt and a genderless permed hairdo, like a lot of college students in the 1970s. She was almost a generation older than most of them, but so were many others. Drugs and jail time and everything else she'd lived through were etched on her craggy, tough-woman face. She was certainly not the coed I'd seen in the varsity movies of the early 1950s or when I arrived at Fresno State in 1967, but that vapid look was mostly history anyhow. More and more of our students were working class, and hard times showed on their faces. Even those who didn't have rough lives now eschewed the college girl look.

"That woman's going after a lot of counseling," the associate executive vice president smirked to Phyllis when he saw Nicky in my office every day. "I hope she's getting some good advice."

She must have; she graduated cum laude in two and a half years. She wrote too, John Rechy–type stories about a peripatetic butch who lives in the underbelly of lesbian life, stories that continued where "Walk With the Wind" left off.

"Is the world ready for stuff like this from a woman?" we asked each other.

It would take twenty more years, but "Walk With the Wind" would sit in bookstore windows as *A Crystal Diary*. She still calls me Lil.

By October my belly was a nice round watermelon, but I'd said nothing to anyone in the Thomas Administration Building. Did they think I'd just gotten fat?

By November it was no longer possible to ignore, but how could they believe what their eyes were seeing? It was easy to get the Pill. Hardly anyone got pregnant by accident anymore. And if they did, abortions were legal. Was it conceivable that an unmarried assistant vice president for Academic Affairs would carry a baby inside that huge abdominal protrusion? No one asked me. When we talked, they kept their eyes trained on my face, on the wall, on the air, anywhere but down.

In bed together, Phyllis and I speculated about how the campus telephone lines must crackle and sizzle, what circumlocutions Polonius must have devised to proclaim it to the president, how the deans must buzz and chatter until they hear our steps at the meeting room door, then scurry to their seats like naughty schoolchildren.

One night Phyllis and I were asleep in her bed when the phone rang. The luminous hands of the clock said 1:10. Phyllis reached for the phone. It was our old vice president, calling from San Francisco, where some national association of university chancellors was holding an annual meeting. "Phyllis?" he slurred. I could hear him all the way over on my pillow. "I heard the craziest thing tonight about Lillian Faderman." Word had gotten out around the country.

"You should have passed the phone over to me," I murmured when she spooned herself around me again and we floated off on one boat to sweet dreams.

But their silly curiosity is of no consequence. What matters is the precious creature forming inside me. I can see it as clearly as though I've placed a periscope in the navel that once attached me to my own mother. I can see its perfect little fingers and toes, its scrunched-up face that soon will unscrunch and be beautiful, its magical little collarbone and ribs and elbows and knees.

"I hope it'll be musical," Phyllis says one evening as we dream together about who this little being will be.

"If musicality is genetic, she won't be," I confess. "I'm practically tone deaf."

"Early training's the key," my music professor insists, and every night she croons to my naked belly, sends her fine contralto right through my navel into the delicate seashell ears inside me. It's a charming old British folk song that she sings. My Jewish child is bound to adore it.

She wanted me to go with her to her parents' home in San Diego for Thanksgiving. "I've told them all about you and the baby," she said.

A silver-haired, blue-eyed family. Her mother was dainty and sheltered-looking, and the house was filled with delicate heirlooms. Her father was kindly, gentle beneath a curmudgeonly exterior, a retired lieutenant colonel who still met every month with the officers with whom he'd helped liberate France thirty years earlier.

"I think it's wonderful about the baby," Phyllis's mother said in her high, sweet voice as we washed the Thanksgiving dishes together. "Just wonderful," and she patted my soapy hand with hers.

On Saturday the MacDougalls came to play bridge with the Irwins, and Phyllis and I got ready to go and see a Woody Allen film. Mr. MacDougall had been in France with Fred Irwin, and he'd kept his poker-stiff military bearing. As I was putting on my lipstick in the guest bathroom, I heard Fred defend me to his old army buddy: "She didn't want a husband, for God's sake; she wanted a baby, and that's her right."

When I'd thought of having a baby, for years it had been for the sake of my mother and Rae: I longed to give them this little entity who would bring new hope and some joy into their lives. I longed to rescue them from the fate Hitler had prepared for their kind—for our kind—by calling a Sarah or an Avrom back into existence and nourishing it so that it might someday, in its turn, add others to our tiny, decimated tribe. But now when I thought of having the baby, my whole body was charged with a powerful feeling for it and it *alone*. There was almost no minute I spent by myself when I didn't protect with fingers laced and strong as steel the belly that sheltered it, this small, unknown being inside me whom I loved already so fiercely and unconditionally, as I'd learned to love from my mother and My Rae.

I go to natural childbirth classes because I want to be awake for that instant when my child takes its first mouthful of air into its lungs. We meet in a large, mirrored room: a long-haired, Earth Mother teacher; eleven pregnant women; and eleven partners who will coach us through labor—ten husbands and Phyllis. The partners learn to take hard Lamaze breaths along with us pregnant women, to push as we will have to push. They sit behind us on the floor, their hands wrapped around our abdomens. In the mirror I see Phyllis's hands around my big stomach, laced as I've often laced my own fingers, cherishing what's inside me. I love what I see.

We didn't go to the campus on the last Monday in January because it was a university holiday, but I hadn't missed a day of work throughout the pregnancy. In all my thirty-four years I'd never been as hardy—not a single cough or sneeze all fall or winter. Not one tiny headache. Not even a broken nail. Now I'd spent the voluptuously free day reading on Phyllis's couch, walking on the ditch bank and watching a fat muskrat build its house, going to the barn with Phyllis to feed a foal who had a burnished gold coat and comically long legs. After dinner we watched the news, and just as MacNeil or Lehrer said his last word, a butterfly began to beat tiny wings against the walls of my womb, wingbeats so soft they almost tickled.

"It's time," I told Phyllis.

"It's January twenty-seventh," she said. "Mozart's birthday."

Twenty minutes later, before we reached Fresno Community Hospital, the butterfly had become a biting, burning panther. I opened the car window and drew great drafts of cooling January air into my lungs. But he didn't let me suffer long.

"It's a boy!" the doctor shouted at my final push, at nine fifty-nine P.M., and I knew that Avrom was who I wanted and needed the baby to be all along.

Fresno had two synagogues, and though I'd never been inside either one, when I was about six months pregnant I went to the one closest to my house, Beth Jacob, to ask the rabbi if he knew of a girl who could live in my home and take care of my baby while I worked.

"My wife would like such a job," Rabbi Schwartz, a little man not much taller than my aunt, said with an incongruous Cockney accent. "She wouldn't live there, but she'd stay until you came home every day."

Bea Schwartz had the rabbi's Cockney accent and wore a leopard-skin coat. Her hair was dyed midnight black, and her red fingernails jutted out an inch beyond the tips of her fingers. She had a distracted expression, a look my mother had sometimes had when I was a child.

I couldn't sleep. "Those fingernails," I wailed.

"But they raised two kids," Phyllis reminded me. "The rabbi said their son is a doctor."

The second day after Avrom was born, he and I came home. I hadn't planned to take all the sixteen weeks' sick leave due me, but now I loved the animal luxury of doing nothing but nestling my baby in my bed, nuzzling his rose-petal cheeks, watching over his sleep, adoring the perfection of the tiny pink nails on his fingers and toes. I knew nothing outside the wonder of him.

But on the fourth day the vice president called. The University Budget Committee needed to see the plans I'd drawn up for the faculty retreat on innovative instruction. Where were they? Clearly an assistant academic vice president could not take weeks away from the university to be with a baby. "I'll be in this afternoon," I told him, and with a troubled heart I telephoned the Schwartzes.

"Not to worry," the rabbi said. "We'll come right over."

Here are our days: I rise at seven, and I nurse Avrom and prepare baby formula for the hours I'll be gone. Bea Schwartz and the rabbi arrive at seven forty-five, and I leave for the university. I call at nine o'clock, at ten, at eleven. Almost always it's Rabbi Schwartz who answers the phone. (Won't the congregation be angry that he's taken other employment?) "He's doing smashing," the rabbi says. "Not to worry."

At noon, Phyllis and I hurry back to Harrison Street so I can nurse Avrom. Almost always, Rabbi Schwartz is walking the floor with my baby in his arms, crooning off-key British lullabies while Bea sits on the couch with a faraway look. Avrom bats his big eyes and smiles toothlessly up at the rabbi.

Phyllis and I lunch on a hunk of bread and a chunk of cheese and hurry back to campus, where I spend the afternoon organizing the spring faculty retreat, thinking all the while of how the rabbi holds my son in his arms.

At five o'clock I go home and nurse Avrom, and Phyllis rushes off to the ranch to feed the animals. But by six-thirty she's back on Harrison Street, cooing over Avrom, carrying him everywhere in her arms while I fix our dinner. We eat it as he slumbers in his blue bassinet at the side of our table. Then I nurse him once more and dandle him, and Phyllis sings to him. Together we place him in his bassinet again before we tumble into my bed. At 2 A.M. he sings to us, sings us awake with his powerful lungs. Sometimes I get up to hold him in my arms and nurse him at my breast. Sometimes Phyllis gets up and goes into the kitchen to warm his bottle, then holds him in her arms and nurses him. The alarm buzzes at six-thirty and we tear away from each other. As I float in and out of a few more snatches of sleep, I hear the front door shut and her car start. She must drive back to the ranch to feed the animals before she goes off to work.

"Let's live together," I tell Phyllis soon, because already we're a family.

"Do you know what my father just said?" She laughed after one of her weekly phone calls to San Diego. "He said that since we're raising Avrom together, why can't we call him Irwin too."

I'd worried since my son's birth: If something were to happen to me, Rae would be too old to take care of him, and my mother and Albert were unthinkable. The indifferent state would ship him off to a place like the Vista Del Mar Home for Orphans, where poor Arthur Grossman was sent when we were kids. They wouldn't care that Phyllis loved him. What could she use to prove her tie? "Yes, that's his name from now on," I said. "Avrom Irwin Faderman."

There are so many people who are glad my son has come into the world.

When he started to talk, he called me *Mommy* and my partner *Mama Phyllis*. We couldn't stop to think about how we looked to people outside because we were too busy living our lives, but now and then word got back to us: some lesbians in Visalia who asked an acquaintance if the "bizarre story" they heard, about "a professor who had herself artificially inseminated," was really true; someone on campus who remarked to a colleague that Phyllis and I were "engaged in a social experiment." How could they know the love among the three of us and the caring? Or that as life made *me*, the family *I* made was the only one I could live in? How could they know that Avrom made up for what Hitler and what Moishe took away, that I loved him with such tenderness and joy and wonder—as though I'd invented motherhood? How could they know he was to me the completion of a sacred mission?

A woman who had a child out of wedlock in 1975 could not become a college president. I wasn't unaware when I chose to get pregnant that it might abort my career as an administrator, but now I knew for sure. My administrative colleagues never said a word about Avrom after he was born—any more than they did before he was born. As far as they were concerned, it was as though the funny protrusion around my abdomen had just magically deflated. Of course they thought me odd. No matter what administrative skills I might have, I would never really be one of them.

But did I want to be, or was it blind ambition that had made me dream of becoming a college president, just as I'd dreamt once of becoming a movie star? I truly missed the classroom. The next school year, I decided, would be my last one in administration. After Avrom's 2 A.M. feedings stopped, my reading started again. I pored over books that would one day prepare me to teach lesbian and gay literature. The books absorbed me and claimed me, as always, in ways that organizing the next faculty symposium never could. What luxury it was: to sit in the den after we put Avrom to bed and lose myself in the written word—especially now in words about love between women, which had changed so much from the days when I found the lugubrious *Twilight Lovers* or *Odd Girl Out* on the paperback book racks in drugstores. But I wished that some historian would place it all in context for me—trace it from the earliest images, trace what it must have been like for women who made their lives together a hundred years ago, two hundred years ago, three hundred years ago, women who loved each other as Phyllis and I did now.

"Why don't you do it?" Phyllis asked.

I laughed at her musician's naiveté. "It takes scholarly skills I don't have. I'm not a historian."

"What skills don't you have?" Phyllis said. *"Become a movie actress,"* *my mother had said.*

I dismissed it that evening, but I couldn't dismiss it permanently. There was no such field as "lesbian history." With whatever scholarly skills I did possess, why couldn't I try to help create it? Who else in the whole country was in as perfect a position as I? I'd done enough work for my dissertation and my two textbooks to have some notion about research. I was a tenured full professor with absolute job security, and whatever my colleagues might think privately, they couldn't punish me for being a homosexual historian any more than they could punish me for being an unwed mother. I had a family that kept me at home, a partner to share responsibilities with me, and when I wasn't at school I had time to work while my infant son slept. Why shouldn't I do it?

"Do it," Phyllis urged again. "You can do it."

My writing too was a sheaf of oats.

RIGHT: *Lillian, Albert, Avrom, and Mother*

BOTTOM LEFT: *Avrom and Grampa Albert Gordin*

BOTTOM RIGHT: *Avrom and Grampa Fred Irwin*

My mother and Albert and Rae come to visit. Albert carries Avrom all over the living room, calling him "Yankeleh." "Maybe I better take him for a while, Dad," I say after he tries for half an hour to teach the baby to say "Good morning, how are you?" in Yiddish, Hebrew, Polish, Russian, and Spanish. But then my mother wants to hold him, and I place him in her open arms. She sits with him on her lap, touches his little fingers with a delicate pinkie, gazes at him with a dreamy look. Is it me she sees? Is it Hirschel? "Avremeleh," she calls him. We let him sleep in his bassinet for a while, then my aunt goes to get him, to hold him, to sing "Raisins and Almonds" to him in her foghorn voice. "Under Avremeleh's little cradle," she blares in Yiddish, "stands a pure white goat . . ." He looks up at her with huge love eyes.

Though my aunt has asked me numerous times during the visit why Roger doesn't come and see his son, before she gets into the back seat of Albert's car for the drive home, she turns to Phyllis to instruct her: "Take care on Lilly and the baby."

"I will," Phyllis promises solemnly. "I'll take very good care of them," and her blue eyes lock with My Rae's.

19 EPILOGUE

1979

PHYLLIS WENT BACK to her department too. They elected her chair because they thought she was the only one who could keep the string professors from strangling one another with catgut, the woodwind professors from soaking one another's reeds in strychnine. She did bring about something of a truce before we went off on sabbatical—to San Diego, where we'd be near Granma and Grampa Irwin. She'd write a music fundamentals text, and I'd expand my lesbian history articles into a book I'd call *Surpassing the Love of Men*.

If I'd been an academic historian, I would have known how difficult it would be to trace love between women from the Renaissance to the present—over two continents and five countries. But I didn't know it. Maybe the editors at Random House and William Morrow didn't know it either, because they both bid on the book as soon as they saw my outline. "I'm going to be published by a New York publisher!" I shouted to my mother over the phone. "Two big publishers love my book!"

"Oh, Lilly," my mother cried, "I'm so proud of you." But then we said no more about it. What could my mother understand about "Romantic Friendship and Love Between Women from the Renaissance to the Present" or about New York publishers?

I laughed at myself when I hung up. My ecstatic squeal echoed still in my ears. "Two big publishers love my book!" It had been me, a ten-

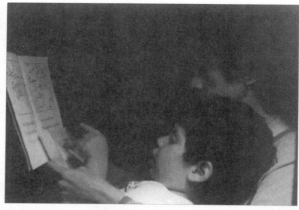

LEFT: *Avrom and Lillian: Avrom reading, age three and a half*

BOTTOM: *Phyllis and Avrom*

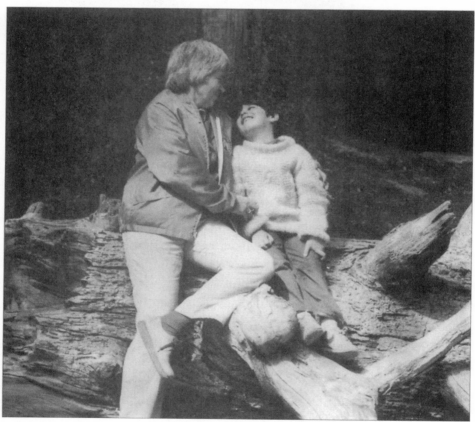

TOP LEFT: *Chanukah*
TOP RIGHT: *Christmas*
BOTTOM: *Phyllis, Avrom, and Lillian*

year-old kid, shouting to Mommy: "RKO and MGM both wanna give me a contract!"

At the end of that sabbatical year, my mother came to San Diego by bus, a last visit. Driving her home to Los Angeles we stopped at Knott's Berry Farm, where she and I had gone a few times with Rae and Mr. Bergman when I was a child. Knott's Berry Farm had been a corny tourist attraction made up mostly of two-dimensional or papier-mâché imitation Hollywood sets—cowboy saloons and gold miners' cabins and hoosegows in which you could have your picture taken as a jailbird. FUN FOR THE WHOLE FAMILY, the billboards between San Diego and L.A. announced, and in recent years Knott's had installed elaborate rides for the kids in order to compete with Disneyland, down the road.

My mother sat on a long bench with four or five other grandparents and exhausted parents, and Phyllis and I stood at a mesh gate, watching our son go round and round a phony lake on a big plastic swan. For no reason at all I glanced back at my mother. The brilliant Southern California sunshine seemed to illuminate just her and none of the others on the bench; she seemed inches taller than all of them. Her eyes were half-closed. She was basking in the warmth and watching her grandson. I'd never seen her like that, so calm, so self-possessed and content, so queenly. Where had the coat of her craziness gone? the old veil of her tragedy that almost always covered her face? I gazed and gazed. *This picture of her, just this, is what I want to hold on to forever.*

She called a few days later, when we were back in Fresno, but the majestic figure in the sunlight had vanished. "The doctor found a big lump," the old hysterical voice screeched into the phone. "A big lump, Lilly! What do you think it is?"

How could it be, when I'd just seen her looking happier than she ever had? "You'll be okay, Mommy. Don't worry now." It was the voice of a ten-year-old—a child trying to sound calm and controlled in front an adult who wasn't. "I'm coming, right away."

When I arrived, my mother was pacing up and down Curson Avenue, the familiar look back on her face, the familiar dishevelment back in her hair and clothes. This time, though, it wasn't my mortality that she was worried about but her own. "What do you think it is, Lilly?" she cried again, though I knew she didn't want to hear the terrible word.

My son is four years old. Is this all she'll get to see of him? The thought comes with despair, rage, then a warp in time: I'm the one who's four years old; my mother is abandoning me. "I'll make us a cup of coffee," I told my mother lightly. I went to her kitchen and stuck my head deep into the cupboard where she kept the Instant Folgers so she wouldn't see my face screwed up in a four-year-old's panic.

At the hospital we sat together in an office, and the doctor, dressed in a natty light-colored suit and a dark shirt, gave my mother a form to sign. "You need to read it first," he said brusquely, and busied himself looking for something in a drawer. I stood at her side and read the words to myself as she held the paper. "What does it mean?" she asked me in Yiddish, her eyes blinking, out of control, as though the fine print on the official-looking paper signified doom.

I couldn't say the words because I wanted to protect her from them. "It just says they'll put you to sleep for a little while," I answered in English, "and then they'll do a test."

"That's only part of what it says." The doctor threw me a disdainful look. He grabbed the paper from my mother's hand and with a finger inexorable as death pointed to the clause he wanted her to see. "Look, here. It says that if I find a malignancy when we're doing the biopsy, you've given your consent for a mastectomy."

"What does he mean?" she asked again in Yiddish, and now I had to say it.

We'd gone to have Thanksgiving dinner with friends in Three Rivers, and I could hear the phone ringing into the dark when we pulled up to our garage. "Lee-lee, the ambulance came for your mother. She's in the hospital very sick, very very sick," Albert yelled into the phone. It was pneumonia, he said. She'd had three months of chemotherapy.

"We'll come with you," Phyllis cried.

"No. Please. I need to be alone with her," I said. "Stay here and take care of our boy."

. . .

My mother is hooked up everywhere to complicated yards of tubes and wires. She tries to tell me something, her hands waving indecipherable messages, her lips moving around the clear tube in her mouth that reaches down to her lungs. "What, Mom? What?" I can't understand. "Tell me later, when they take the tube out of your mouth." But she won't stop. Now she points to her lips, pulls my chin to her, pulls me close to her face. It frightens me. What does she want from me? "I don't understand," I cry, frustrated. It had always been so hard for me to understand her. But she won't rest. She points to my lips now, pulls my chin to her. "My face?" I'm desperate. "What about my face?"

Then I get it. So simple. "You want me to kiss you?" I hear my aunt, who's standing behind me, make a muffled sound. My mother nods and sighs deeply, and her body seems to relax for the first time. I kiss her face over and over and call her "my darling." When I leave the room for a minute, Rae runs behind me. "Wash your mouth good with soap," she whispers loudly. "Pneumonia is catching."

I go into the bathroom and scrub my lips as Rae directed, but then I'm sorry I did it, and my lips hurt from the disinfectant soap. All that day I kiss my mother over and over and call her "my darling." I won't scrub my lips anymore. I stand by her side and hold her hand. What can I tell her? "I sent my editor Part One of my manuscript, and she says it's going to be a very important book." "Avrom's kindergarten teacher says he's reading at a third-grade level."

She squeezes my hand, and her lips seem to smile around the tube before we lapse into silence, then I kiss her again. There isn't any more to say. But there doesn't need to be.

As a child I had little to say to my mother that I thought she could understand, yet I had a million kisses for her. When I grew up I was usually too angry to give her kisses. I couldn't bear to witness her pain anymore, I couldn't bear that she'd been always a victim. Why hadn't she known how to make a decent life for herself? But it comforts me now, it comforts her too, I can see, when I kiss her again and again as I used to.

Have I really told her everything I need to? "It'll be all right, Mommy," I say now. Not you'll be all right. I can't lie to her.

"It'll be all right," I say again after a few minutes, and she nods her head yes.